D0962363

THE
TEACHING
MINISTRY
OF THE
CHURCH
2ND EDITION

THE
TEACHING
MINISTRY
OF THE
CHURCH
2ND EDITION

EDITED BY

WILLIAM R. YOUNT

ACADEMIC
NASHVILLE, TENNESSEE

6 7 8 9 10 11 12 • 19 18 17 16 15
LB

TABLE OF CONTENTS

PART THREE
PREPARATION FOR TEACHING

AUTHORS

Johnny Derouen[1]
Assistant Professor in Student Ministry

Ph.D., Student Ministry, 2005
Southwestern Baptist Theological Seminary

Robert DeVargas
Assistant Professor of Communication Arts

Ph.D., Foundations of Education, 1998
Southwestern Baptist Theological Seminary

Esther Díaz-Bolet
Assistant Professor of Administration

Ph.D., Administration, 1999
Southwestern Baptist Theological Seminary

Octavio J. Esqueda
Associate Professor of Foundations of Education

Ph.D., Higher Education, 2003
University of North Texas, Denton, Texas

Scott Floyd
Professor of Marriage and Family Counseling

Ph.D., Psychology and Counseling, 1990
Southwestern Baptist Theological Seminary

Karen Kennemur
Instructor in Children's Ministry

Ph.D., Childhood Education (ABD: 2008)
Southwestern Baptist Theological Seminary

Margaret Lawson
Associate Dean of Master's Programs,
and Associate Professor of Foundations of Education

Ph.D., Foundations of Education, 1994
Southwestern Baptist Theological Seminary

---

[1] All chapter authors are faculty members serving the School of Educational Ministries, Southwestern Baptist Theological Seminary, Fort Worth, Texas, in October 2007.

Marcia McQuitty
Professor of Children's Ministry

Ph.D., Childhood Education, 1994
Southwestern Baptist Theological Seminary

Mike McGuire
Associate Professor of Marriage and Family Counseling

Ph.D., Marriage and Family Counseling, 1992
Texas Woman's University, Denton, Texas

Bob Mathis
Assistant Dean and Professor of Administration

Ph.D., Church Administration, 1984
Southwestern Baptist Theological Seminary
Ed.D., Higher Education Administration, 1995
University of Southern Mississippi

Terri Stovall
Dean and Associate Professor of Women's Studies

Ph.D., Administration, 2001
Southwestern Baptist Theological Seminary

Bob Welch
*Dean, School of Educational Ministries, and
Professor of Administration*

Ph.D., Administration, 1990
Southwestern Baptist Theological Seminary

Rick Yount
Assistant Dean and Professor of Foundations of Education

Ph.D., Foundations of Education, 1978
Southwestern Baptist Theological Seminary
Ph.D., Educational Research, 1984
University of North Texas

FOREWORD

Daryl Eldridge

President, Rockbridge Seminary
Former Dean, School of Educational Ministries, SWBTS,
Fort Worth, Texas
Editor of the first edition of
The Teaching Ministry of the Church (1995)

T he world has changed dramatically since the first edition of *The Teaching Ministry of the Church*. The rise of Islamic fundamentalism, the proliferation of religious sects, and the secularization of the culture have only increased the importance of producing fully developed followers of Jesus Christ. In the face of such changes, Sunday school, the mainstay for discipling believers, is declining in nearly every denomination. Bible readership is also declining among Christians. The spiritual transformation of believers comes into question when Christians are just as likely to divorce and cheat on their income tax as non-Christians. How will the church respond to these challenges?

Teaching is one of God's primary activities. Job proclaimed, "God is exalted in his power. Who is a teacher like him?" (Job 36:22 NIV). God wants us to know Him. From the beginning of time, through various means, He has revealed to us His character. It wasn't enough simply to record the stories of God's continual effort to reveal Himself to us. God left heaven and invaded our presence in the form of a teacher, the favorite designation of the Son of God.

Jesus' parting words to His student-friends were not "Go, worship," but, "Make disciples." The commission of every believer is: "As you go, **make disciples** of all nations, teaching them to observe everything I have **taught** you. And remember, no matter where you go, for as long as eternity, I am with you" (Matt 28:19–20, my translation). The power of the Trinity continues to teach us through the Holy Spirit. Jesus delivered on His promise, "But the Counselor, the Holy Spirit—the Father will send Him in My name—will teach you all things and remind you of everything I have told you" (John 14:26).

The early disciples understood their mission and spent their energies teaching others what Jesus imparted to them. The early church was taught to "let the message about the Messiah dwell richly among you, teaching and admonishing one another in all wisdom" (Col 3:16). The simple truth is that the church that fails to teach will fail in its mission and therefore will cease to be the church.

In recent years worship services have been the front door for many churches rather than small-group Bible study. Worship attendance exceeds Sunday school attendance in most churches. While worship is vitally important to the believer, Christians have been lulled into thinking that a sermon is discipleship. John Wesley said he could preach to thousands of people, but he would see little change in the lives of listeners. However, if he could get people in a small band of followers, transformation could take place. He understood the power of discipleship in small groups.

Unfortunately, too many church members have assumed that discipleship is optional. They have falsely assumed they can say the sinner's prayer and be done with it. Gary Thomas warned us:

> When our goals reach beyond making it into heaven to a life of ministry and impact here on earth, maturity does matter. I can be immature and reach heaven. I'm not sure, however, that I can remain immature and see hell break apart at my feet. If I am steeped in habitual sin, if I remain a spiritual adolescent, I cannot threaten hell, not while kissing its feet or lusting after its trinkets.
>
> The goal I adopted—see hell break apart at my feet—encourages me to grow, not just for my own sake, but for the sake of others.[2]

This book is important because this generation will only see hell break apart at its feet when we take seriously the mission of making disciples. This book is a guidebook not just for those responsible for the teaching and administration of the discipleship ministries of the church but for anyone who is passionate about seeing Christians

---

[2] Gary Thomas, *Seeking the Face of God: The Path to a More Intimate Relationship with Him* (Nashville: Thomas Nelson, 1994), 29.

grow in their faith. It provides a biblical and theological rationale for the teaching ministry of the church.

The teaching ministry involves all ages and a variety of strategies for equipping the saints for ministry. It involves both instruction and administration. The reader will explore how people learn as they journey through the stages of life and will consider the implications for reaching and ministering to these age groups. The book also provides practical help in the structure of the teaching ministry of the church.

The reformation of the church in the twenty-first century will be the deployment of all believers as ministers. Volunteers are the workforce of the teaching ministry. Volunteers require enlistment, training, supervision, and celebration. The responsibility of pastors and church leaders is to equip believers for ministry. Regardless of your specific leadership responsibilities in the church, your success as a leader will depend on your ability to lead volunteers, for which this book will be a tremendous help.

There is not a better time to be in ministry. The advancements in technology and travel make it possible for us to reach the world for Christ like never before. While secular adults may not be turning to the church, they are interested in spiritual things. We have the opportunity to engage the culture, dialogue with those who do not know our Lord, and teach them about the Jesus who changed our lives.

If you did not know that the apostle Paul's letter was written nearly 2,000 years ago, you would think it was crafted for our generation. He wrote, "Pay careful attention, then, to how you walk—not as unwise people but as wise—making the most of the time, because the days are evil" (Eph 5:15–16). May this generation be faithful to make disciples in all nations that we might see hell break apart at our feet.

PREFACE TO THE
SECOND EDITION

Rick Yount

H e stood before a solemn assembly in the seminary chapel. Students, faculty, and administration had gathered on that warm September morning in 2007 to commemorate the installation of a new academic chair. He spoke solemn words from Paul's charge to the leaders of the church at Ephesus—apostles, prophets, pastors, and teachers. These leaders were given to the Church, the apostle wrote by inspiration of the Holy Spirit, by none other than Christ Himself (Eph 4:7,11), and that for an express purpose: "for *the training of the saints* in the work of ministry, to build up the body of Christ" (Eph 4:12; emphasis mine).

The speaker was Jack D. Terry, special assistant to the president, who, over a lifetime of educational ministry, had served as vice president for development, dean of the School of Educational Ministries, professor of foundations of education, minister of education, and longtime Bible teacher of adults in his own local church. The chair was the Jack D. and Barbara Terry Chair of Christian Education. Its first recipient, honored this day as well, was Dr. Wesley Black, associate dean of Ph.D. studies and professor of student ministries in the School of Educational Ministries.

There, before the entire seminary family, Terry laid out the core principle that had guided his ministry: to help members of churches grow spiritually, to equip them thoroughly, and to engage them wholeheartedly in the work of ministry. The perspective of Paul, he concluded, could be summed up succinctly in a marketing slogan made popular by The Home Depot: "You can do it. We can help."

The message was a timely one. The Lord's parting imperative was to "make disciples" by "baptizing them," the ministry of evangelism, and "teaching them to observe" what Jesus commanded, the ministry of discipleship (Matt 28:19–20). These tasks cannot be accomplished by professional ministers alone. It was never the Lord's intention that they should be.

The Church is the Lord's compassionate army. Every member is a minister, gifted by God to carry out supernatural ministry in the Spirit's power—*able to do* in the world what God calls them to do. Those called to Christian leadership are, according to Paul, doer-trainers: ministering and equipping others to minister. *We can help.*

What are the educational ministries of the Church? What are our goals? How do we organize the process? How do we evaluate our efforts? You hold in your hands a collection of passionate essays written to answer these vital questions. While we have structured the text around core themes in Christian education, each chapter takes its flavor, its focus, and its priorities from the one who wrote it—professor-practitioners who live and breathe the content they have written.

We gratefully stand on the shoulders of those who produced the first edition: editor Daryl Eldridge, who graciously wrote the foreword for our present volume, Norma Hedin, Terrell Peace, William "Budd" Smith, and Jack Terry Jr.

We have written with you, the reader, in mind. We pray for your personal growth as you depend on the Lord to teach you through these pages, and more, for those you will teach in Jesus' name.

Fort Worth, Texas
October 2007

Part One

THEOLOGICAL FOUNDATIONS

FOR THE TEACHING MINISTRY

OF THE CHURCH

Chapter 1

A THEOLOGY OF CHRISTIAN EDUCATION

Rick Yount

Then **we will no longer be little children**, tossed by the
waves and blown around by every wind of teaching,
by human cunning with cleverness in the techniques of deceit.
But **speaking the truth in love,** let us **grow in every
way into Him who is the head—Christ**.
From Him the whole body, fitted and knit
together by every supporting ligament,
promotes the growth of the body for building up itself in
love by the proper working of each individual part.
(Eph 4:14–16)

Teaching into the Unknown

I stood at the front of the room and stared into what I can only
describe as a deep, dark pit of unknown. As I looked into the
eyes of my students, I felt isolated, completely alone. A Kazakh
wind blew across the building, rattling the windows, making the sub-
zero temperature outside seem all the more cold.

Of the 17 students sitting before me, eight had made a treacher-
ous journey over ice-covered mountains from Bishkek, Kyrgyzstan.
They had driven all night, 300 miles, 10 hours, in order to arrive in
time for the class. This class, *my class*. What were they thinking?
What did they expect? What did they already know? Would the

3

materials I prepared actually help them, their teaching ministries, their churches?

What I needed was a compass to steer me in the right direction until we—these students and I, *together*—could discover common landmarks that would unite us in a common cause, a common journey. And lead us to a common outcome of growth in the Lord.

Fortunately, I had such a compass. What I lacked at this particular moment was any evidence that my compass was relevant to these Russian Baptists who lived and worked 11 time zones east of Fort Worth. There was only one way, one terrifying way, to find out. I silently voiced a prayer for help and stepped into the darkness. I could only hope my words would find fertile soil.

A Theology

Literally, the word *theology*, a combination of *theos* (God) and *logos* (study, discourse), means "the study of God," His nature and attributes. A. H. Strong extends this definition to include "the whole range of Christian doctrine . . . of those relations between God and the universe in view of which we speak of Creation, Providence and Redemption."[1] Klaus Issler echoed this classic sentiment in his contemporary definition: theology is "the study of God—who God is and what he has provided for his creation, both now and forever."[2]

Theology is both science and philosophy. It is *science* in that it discovers the facts and relations that exist between God and the finite universe, that in turn are based on God's works and activities. Just as physical science discovers facts about gravity and aerodynamics and orders those facts into their natural and proper relationship to produce the rational basis for flight, so, in the same way theology discovers facts about God's creative, sustaining, and fulfilling work in the universe, including mankind, and produces the rational basis for God-ordered life, purpose, and destiny. Theology is *philosophy* in that it "exhibits these facts in their rational unity, as connected parts

[1] A. H. Strong, *Systematic Theology* (Valley Forge: Judson, 1907; 32nd printing, 1979), 1.
[2] K. Issler, "Theological Foundations of Christian Education," in Michael Anthony, *Introducing Christian Education: Foundations for the Twenty-first Century* (Grand Rapids: Baker, 2001), 35. Issler's chapter is highly recommended for anyone desiring a thorough treatise on the theological foundations of Christian education.

of a formulated and organic system of truth" that is brought into contact with the human mind through revelation.[3]

Theology is our beginning point. Here is the foundation of our text: God exists, and in His very nature, He is Teacher. Further, the Church is, at its heart, a teaching institution, drawing the lost to faith and spiritual regeneration, prompting believers to transformation and sanctification, and equipping the saints for works of service in the real world.

Education

The term *education* has become an increasingly loaded term for the Church, especially in theological circles. A theologian friend of mine recently remarked that my continued use of the term "tainted me." He could not tell me why, exactly, but the term had taken on a "liberal" connotation. It would be far better, he said, to use words like *discipleship* or *equipping*, or even the term popularized by our Catholic brethren: *spiritual formation*.

Even educational experts differ on both the meaning and methods of education. Dr. Jack Terry introduced me to the debate in 1974 in my first philosophy of education class. He noted that there are two different Latin roots of the English word *education*. They are *educare*, which means "to train or to mold," and *educere*, meaning "to lead out."

Forty years later the debate continues. Bass and Goode contrast these two perspectives of education and raise the question whether balance between the two camps can ever be achieved. *Educare* emphasizes the preservation of knowledge and the shaping of the next generation in the image of their parents. *Educere* emphasizes the preparation of a new generation for the changes that are to come, equipping them for the solving of problems yet unknown. *Educare* calls for direct instruction, subject mastery, and becoming good, reliable workers. *Educere* calls for questioning the givens, thinking "outside the box," and creating new ways of seeing the world.[4] Unfortunately, the recommendations forwarded in the article—

---

[3] Strong, 2.

[4] See V. R. Bass and J. W. Good, "Educare and Educere: Is a Balance Possible in the Educational System?" *Educational Forum* (Winter 2004), http://findarticles.com/p/articles/mi_qa4013/is_200401/ai_n9389288.

balancing old *(educare)* and new *(educere)*, involving "stakeholders" in decision-making and increasing resources, leave us with little more than rehashed word magic. The system itself is confused, and no one, it seems, is able to speak to the confusion.

Regardless of the endless theoretical and political debates, the result has been high school graduates by the tens of thousands who cannot make change, spell, or speak standard English. Fortunately, the term *education* in "Christian education" has a very different meaning.

Christian Education

Issler reached back to Nevin Harner's 1939 definition as the basis for his discussion of the theological foundations of Christian education: "Christian education is a reverent attempt to discover the divinely ordained process by which individuals grow in Christlikeness, and to work with that process."[5] There is much here to embrace. It is a *reverent* attempt, a journey, made in humility, of a truth-seeker. This truth is revealed to, not discovered by, the one who humbles himself under the mighty hand of God.[6] The attempt focuses on the divinely ordained *process* of growth. Growth is not instantaneous but sequential. Not immediate but progressive. The attempt focuses on the *divinely ordained* process of growth. Just how does *God intend* a learner to move from lost rebel to found child? From "babe in Christ" to "well-equipped saint"?

This divinely ordained process of growth moves in a specific direction: *Christlikeness.* I like this focus on Christ and the goal to grow to be like Him. Strong does not hesitate to place Christ at the center of theology:

> That Christ is the one and only Revealer of God, in nature, in humanity, in history, in science, in Scripture, is in my judgment the key to theology. . . . What think ye of Christ? is still the critical question, and none are entitled to the name of Christian who, in the face of evidence he has furnished us, cannot answer the question aright.[7]

---

[5] Issler, 35.
[6] 1 Pet 5:6.
[7] Strong, vii, ix.

The work of Christian education is to analyze that divinely ordained process of supernatural transformation as it intersects relevant life changes in preschoolers, children, youth, and adults who
live in a natural world. This interaction of supernatural and natural
processes of change carries the theological issues of conversion, regeneration, sanctification, and transformation into the realm of the
social sciences—particularly educational psychology—as we deal
honestly with changes in the cognitive (knowledge and understanding), affective (values and preferences), and behavioral (skills and
habits) areas of life. The work of Christian education carries us into
the Church and out into the world through ministry.

Issler states "the essential question" that Christian education
must answer: How do we educate Christians?[8] Dallas Willard goes
a step further, detailing what the process looks like: "[Our goal is]
transforming disciples inwardly, in such a way that doing the words
and deeds of Christ is not the focus but the natural outcome or side
effect."[9] That is, becoming like Christ inwardly so that we naturally
behave like Christ outwardly. None of us, of course, will become like
Christ since He is God. But in moving toward Him, in "growing up
into" Him (Eph 4:15 KJV), we become better than we were and more
like what He created us to be.

Dennis Williams goes farther still, summarizing several evangelical definitions for Christian education this way: "Bible-based, theologically sound, Holy Spirit-empowered, the elements of teaching/
learning/growth/equipping, change, the church, evangelism, and
service. Christian education, then, is more than merely teaching
Christians."[10]

A Theology of Christian Education

Williams's words carry me back to my fervent, fearful prayers
in the early 1970s, as I struggled to find ways to teach deaf college
students in my Bible class. "Lord, how should I teach so that these
learners will grow up into You?" I struggled with teaching into the

---

[8] Ibid.

[9] D. Willard, *Renovation of the Heart: Putting on the Character of Christ* (Colorado
Springs: NavPress, 2002), 240.

[10] D. Williams, "Christian Education," *Evangelical Dictionary of Christian Education*,
ed. Michael Anthony (Grand Rapids: Baker Academic, 2001).

unknown. What did these deaf college students know? What had
been their experiences with the Lord, with Church, with Scripture?
What did they need to grow toward the Lord, and after conversion,
to grow up in the Lord? How should I prepare my "lessons"? What
should be the focus of my teaching?

Over the next three years of teaching these college students,
the Lord brought experiences into the classroom that answered all
these questions. Over five years of masters' and doctoral studies in
Foundations of Education at Southwestern Seminary, the Lord laid
strong theological, philosophical, and psychological foundations
under my experiences and produced, in the end, a concise theology
of Christian education. Those of you familiar with 30 years of the
Disciplers' Handbook, or the first chapter of *Created to Learn* (1996),
or the framework of *Called to Reach* (2007) will recognize it immediately. I ask for your patient indulgence as I lay it out once again for
new readers.

A Theology of Christian Education: The Disciplers' Model

No single model can encompass the whole of Christian growth.
Like Piaget's table of three cones,[11] the "truth" of the cones remains
the same even as their appearance changes as one moves around
the table. So the truth of God's plan for the spiritual formation of
disciples—justification (conversion, regeneration), sanctification
(discipleship, being equipped), and final glorification—does not
change; but we can see His plan from many different perspectives.
There are many helpful models, which is why I am using the indefi-
nite article—"a" theology of Christian education.

The Disciplers' Model is the answer to that simple yet profound
question I prayed for during those early years. While it may sound
sanctimonious—perhaps a bit self-serving—to claim that this model
of mine is "the Lord's answer," I know of no other way to say it. I
cannot claim any right of creation or discovery. My intent is to honor
the Lord who answered my prayers and who gave me the means
to teach into the Deaf unknown with confidence and into many
unknowns since. The Disciplers' Model became, and remains, my

---

[11] Picture a table with three cones, a larger one behind, and two smaller ones in
front. As one moves around the table, the two-dimensional perception of the cones
changes, while the three-dimensional reality remains constant.

teaching compass. And now, after 30 years, I can say that this simple model represents a divinely ordained process that has never failed to move my students or me in the direction of spiritual growth and Christlikeness.[12]

The surrounding circle of the model represents the Holy Spirit as Teacher, the One who holds all the other elements together in a balanced synergism. In our text we will look closely at "**God as Teacher**," with **chapters 3, 4, and 5 detailing Father, Son, and Spirit as Teacher.** God is, in His very nature, a Teacher. The more we imitate His methods and manners, and the more we allow Him to teach through us, the more effective we will be in facilitating spiritual growth.[13]

The two foundation stones of the model are the Bible (eternal truth) and needs of learners (present needs). In every teaching encounter of Jesus, we see Him conveying eternal truths to learners in the context of their immediate (though not always well-perceived) needs. **Chapter 6, "The Bible as Curriculum,"** provides a theological analysis of Scripture as the central focus of Christian teaching, whatever other curricular helps we choose. **Chapter 12, "How to Study the Bible,"** provides practical helps in "rightly dividing the Word of Truth" in preparation for teaching. **Chapter 7, "The Disciple,"** focuses on the general needs of all learners and the process of discipling, while chapters **15, 16, 17, and 18** detail specific needs of **preschoolers, children,**

The Disciplers' Model

Growth

Think Relate Value

Bible Needs

Holy Spirit

---

[12] Am I, after these 30 years, like Christ? No. Am I more like Christ today than I was 30 years ago? By all means. I still frustrate my wife and embarrass my children. I still anger (or disappoint) my students. My (lack of) warm social skills call for gracious patience on the part of dear colleagues. But I am better today than I was before. Because of Him.

[13] For those unfamiliar with the Disciplers' Model, and wanting to learn more, you can find much more extensive discussions in *The Disciplers' Handbook: From Transmitting Lessons to Transforming Lives* (1979; 9th ed., 2006), which can be downloaded as PDF files free of charge from the North American Professors of Christian Education Web site (http://www.NAPCE.org).

youth, and adults, as well as suggested methods for helping learners
in these age groupings grow spiritually.

Three pillars define the process of spiritual growth. The left pillar
focuses on helping learners think. It stands on the left foundation
stone, the Bible, and emphasizes the need to understand the meaning of Scripture for daily living. Here we help learners contrast their
own personal perceptions of subjective truth with the eternal truth
of God. The right pillar focuses on helping learners integrate the
values of Scripture into personal priority systems. It stands on the
right foundation stone, learner needs, and emphasizes the personal
relevance of God's Word for "my needs." Here we help learners
contrast their own emotional turmoil with emotional maturity that
comes from God. **Chapter 11, "The Goal of Christian Education:
Christlikeness,"** analyzes these two processes in detail.

The central pillar focuses on helping learners establish relationships. Churches are communities of faith in which we pray, "*Our*
Father in heaven." Part of the process of growing spiritually is connecting with other believers in meaningful ways, and this happens
best in small, interactive classes and even smaller groupings within
classes. We cannot grow alone, no matter how independent or self-
reliant we may choose to be. These relational aspects are covered in
chapter 8, "The Church's Role in Teaching," and **Chapter 9, "The
Family's Role in Teaching."**

The capstone of the model is our goal, growth in Christ. We lead
learners to think beyond personal perceptions by asking questions
and posing problems. More than engaging them in an academic
pursuit of truth, we help them consider their perceptions in light of
God's message. We move them beyond a simple acquaintance with
Bible stories to actually *living biblically*. This is rational growth.

We lead learners to remove emotional "smiley face" masks and
become more real by sharing ourselves and listening, to move toward
emotional maturity by "putting off" negative attitudes in the discipling group, to overcome personal hurts through mutual support in
the love of Christ. This is emotional growth.

We lead learners to relate meaningfully with others, *receiving from
them freely* when in need, and *giving freely to them* when they are in
need, to move them into ministry with others in the name of the One

who freed them from self-centeredness and its resulting stagnation. This is relational growth.

Thinking, feeling and valuing, and relating are aspects of spiritual growth in Christ. **Chapter 10, "The Pastor as Teacher,"** provides guidance as we engage believers and encourage them to become pastor-teachers in their own right. **Chapter 11, "The Goal of Christian Education,"** provides the capstone for the theological section of the text and defines a means to lead believers to develop toward Christlikeness.

A Theology of Christian Education *Organization*

For theology to take root in a local congregation, it needs a framework, an anchor. The Disciplers' Model itself is organized, but to engage a given congregation, there must be organizational connections between theory and practice. Our text is more than a teaching text. It is designed to help leaders and congregations develop a plan for growth. **Chapter 2, "A Theology of Organization,"** provides the biblical basis for such an organizational structure. **Chapter 13, "Planning to Teach,"** and **Chapter 14, "Creating an Unforgettable Lesson,"** provide specific details for organizing learning experiences. **Chapter 19, "How to Select Curriculum,"** provides practical helps for choosing the right materials from a wide variety of sources. **Chapter 20, "Teacher Training,"** provides practical guidance in setting up, maintaining, and conducting ongoing teacher training efforts. **Chapter 21, "Administrating Educational Programs,"** provides specific guidelines for coordinating the many avenues for spiritual growth within the congregation. **Chapter 22, "Ministering Alongside Volunteers,"** provides guidance in enlisting, organizing, training, and supporting the many volunteers needed for a multi-faceted Christian education program. **Chapter 23, "Evaluating the Teaching Ministry,"** provides practical guidelines for analyzing present strengths and weaknesses in a congregation's Christian education enterprise.

These administrative guidelines and suggestions provide "the cup," the container, which delivers Living Water to the thirsty and Living Bread to the hungry. The Disciplers' Model provides a picture of the process by which Water and Bread are assimilated into the system, individually and collectively, that we might "grow in every way into Him who is the head—Christ" (Eph 4:15).

Teaching into the Unknown—Revisited

I was teaching into the unknown, using my educational compass, but not knowing whether it could guide me in this unknown land. During a session on that first, frigid day in Kazakhstan, I asked a question. A student in the back of the room raised his hand and answered. It was a good answer, and it led me to elaborate. When I paused, the student raised his hand and said, "I wish to apologize to the professor for the inadequacy of my answer. I will endeavor to do better in the future." Apparently, my additional comment made him think I considered his answer incomplete. "Your answer was fine. You answered the question well. My additional comment was not a criticism of your answer but merely a way to extend the thought. I call that teaching. No apology is needed." During the next break he moved his things from the back of the room to the front and joined the discussions.

Later in the week I decided to use small groups to integrate my presentation with what they experienced in their own churches. I gave a brief overview of a portion of the material and then divided the students into six groups. I asked them to consider ways they were already using the material in their churches. They looked perplexed. I explained again, and all but one group set about doing their best. The one group called me over and, through my translator, asked what I wanted exactly. I explained the assignment again.

My translator turned to me and said, "They do not understand what you want. *They cannot do what you are asking.*" It made me a little angry, quite frankly. It reminded me of all the hearing folks I met years ago who claimed that Deaf people could not "discuss Bible passages"—that they needed simple teaching, "on their level." What I discovered was that it was usually the sign language limitations *of the hearing leaders* that was at fault, not the mental or social or language limitations of the Deaf. Experiences with groups of Deaf youth and adults demonstrated that they did well with question-and-answer approaches, with discussion, and with problem-solving activities once they were given the opportunity. No, these Russian

Baptist leaders could do exactly what I was asking. They just needed a little prompting.

I turned to the interpreter and said, "They *can* do what I am asking, and they *will* do what I am asking, and *you* will be amazed!" The words surprised me, so I prayed, hoping that the Lord had prompted them! I told her to tell the group to do the best they could. She rolled her eyes and did as I asked. They rolled their eyes and turned to the task.

A few minutes later I asked for reports. No one moved. I asked again, "Who will come and share your group's conclusions?" One of the members of a group elbowed another and told him to report. He obediently walked to the front and began, timidly, to report. His statements were tentative and rather simple, but they were correct. With each point he made, I responded with some of the affirming words I'd learned in Russian: "good," "yes," "I agree," "correct," "excellent." With each affirmation his confidence grew, and he shared more. It took little encouragement to get the second and third and fourth reporters to the front.

We moved to the second section of material, and during the process of their group work, the time for tea break arrived, which Russians take quite seriously. Discussion on the material continued as they walked to the dining hall, and during the 20-minute teatime, and on their way back. Once back in the classroom, they quickly reassembled in their groups. Discussion was more lively now, practical applications deepened, diagrams were created and redrawn to explain points. Students made more discoveries and raised deeper questions about church practices and how they fit into the material. The darkness of the unknown was receding. They were behaving like students the world over.

In the midst of the third session of "rowdy" discussions, my translator looked at me with an amazed expression on her face and said, "I've never seen anything like this." Praise the Lord!

In the last session, while discussing the Holy Spirit as Teacher, one student, an academic vice president from Bishkek, stepped to the marker board and drew what looked like a tongue hanging down from the surrounding circle of the model. He explained that it was a handle, making the circle into a magnifying glass. "The Holy Spirit is a magnifying glass. Only He can show us truly"—and at this point, he began pointing to the various parts of the model—"what the Bible says, what our needs are, how we need to think and value, how to teach so our people can grow in Christ." I was so impressed that I violated the old Soviet code of educational practice ["Teachers must never allow students to know they've learned from them"]. I told him I had never thought of that before but that I would certainly use it from now on. This experienced academic dean simply beamed with delight. There were scores of such "moments" during the week. The final exam came, and all the students passed.

As we met for the last time, one of the students, the president of the Russian Baptist Union in Central Asia, stood and spoke for the class. "Thank you for this class. You have not only taught us how to teach, but more importantly you have shown us how to teach. We will never teach our classes the same way again. Please come again."

The Bishkek contingent made their way to their vans for the long trek back over the mountains. I went to get my bags. I was so thankful to the Lord for the good response. Thirty minutes later, the building secure, I got into the car and noticed that all the students were standing next to their vans. It was well below freezing outside, but there they stood, hats removed, waiting. Waiting for what? As we drove past them, they turned to face the car as we made our way out the drive, waving good-bye. I am not a weeper, but I wept at that sight. As we turned the corner, they tumbled into the vans, and headed home. The Holy Spirit had brought us together, built relational bridges, and shined the Lord's resurrection light into the darkness of the unknown.

I feel strange sharing the story, as if it is something I should simply treasure in my heart. But the words illustrate the point. The Compass can lead us even as we teach into the unknown. Life and Light had grown in the darkness that week, and it was Christ. The Compass is a theology of Christian education—Bible based, Christ centered, learner oriented—that led me through the early unknowns of that week, that led us all to a level above both our cultures, and that opened the door for further teaching opportunities.

It is this same theology of Christian education that we offer you through the pages of this text. To this end—growth in Christ—we all have labored over these months. To this end we have prayed and studied and written. May Christ be lifted up, and may the Church be strengthened, as you give yourself first to the Lord and then to the heartfelt words written in these pages. Lord Jesus, make it so!

Chapter 2

A THEOLOGY OF
ORGANIZATION:
WORKING TOGETHER

Bob Welch

Since God is not a God of disorder but of peace . . .
everything must be done decently and in order.
(1 Cor 14:33,40)

Asa professor of church administration, I am frequently
asked to advise pastors and other ministers about the organization of their churches. I analyze various structuring
documents like organizational charts, the constitution and bylaws,
and policy manuals. I ask questions like, "How many individuals do
you directly supervise?" and "How is the laity of the church organized to exercise their spiritual gifts?"

From these observations I can quickly determine the underlying
philosophy and theology for conducting the affairs of the church.
Research clearly demonstrates that the *minister who does not have a
proper grasp of the biblical role of leadership is destined for a weak and
often unsatisfactory ministry.*[1]

A Pastor in Distress

I recently recognized this very fact in my own pastor. The press
of administrative details of the church was driving him from effective pastoral ministry. The harder he worked, the less he was able to
accomplish the work God called him to do in our church. I strongly

---

[1] For a summary of research conducted in staff mortality, see the preface to Robert Welch,
Church Administration: Creating Efficiency for Effective Ministry (Nashville: B&H, 2005).

16

encouraged him to call an associate pastor for administration who could assist him in these details. While I fully understood his need to do so, and the benefits he would gain, I wondered whether he saw the need and would carry through.

Organization Is Natural

I stand in awe of the beauty and wonder of nature. I love to look into the evening sky and view hundreds of stars that shine down from their places millions of miles away. As I study the heavens through my telescope, this grandeur is magnified a thousand times over. With each morning's sunrise, the splendor of our own planet reveals itself in a burst of color, movement, and power.

Having been trained as a scientist, I am spellbound at the intricate design of the creation of our heavenly Father. From the one-celled amoeba, whose exact organization is mirrored millions of times over in a laboratory beaker, to the complex creature called human, whose essence is made up of millions upon billions of single cells, one sees the handiwork of the remarkable Creator.

Just think of it! When you plant an apple seed, you always get an apple tree. Further, that tree produces apples, and those apples produce seeds that will produce more apple trees. Ever wonder why the apple seed does not produce a pear tree? Or a lemon tree? All three are fruit trees and serve the same general purpose—to provide fruit to eat. Why did God, in His creation, bring order and organization to the various elements of our world? Why do fungus and mold differ from the grass? Why does grass differ from the rosebush? And why does the rosebush differ from the oak tree? Even among trees, why does the oak tree, with all its strength and usefulness, differ significantly from the giant sequoia tree of coastal California? To the Christian the answer is simple: because God in His creative act ordered it so.

Since the beginning of time mankind has accepted the concept that creation, so intricate in design, required a Creator, a Designer. Scientists over the past hundred years or so have postulated theories that our universe, including the earth and mankind, evolved by happenstance. Foremost in this change of view was the work of Charles Darwin in the middle part of the nineteenth century. His theory of evolution (often called Darwinism) concluded that, through a random combination of chemicals and environments, the organisms and life forms we see today evolved. Darwin provided an intellectually acceptable alternative to the ordered design of God.

You might think my primary objection to Darwin's theory, being a Creationist, is its obvious religious significance. But far more troubling for me, as a scientist, is its weakness from a scientific perspective. Every scientific venue—chemistry, biology, mathematics, geology, physics—has refuted the theory. Darwinism cannot be demonstrated as an acceptable theory because it cannot be duplicated in the laboratory, which is the standard proof a theory requires.

Specifically, when a mutation occurs in nature—an event required to produce a different species—its modification cannot be sustained to the next generation. Generally, both the laws of probability, which stand against mutational changes in the first place, and the second law of thermodynamics, which demands atrophy (decline) in those changes which spontaneously occur, determine that modifications must grow worse, not better, unless acted on from an Outside Force. And science declines to consider the Outside Force.[2]

This rejection of the supernatural, as part of the natural order of things, places some Darwinists in a bind. They are abandoning their support of evolution theory, because the theory cannot be verified empirically. Yet they continue to seek a "natural explanation" for life as we know it.

The Bible directly speaks to the natural order of the universe in its opening verse: "In the beginning, God created the heavens and the earth" (Gen 1:1). As I look at the story of creation in the first chapters of Genesis, I am captured by the progression—the sequence—of the creation events. First light from darkness, then separation of waters; vegetation and the biological creatures appear after land, water, and food are available. God's ultimate creation was man, who was placed in charge (dominion) over it all. There was order, and it was good.

---

[2] For a comprehensive defense of the biblical account of the creation and a discussion of the questions surrounding the evolutionist from a contemporary scientist's view see: Phillip Johnson, *Darwin on Trial* (Downers Grove, IL: InterVarsity Press, 1993; the perspective of a lawyer); Luther Sutherland, *Darwin's Enigma: Ebbing the Tide of Naturalism* (Green Forest, AR: Master Books, 1997); J.C. Sanford, *Genetic Entropy & the Mystery of the Genome* (Downers Grove, IL: InterVarsity Press, 2005); Michael Behe *Darwin's Black Box* (New York: Simon & Schuster, 2000); and John Ashton, *In Six Days: Why Fifty Scientists Choose to Believe in Creation* (Green Forest, AR: Master Books, 2000). Each of these authors takes the tenets of Darwin's evolution and discredits the theory from a variety of scientific disciplines.

I am a young earth scientist who views the earth as being thousands, not millions, of years old. Even secular historians have difficulty dating "civilizations" much older than several thousands of years. Therefore, when the Bible speaks of civilizations like the Egyptian and Sumerian, with sophisticated political, military, and religious systems, it describes a humankind created with a sense of order and organization from the very beginning of man.

Organization Is Biblical

Joseph's Example

In the earliest parts of the Bible, we find evidence of innate human organizational philosophy. Much of the early part of Genesis details the family structure of the patriarchs: Abraham, Isaac, and Jacob (later called Israel) lived by family and community rules.

As we move into the later part of Genesis, we find the son of Jacob prominently engaged in organization. Joseph's story is told from Genesis 37 onward. Joseph was the favored son of Jacob and was sold into Egyptian slavery at age 17 by his jealous brothers. He first served in the household of Potiphar, captain of the guard and an officer to the pharaoh. Because of his excellent service, he was put in charge of the entire household. The context of the biblical story develops around his wrongful placement in prison and his ultimate release because of his God-given ability to interpret Pharaoh's dreams. In Genesis 41, Joseph suggests practical ways to deliver Egypt from a future famine.

> The proposal pleased Pharaoh and all his servants. Then Pharaoh said to his servants, "Can we find anyone like this, a man who has the spirit of God in him?" So Pharaoh said to Joseph, "Since God has made all this known to you, there is no one as intelligent and wise as you. You will be over my house, and all my people will obey your commands. Only with regard to the throne will I be greater than you." (Gen 41:37–40)

Organization in the court of the pharaoh not only saved Egypt from starvation but also provided an escape for Jacob's family and the movement of the nation of Israel into Egypt. This movement of

the covenant people from the promised land would set the stage for
a second example of God's use of organization during the time of the
exodus.

Jethro's Advice

The story of Moses and his leadership in the exodus of Israel from
Egypt 400 years later teaches an important organizational axiom:
no matter how good we are, we cannot do it alone. For 40 years Moses
lived in the household of the Egyptian pharaoh. He was groomed
as a member of the ruling family, which included military training,
as well as education in the history and politics of the cultures of his
day. His career as an Egyptian leader came to an end when he killed
a taskmaster who was abusing a Jewish slave. As a result, Moses
spent 40 years as an exile in the Midianite Desert in the household of
Jethro, a Midianite priest.

Moses was called by God to free Israel from slavery and to return
her to the promised land. In Exodus 18, we find Jethro bringing
Moses' family to him in the wilderness. Jethro notices that things are
not going well for Moses. In fact, we might say that the term "disor-
ganization" would be kind. In verse 14, Jethro asks Moses,

> "What is this thing you're doing for the people? Why
> are you alone sitting as judge, while all the people stand
> around you from morning until evening?"
>
> Moses replied to his father-in-law, "Because the people
> come to me to inquire of God. Whenever they have a dis-
> pute, it comes to me, and I make a decision between one
> man and another. I teach [them] God's statutes and laws."
> (Exod 18:14–16)

One would think Jethro would be proud of his son-in-law's devotion
to God's call for leadership. But such is not the case. Jethro declares,
"What you're doing is not good." Notice Jethro's explanation to
Moses. He faults Moses for poor leadership: "You will certainly wear
out both yourself and these people who are with you, because the
task is too heavy for you. You can't do it alone" (Exod 18:18). Then
Jethro gives sage advice that many in ministry miss even to this day.
Jethro told Moses that his leadership role was to represent the people
to God. He was to be the principal **teacher**, to teach them God's stat-

utes and laws as well as to teach them the way to live and what they must do. That was Moses' role, his responsibility.

Jethro then advises Moses to delegate other leadership responsibilities to selected men who were able, God-fearing, trustworthy, and hated bribes. Leaders would be assigned to various sized groups of people based on their ability. A principle to be learned from this structure is that, **from the lowest to the highest leader, each person was subordinate to someone, with ultimate authority vested in Moses.**

> "Now listen to me; I will give you some advice, and God be with you. You be the one to represent the people before God and bring their cases to Him. Instruct them about the statutes and laws, and teach them the way to live and what they must do. But you should select from all the people able men, God-fearing, trustworthy, and hating bribes. Place [them] over the people as officials of thousands, hundreds, fifties, and tens. They should judge the people at all times. Then they can bring you every important case but judge every minor case themselves. In this way you will lighten your load, and they will bear [it] with you." (Exod 18:19–22)

Jethro describes the expected result of sharing responsibility, while at the same time retaining authority.

> "If you do this, and God [so] directs you, you will be able to endure, and also all these people will be able to go home satisfied."
> Moses listened to his father-in-law and did everything he said. (Exod 18:23–24)

Here are some key elements to this lesson from Exodus 18:

- God calls out individuals to provide leadership.
- Some tasks can be accomplished alone; others require the help of others.
- There may be dire consequences if a leader does not delegate responsibilities to others in the group.
- By assigning portions of a task to a subordinate, leaders are able to focus on the principal elements of their God-assigned task.

- Persons who are given jobs by leaders should meet certain limiting qualifications for the assignment.
- The wise leader will assign responsibilities based on the ability of the person to perform the task.[3]

The First Deacons

Let's visit this lesson of organization as it is played out in a situation recorded by Dr. Luke in the Acts of the Apostles. In chapter 6 we find a racial dispute in the first-century church. In this situation the widows of some Hellenistic Jews, that is, Jews of Greek language and culture, were not being cared for equally with the widows from the Hebraic Jewish community. The Hebraic Jews were responding to the teachings of Moses (Exod 22:22; Deut 10:18; 24:17–22) that required caring for widows and orphans. The Hellenistic Jews felt that the church should provide care equally to all widows.

How did the apostles, the leaders of the church, respond to this problem? They called the whole congregation to a meeting. Listen to their words in Acts 6:2–4:

> Then the Twelve summoned the whole company of the disciples and said, "It would not be right for us to give up preaching about God to wait on tables. Therefore, brothers, select from among you seven men of good reputation, full of the Spirit and wisdom, whom we can appoint to this duty. But we will devote ourselves to prayer and to the preaching ministry."

Note the similarity of the response to that of Exodus 18:

- The apostles stated their leadership role—prayer and ministry of the Word.
- The persons to be placed in charge of waiting on tables were to be selected from among their number.
- There were specific qualifications of those to be selected— "men of good reputation, full of the Spirit and wisdom."
- The apostles would delegate these selected workers their task.
- The word "select" indicates an election process, and those chosen were keenly interested in the service of ministry.

---

[3] Robert Welch, *Church Administration*. In the first four chapters of the text, the author provides practical application of the biblical principles noted here.

- The apostles would lay hands on the selected men in commissioning them to this task.

Verse 7 provides the results of this organized ministry: "So the preaching about God flourished, the number of the disciples in Jerusalem multiplied greatly, and a large group of priests became obedient to the faith."

The sharing of responsibility and leadership, seen in Jethro's advice and the commissioning of deacons, underscores the general wisdom expressed in Eccl 4:9–12.

> Two are better than one because they have a good reward for their efforts. For if either falls, his companion can lift him up; but pity the one who falls without another to lift him up. Also, if two lie down together, they can keep warm; but how can one person alone keep warm? And if somebody overpowers one person, two can resist him. A cord of three strands is not easily broken.

We see this wisdom displayed in the life of Jesus Himself, as He chose 12 "to be with Him" (Mark 3:14).

The Twelve Apostles

While God often calls and empowers individuals to ministry tasks, He also assigns responsibilities to groups. The 12 apostles provide the obvious example. Dr. Luke records the appointment of the Twelve in Luke 6:12–16.

> During those days He went out to the mountain to pray and spent all night in prayer to God. When daylight came, He summoned His disciples, and He chose 12 of them—He also named them **apostles**: Simon, whom He also named Peter, and Andrew his brother; James and John; Philip and Bartholomew; Matthew and Thomas; James the son of Alphaeus, and Simon called the Zealot; Judas the son of James, and Judas Iscariot, who became a traitor.

Jesus' ministry was well underway at this time, and He had many followers. Why would He choose to invest time and energy in the lives of a select dozen? Perhaps the term *apostle* itself provides a key. The *Holman Illustrated Bible Dictionary* gives the meaning of the word derived from the Greek *apostolos* as "one who is sent." In its primary meaning, the term refers to these 12 whom Jesus chose to train for the task of carrying His message to the world. These men had been with Jesus from the beginning of His ministry and were witnesses to His resurrection. He commissioned them for this very task following His resurrection from the dead.

Jesus knew that His short time on earth would be insufficient for Him to spread the good news of His saving grace throughout the world. Jesus empowered others to carry out that task in His place. After pouring His life into these chosen apostles through teaching and example, Jesus accomplished on the cross what He alone could accomplish—our salvation. But then Jesus delegated an assignment to them (Matt 28:16–20):

> The 11 disciples traveled to Galilee, to the mountain where Jesus had directed them. When they saw Him, they worshiped, but some doubted.
>
> Then Jesus came near and said to them, "All authority has been given to Me in heaven and on earth. Go, therefore, and make disciples of all nations, baptizing them in the name of the Father and of the Son and of the Holy Spirit, teaching them to observe everything I have commanded you. And remember, I am with you always, to the end of the age."

They had been called, trained, organized, and now commissioned. Jesus reminds them that He will always be with them as their supervisor, reemphasizing a promise He made earlier in the upper room: "I will not leave you as orphans, I am coming to you" (John 14:12), meaning, of course, His presence with them in the person of the Holy Spirit.

The Church

No sense of biblical organization appears more vividly than the organization of the church itself, as described by Paul. The church became the quintessential manifestation of God's divine organization to spread the good news of His Son to the whole world. Read how Paul described the church to the believers in Corinth in 1 Corinthians 12:

> Now there are **different gifts, but the same Spirit**. There are **different ministries, but the same Lord**. And there are

different activities, but the same God is active in everyone and everything. A manifestation of the Spirit is given
to each person to produce what is beneficial. (vv. 4–7)

. . . For as the body is one and has many parts, and all the
parts of that body, though many, are one body—so also is
Christ. (v. 12)

. . . Instead, God has put the body together, giving greater
honor to the less honorable, so that there would be no division in the body, but that the members would have the
same concern for each other. (vv. 24b–25)

. . . Now you are the body of Christ, and individual members of it. And God has placed these in the church:

first apostles, second prophets, third teachers,
next, miracles, then gifts of healing, helping,
managing, various kinds of languages.
Are all apostles? Are all prophets?
Are all teachers? Do all do miracles?
Do all have gifts of healing? Do all speak in languages?
Do all interpret?

[No, is the obvious answer. We need each other!]

But desire the greater gifts.
And I will show you an even better way.
(vv. 27–31; leading into the "love chapter," chapter 13)

To the church at Rome Paul wrote in Romans 12:4–5: "Now as we
have many parts in one body, and all the parts do not have the same
function, in the same way we who are many are one body in Christ
and individually members of one another."

And finally to the church at Ephesus, Paul described the leadership role responsibilities in the church and the objective of their
guidance:

And He personally gave some to be apostles, some prophets, some evangelists, some pastors and teachers, for the
training of the saints in the work of ministry, to build up
the body of Christ, until we all reach unity in the faith and
in the knowledge of God's Son, [growing] into a mature
man with a stature measured by Christ's fullness. Then we

will no longer be little children, tossed by the waves and
blown around by every wind of teaching, by human cunning with cleverness in the techniques of deceit. But speaking the truth in love, let us grow in every way into Him
who is the head—Christ. From Him the whole body, fitted
and knit together by every supporting ligament, promotes
the growth of the body for building up itself in love by the
proper working of each individual part. (Eph 4:11–16)[4]

Leaders

In his later years Paul wrote Timothy, his "son in the faith," and
described for him the leadership he expected in the church. He calls
the leaders (1) "elders," a term of maturity and wisdom; (2) "bish-
ops," a term of spiritual authority; (3) "presbyters," a term of leadership authority; and (4) "pastors," a term of shepherding care. In
these verses Paul gave specific criteria in selection and qualification
of these men whom the Holy Spirit would call out for the direction
and work of the church. They were to be individuals who

must be above reproach, the husband of one wife, self-con-
trolled, sensible, respectable, hospitable, an able teacher,
not addicted to wine, not a bully but gentle, not quarrel-
some, not greedy—one who manages his own household
competently, having his children under control with all
dignity. (If anyone does not know how to manage his own
household, how will he take care of God's church?). He
must not be a new convert, or he might become conceited
and fall into the condemnation of the Devil. Furthermore,
he must have a good reputation among outsiders, so that
he does not fall into disgrace and the Devil's trap. (1 Tim
3:2–7)

While many other texts from Scripture could be included in this
introduction to the biblical role of organization, these few included
here make clear that God is a God of order (1 Cor 14:40). God's creation, from atom to galaxy, displays for all to see God's eye for design
and detail. The progression of recorded history is stamped clearly
with the footprint of a resolute, ordered plan that from the beginning

---

[4] See chapter 11, "The Goal of Christian Education," for a full exegesis of this seminal
passage.

had as its goal the redemption of God's creation back unto Himself. In the Church we find the creation of an organism and organization to proclaim the gospel of good news of salvation through His Son Jesus Christ. Even the admonition passages of Christ's last instructions define a progression. We are to make disciples worldwide by (1) baptizing them, that is, evangelism, and (2) teaching them, that is, discipleship (Matt 28:19–20). And we are to do this from our hometown to our local Judea, our adjacent Samaria, and to the whole world. Wherever there are disunity and disorder, we find human activity without God's design and direction.

A Pastor's Distress Relieved

Is organization biblical? My pastor believes in organization. Our church called an administrator, an "ad-minister," who is now responsible for the everyday operational elements of the church. The pastor, as well as every minister on our staff, now has greater freedom, like the apostles of old, to give themselves fully to the ministry they were called to fulfill by the Holy Spirit.

Conclusion

As you read the chapters that follow, keep in mind the biblical admonition for being "fully trained." The writers of our text have given themselves to the Lord in order to fulfill what He expects: to provide adequate instruction so that you will be able to perform the ministry the Holy Spirit has placed on you. Jesus said: "Can the blind guide the blind? Won't they both fall into a pit? A disciple is not above his teacher, but everyone who is fully trained will be like his teacher" (Luke 6:39–40). An old Latin proverb says the same thing a different way: "By learning you will teach; by teaching you will learn." The one called to be a student of Christ is compelled not to learn simply for the sake of learning (or to get a degree), but *to learn for the sake of teaching others*. May God bless your learning now, that you may become effective teachers of others, who will, in turn, bless those they teach.

Discussion Questions

1. Why would scriptural references to the assignment of responsibility include statements of qualification for that ministry calling?
2. How does one know whether adequate and appropriate instruction has been given to allow someone to carry out the ministry they've been called to by the Spirit? Does it make a difference whether the minister is professional paid staff or lay volunteer?
3. Why is it appropriate to establish a scriptural foundation when discussing a new ministry of the church?

Additional Resources

Blanchard, Ken, Bill Hybels, and Phil Hodges. *Leadership by the Book.* New York: William Morrow and Company, 1999.

Gangel, Kenneth O. *Feeding and Leading.* Grand Rapids: Baker, 2000.

Rush, Myron. *Management: A Biblical Approach.* Colorado Spings: David C. Cook, 2001.

Shawchuck, Norman, and Roger Heuser. *Leading the Congregation.* Nashville: Abingdon, 1993.

Welch, Robert. *Church Administration: Creating Efficiency for Effective Ministry.* Nashville: B&H, 2005.

Part Two

BIBLICAL FOUNDATIONS FOR

THE TEACHING MINISTRY

Chapter 3

GOD AS TEACHER

Octavio J. Esqueda

The hidden things belong to the LORD our God,
but the revealed things belong to us and our children forever,
so that we may follow all the words of this law.
(Deut 29:29)

I am a big-picture person. I am constantly trying to find the relationship among all areas of life. I see all disciplines as interrelated with one another. I find the term *compartmentalization* problematic because things need to come together at some point for me to understand them accurately. I also aspire to discover the source of who I am and the meaning of what I do. Fortunately, in God I find the purpose and explanation of my life.

Christian ministry also finds its *raison d'être* in the God of the universe. The church exists to glorify God as its single purpose.[1] Consequently, we have Christian education because God is a teacher. He is our model and source of teaching. God uses different methods to teach humanity. In Him, therefore, we find the model for creativity in our teaching.

This chapter introduces several concepts that will be developed further through this book. I will attempt to present a big theological picture of Christian teaching. The first section will address the value of theology, explain how God the Father is a teacher because He reveals Himself to humanity, and describe that God's ultimate purpose of His revelation is that we may know Him and obey Him. The second section explains how God is described as a teacher in

---

[1] A. Malphurs, *A New Kind of Church: Understanding Models of Ministry for the 21st Century* (Grand Rapids: Baker, 2007), 84.

31

the Bible and provides examples of His teaching in both the Old and New Testaments.

The Importance of Theology

All Christians are theologians. Theology is central to the teaching ministry of the church and to every dimension of our lives. The word *theology* means "the study of God." It comes from the Greek words *theos* (God) and *logos* (speech, reason, word). To do theology is to reflect on God. Our theology, or the lack of it, affects the way we think and live. A. W. Tozer once said:

> What comes to our minds when we think about God is the most important thing about us. . . . The gravest question before the church is always God Himself, and the most portentous fact about any man is not what he at any given time may say or do, but what he in his deep heart conceives God to be like. We tend by a secret law of the soul to move toward our mental image of God. [2]

Theology and ministry are like the two sides of a dollar bill. The two faces are inseparable for the bill to have value. It is impossible to separate them completely because they belong to the same bill. Although we may look at one side at a time, in reality both sides must go together. In the same way, we cannot serve a God we do not know, and we cannot know God and fail to serve Him. Some have argued that Christian teachers are "practical theologians." Yet we *all* must be theologians and practitioners at the same time. God is the source and model for Christian teaching. We are theologians who proclaim God's truths that affect our everyday lives.

Since theology affects our lives completely, believers should be wise to develop into good theologians. God said that the most important thing we can do as human beings is to know Him and understand Him in order to do His will (Jer 9:24). Therefore, the central question is, How can we know God so we, as teachers, can teach His ways? The answer is found in God's revelation.

---

[2] A. W. Tozer, *The Knowledge of the Holy: The Attributes of God: Their Meaning in the Christian Life* (New York: Harper & Row, 1961), 1.

God's Revelation

We can know God because He reveals Himself to us. The word *revelation* means "disclosure." The God of the universe has taken the initiative to manifest Himself to us so we, as finite beings, can know Him, the infinite God. The Lord, then, is at the center of everything, and as the Creator, He determines and explains everything that exists. The Bible opens with the affirmation that God exists, and He created the heavens and the earth. Only in Him do we find purpose and meaning in our lives. As C. S. Lewis said, "I believe in Christianity as I believe that the Sun has risen—not only because I see it, but because by it, I see everything else."[3]

God reveals Himself to us in two basic ways—through general revelation and special revelation. God discloses Himself to human beings in a general way though creation and conscience (Ps 19). God uses creation to teach us about His power. Theologian Millard Erickson points out that general revelation "is God's communication of himself to all persons at all times and in all places."[4]

God reveals Himself in special ways through His Word: the incarnate Word (*logos*) of God, Jesus Christ, and the written Word of God, the Bible. Christ is, therefore, the central focus of God's revelation, and the way we can know Christ is through the written Word of God. Through special revelation human beings are able to "identify God, understand something about him, and point others to him."[5]

Consequently, the Bible then must be the content of our teaching. Christian teaching is based on Christ and focused on the Scriptures. The Word of God is the main curriculum in Christian education (see chapter 6, "The Bible as Curriculum"). Christian teaching is the exposition of the Bible to people. Sometimes at the end of a sermon, I have thought to myself, *Great message, wrong passage,* or worse, *Great message, no passage.* Christian teaching and preaching must be based on the Bible. Christian teachers are messengers of God's revelation.

---

[3] A. McGrath, *Christian Theology: An Introduction,* 4th ed. (Malden, MA: Blackwell, 2007), 102.
[4] M. Erickson, *Christian Theology,* 2nd ed. (Grand Rapids: Baker, 2000), 178.
[5] Ibid., 223.

God *Is* the Teacher

Every time the Lord reveals Himself to us, He is teaching us. Therefore, God, by His very nature, is a teacher. In fact, we teach because God is a teacher. Christian teaching exists because God is a teacher. The teaching ministry of the church finds its purpose in the active teaching of God. Job 36:22 says, "Look, God shows Himself exalted by His power. Who is a teacher like Him?" No one is a teacher like God. Therefore, it is good to be taught by Him. Psalm 94:12 says, "Lord, happy is the man You discipline and teach from Your law." The result of His teaching is blessing; we find goodness only in Him. Our main goal in life should be to know God because only in Him are we complete. Fortunately, it is His very nature to teach us!

In Psalm 25, we find the attitude God expects from us when we receive His instruction. The psalmist asks the Lord: "Show me," "Teach me," "Lead me," and "Remember me." He recognizes that to receive God's teaching is an act of grace. Therefore, we should be teachable and desire His message:

> Make Your ways *known to me*, Lord
> *teach me* Your paths.
> *Guide me* in Your truth and *teach me*,
> for You *are* the God of my salvation;
> I *wait* for You all day long.
> *Remember*, Lord, Your compassion
> and Your faithful love,
> for they [have existed] from antiquity.
> Do not remember the sins of my youth
> or my acts of rebellion;
> in keeping with Your faithful love, *remember me*
> because of Your goodness, Lord.
> The Lord *is* good and upright;
> therefore *He shows* sinners *the way*.
> *He leads* the humble in what *is* right
> and *teaches them* His way. (Ps 25:4–9, emphasis added)

Every time the Lord manifests Himself to us, He is teaching us. God is a teacher. Moreover, God is *the* teacher. His objective is that we follow His instruction. When God teaches, He looks forward to our compliance with His desires. The result of His instruction is not information but our action and a change of lifestyle. The following passages make this situation clear:

> I will instruct you and show you *the way to go*;
> with My eye on you, I will give counsel.
> (Ps 32:8, emphasis added)

> And many peoples will come and say,
> "Come, let us go up to the mountain of the LORD,
> to the house of the God of Jacob.
> He will teach us about His ways
> so that *we may walk in His paths*."
> For instruction will go out of Zion
> and the word of the LORD from Jerusalem.
> (Isa 2:3, emphasis added; cp. Mic 4:2)

When we receive God's words, we ought to follow them. He shows us the way in which we should go and the path in which we should walk. When God speaks, we need to obey. This is God's simple but indispensable expectation when He teaches.

God's Primary Educational Goal

Faith should be our appropriate response to the knowledge of God we receive through the revelation (disclosure) He has made of Himself. The Bible says that without faith it is impossible to please God (Heb 11:6). When God teaches us through His revelation, He expects us to respond in faith, believe Him, and obey Him. We can know God and recognize Him as God when we trust Him completely.

God expects our complete obedience in love. He does not take the initiative to speak to us just to satisfy our curiosity but to change us according to His will. Thus, obedience is the purpose of God's revelation to us as Deut 29:29 says: "The hidden things belong to the Lord our God, but the *revealed* things belong to us and our children forever, so that we may *follow* all the words of this law" (emphasis added). Every time God speaks to us, we are wise to comply with His words. Every time we teach the Bible, our expectation is that our students will obey God's Word.

Deuteronomy 6:4–5 summarizes God's educational goal for the Jewish people: "Listen, Israel: The LORD our God, the LORD is One. Love the LORD your God with all your heart, with all your soul, and with all your strength. These words that I am giving you today are to be in your heart." This passage, known as the *Shema* from the Hebrew word for "hear," constitutes the "basic confession of faith in Judaism."[6] All Jewish believers were to recognize the Lord as God and to love (obey) Him with all their being.

In the New Testament our Lord Jesus Christ also made the claim that the summary of God's written revelation is to love Him completely and to love our neighbor as ourselves (Matt 22:37–40). As a matter of fact, loving Jesus above everyone else is a requirement to follow Him (Matt 10:37–39). We must love Christ preeminently in order to be His disciples.

We prove that we love God when we follow His commandments. The purpose of Christian teaching is our transformation. We need to "be transformed by the renewal of" our minds (Rom 12:1–2) in order to see life as God sees it. We transform our minds when we change our thinking according to God's revelation. Only when we adapt our thoughts to God's can we understand His will. The teaching of the Bible must affect every area of our lives.

The goal of Christian education is to present everyone perfect in Christ Jesus (Col 1:28). Our final examination measures whether we are like Christ, behaving and living like Him. Therefore, we teach to change lives![7] The application of the Bible becomes, then, the key section for a lesson. God's standards should affect how I relate to my wife, students, and the people with whom I rub shoulders every day.

Examples of God as Teacher in the Scriptures

The Bible provides a record of God's different methods of teaching human beings. Our God is creative and has related with His people in diverse and varied ways. He chose a way to communicate His messages according to the context and situation of His people, the "learners." In the Bible we find the record of God's desire to com-

---

[6] E. D. Radmacher, ed., *Nelson's New Illustrated Bible Commentary* (Nashville: Thomas Nelson, 1999), 243.

[7] H. Hendricks, *Teaching to Change Lives* (Sisters: Multnomah, 1987).

municate with humanity. The Holy Scriptures tell us the story of salvation: God's intent to restore us to Himself in the context of the history of revelation.[8] The Old and New Testaments describe God's methods of unfolding this story. The Bible, then, is God's teaching book.

Old Testament

God created humanity so that He could enjoy a personal relationship with us. He created both men and women in His own image (Gen 1:27). Adam and Eve, the first human beings, had the benefit of listening to the Creator's voice and hearing His instruction (Gen 2:16). However, they sinned against God, and that relationship was affected profoundly (Gen 3). The connection between God and humanity was broken because of sin (Rom 5:12). Therefore, the main plot of the Bible is the story of redemption.

The Lord established a covenant with Abraham and his descendents. God chose Abraham, and through him He planned His redemptive plan of salvation (Gen 12:1–3; Gal 3:8). He taught the first Hebrew patriarchs in different ways: dreams, theophanies, angels, miracles, and His audible voice. Jacob, Abrahams' grandson, became Israel, the father of 12 sons who would form the Jewish people (Gen 35:9–12).

After they spent over 400 years in Egypt, with freedom at the beginning as residents but later as slaves, God called Moses to liberate His people. God appeared to Moses in a burning bush. Moses was able to receive God's instruction as if they had a face-to-face conversation. The mighty hand of God performed many miracles to teach about His power and existence. The plagues against Egypt ended with the death of every Egyptian firstborn. God culminated His victory by opening and closing the Red Sea to deliver Israel and to slay his oppressors. Everyone learned about God's power and majesty.

The Lord established a covenant with the people of Israel on Mount Sinai after their deliverance from Egypt (Exod 19:5–6). God promised them that He would be their God and they would be His people if they obeyed His commandments (Jer 11:4). The Lord wanted to be at the center of their lives. From that moment "every

---

[8] J. I. Packer, "God Has Spoken," in *The Christian Theology Reader*, ed. Alister McGrath, 3rd ed. (Malden, MA: Blackwell, 2007), 167.

aspect of Hebrew culture by design aided in the process of forming the belief of the faith community."[9] Every social activity had the intention of placing God as the focal point. God established feasts and festivals for the Hebrew community as opportunities for instruction about His intervention in their daily lives. Through these activities every person learned about their history and God's generosity.[10] We can learn that "teaching" happens at different times and circumstances, not only inside of a classroom.

The Hebrew community celebrated three main national festivals: Passover, Pentecost, and Tabernacles. The Passover commemorated the deliverance from slavery and oppression in Egypt. Also known as the Festival of Unleavened Bread, this holy convocation was held on the fourteenth of the first month (Nisan). During seven days every person in the community had to eat unleavened bread (Lev 23:6). God was teaching them to remember His holiness, the seriousness of sin, and its consequences. It was also an opportunity to remember God's provision to cleanse His people's sins and offer them salvation.

The Festival of Pentecost was celebrated 50 days after the Passover (Lev 23:26). This special day commemorated the giving of the law. Also known as the Festival of Weeks, this holy celebration took place at the end of the wheat harvest on the sixth day of the month of Sivan. Every person was reminded that the Lord is the One who provides. Therefore, they gave Him back from their firstfruits as God blessed them (Deut 16:10). God taught them, as an agricultural society, to keep in mind His goodness through the fruits of their labors. Even though they worked hard, the Lord made their harvest possible.

The Festival of Tabernacles, also known as the Festival of Booths, commemorated the journey of the people of Israel in the wilderness. This special feast lasted seven days; the people dwelt in booths to remember their wanderings as the Hebrew people left Egypt (Neh 8:14). The people of Israel gathered at the end of the fruit harvest to focus on the Lord's deliverance and to recommit their total dependence on Him. God was teaching them that disobedience to His will brings affliction and purposeless living.

---

[9] J. R. Estep Jr., ed., *C.E.: The Heritage of Christian Education* (Joplin: College Press, 2003), 2.

[10] W. Barclay, *Educational Ideas in the Ancient World* (Grand Rapids: Baker, 2003).

God commanded the people of Israel to celebrate other special days. The Sabbath was observed as a holy day (Lev 23:3). Every week the Hebrews devoted a whole day to the Lord. They were commanded to rest because God rested after He created the world. Later on, a main purpose of the synagogue Sabbath services was religious instruction.[11] The people of Israel focused on God and His teachings. The Day of Atonement was a holy convocation for the people to afflict their souls and offer sacrifices for the sins of the nation (Lev 23:27). They remembered that their God was a holy God and that sin goes against His nature. Every occasion was a teachable situation, as Siew points out:

> Through a system of elaborate celebrations, the people remembered their humble beginnings (Passover/Feast of Unleavened Bread), celebrated God's sustained grace (Feast of Weeks, Feast of Ingathering), received cleansing (Day of Atonement), and regularly consecrated themselves to holy service (Sabbath, New Moon).[12]

Old Testament laws and regulations told the Hebrew people how to relate correctly to the holy and majestic Creator. Acts of obedience were the appropriate reaction to God's teaching.

The Hebrew sacrificial system was also a response to the holiness of the Lord. Priests interceded before God by offering sacrifices on behalf of the people and themselves.[13] Priests were also educators: First, they provided religious instruction to younger priests. Second, they instructed people regarding offerings, festivals, and all special days in the Hebrew calendar.[14] We learn that God also uses people to teach His truths to others.

God was supposed to be central in everyday life activities. Everything in the culture was intended to point people toward God. The Hebrew mind-set emphasized a holistic approach to see life under the Lord's authority with the main goal of pleasing Him in every

---

[11] Barclay, 24.

[12] Yau-Man Siew, "Hebrew Education through Feasts and Festivals," in *Evangelical Dictionary of Christian Education*, ed. Michael Anthony (Grand Rapids: Baker Academic, 2001), 325.

[13] J. L. González, "Priesthood," in *Essential Theological Terms* (Louisville: Westminster John Knox, 2005).

[14] M. J. Anthony and W. S. Benson, *Exploring the History and Philosophy of Christian Education: Principles for the 21st Century* (Grand Rapids: Kregel, 2003).

area and with every decision.[15] God did not want them to compartmentalize their religious duties from the rest of their lives. God's
teaching ought to relate to everything we are and do. This reality
permeates the Old Testament story as Reed and Prevost point out:

> The history of the Jews is a record of their relationship
> with God as expressed in covenant. Their educational sys-
> tem arose as an instrument to pass on that relationship to
> subsequent generations. It also was an act of obedience to
> God's commands within the covenant. The Jews believed
> that, as God has chosen them, God was concerned with the
> means by which they should educate and be educated.[16]

New Testament

The New Testament focuses on Jesus Christ, how He completes
the plan of salvation and the reestablishment of God's dominion over
His creation.[17] Jesus brings fulfillment to Old Testament prophecies
of salvation and restoration. He is the main object of God's revelation, as Heb 1:1–2 affirms: "Long ago God spoke to the fathers by the
prophets at different times and in different ways. In these last days,
He has spoken to us by [His] Son, whom He has appointed heir of all
things and through whom He made the universe." God uses different
methods to teach humanity, but His supreme revelation is through
His Son. In Jesus human beings can see and comprehend God (John
14:9). Chapter 4 further explores the role of Jesus as Teacher.

God also teaches through His Spirit (John 14:26). Chapter 5 develops the Spirit's role. God uses believers to instruct one another
(Rom 15:14). The Lord accomplishes His purposes through His
Word (John 17:17). God communicated in the New Testament
through different instructional methods like miracles, the apostles, and the church. The Lord is not limited to only one way of
teaching.

We can conclude that God is the model of creativity in teaching. He reveals Himself in different and varied ways. He teaches
people according to their circumstances. He is not limited to a single

---

[15] W. R. Yount, *Created to Learn* (Nashville: B&H, 1996).
[16] J. E. Reed and R. Prevost, *A History of Christian Education* (Nashville: B&H, 1993), 45.
[17] D. L. Bock, "Introduction," in *A Biblical Theology of the New Testament*, ed. R. B. Zuck and D. L. Bock (Chicago: Moody, 1994).

teaching technique but uses diverse methods throughout history. Therefore, we should follow His example when we teach His Word. Creativity becomes necessary in Christian education because God is creative.

I still remember a Sunday school class when I was a teenager because of the teacher's creativity in presenting God's message. As I was approaching the classroom, I noticed something unusual. The setting was like a funeral service. At the center of the classroom was a black coffin. Everything was dark, and the smell of coffee was filling the air. The teacher told us that someone had died and that we were to mourn the death of that person. He taught about death and our destiny after we die. At the end of the lesson, he asked us to decide whether the dead person in the coffin would spend eternity with God. He told us to look at the face of the dead person, one by one, and then guess his destiny. As I reluctantly looked inside the coffin, I realized it had a mirror. As I saw my face there, I thought about the imminence of death and the importance of making a decision for Christ while we are still alive. That teacher was creative and wanted to present God's message in different ways so his students could learn.

Our Lord provides the greatest example of diverse teaching methods. Michael Lawson summarizes the diverse methodology of the Creator:

1. He spoke directly and audibly from heaven.
2. He wrote on tablets of stone.
3. He became flesh.
4. He revealed Himself in supernatural beings.
5. He gave vivid dreams and visions.
6. He wrote on the walls of a palace.
7. He made an animal talk.
8. He voiced truth through human prophets.
9. He composed poetry.
10. He provided visual reminders of promises.[18]

---

[18] M. S. Lawson, "Biblical Foundations for a Philosophy of Teaching," in *The Christian Educator's Handbook on Teaching: A Comprehensive Resource on the Distinctiveness of True Christian Teaching*, ed. K. O. Gangel and H. G. Hendricks (Grand Rapids: Baker, 1988), 62.

Conclusion

Christian teaching exists because God is a teacher. Pazmiño in his excellent work, *God as Teacher*, concludes, "God as the creator is the educator from whom all content of education issues."[19] The Lord's desire to communicate with His creation establishes the foundation of Christian education. God's self-revelation is the source of teaching. Therefore, the content of our teaching must be God's written revelation (the Bible).

We teach to change lives. Our goal is to see life as God does. We need to renew our understanding, to adjust our thoughts and actions so we can understand God's will (Rom 12:2). God's expectation is the same every time He teaches: complete obedience. Therefore, we must expect obedience to God's Word when we teach. Application, then, becomes central in Christian education. The goal is transformation not merely information. The purpose of our teaching must be communicating God's truth in ways that "create genuine understanding and the desire to change in accordance with God's self-revelation."[20] To follow God's example, we also need to be creative when we teach.

God helps us see the big picture of life and ministry. In Him we find meaning and purpose for everything we do. All aspects of the teaching ministry of the church center on God. Our theology affects our existence and service to the Lord. He desires to communicate with us and reign over us, as John Calvin concluded:

> For how can the idea of God enter your mind without
> instantly giving rise to the thought, that since you are his
> workmanship, you are bound, by the very law of creation,
> to submit to his authority?—that your life is due to him?—
> that whatever you do ought to have reference to him? If so,
> it undoubtedly follows that your life is sadly corrupted, if
> it is not framed in obedience to him, since his will ought to
> be the law of our lives. On the other hand, your idea of his

---

[19] R. W. Pazmiño, *God as Teacher: Theological Basis in Christian Education* (Grand Rapids: Baker Academic, 2001), 33.

[20] M. Young, "Biblical Foundations for a Philosophy of Teaching," in *Evangelical Dictionary of Christian Education*, ed. M. Anthony (Grand Rapids: Baker Academic, 2001), 80.

nature is not clear unless you acknowledge him to be the
origin and fountain of all goodness.[21]

Discussion Questions

1. Explain the relationship between theology and Christian
    education.
2. How does God's revelation affect the content of Christian
    teaching?
3. What methods does God use to teach today in comparison with
    the methods He used in both the Old and New Testaments?
4. Explain God's educational goal with the *Shema*.
5. Why is creativity important for a Christian teacher?

Bibliography

Anthony, Michael J., and Warren S. Benson. *Exploring the History and
Philosophy of Christian Education: Principles for the 21st Century.*
Grand Rapids: Kregel, 2003.

Barclay, William. *Educational Ideas in the Ancient World.* Grand
Rapids: Baker, 2003.

Bock, Darrell L. "Introduction." In *A Biblical Theology of the New
Testament*, ed. Roy B. Zuck and Darrell L. Bock. Chicago: Moody,
1994.

Calvin, J., and H. Beveridge. *Institutes of the Christian Religion.*
Translation of *Institutio Christianae religionis*. Reprint, with new
introd. Originally published: Edinburgh: Calvin Translation
Society, 1845–1846 (I, ii, 2). Oak Harbor, WA: Logos Research
Systems, Inc, 1997.

Erickson, Millard. *Christian Theology.* 2nd ed. Grand Rapids: Baker,
2000.

Estep, James Riley, Jr., ed. *C.E.: The Heritage of Christian Education.*
Joplin: College Press, 2003.

González, Justo L. "Priesthood." In *Essential Theological Terms.*
Louisville: Westminster John Knox, 2005.

---

[21] J. Calvin and H. Beveridge, *Institutes of the Christian Religion*. Translation of:
Institutio Christianae religionis. Reprint, with new introd. Originally published:
Edinburgh: Calvin Translation Society, 1845–1846. (I, ii, 2) (Oak Harbor, WA:
Logos Research Systems, Inc, 1997).

Hendricks, Howard. *Teaching to Change Lives*. Sisters, OR: Multnomah, 1987.

Lawson, Michael S. "Biblical Foundations for a Philosophy of Teaching." In *The Christian Educator's Handbook on Teaching: A Comprehensive Resource on the Distinctiveness of True Christian Teaching*, ed. Kenneth O. Gangel and Howard G. Hendricks. Grand Rapids: Baker, 1988.

Malphurs, Aubrey. *A New Kind of Church: Understanding Models of Ministry for the 21st Century*. Grand Rapids: Baker, 2007.

McGrath, Alister. *Christian Theology: An Introduction*. Malden, MA: Blackwell Publishing, fourth edition, 2007.

Packer, James I. "God Has Spoken." In *The Christian Theology Reader*, 3rd ed., ed. Alister McGrath. Malden, MA: Blackwell, 2007.

Pazmiño, Robert W. *God as Teacher: Theological Basis in Christian Education*. Grand Rapids: Baker, 2001.

Radmacher, Earl D. ed., *Nelson's New Illustrated Bible Commentary*. Nashville: Thomas Nelson, 1999.

Reed, James E., and Ronnie Prevost. *A History of Christian Education*. Nashville: B&H, 1993.

Tozer, A. W. *The Knowledge of the Holy: The Attributes of God: Their Meaning in the Christian Life*. New York: Harper & Row, 1961.

Yau-Man Siew. "Hebrew Education through Feasts and Festivals." In *Evangelical Dictionary of Christian Education*, ed. Michael Anthony. Grand Rapids: Baker Academic, 2001.

Young, Mark. "Biblical Foundations for a Philosophy of Teaching." In *Evangelical Dictionary of Christian Education*, ed. Michael Anthony. Grand Rapids: Baker Academic, 2001.

Yount, William R. *Created to Learn*. Nashville: B&H, 1996.

Chapter 4

JESUS, THE MASTER TEACHER

Rick Yount

So as He stepped ashore, He saw a huge
crowd and had compassion on them,
because they were like sheep without a shepherd.
Then He began to teach them many things.
(Mark 6:34)
When Jesus had finished this sermon, the
crowds were astonished at His teaching,
because He was teaching them like one who
had authority, and not like their scribes.
(Matt 7:28–29)

God revealed Himself as Teacher. Jesus clearly connected Himself to the Father when He stated, "I and the Father are one" (John 10:30). It is no surprise then that Jesus, though He preached the good news and met many physical needs, was known best as *Rabonni*, Master, Teacher.

Further, Jesus connected Himself to the Father *specifically* as Teacher: "For I have not spoken on My own, but the Father Himself who sent Me has given Me a command as to what I should say and what I should speak. I know that His command is eternal life. So the things that I speak, I speak just as the Father has told Me" (John 12:49–50). And again, "Don't you believe that I am in the Father and the Father is in Me? The words I speak to you I do not speak on My own. The Father who lives in Me does His works" (John 14:10). When the Pharisee Nicodemus met with Jesus at night, he acknowledged, "We know that You have come from God as a teacher" (John

45

3:2). Jesus came teaching what He had learned from His Father. And what was the result? Sherwood Eddy, in his classic *Maker of Men,* writes:

> He was allowed less than three years in which to do His work; little more than a year in His public ministry, and a year in retirement training His pathetic remnant. He was cut off in His young manhood, a little past the age of thirty. Socrates taught for forty years. Plato for fifty. Aristotle had lived long and filled libraries with his learning. Buddha and Confucius had fulfilled their three score and ten. [Jesus] was among a crushed people, under an oppressive legalism, zealously opposed and hated by scribes and Pharisees, betrayed by Jews and crucified by Gentiles. He left no book, no tract, or written page behind Him. He bequeathed no system, no philosophy, no theology, no legislation. He raised no armies, held no office, sought no influence, turned His back forever on might, magic, and cheap miracle.
>
> Yet He transformed the bigoted Jew and universalized his religion; He showed the philosophizing Greek the highest truth; He won the proud Roman to plant the cross on his standard instead of the eagle; He stretched out His hand to the great continents and transformed them—to Asia, to savage Europe, to darkest Africa, to America.[1]

Since Christian teachers desire a Christ-centered teaching ministry, it is natural to focus attention on Jesus as Master Teacher, the Example, the Model. God the Teacher in flesh. What kind of students did He have? What characteristics did He display? What methods did He use? What principles did He espouse?

In exploring these questions, we risk the danger of trampling the beauty of what we analyze. A botanist, for example, may carefully dissect a delicate flower and yet destroy it in the process, reducing it to wilted bits. We analyze Jesus in His role as Teacher with an intentional sense of awe and reverence. We honor Him as Lord even as we study Him and imitate Him as the Model of how we should teach.

---

[1] S. Eddy, *Maker of Men* (New York: Harper & Bros., 1941).

The Students of Jesus

A friend of mine, a fellow minister of education, invited me to join him for a cup of coffee at a local cafe. He was as depressed as any minister I'd ever known. As he poured out his heart, he returned again and again to the same lament: "If only I had a few committed people to work with!" and "If only we had some church members with the leadership skills to direct our programs!" Seminary had taught him about programs for children and youth and adults; singles and seniors; outreach and in-reach; organization and enlistment; church councils, weekly workers' meetings, and appreciation banquets. Where do we find the people to make these programs come to life? Where do lay leaders come from? Seminary had exposed him to a wide variety of *Christian ministry ideals*. He found himself in the *ordeal of local church ministry*, and he was sinking fast.

His experience is not unique. I suppose every minister has had feelings like these from time to time. But we are not called to some abstract, academic ideal. We are called "for the training of the saints in the work of ministry," or, as *The Message* has it, "to train Christians in skilled servant work" (Eph 4:12). We take the saints as they are, and disciple them—helping them grow to become all God intended them to be. That is our calling. And that is exactly what Jesus did with His disciples.[2]

We tend to think of the disciples—especially Peter, James, and John—as great men of faith. This they became. But they were not "great men of faith" when Jesus chose them. Though they were chosen carefully and prayerfully (Mark 6:12–16), they were very human. Let's look at some of the basic characteristics of the 12 men Jesus chose as His closest students.

The Disciples Were Imperfect

Scripture provides us ample evidence that the Twelve were rough in character and demeanor. James and John, the sons of Zebedee, were so short-tempered that they were nicknamed the "Sons of Thunder" (Mark 3:17). On one occasion when a Samaritan town did not welcome Jesus appropriately, James and John suggested He call

---

[2] See chapter 22, "Ministering alongside Volunteers," for practical help in this essential ministry.

fire down from heaven to destroy it. Jesus rebuked them for their outburst and went on to another village (Luke 9:54–55).

Simon was impetuous and unstable. Though Jesus gave him the name Peter (*Petros,* "rock," Matt 16:18), Peter gave little evidence of stability. Jesus told the disciples about His impending death in Jerusalem, but Peter protested. When the guards came for Jesus in Gethsemane, Peter drew a sword and cut off Malchus's ear (John 18:10). Though Peter had bragged that he would die for Jesus (John 13:37), he later denied being a disciple to a servant girl, to one of the men standing by the courtyard fire, and to one of the high priest's relatives (John 18:17, 25–27). Peter was impetuous and unstable, even after three years of living with the Master.

Thomas was a realist. He had been absent the first time Jesus had appeared to the disciples (John 20:24). "So the other disciples kept telling him, 'We have seen the Lord!' But he said to them, 'If I don't see the mark of the nails in His hands, put my finger into the mark of the nails, and put my hand into His side, I will never believe!'" (John 20:25). Where had Thomas been the last three years? He had witnessed many miracles at the hands of Jesus. He had lived and worked with these men. Why was he so stubborn?

And yet he was honest. When the facts presented themselves, he did not hesitate to act on them. A week later Jesus stood among them and invited Thomas to inspect His wounds. Thomas's reaction was immediate and absolute: "My Lord and my God!" (John 20:28).

Then the political power brokers, Judas Iscariot and Simon the zealot, saw in Jesus a potential Jewish King who might overthrow Roman oppression. Further, Judas was a thief, pilfering money from the common purse, which he was responsible to keep (John 12:4–6). The disciples were far from perfect.

The Disciples Were Slow to Learn

Jesus chose the Twelve during His first year of ministry.[3] For nearly three years they lived with Him, following Him and observing many miracles. But they were so slow to learn. He talked to them

---

[3] A. B. Bruce, *The Training of the Twelve,* 4th ed. (New York: A. C. Armstrong & Sons, 1894; reprint, New Canaan, Conn. Keats Publishing, 1979), 12. See also A. Edersheim, *The Life and Times of Jesus the Messiah,* vol. 1 (London: Longmans, Green and Co., 1890; reprint, Grand Rapids: Eerdmans, 1969), 348.

of His impending death and resurrection (Matt 16:29), and yet they were shocked when He actually died and they were surprised by His resurrection (Luke 24:6–11). Even when He appeared to them after His resurrection, some of them doubted (Matt 28:17)! They were slow to learn.

The Disciples Were Self-centered

As Jesus and the Twelve made their last journey to Jerusalem, the cross dominated Jesus' thoughts. Peter, however, could only think of the sacrifices *they* had made. "Look, we have left everything and followed You. So what will there be for us?" (Matt 19:27).

At another time Jesus and the disciples were making their way across the Sea of Galilee. A violent storm arose and nearly swamped the boat. What was their reaction? "Teacher! Don't you care that we're going to die?" (Mark 4:38). Jesus clearly revealed their self-centeredness: "Why are you fearful? Do you still have no faith?" (Mark 4:40). He had told them they were going over to the other side (Mark 4:35)—drowning in a storm had not been part of His plan.

Still another example of their self-centeredness is revealed at the arrest of Jesus. We've already noted Peter's false bravado: "I will lay down my life for you" (John 13:37). And again, "Even if everyone runs away because of You, I will never run away!" (Matt 26:33). Then Jesus told Peter he would disown Him three times before morning (v. 34). "'Even if I have to die with You . . . I will never deny You!' And all the disciples said the same thing" (v. 35). But when Jesus was arrested, "all the disciples deserted Him and ran away" (v. 56), and Peter succeeded in protecting himself through the night by denying Jesus three times (vv. 69–75).

The Disciples Were Uneducated and Unprofessional

The center of higher learning in Jesus' day was Jerusalem, and many of the inhabitants of Judea were well educated in the Law. Galilee was a different matter. Galilee provided rich soil for farming, an abundance of hard workers for a vast array of trades and businesses, and a bountiful lake for fishing. Its beauty may have led some to meditation and prayer, but it certainly did not evoke the dark fanaticism of the religious in Jerusalem. So, while Galilee was home to "generous spirits, warm hearts, simple manners, and earnest

piety," it was looked down on by the rabbinic leaders in the south.[4]
Edersheim reports the following common saying: "If a person wishes
to be rich, let him go north; if he wants to be wise, let him come
south."[5]

Jesus began and built His ministry in Galilee (Luke 23:5) and
chose men of the north to be His disciples. They were not educated
men, but they hungered for real righteousness, being sick of the righteousness then in fashion. They demonstrated basic elements of faith
and devotion. They displayed a willingness to grow and to learn.
Jesus saw great potential in these men.[6] That's why He could call unstable Simon "*Petros*," because He saw the "rock" that Simon would
ultimately become.

The Disciples Were Apprentices, Not Mere Learners

The differences between north and south can also be seen in two
words used for "learner." Coleman makes the distinction between
mathetas (practical apprentice) and *talmid* (academic scholar).[7] A.
B. Bruce underscores the idea of *mathetas* when He writes that Jesus
"desired not only to have disciples, but to have about Him *men whom
He might train to make disciples of others*" (emphasis mine). And
again, "The careful, painstaking education of the disciples secured
that the Teacher's influence on the world should be permanent; that
His kingdom should be founded on the rock of deep and indestruc-
tible convictions in the minds of a few, not on the shifting sands of
superficial evanescent impressions on the minds of the many."[8]

The disciples were not trained, but they were *trainable*. They had
not been taught, but they were *teachable*. Nothing more in learners
should a teacher desire, and nothing more does a teacher need!

The disciples were rough-hewn, imperfect, self-centered, and
untrained when Jesus prayerfully chose them. That is, they were normal people with all the problems and potential of people today. Yet
from among these Twelve came leaders who turned the entire known
world upside down for the Lord.

---

[4] Edersheim, *Life and Times of Jesus the Messiah*, vol. 1, 224–25.

[5] Ibid., 223.

[6] Bruce, *Training of the Twelve*, 5–8.

[7] L. Coleman, *Why the Church Must Teach* (Nashville: Broadman, 1984), 23.

[8] Bruce, 13.

How can we teach so that our learners become *mathetas* and, in time, leaders and teachers of others? What can we glean from Jesus' words and actions that will help us develop our skills in the teaching ministry of the church? It is to the Teacher that we now humbly and carefully turn our attention.

The Characteristics of Jesus as Teacher

In both the Ten Commandments and the Sermon on the Mount, "Who we are in the Lord" comes before "What we do for the Lord." Our best teaching flows out of our hearts—who we are—not merely from mouths or methodologies. So before we look at the methods of Jesus, we need to learn something of the person of Jesus.

Jesus Was What He Taught

Years ago I explained how "Jesus was the Model of what He taught," but what some students understood by that missed my intention. Jesus did not "model His teaching" like some runway queen parading the latest fad. His lifestyle was no put-on, conceived to reinforce His words. Jesus simply lived what He taught. What He taught flowed out of who He was.

One day, after Jesus finished praying, an observant disciple asked Jesus to teach them to pray (Luke 11:1–2). Educators call this a "teachable moment." Creating a climate of teachable moments, particularly in a formal class setting, is difficult. Jesus wasted no time responding to the request of the disciple.

Teaching naturally flowed from Jesus' life. His words and actions reinforced each other with an authority that amazed His hearers. "What we are" speaks more loudly than "what we say." Faith learning is more "caught from" than "taught by" a teacher. Some 30 years after Jesus had ascended to heaven, Peter wrote to pastors, "Shepherd God's flock among you . . . *not lording it over those entrusted to you, but being* examples *to the flock*"[9] (1 Pet 5:2–3, emphasis mine). Jesus

---

[9] Consider this command of Peter, the *pastor's* pastor, learned from the Master, when you consider the meaning of "pastoral authority." I had the privilege of preaching in a Kyrgyz Baptist church in Bishkek, Kyrgyzstan, in June 2007. The pastor translated my Russian into Kyrgyz. After the meeting I said to him, "You have a fine church here." He responded by pointing heavenward and saying, "It is His church. I am only His servant." He understood Jesus' meaning ("It shall not be so among you!") and Peter's admonition against "lording over."

was the Example to Peter, to the Twelve, and to all who would follow Him. If we wish to pattern our teaching after Jesus, we will strive
to be living examples of what we teach.

Jesus Was Comfortable with People of All Kinds

Effective teachers, that is, "lifechangers," establish rapport with
learners. Rapport building is a social skill that requires some degree
of sensitivity to those we teach. The Scriptures reflect Jesus' amazing ability to be at home with a wide range of people—whether they
were poor or wealthy; Jew, Gentile, or Roman; male or female. Let's
look at just a few examples.

- Jesus spoke confidently with Nicodemus, a devout Jewish
  leader. He showed no anxiety as He taught the "up-and-out"
  member of the ruling Sanhedrin (John 3).
- He invited Himself to dinner at the home of the "down-and-
  out" tax collector Zacchaeus. He demonstrated no discomfort
  being in the company of wealth (Luke 19). He chose another
  tax collector, Matthew, as one of His disciples (Matt 9:9–12).
- He conversed openly with an "out-and-out" Samaritan
  woman who had come to draw water from a well. He broke
  with the social customs of His day: a respectable man did
  not talk with women in public, nor a respectable Jew to
  Samaritan "half-breeds." But Jesus drew this Samaritan
  woman to faith in Himself. And through her He reached into
  her village (John 4:28–30).
- Jesus healed the demon-possessed daughter of a heathen
  woman after He taught her who He was (Matt 15:22–28).[10]

---

[10] The Canaanite woman entreats Jesus, "Lord, Son of David, have mercy on me!"
Jesus' behavior appears rude: "Jesus did not answer a word" (Matt 15:23). When she
continued, "Lord, help me!" (v. 25), His language sounds strangely harsh: "It is not
right to take the children's bread and toss it to their dogs" (Matt 15:26). Edersheim
explains that the woman's approach to Jesus was "not as the Messiah of Israel but
an Israelitish Messiah—this was exactly the error of the Jews which Jesus had encountered and combated, alike when He resisted the attempt to make Him King, in
His reply to the Jerusalem Scribes, and in His Discourses at Capernaum. To have
granted her the help she so entreated, would have been, as it were, to reverse the
whole of His teaching, and to make His works of healing merely works of power. . . .
And so He first taught her, in such manner as she could understand—that which
she needed to know, before she could approach Him in such a manner—the relation
of the heathen to the Jewish world [dogs, children] and of both to the Messiah, and

• The disciples rebuked parents for bringing their little children to Jesus, but Jesus welcomed them: "Leave the children
alone, and don't try to keep them from coming to Me, because the kingdom of heaven is made up of people like this"
(Matt 19:14).

Besides these instances Jesus surrounded Himself with people of
all kinds. He healed all sorts of diseases in crowds and drove out
demons from the possessed (Mark 1:34). He healed the deaf (Mark
7:32 ff) and the blind (John 9:1 ff), the lame (Matt 21:14) and the
leprous (Matt 8:3). During His arrest He healed the ear of Malchus,
one of the high priest's servants (Luke 22:51; John 18:10).

We naturally tend to stay with "our own kind." Discomfort
mounts as we deal with people much richer or poorer than ourselves. It isn't easy to deal with people of a different race, language,
or age bracket. To do so requires an extra degree of energy and commitment. But teachers who build bridges to all people are the most
effective.

Jesus Was Compassionate Toward His Learners

Jesus protected the disciples from harm (John 17:12). He gave the
disciples instructions before He sent them out (Matt 10). Whether
He used a strong rebuke (Matt 16:23; Luke 24:25) or a gentle explanation (Matt 16:21; Luke 24:27), His focus was on the disciples' welfare: "The Son of Man did not come to be served, but to serve, and to
give His life—a ransom for many" (Matt 20:28).

Jesus cared more for learners than lessons. One day Jesus was
teaching about fasting (Matt 9:14–17). Jairus, ruler of the local
synagogue, appeared and asked Him to attend to his sick daughter.
Which was more important to Jesus, finishing His lesson on fasting,
or helping Jairus and his daughter? "Jesus and His disciples got up
and followed him" (v. 19). In all these ways Jesus demonstrated His
compassion for learners.

We will be more effective as teachers when we care for the people
we teach: accepting them, visiting them, gently directing them, looking out for their welfare. Effective disciplers can honestly say to their

---

then He gave her what she asked" (Edersheim, *Life and Times of Jesus the Messiah*,
vol. 2, 39).

learners, "You are not here for me; I am here for you." Such a view comes from a heart of compassion.

Jesus Had a Strong Self-concept

Our society has gone overboard with the idea of self-esteem and positive self-concept. Fifteen years ago *Newsweek* reported that American high school students were significantly more *confident* (subjective perception) in their math and science skills than were their Japanese counterparts. The only problem was that Japanese high school students were significantly more *competent* (objective achievement) in math and science than American students.[11] Things have only gotten worse as we have worshipped "feel good" at the expense of "think well" and "do well." The result, which many of us have predicted for 30 years, has been more self-esteem problems than ever. Jesus provided the proper perspective of self-concept, as well as the appropriate self-esteem that results from it. He demonstrated a healthy self-concept in five ways.

1. Jesus was a man on a mission. Jesus did what He did because He was sent by the Father (John 5:23)—given a mission—and this gave Him focus. His work was what the Father had given Him to do (John 5:19–36), a visible expression of the Father working through Him (John 14:10). Jesus' self-concept was based on a "Father first" perspective rather than the "me first" philosophy of our day. He sought His Father's will and did it, not turning to the left or right. He was a man on a mission, and knowing this generated focus to teach with authority.

Each of us has a personal yoke, *His* yoke, which is our mission to perform. When we find and accept that mission, we find rest and refreshment in the Lord and learn from Him (Matt 11:28–30). In short, we find our selfhood as God created us to be. This discovery of "self" is far better than trying to make something of ourselves for the Lord! Find the Lord's place for you and give yourself—first to *Him* and then to *it*.

2. Jesus was a man of dynamic humility. Nowhere in the Gospels do we find Jesus demanding worship from the disciples. Jesus did not fret when He experienced a lack of recognition, nor did He

---

[11] J. Adler, et al., "Hey, I'm Terrific: The Curse of Self-Esteem," *Newsweek* (17 February 1992): 46–51.

grumble when those He healed weren't more grateful or when the religious leaders didn't give Him the respect He deserved. Though He did not demand worship, He did, on at least one occasion, acknowledge it when given. But look how He used it:

> "You call Me Teacher and Lord. This is well said, for I am.
> So if I, your Lord and Teacher, have washed your feet, you
> also ought to wash one another's feet. For I have given you
> an example that you also should do just as I have done for
> you. I assure you: A slave is not greater than his master,
> and a messenger is not greater than the one who sent him.
> If you know these things, you are blessed if you do them."
> (John 13:13–17)

Jesus came as the humble "Suffering Servant" (Isa 53; Matt 16:21). Yet His humility was not passive. He never played the victim, apologetically kicking the dirt because people—His own people—rejected Him. His was a dynamic humility, an energetic submission. Even when He stood before Pilate, the one man who, humanly speaking, could rescue Him from the cross, we see our Lord submissive and powerful: "You would have no authority over Me at all . . . if it hadn't been given you from above" (John 19:11). Jesus did not put Himself down, except to exalt the Father (Luke 18:19). He never belittled His ministry. He never grinned with embarrassment when people praised Him. He displayed the dignity of authority.

While He never demanded worship, neither did He reject worship when it was given. When the rich young ruler fell on his knees before Him, Jesus gave no sign of discomfort. He simply dealt with the man's desire (eternal life) and his need (to be rid of his life-choking wealth). Sadly, he chose to reject Jesus' solution (Mark 10:17–22). When Thomas saw Jesus after the resurrection and exclaimed, "My Lord and my God!" Jesus gave no indication that Thomas's adoration was out of line (John 20:28–29). Jesus' dynamic humility was a vigorous meekness, a vital submissiveness, an aggressive lowliness.

We are in trouble if we expect others to praise us for our good work. Sooner or later we will be disillusioned. The best course is to do good and let go all thought of it: "Don't let your left hand know what your right hand is doing" (Matt 6:3). We are in trouble if we cannot accept another's praise without embarrassment. This usually indicates some level of self-consciousness. The best course is to accept compliments graciously, without dwelling on them. Such dynamic humility frees us from social traps of disillusionment and self-consciousness.

3. Jesus' calmness under attack. Jesus' self-concept is shown by calmness when attacked. He healed two demon-possessed men[12] by casting the demons into a nearby herd of pigs. Those tending the pigs ran into town and told what had happened. The whole town went out to confront Jesus over their loss "because they were gripped by great fear" (Luke 8:37). They feared Jesus' power and were angry over their loss. There is no more volatile mix of human emotions than fear and anger. They begged Jesus to leave (Matt 8:34). How did Jesus react? Apparently without a word of defense or explanation He "got into a boat, crossed over, and came to His own town" (Matt 9:1).

How many of us would attempt to defend ourselves and our actions? How many of us would want to explain to the villagers what had happened—the very Son of God had just now restored two men to their right minds by casting out a legion of demons? How many would beg them to understand that what had been done was for the best? Jesus simply left quietly.

4. Jesus' patience with His disciples. As we have seen, the disciples had many weaknesses, yet Jesus never gave up on them. "I guarded them and not one of them is lost, except the son of destruction, so that the Scripture may be fulfilled" (John 17:12).

He demonstrated patience when the disciples lacked faith during the storm: "Why are you fearful? Do you still have no faith?" (Mark 4:40). He demonstrated patience when they were unable to heal the demon-possessed boy. Why? "Because of your little faith" (Matt 17:20). He demonstrated patience when they fell asleep in the garden: "So, couldn't you stay awake with Me one hour?" (Matt 26:40). He never gave up on His disciples because they were a part of His mission: "I pray for . . . those You have given Me, because they are Yours" (John 17:9).

---

[12] Mark and Luke record that Jesus healed one demon-possessed man (Mark 5:1; Luke 8:26). Edersheim explains this by saying, "From these tombs the demonized, who is specially singled out by Mark and Luke, as well as his less prominent companion, came forth to meet Jesus" (*Life and Times of Jesus the Messiah*, vol. 1, 607). See Matt 8:28.

Insecure teachers easily lose patience with students because they see a negative reflection on their own teaching ability when students fail. Secure teachers patiently try again, until their learners master the subject.

5. Jesus' self-concept was tied to identification with the Father through prayer. We emphasized at the beginning of the chapter the dependence of Jesus on the Father for His work and teaching. The ongoing connection between Them was prayer. "Very early in the morning, while it was still dark, He got up, went out, and made His way to a deserted place. And He was praying there" (Mark 1:35). On another occasion we are told specifically that Jesus "spent all night in prayer to God" (Luke 6:12). Luke tells us that Jesus *often* prayed in lonely places (Luke 5:16). Jesus reinforced the importance of prayer through the parable of the persistent widow: "to pray always and not become discouraged" (Luke 18:1). Further, Jesus underscored the importance of *asking the Father*, who "gives good things" (Matt 7:11), does what we ask in Jesus' name (Matt 18:19; John 15:16; 16:23), and gives the Holy Spirit (Luke 11:13).

Prayer—the personal connection with the heavenly Father—was an essential part of Jesus' self-concept. And if Jesus, the Second Person of the Trinity (Matt 28:19), in whom the "entire fullness of God's nature dwells bodily" (Col 2:9), needed time alone in prayer, how much more do we?

Prayer is the connection. The Word is the means. The Spirit is the power. Jesus is our Lord and Example. All combine to remake us after His image.

A healthy self-concept, a godly sense of self-esteem, is important: "Love your neighbor *as yourself*" (Lev 19:18; Matt 19:19). For Christians, knowing to whom we belong is an essential part of learning who we are. And knowing who we are in the Lord gives us the confidence we need to teach others. As we make this holy journey, we will find that our self-concept takes care of itself, because Jesus came so we "may have life and have it in abundance" (John 10:10).

Jesus Knew His Learners

One of the reasons Jesus' teaching was so special is that it focused on the real-life needs of those whom He taught. Jesus knew His learners, and He used that knowledge to focus His teaching for maximum effectiveness in each situation. Jesus understood the balance of Scripture and learner needs.[13]

Jesus' knowledge was both divine and human. Being divine, He could read the hearts and minds of the people around Him. When the Pharisees claimed Jesus' miracles were done by Beelzebub, the prince of demons,[14] Matthew tells us Jesus knew their thoughts (Matt 12:24–25). When many people believed in Jesus because of the miracles, John writes, "He did not need anyone to testify about man; for He Himself knew what was in man" (John 2:25). Later, when many of His followers began to desert Him, John tells us, "Jesus knew from the beginning those who would not believe and the one who would betray Him" (John 6:64).

Mark gives us the clearest picture of Jesus' ability to discern the thoughts of others. Men, wanting to get their paralytic friend to Jesus, lowered him through the roof of a crowded house. "Seeing their faith, Jesus told the paralytic, 'Son, your sins are forgiven'" (Mark 2:5). Some of the scribes were thinking to themselves: "Why does He speak like this? He's blaspheming! Who can forgive sins but God alone?" Immediately Jesus knew what they were thinking, and He said to them, "Why are you reasoning these things in your hearts?" (Mark 2:5–8).

Even though Jesus had supernatural power to read hearts and minds, He also depended on His human knowledge of people. Much of what He knew about people He learned through observation, conversation, or by asking questions. To Peter: "What do you think, Simon?" (Matt 17:25). To the Pharisees: "What do you think about the Messiah? Whose Son is He?" (Matt 22:42). To Pilate: "Are you asking this on your own, or have others told you about Me?" (John 18:34).

Whether Jesus used divine or human knowledge, He *used that knowledge in order to teach*. He knew the Samaritan woman's need for water and, on a deeper level, a satisfying marriage and, deeper still, salvation. So He used water and husbands to teach her about

---

[13] Jesus' dual focus on teaching eternal truth to learner need is the source for the foundations stones of the Disciplers' Model.

[14] Edersheim renders the name "Beelzebul" rather than "Beelzebub," which is a reference to Baalzebub, the "fly-god of 2 Kings 1:2." He retranslates "Beel" (master) and "zibbul" (sacrificing to idols), so "Beelzebul" means the "lord or chief of idolatrous sacrificing," vol. 1, 648.

Himself. Jesus understood the heathen woman's ignorance of the true Messiah, and so He taught her about Himself with children and dogs and then granted her request. Nicodemus was a teacher of Israel (John 3:10). Yet he did not understand the spiritual meaning of what he taught until Jesus instructed him. Jesus knew His learners and used that knowledge to focus His teaching.

Disciplers study general characteristics of those they teach.[15] They learn specifics of the learners in their classes through conversation, sharing, questions, and prayer requests. What we learn, we use to focus teaching preparation and execution to connect with our learners as they are.

Jesus Was a Master of the Old Testament

While the scribes and Pharisees embellished the Old Testament with their own corollaries and exceptions, Jesus displayed a fluent mastery of Scripture. For example, the Pharisees hated Jesus because He healed people on the Sabbath (Matt 12:9–14). They justified their indignation by reckoning Jesus' healing as "work," forbidden on the Sabbath (Exod 20:8–11). Jesus pointed out their hypocrisy and *interpreted the Law in light of the whole Old Testament:* "What man among you, if he had a sheep that fell into a pit on the Sabbath, wouldn't take hold of it and lift it out? A man is worth far more than a sheep, so it is lawful to do good on the Sabbath" (Matt 12:11–12).

The Pharisees considered principles more important than people and derived their power from holding principles over people. Jesus explained it this way: "[The Pharisees] tie up heavy loads that are hard to carry and put them on people's shoulders, but they themselves aren't willing to lift a finger to move them" (Matt 23:4).

Jesus saw people as more important than arbitrary principles. Religious leaders twisted the Old Testament to fit their own purposes of power and control. The "Sabbath rule" was one example of this. They would rather an invalid remain unhealed than accept Jesus' violation of *their interpretation* of Sabbath rest. Indignant because Jesus had healed on the Sabbath, the synagogue ruler said to the people,

---

[15] A simple search for "Teaching Preschoolers" at www.amazon.com on October 2, 2007 revealed 48 books on preschooler characteristics and activities. Denominational publishers produce books on age groups (preschool, children, youth, adult) and target groups (singles, young marrieds, senior adults).

> "There are six days when work should be done; therefore
> come on those days and be healed and not on the Sabbath
> day."
>
> The Lord answered him, "Hypocrites! Doesn't each one
> of you untie his ox or donkey from the feeding trough
> on the Sabbath and lead it to water? Satan has bound this
> woman, a daughter of Abraham, for 18 years—shouldn't
> she be untied from this bondage on the Sabbath day?"
> When He said this, all his opponents were humiliated,
> but the people were delighted with all the wonderful things
> He was doing. (Luke 13:14–17)

Which was primary in the Old Testament, principles or people, rules
or relationship? Jesus spoke plainly when He said, "The Sabbath was
made for man, not man for the Sabbath" (Mark 2:27). Even the Old
Testament accuses the Pharisees:

> Would the LORD be pleased with thousands of rams,
> or with ten thousand streams of oil?
> Should I give my firstborn for my transgression,
> the child of my body for my own sin?
> He has told you men what is good
> and what it is the LORD requires of you:
> Only to act justly,
> to love faithfulness,
> and to walk humbly with your God. (Mic 6:7–8)

When the Pharisees threw the adulterous woman at Jesus' feet, their
intent was to uphold the law and trap Jesus (John 8:5–6). The law
was clear: there was no shade of gray: "must be put to death" (Lev
20:10). They cared nothing for the woman. Their intent was to destroy this One who questioned their authority and power. Principle
and power, not people.

In contrast to the Pharisees, Jesus cared for the woman and led
her away from her sin. He displayed the loving-kindness of Yahweh,
God of Israel. His challenge, "The one without sin among you should
be the first to throw a stone at her" (John 8:7), refocused their attention on their own need of salvation from sin. The oldest, and
evidently the wisest, were the first to understand Jesus' meaning.
They dropped their stones and left, followed by the younger men,

who may have been more passionate and less ready to miss a "God-honoring" killing.

Jesus acted as He did because He was Master of the heart of the Old Testament. In a fanatically religious nation, religion was the means to power. The scribes and Pharisees were trapped, as it were, by their own egotistical need for power. The Word of God was merely another tool to be used to maintain control.

Jesus rejected this hypocrisy, knowing that the Old Testament was God's Word, the revelation of His Father. Jesus analyzed the teachings of the Law and the Prophets and synthesized the central thrust of the Father's perfect loving-kindness in two brief statements of relationship: "Love the Lord your God," and "love your neighbor as yourself" (Matt 22:37–40). These were not new teachings. Jesus was quoting the Old Testament, specifically Deut 6:5 ("*Love the* LORD *your God* with all your heart and with all your soul and with all your strength") and Lev 19:18 ("Do not seek revenge or bear a grudge against one of your people, but *love your neighbor as yourself.* I am the LORD"; emphasis added). But He went beyond knowledge of the Scripture and mere understanding. He expanded the Old Testament in His "you have heard that it was said . . . but I tell you" teachings (Matt 5:21–22,27–28,33–34,38–39,43–44).

Have you noticed the balance in Jesus' teaching? He was Master of the Scripture, and yet He focused that mastery on *teaching people* where they were. People were His focus. Scripture was His means. As He applied Old Testament Scripture to real problems in His students, He provided solutions uniquely suited to each one.

Disciplers are stretched in the same way. On the one hand, we focus on scholarship: "Be diligent to present yourself approved to God, a worker who doesn't need to be ashamed, correctly teaching the word of truth" (2 Tim 2:15). Commentaries, study aids, Bible dictionaries,[16] and Bible handbooks provide windows into the text. Yet we focus all the fruit of our study at the point where learners live in the now, leading them as scholar-counselors away from chaos and into truth.

---

[16] It is important to use a *Bible* dictionary rather than a general English dictionary to define Bible words. The English dictionary gives us the way words are commonly used in contemporary American speech. Bible dictionaries give us definitions and explanations of word usage in biblical times.

Jesus' Methods of Teaching

Now that we have an idea of who Jesus was, let us explore the way He taught. We do not focus here on typical teaching methods—lecture, question and answer, small-group discussion[17]—but rather on His primary emphases in teaching. We will look at 10 such areas.

Jesus Established Relationship with His Learners

Teaching from mouth to ear is very different from teaching heart to heart. If "getting the lesson across" is the main goal, there is little need for relationship between teacher and student. But if transforming students toward Christlikeness is the goal, a warm positive relationship is essential.

Jesus "appointed 12 . . . to be with Him" (Mark 3:14). Bruce indicates that their selection passed through three stages. In the first stage, the Twelve, as well as others, believed in Jesus as the Messiah, the Christ,[18] and occasionally accompanied Him at their convenience. The second stage involved leaving their secular occupations and traveling with Him. The third stage began when they were chosen by the Lord and formed into a select band to be trained for the great work of apostles.[19] The apostles lived together and ate together. They witnessed the miracles of Jesus together. They suffered rejection together. All the while, Jesus loved them, taught them, protected them.

Like coals in a fire, their mutual support and service strengthened them. Pull a coal from the fire, and it soon cools down. Peter's denials. Thomas's doubt. Scattering at Jesus' arrest. Despite obstacles, Jesus fanned the individual sparks of the Twelve into a family of fire, and within that context He taught them.

We build relationships with individuals, teacher to learner, and encourage relationships among learners as well. As we interact, we learn from one another and teach one another. One learner's answer raised a question for another. A third learner's question caused several others to think in different ways. A matrix of relationships generates multidirectional, multilayered teaching.

---

[17] If you are interested in specific teaching methods, consult Yount, *Called to Teach* (Nashville: B&H, 1999)

[18] "The Anointed One of Israel," the Messiah (Hebrew, OT), the Christ (Greek, NT).

[19] Bruce, *Training of the Twelve*, 11–12.

Jesus Stimulated and Maintained Interest

Jesus stimulated interest with dramatic illustrations and exaggeration. His illustrations included an unmerciful servant (Matt 18:23–35), equal wages for unequal work (Matt 20:1–16), murdering tenants (Matt 21:33–43), undeserving wedding guests (Matt 22:1–14), unprepared virgins (Matt 25:1–13), wise and foolish investors (Matt 25:14–30), wise and foolish builders (Luke 6:46–49), a good Samaritan (Luke 10:30–37), a rich fool (Luke 12:16–21), a lost sheep, coin, and son (Luke 15:3–32), a shrewd manager (Luke 16:1–13), a rich man in hell (Luke 16:19–31), and the condemned Pharisee and forgiven tax collector (Luke 18:9–14). Such stories seized the hearts of Jesus' listeners because they came directly out of their own frustrations and disappointments.

Jesus stimulated interest through exaggeration. If your hand or foot causes you to sin, "cut it off" (Mark 9:43,45). If your eye causes you to sin, then "gouge it out" (Mark 9:47). The only way to be Jesus' disciple is to "hate [your] own father and mother, wife and children, brothers and sisters—yes, even [your] own life." Jesus made a dramatic point about priorities. If one puts family or self ahead of Him, he "cannot be My disciple" (Luke 14:26). Sound too strong? Jesus merely personalized one of the Commandments: "Do not have other gods besides Me" (Exod 20:3). Illustrations and exaggerations helped to stimulate interest.

Jesus not only secured the interest of learners; He maintained it. He asked questions. He focused His teaching from the perspective of His students. He used parables with the masses but explained them when He was alone with His disciples (Mark 13:10–18; 5:33–34). Those who truly hungered for righteousness would follow, learn, and grow. Those who were merely curious would fall by the wayside.[20] We stimulate interest in Bible studies by means of "learning readiness" activities: raising questions, sharing a personal testimony, providing a demonstration. We maintain interest with stories, questions, and discussions of various types. See chapter 13, "Planning to Teach," for specific examples.

---

[20] And Jesus let them go. So why do we pursue disinterested lost people with such abandon? Are we more serious about evangelism than Jesus, or are we merely tossing His pearls at swine?

Jesus Taught by Example

Jesus inspired His disciples to imitate Him. Pray as I prayed. Love as I loved you. Serve as I served. Take up your cross as I took up Mine. Care for the sheep as I cared for the sheep. Finish your course as I finished Mine. But here we focus on His method.

Jesus pointed to faithful behavior as examples to His disciples: the widow who gave all she had, the Roman centurion who believed Jesus could heal by spoken word, children who ran to Him, the boy who gave his lunch to Jesus and then ate his fill, the persistent Syro-phoenician woman, the woman with an issue of blood. He pointed to bad examples of faith: religious zealots, legalistic scribes, puffed-up Pharisees, corrupt politicians. He pointed to examples from nature: wind, seeds, sheep and goats, pearls. Tangible examples provide mental imagery that fills two-dimensional words with meaning. We will teach more effectively as we focus attention and thinking by means of examples.

Further, the best teachers are case studies of what they teach and help learners themselves to become living examples of biblical truth. Peter wrote to young pastors to be *"examples* to the flock" (1 Pet 5:3; emphasis added). Transforming Bible study—whether in church or college or seminary—molds teachers and learners into better examples of the Truth rather than mere living libraries of it.

Jesus Taught People More Than Lessons

Not once in Scripture do we find Jesus saying, "Our lesson for to-day is Leviticus, scroll 3." His teaching flowed out of the needs of the people He taught. It flowed out of problem situations they presented. It flowed out of the real crises of life.

This is not to say that lesson planning or organized curriculum is unnecessary. None of us can teach like Jesus did, so adhering to specific principles of lesson planning helps us order our structure and methods.[21] Curriculum writers provide enormous assistance to teachers in our churches. Well-designed materials target a wide range of issues relevant to growing in the Lord.[22] But the prime emphasis of disciplers is the *people in the chairs*, not the lines in the les-

---

[21] See chapter 13, "Planning to Teach."
[22] See chapter 19, "Selecting and Evaluating Curriculum."

son. God's Word is Truth. But it becomes "truth that matters to me" for learners as it intersects learners where they live.

Many teachers in our churches, both volunteer and professional, do not understand this balance. The goal for many is to "cover the lesson"—that is, ensure that every assigned verse is discussed. When teachers aggressively pursue this goal, learner questions are ignored, learner comments are curtailed, and the sharing of relevant personal experiences is restricted. "Mildred, I wish we could discuss your question, but I have four more verses to cover." This teacher may cover the lesson, but he hasn't taught Mildred. Expect interruptions and questions. *No, welcome them!* Because these provide fertile ground for learning. Encourage openness. Teach people, not lessons.

Jesus Emphasized Character More Than Content

The Pharisees knew their content. They memorized the five books of Moses. They mastered the myriad details of proper prayer, almsgiving, and fasting. Their religion was a superficial, technical, external show of rote actions and memorized rules, a tedious rule book that led them to become "sanctimonious faultfinders."[23] They were so good at religious regimentation that they were held up as the standard to be followed.

Jesus was more interested in internal character than external show. Character focuses on the head: knowing what God has said and understanding what He expects. Character focuses on the heart: committed to God's message and devoted to His kingdom priorities. Character focuses on the hand: employing spiritual gifts and natural abilities to accomplish God's mission in the world. This trilogy forms the basis for character-building teaching.[24] How do we help learners know God's Word and understand its meaning? How do we inspire commitment to God's way of life and galvanize devotion to His priorities? How do we provoke awareness and engagement of gifts toward accomplishing God's mission to the world? By teaching to build character.

For learners to grow in character, they must have freedom to think and decide for themselves. Jesus understood this. His disciples

---

[23] Bruce, *Training of the Twelve*, 27.
[24] See chapter 11, "The Goal of Christian Education: Christlikeness" for an in-depth discussion of this trilogy.

freely chose to follow Him. The rich young ruler freely chose not to. Judas chose to betray Jesus. Thomas chose to doubt. Peter chose to deny the Lord. The disciples chose to run away when Jesus was arrested. The Pharisees hated this freedom because their basic desire was to gain power and maintain control.[25] For all their religious power, the Pharisees were "like whitewashed tombs, which appear beautiful on the outside, but inside are full of dead men's bones and every impurity" (Matt 23:27).

Jesus Focused on Ever Smaller Groups

"Large crowds followed [Jesus] from Galilee, Decapolis, Jerusalem, Judea and beyond the Jordan" (Matt 4:25). Throughout His ministry Jesus taught the crowds. From the crowds Jesus chose two specific groups of workers. He first chose the Twelve (Matt 10:1ff) to be trained as apostles to carry on the work after He left. Later "the Lord appointed seventy-two others and sent them two by two ahead of him to every town and place where he was about to go" (Luke 10:1 NIV). The Twelve were chosen to be with Him; the seventy-two to go before Him. Both groups were given power to drive out demons, but only the Twelve were given power to heal diseases (cf. Matt 10:1 and Luke 10:1,17).

From the Twelve, Jesus chose three for special attention: Peter, James, and John. These three men experienced things with Jesus that the other nine did not.

- They witnessed the transfiguration of Jesus (Matt 17) while the nine remained at the bottom of the mountain.
- They accompanied Jesus into the home of Jairus when Jesus raised his daughter from the dead (Mark 5:37) while the nine remained outside (Luke 8:51).
- When Jesus and the disciples went to Gethsemane, the nine stayed back while the three moved forward with Jesus into the garden (Mark 14:32–33).

The apostle Paul tells us that Peter, James, and John became pillars in the early church as a result of their advanced training and personal attention (Gal 2:9).

---

[25] See Matt 12:1–8 and 15:1–11 for two vivid examples of this.

Of the three, Jesus paid the greatest attention to Simon. He gave Simon the new name of Peter (*Petros,* rock; John 1:42). He healed Peter's mother-in-law (Matt 8:14–15). He allowed Peter to try something miraculous—walking on water—and fail (Matt 14:28–33). Jesus recommissioned Peter after he denied Him (John 21:15ff). Peter served his Lord faithfully until his death.

Noted Christian educator Howard Hendricks once said he was finished with building great churches. He wanted to give the rest of his life to *building great people.* "Even if you build a church of 3200 people, if none of them develops, 3200 times 0 still equals 0. But 1 times 1 equals 1, and that is 100 percent better. The question you must ask is 'Whose life are you impacting?'"[26] This approach to teaching ministry is certainly in line with that of Jesus, who poured Himself into ever-smaller groups.

Jesus Recognized the Worth of His Learners

Local church ministry is people intensive. We plan programs, but without people to lead and staff the programs and reach others to participate in them, our planning is in vain. In the hustle and bustle of church ministry, it is easy to focus on "getting the job done" and take for granted the very ones who are doing the job. In this kind of corporate-hive atmosphere, learners are simply the means by which ministry is done. This utilitarian view of people tells worker-bees that they are valuable so long as they produce. "Fail to meet organizational standards and you'll be replaced by someone more dedicated to the corporate-hive." In such a system leaders can easily abuse the very people of God in the name of reaching strangers (who are then abused in order to "win" more).

The disciples were not the *means* of Jesus' ministry. They were the *end* of it. Jesus did not use (that is, *abuse*) His disciples to reach the crowds. In fact, Jesus pulled away from the crowds in order to teach the disciples. They were not tools in the hands of a clever public relations man but rather beloved friends (John 15:15). Jesus poured His heart into them, and after He left, they carried on His work.

---

[26] Student report on conference notes, Howard Hendricks, February 10, 1992. Dr. Hendricks was professor of Christian education at Dallas Theological Seminary in Dallas, Texas, at the time.

Many church members are hungry for pastors and ministers who care about them for who they are and not merely for what they can do for the minister's career. Before being challenged to reach "10 more next Sunday," they would like to know that we've noticed them, that we care for them, that we love them. Our flocks are worthy of compassion, and we are called to lead with compassion. See chapter 22, "Ministering alongside Volunteers," for practical ways to do this.

Jesus Emphasized Quality of Effort over Quantity of Learners

The "quality versus quantity" debate has long raged in Baptist circles. Those who emphasize "quality Bible study" in Sunday school may create classes that are self-satisfied, self-sufficient, internally focused, and indifferent toward outsiders. *Cloistered cliques.* Those who emphasize "quantity" through outreach efforts may create classes that are shallow and spiritually stagnant, and whose members are indifferent to one another. *Exhausted strangers.*

The Great Commission calls for both reaching (evangelism) and teaching (discipleship). Jesus' preference between the two is clear, and Bruce's description bears repeating:

> The careful, painstaking education of the disciples secured that the Teacher's influence on the world should be permanent; that His kingdom should be founded on the rock of deep and indestructible convictions in the minds of a few, not on the shifting sands of superficial evanescent impressions on the minds of the many.[27]

Measures of spiritual vitality are constantly tied to the circus sideshow measure of how many people gathered, rarely to what actually happened in those people because they gathered. Jesus never bragged about the crowds of people who gathered around Him to be healed or fed or taught. *Attendance* was not His concern; *people* were. Yes, numbers are people. But when leaders become overly concerned about "10 more next Sunday," they seldom care about *who those 10 are.*

Later, as Jesus increased His emphasis on "denying self" and "taking yokes" and "bearing crosses," people began to drift away. As the crowds left Him, Jesus did not change His message. The rich young

---

[27] Bruce, *Training of the Twelve,* 13.

ruler walked away from Jesus, unwilling to pay the cost of discipleship. But Jesus did not change His message. *He did not evaluate the
quality of what He was doing by the quantity of people following Him.*
He knew He was in the Father's will, and He was faithful.

There were money boxes in the temple where the faithful deposited their tithes and offerings. The coins were deposited in metal
cones made in the shape of a trumpet.[28] When a person dropped
several coins into the opening, they clinked and clanked as they fell
through the cone. The Pharisees loved to pour a bag of coins into the
box so that people nearby would hear the ringing of the trumpets
and turn to see who had made such a large offering.

One day Jesus sat near the offering boxes, watching the crowd
putting their money into the temple treasury. Several rich worshippers poured in their coins and sounded the trumpets. Brrrrr-ring!
Then a poor widow happened by and put in two small copper coins,
worth only a fraction of a penny. Tink-tink-tink. Tink-tink-tink.
Calling His disciples, Jesus said, "This poor widow has put in more
than all those giving to the temple treasury. For they all gave out of
their surplus, but she out of her poverty has put in everything she
possessed—all she had to live on" (Mark 12:41–44). It was the quality of the gift, not its quantity, that caught Jesus' eye and evoked His
praise.

When we find ourselves in small places—in a Sunday school class,
a small church, a difficult mission field—let us not fret over numbers, but let us give ourselves to these few, giving the Lord our best
efforts, and leave the results to Him.

Jesus Emphasized Action More than Knowledge

Jesus defined the terms *wise* and *foolish* not on the basis of what
one knows, but on the basis of what one does with His words (Matt
7:24,26). When our students leave our classes, have we helped them
to practice what they've learned from God's Word? They have heard
the words, but do they put them into practice? If we haven't, then
Jesus says we have sent them out as fools. When your congregation
leaves the sanctuary after worship, they have heard the words, but do

---

[28] Edersheim, *Life and Times of Jesus the Messiah,* vol. 2, 387.

they practice them? If they do, then Jesus says we have sent them out as wise.

Encouraging students to practice what they learn in the study of God's Word is worthy of serious attention. This can be achieved through assignments done during the week, case studies in class, personal experiences related to the subject, and even class mission projects. Putting the Word into practice is essential in developing biblical wisdom in our learners.

Jesus Focused on Structure More than Detail

As a master of the Old Testament, Jesus taught its key themes. Jesus majored on truth, the Pharisees on trivia. Jesus majored on love, the Pharisees on legalism. Jesus majored on justice, the Pharisees on judgment.

When we teach, say, the story of the good Samaritan, are we more interested in covering every verse in the story or helping our learners become "better good Samaritans"? Do we curtail questions from learners in order to complete our lectures? When there are five major truths in a given lesson, are we more inclined to cover all five equally, or would we rather choose the one that relates best to our class needs and focus on it?

The pinnacle of our teaching ministry is lifting high the Lord Jesus and letting Him draw all our learners to Himself. There is no greater reward in teaching than to see a life transformed by the love and power of the Lord. May God grant you many such rewards as you offer your teaching ministry to Him.

It is easy to get lost in the details of a particular study and miss the central truth God is conveying. My teenage son was an active Bible driller at our church back in the early 1990s. He had just passed the associational drill competition with flying colors and was headed to the state competition. He knew his memory work! We were practicing his verses one day. After he perfectly quoted an Old Testament verse, I asked him what it meant. He sighed heavily, rolled his eyes, and said, "We don't have to know what the verses *mean*, Dad. We're just supposed to memorize them!" Great on details. Weak on meaning. So I explained the meaning of the verse. Take care not to lose your learners in a mass of detail, even if the detail is God's Word.

Jesus Stressed Long-Term Rather than Immediate Results

We have already noted that Jesus consciously poured His life into a select band of believers, who could then carry on His mission after He left. He did this even though He could have drawn a crowd anywhere He went with His dramatic teaching and miraculous works. Jesus made this choice because the in-depth training of the Twelve formed the foundation for the early church, which then carried His gospel around the world.

In one sense Jesus' training of the Twelve was preparation for ministry. His words and explanations and parables formed the raw material out of which the disciples learned to be apostles. But even at the end of Jesus' ministry, as He prepared to return to the Father, the disciples were ill-suited to take on the power of the Sanhedrin and the power of Rome. They had been trained, but they lacked the power to carry out their mission. However, Jesus promised them that they would "receive power when the Holy Spirit has come upon you, and you will be My witnesses in Jerusalem, in all Judea and Samaria, and to the ends of the earth" (Acts 1:8).

And so, on the day of Pentecost, the Holy Spirit filled the believers and empowered them to do all that Jesus had commanded them. They had been prepared. Now they were transformed. The day of Pentecost forever divided history into two eras: the first, in which the Holy Spirit was imparted to God's chosen for specific purposes and short periods; and the second, in which the Holy Spirit takes up permanent residence (Eph 1:13) in the life of the believer in Jesus (1 Cor 12:3).

Jesus knew He had to return to the Father so that He could send the Spirit to dwell in the hearts of all believers everywhere: "Nevertheless, I am telling you the truth. It is for your benefit that I go away, because if I don't go away the Counselor will not come to you. If I go, I will send Him to you" (John 16:7). But the work of the Counselor, the Holy Spirit, is to glorify Jesus, not Himself (John 16:14). The Holy Spirit does not speak on His own, but speaks only what He hears—presumably from Jesus (John 16:13). And in His earlier teaching on the Holy Spirit, Jesus intimated that He Himself would be coming to them (John 14:16,18). Both Peter and Paul used the terms *Holy Spirit* and *Spirit of Christ* interchangeably—so when

Christians say that Jesus "lives in our hearts," we reflect this dual meaning.

The point here is that the teaching of Jesus provided the raw material for the transformation that took place at Pentecost by the Holy Spirit. The Spirit called to remembrance all that Jesus had taught the disciples and used that teaching to grow them into the leaders of the early church. See chapter 5, "Holy Spirit as Teacher," for more.

Paul writes to the Corinthians, "I planted, Apollos watered, but God gave the growth. So then, neither the one who plants nor the one who waters is anything, but only God who gives the growth" (1 Cor 3:6–7). We may teach or preach our hearts out, week after week, and see little spiritual fruit resulting from our efforts. Then one Sunday, for no apparent reason, the Lord moves in the hearts of several of the members, and a spiritual breakthrough occurs. There is an insidious temptation to do "whatever works" in order to make the church grow. This is fleshly, worldly thinking. Ends seem to justify the means. But it is not we who build the Church—God does. "Unless the Lord builds a house, its builders labor over it in vain" (Ps 127:1a).

Does this mean we do nothing but simply wait for God to do whatever He is going to do? No. Paul continues, "The one who plants and the one who waters are equal, and each will receive his own reward according to his own labor" (1 Cor 3:8). There is a work to be done. What is that work? Praying and teaching the Word: that is our labor. And God grows His Church by His Spirit in His time and in His way.

Discussion Questions

1. How do you react when you work hard to do a good job but no one congratulates you on your efforts? When you serve faithfully in a difficult position and few seem to notice? When you've done your best to be fair, honest, and open in a church issue and people accuse you of petty self-interest? (*Dealing dynamically with frustration.*)

2. How do you react when someone you've helped says, "Thank you"? When someone in your church praises you to your face?

When someone praises you in a public gathering? (*Dealing humbly with praise.*)
3. Discuss human characteristics and methods of Jesus that you possess and use by His grace.
4. Discuss human characteristics and methods of Jesus that you lack and need His help to develop.

Suggested Reading

Bruce, Alexander Balmain. *The Training of the Twelve.* 4th ed. New York: A. C. Armstrong & Sons, 1894. Paperback reprint, New York: Cosimo Classics, 2007.

Edersheim, Alfred. *The Life and Times of Jesus the Messiah.* Vol. 1. London: Longmans, Green and Co, 1890; reprint, Peabody: Hendrickson, 1993.

Willard, Dallas. *Renovation of the Heart: Putting On the Character of Christ.* Colorado Springs: NavPress, 2002.

_____. *The Divine Conspiracy: Rediscovering Our Hidden Life in God.* San Francisco: HarperSanFrancisco, 1997.

Zuck, Roy B. *Teaching as Jesus Taught.* Eugene, OR: Wipf & Stock, 2002.

Bibliography

Adler, Jerry, et al. "Hey, I'm Terrific: The Curse of Self-Esteem." *Newsweek*, 17 February 1992.

Bruce, Alexander Balmain. *The Training of the Twelve.* 4th ed. New York: A C Armstrong & Sons, 1894; reprint, New Canaan, CT : Keats, 1970

Coleman, Lucien. *Why the Church Must Teach.* Nashville: Broadman, 1984.

Eddy, Sherwood. *Maker of Men.* New York: Harper & Bros., 1941.

Edersheim, Alfred. *The Life and Times of Jesus the Messiah.* Vol. 1. London: Longmans, Green and Co., 1890; reprint, Grand Rapids: Eerdmans, 1969.

Chapter 5

THE HOLY SPIRIT
AS TEACHER

Octavio J. Esqueda

Not by strength or by might,
but by My Spirit, says the LORD of Hosts.
(Zech 4:6)

T he Holy Spirit is essential in Christian teaching. God collaborates with Christian teachers through the Holy Spirit in order to accomplish His purposes. Both teachers and students need the Spirit's illumination to understand and apply the Scriptures.

The Rooster's Hidden Meaning

In 1996 Gabriel García Márquez, winner of the Nobel prize for Literature in 1982, shared a story related to one of his novels that illustrates the privilege Christian teachers and students enjoy with the Holy Spirit.[1] His son was taking a literature course in high school. The teacher required the reading of *El coronel no tiene quien le escriba* (*No One Writes to the Colonel*), a novel by García Márquez.[2] In that novel a rooster appears in different sections of the story.

---

[1] I had the opportunity of spending four days with Gabriel García Márquez. He is one of the best Latin American writers and a leader of the literary movement known as "magic realism." García Márquez shared during these days about his life and work to a select group of 26 people from all around the world as part of a lecture series sponsored by the University of Guadalajara's *Cátedra Julio Cortázar*. Angelica, my wife now but my fiancé at that time, and I were the only two literature students taking part in these lectures. The rest of the participants were professors and scholars who had specialized in the literary work of García Márquez.

[2] G. G. Márquez, *El coronel no tiene quien le escriba* (Barcelona: Random House, 1999).

The old, poor colonel expects to make some money with the rooster to support his wife during their final years. The high school teacher explained to the class how this rooster was essential for a clear understanding of the book. "The rooster is the hidden main character of the novel," the teacher concluded.

At the end of the day, the son of García Márquez went home and told his dad that his class talked about one of his novels. He asked his dad about the real meaning of the rooster. Gabriel García Márquez was puzzled by the question and answered, "What rooster? The rooster is just that, a simple rooster! There is not a hidden meaning whatsoever."

Every student and the teacher left the class with a misconception of the novel. Only one person had direct access to the author and received the correct instruction about this work because of the father-son relationship.

A Personal Relationship with God through the Spirit

All born-again Christians are indwelt by the Holy Spirit and enjoy direct access to the Father. The Holy Spirit inspired the Scriptures, and He enables believers to understand the biblical text through His work of illumination. We have direct access to the Author of the Scriptures! The Holy Spirit helps us to understand, follow, and obey the Father. The Bible is the only book in which all Christians benefit from a personal relationship with the Author and can go directly to Him at any time.

The Holy Spirit Is Central in the Teaching-Learning Process

The role of the Holy Spirit is essential in the supernatural transformation of learners through Christian education. The Holy Spirit is vital for *all* spiritual tasks. Therefore, Christian education apart from the Holy Spirit is meaningless. Fred Dickason points out, "The Holy Spirit is the sovereign, most wise, and ultimate teacher of spiritual truth. He makes God's truth relevant to the persons involved and enables application that causes life and growth. Our teaching and learning efforts are in vain unless we cooperate with the Spirit."[3]

The Holy Spirit helps Christian teachers by giving them discernment of God's truths and empowering them to instruct students in a way that produces spiritual transformation. As the author of God's written revelation, the Spirit helps both teachers and students to understand the Bible's message through illumination. The purpose of illumination is to understand biblical truths. Only the Holy Spirit creates the necessary change so that believers can achieve the goal of becoming more like Christ. The following illustration[4] summarizes the work of the Holy Spirit in the teaching learning process:

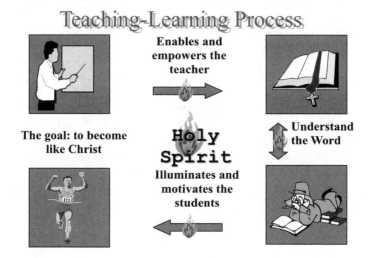

The Holy Spirit makes Christian education dynamic and distinct from any other type of education. Zuck argues that three factors define Christian education: "(1) the centrality of God's written revelation, (2) the necessity of regeneration, and (3) the ministry of the Holy Spirit."[5] The Holy Spirit, then, plays *the* vital role in Christian teaching.

---

[3] C. F. Dickason, "The Holy Spirit in Education," in *Christian Education: Foundations for the Future,* ed. Robert E. Clark, Lin Johnson, and Allyn K. Sloat (Chicago: Moody, 1991), 121.

[4] Illustration developed by the author for use in teacher training conferences.

[5] R. B. Zuck, *Spirit-Filled Teaching: The Power of the Holy Spirit in Your Ministry* (Nashville: Word, 1998), 2.

Although most Christians affirm the importance of the Holy Spirit in ministry, we can at times fail to practice what we claim to believe. A few years ago, I was a committee member for the educational program of a local church. We always started our meetings with prayer, as most Christian gatherings traditionally do. On one particular occasion, a committee member, a respected deacon of the church, arrived just a few minutes late to our meeting. He apologized for being late, and the committee leader responded, "Don't worry, you *just* missed the prayer." He answered with a combination of relief and irony, "It's OK then. I have heard many prayers in life." In this case prayer was nothing more than the first item on the agenda. Tragically, we can make the same mistake in our teaching ministry.

Since the role of the Holy Spirit is essential and God's work relies primarily on His power (Zech 4:6), we would be more effective if we spent more time praying and less time planning or talking. Our actions reflect our convictions more than our words do. Christian teachers are most effective when they bathe their lesson planning and teaching with prayer. Prayer, then, is the essential element in the teaching-learning process.

Names of the Holy Spirit Relating to Teaching

Scripture reveals several names for the Holy Spirit that connect Him to the ministry of teaching. These include "the Spirit of truth," "the Revealer of God," and "Counselor-Helper."

Holy Spirit as Spirit of Truth

The Holy Spirit is truth, as John 16:13 states: "When the *Spirit of truth* comes, He will guide you into all the truth." God the Father is truth (Deut 32:4) and the Son is truth (John 14:6). Therefore, the Word of God is also truth (John 17:17). As the Spirit of truth (John 14:17), the Holy Spirit guides believers to discover and understand truth.

Consequently, all truth is God's truth. Christian educators need not be afraid of finding truth in secular sources because a distinction does not exist between sacred and secular truth.[6] It is common for

---

[6] F. E. Gaebelein, *The Pattern of God's Truth: The Integration of Faith and Learning* (Winona Lake, IN: BMH Books, 1968).

seminary students and believers in general to struggle with "secular" knowledge with implications for Christian ministry. However, since the Trinity is the source of faithfulness, God is present wherever truth is found. Truth is an attribute of the Godhead that emphasizes reliability and steadfastness. For that reason we can trust in the faithfulness of God and His Word.[7] Truth cannot contradict itself in order to remain truthful. With the Bible as the standard, believers should not be afraid of pursuing knowledge regardless of the source. Truth is always sacred because it flows from the Godhead.

Another implication of the Holy Spirit as the source of truth is the realization that God hates lying and falsehood. Proverbs 6:16–19 contains a list of the things that God detests. The list includes "a lying tongue" (v. 17) and "a false witness who speaks lies" (v. 19) as part of the seven things God loathes. Only falsehood is repeated twice on the list! Jesus referred to Satan as the father of lies (John 8:44). Christians must "gird their waist with truth" in order to stand against the wiles of the devil (Eph 6:14). Therefore, God expects His children to reject falsehood and pursue righteousness and truth (Eph 4:22–25). It is better for Christian teachers to admit their ignorance when students ask questions than to invent answers to avoid appearing uninformed. All believers need to walk in truth because the Spirit is truth (1 John 5:6). Apart from the Spirit, God's truth remains elusive![8] Christian teachers are messengers of truth—a big responsibility indeed.

The Holy Spirit as the Revealer of God

The Holy Spirit is God (Acts 5:3–4; 2 Cor 3:18). As the Third Person of the Godhead, He is the main agent in divine revelation.[9] He reveals God because the Spirit is God. The Spirit can understand the deep things of the Father and the Son and is able to reveal them to believers. The apostle Paul explains the reason the Holy Spirit can unveil God:

---

[7] K. J. Vanhoozer, "Truth," in *Dictionary for Theological Interpretation of the Bible,* ed. Kevin J. Vanhoozer (Grand Rapids: Baker Academic, 2005).

[8] A. McGrath, *Christian Theology: An Introduction,* 4th ed. (Malden, MA: Blackwell, 2007).

[9] J. D. Pentecost, *The Divine Comforter: The Person and Work of the Holy Spirit* (Grand Rapids: Kregel, 1997).

> What no eye has seen and no ear has heard, and what has
> never come into a man's heart, is what God has prepared
> for those who love Him. Now God has revealed them to us
> by the Spirit, for the Spirit searches everything, even the
> deep things of God. For who among men knows the con-
> cerns of a man except the spirit of the man that is in him?
> In the same way, no one knows the concerns of God except
> the Spirit of God. Now we have not received the spirit of
> the world, but the Spirit who is from God, in order to know
> what has been freely given to us by God. (1 Cor 2:9–12)

It is through the ministry of the Holy Spirit that we comprehend
God's truths. A person needs the Holy Spirit in order to understand
God and receive His instruction (v. 14). Through the Spirit of God,
we can possess the mind of Christ (v. 16). Only with the help of the
Spirit of wisdom and revelation can we know God better (Eph 1:17).
Again, dependence on the Holy Spirit is imperative for Christian
teachers.

Zuck defines evangelical Christian education as "the Christ-
centered, Bible-based, student-related process of communicating God's
written Word through the Power of the Holy Spirit, for the purpose of
guiding individuals to know and to grow in Christ."[10] Spiritual preparation through prayer is an essential element in Christian teaching.
Professors should pray for their students during the week with the
expectation that the Holy Spirit will teach them deep things between
class sessions and use them to teach others. Christian teaching is a
process that lasts more than the actual lesson because of the continuing teaching of the Holy Spirit beyond the session.

The Holy Spirit as Counselor-Helper

Jesus referred to the Holy Spirit as our "Counselor" or "Helper"
(John 14:26). The Greek word used in this passage to describe the
work of the Holy Spirit is *paraclete*. It literally means "one called
alongside." The purpose of the Holy Spirit is to help and counsel
believers into Gods' truths. God the Holy Spirit lives in us as believers in Christ to assist us in our understanding of the Father and to
respond in obedience to His Word. Therefore, Christian teaching
cannot succeed apart from the "counsel" of the Holy Spirit. The Holy

---

[10] R. B. Zuck, *Spirit-Filled Teaching,* ix

Spirit is the main motivator in Christian education. Only the Spirit knows our students completely and can meet their needs.[11]

Jesus requires His followers to love Him completely and supremely above all other relationships (Matt 10:37–39). To be true disciples of Christ, we need to love Him with all our being. The proof of our love is obedience to His commandments (John 14:15,20). We need to keep His words, which are the same as the Father's: "The one who doesn't love Me will not keep My words. The word that you hear is not Mine but is from the Father who sent Me" (John 14:24). Remembrance and compliance to Jesus' words are imperatives for His disciples.

However, how were the original disciples able to remember His words? The answer: through the Holy Spirit. Jesus was present with His disciples, but the Holy Spirit now dwells with Christ's followers (John 14:16). Through the Holy Spirit, Jesus' followers can benefit from Jesus' presence: "I *[Jesus]* will not leave you as orphans; I am coming to you" (John 14:18). The Father sends the Spirit to Jesus' disciples. "But the Counselor, the Holy Spirit—the Father will send Him in My name—will teach you all things and remind you of everything I have told you" (John 14:26). The Holy Spirit helped Jesus' disciples to remember His teachings. The Spirit leads believers into the truths that Jesus lived and taught.[12] The Holy Spirit's instruction is always about Jesus and goes beyond His teaching only in deepening our understanding of His words.[13]

Teaching Ministries of the Holy Spirit

The Holy Spirit ministers to us, and through those ministries He teaches us. He operates in various ways to fulfill God's purposes. For example, He was actively involved in creation (Gen 1:2; Job 33:4; Ps 104:30) and empowered the conception of Jesus (Luke 1:35). Moreover, the Holy Spirit plays the vital role in the relationship between Christians and the Church. The Spirit carries out every aspect

---

[11] N. N. Pérez, *Jesús, el Maestro: Su plan educativo transformador* (Río Piedras, PR: Palabra y Más, 2006).

[12] M. M. Turner, "Holy Spirit," in *Dictionary of Jesus and the Gospels*, ed. Joel B. Green, Scot McKnight, I. Howard Marshall (Downers Grove, IL: InterVarsity, 1992).

[13] J. M. Hamilton Jr. *God's Indwelling Presence: The Holy Spirit in the Old and New Testaments* (Nashville: B&H Academic, 2006).

of the work of the Church through different ministries, and in doing so, He teaches.

The Holy Spirit makes possible the salvation of humanity. He convicts of sin (John 16:8) and regenerates sinners so their relationship with God can be restored (Titus 3:5). The Holy Spirit incorporates us into the body of Christ during His baptism (1 Cor 12:13). Salvation and the reception of the Holy Spirit occur simultaneously as two sides of the same coin. The Holy Spirit makes us new persons and dwells in all Christians (John 14:7). Every believer receives the Spirit at the moment of conversion:

> To receive the Spirit is to begin the Christian life (Galatians 3:2–3); righteousness through faith and the promise of the Spirit are equivalently regarded as "the blessing of Abraham" (vv. 1–4); to be baptized in the Spirit is to become a member of the body of Christ (1 Corinthians 12:13); if anyone does not "have the Spirit of Christ" that person does not belong to Christ, is not a Christian (Romans 8:9); only reception of the Spirit makes it possible for us to be children of God, to call on God as Father (vv. 14–17); the divine seal establishing the bond between God and the believer is now the Spirit himself, not circumcision (and not baptism—2 Corinthians 1:22; Ephesians 1:13–14).[14]

All believers are called to share the good news of salvation through Jesus Christ. We are to be faithful in our efforts to witness. However, it is the Spirit who does the supernatural work of conversion.

We noted above that the Holy Spirit guides believers into God's truth (John 16:13), but He does more. He illuminates our understanding of God's calling, power, and the riches of His grace (Eph 1:18–19). The Spirit enlightens our minds to understand God's revelation. Through the ministry of illumination, the Holy Spirit enables believers to discern the meaning of God's message, receive it as from God, and apply it to our lives.[15] Consequently, we should live and teach according to the guidance of the Holy Spirit. In fact, "all our

---

[14] J. D. G. Dunn, "The Doctrine of God the Holy Spirit," in *The Portable Seminary: A Master's Level Overview in One Volume*, ed. David Horton (Bloomington, MI: Bethany House, 2006), 154–55.

[15] R. B. Zuck, *Spirit-Filled Teaching*.

ministry, whatever form it may take, is to be done in the power of the Holy Spirit"[16] if it is to be effective and produce fruit that abides.

Sometimes the Holy Spirit does His work in subtle ways. In 2003, I was invited to teach a Christian education course at a Bible seminary in Guatemala City. My wife and I arrived there on Saturday evening and the one-week course started the following Monday.

Our host told us that he would pick us up the next morning to attend a church service. That Sunday morning I heard someone knocking on the door a few minutes before the time we were expecting our host. When I opened the door, I recognized him and said, "I thought you said that you will come later."

He replied, "Yes, I will come back in 15 minutes. I just came *now* to let you know that *you are the preacher this morning.* I forgot to tell you last night."

I had just a few minutes to prepare a sermon without knowing anything about the congregation. I had studied Isaiah 40 before, and I decided to preach through that chapter. The passage talks about the God of hope and how He is able to keep His promises. Therefore, we can receive His comfort and trust Him.

After the service a leader from the church came to me and told me that the message was exactly what the congregation needed. A family from the church had an accident that week that shocked the church family. The whole church was grieving, and I did not know about it, but the Holy Spirit led me to choose a Bible passage that spoke to the church's needs. The Spirit illuminated the minds and hearts of the people to understand the Word and receive God's comfort.

The Bible is the Word of God because the Holy Spirit inspired the writers. Second Peter 1:21 states, "For prophecy never came by the will of man, but holy men of God spoke *as they were* moved by the Holy Spirit." The Spirit is the Author of the Scriptures. Inspiration "is that supernatural work of the Holy Spirit whereby He so guided and superintended the writers of Scripture that what they wrote is the Word of God, inerrant as originally written."[17] The following chapter, "The Bible as Curriculum," further develops the nature of the Word of God.

---

[16] W. Grudem, *Systematic Theology* (Grand Rapids: Zondervan, 1994), 649.

[17] Zuck, *Spirit-Filled Teaching*, 31.

The teaching ministries of the Holy Spirit are also essential for the
Christian life. Believers are commanded to be filled with the Spirit in
order to live as God intended (Eph 5:18). To be filled with the Spirit
means to yield complete control to the Spirit's direction and authority. This filling influences every aspect of believers' lives. Christian
character, worship, and ministry are made possible only as a result
of the Holy Spirit's filling.[18] A life controlled by the Holy Spirit produces fruit (attitudes and qualities) that please God: "But the fruit of
the Spirit is love, joy, peace, longsuffering, kindness, goodness, faithfulness, gentleness, self-control. Against such there is no law" (Gal
5:22–23). The word "fruit" is singular but has a collective connotation. The essence of the Christian life is to let the Holy Spirit direct
our actions. Therefore, it is impossible to please God apart from the
Holy Spirit. Any teaching ministry to be effective requires teachers
filled with the Holy Spirit because this filling is a "divine empowering for a specific ministry."[19]

The Gift of Teaching

The Holy Spirit bestows special abilities on every Christian for the
spiritual edification of the Church. The Spirit provides these gifts as
part of God's grace (*charisma*) to all believers. The Bible mentions
the spiritual gift of teaching in three different passages: Rom 12:7;
1 Cor 12:28; and Eph 4:11. The Spirit uses gifted teachers to prepare,
equip, and train Christians to serve one another within the body of
Christ.[20]

The gift of teaching is the ability to explain God's truth to people.
This gift is connected in some instances to the gift of pastor as in
Eph 4:11 but could be given alone.[21] Although *all* believers are called
to teach God's Word to people (Matt 28:20), the Holy Spirit especially empowers some individuals with the gift of teaching. Millard
Erickson points out four important considerations about spiritual
gifts according to 1 Corinthians 12 and 14:

[18] E. Woodcock, "The Filling of the Holy Spirit," in *Bibliotheca Sacra* 157 (January-
March 2000): 68–87.

[19] Ibid., 83.

[20] G. C. Newton, "Holy Spirit," in *Evangelical Dictionary of Christian Education*, ed. M.
J. Anthony (Grand Rapids: Baker Academic, 2001), 340.

[21] C. C. Ryrie, *Basic Theology: A Popular Systematic Guide to Understanding Biblical
Truth* (Chicago: Moody, 1999).

1. The gifts are bestowed on the body (the church). They are for the edification of the whole body, not merely for the enjoyment or enrichment of the individual members possessing them (12:7; 14:5,12).
2. No one person has all the gifts (12:14–21), nor is any one of the gifts bestowed on all persons (12:28–30). Consequently, the individual members of the church need one another.
3. Although not equally conspicuous, all gifts are important (12:22–26).
4. The Holy Spirit apportions the various gifts to whom and as He wills (12:11).[22]

The use of spiritual gifts could be neglected in some local churches because of the difficulty of clearly identifying the gifts among believers. The Bible does not provide a checklist or question-naire for discovering spiritual gifts. However, Scripture clearly men-tions the importance of spiritual gifts and their relationship to the spiritual growth of the church (Eph 4:11–16). How can church lead-ers discover the spiritual gifts in their congregations? They can do it only by spending time with their members. There are no shortcuts. Spiritual gifts inventories can be helpful, but a close relationship with people is essential. A relationship (discipleship) is necessary to get to know believers and their gifts. It takes time to equip people to do the work of ministry.

Christians with specific spiritual gifts should exercise them in every area of the church. For example, in local churches people with the spiritual gift of teaching should be the ones "formally" teaching in the congregation and instructing others how to teach. Unfortunately, in some cases the teachers are the ones available or willing, not necessarily the ones gifted by the Spirit, to do it. In these instances the local church is missing God's empowerment that causes the growth of the body (Eph 4:16). Spiritual gifts are closely related to the Spirit's filling: "No matter how gifted or spiritual a teacher may be, learning and growth towards Christ-likeness will not

---

[22] M. J. Erickson, *Christian Theology*, 2nd ed. (Grand Rapids: Baker, 2000), 892.

take place unless a learner allows the Holy Spirit to work within his or her heart."[23]

Conclusion

Through the Holy Spirit the God of the universe, the mighty Creator, dwells in all believers and empowers them to serve Him. It is amazing and humbling to realize that the Lord partners with us in the teaching ministry of His church! This point is underscored by Zuck, who writes, "Christian education is a cooperative process, a venture involving both the human and the divine. Human teachers communicate and exemplify truth; the Holy Spirit seeks to provide guidance, power, illumination, and insight to the teachers."[24]

The Holy Spirit does not replace Christian teachers. He chooses to teach through us and through our ministry to others, as we rely on His power to accomplish His purposes in building the Lord's Church. What a great Teacher, and what a great honor to be channels of His teaching to others!

Discussion Questions

1. Why is the Holy Spirit essential in Christian teaching?
2. Since the Holy Spirit is truth, why do some believers differentiate between *sacred* and *secular* truth?
3. How does the Holy Spirit serve as a counselor-helper in the teaching-learning process?
4. Is it possible to serve God apart from the Holy Spirit? Explain.
5. In what ways can we partner with the Holy Spirit to help us teach? Some use "dependence on the Spirit" as an excuse for poor preparation. How would you explain that this attitude is a misconception of the Spirit's role?

---

[23] G. Newton, "The Holy Spirit in the Educational Process," in *Christian Education: Foundations for the Twenty-first Century*, ed. Michael J. Anthony (Grand Rapids: Baker Academic, 2001), 127.

[24] R. B. Zuck, "The Role of the Holy Spirit in Christian Teaching," in *The Christian Educator's Handbook on Teaching: A Comprehensive Resource on the Distinctiveness of True Christian Teaching* (Grand Rapids: Baker, 1988), 37.

Bibliography

Dickason, Fred C. "The Holy Spirit in Education." In *Christian Education: Foundations for the Future*. Ed. R E. Clark, Lin Johnson, and Allyn K. Sloat. Chicago: Moody, 1991.

Dunn, James D. G. "The Doctrine of God the Holy Spirit." In *The Portable Seminary: A Master's Level Overview in One Volume*. Ed. D. Horton. Bloomington, MI: Bethany House, 2006.

Erickson, Millard J. *Christian Theology*. 2nd ed. Grand Rapids: Baker, 2000.

Gaebelein, Frank E. *The Pattern of God's Truth: The Integration of Faith and Learning*. Winona Lake, IN: BMH Books, 1968.

García Márquez, Gabriel. *El coronel no tiene quien le escriba*. Barcelona: Random House, 1999.

Grudem, Wayne. *Systematic Theology*. Grand Rapids: Zondervan, 1994.

Hamilton, James M., Jr. *God's Indwelling Presence: The Holy Spirit in the Old and New Testaments*. Nashville: B&H Academic, 2006.

McGrath, Alister. *Christian Theology: An Introduction*. 4th ed. Malden, MA: Blackwell, 2007.

Nales Pérez, Nereida. *Jesús, el Maestro: Su plan educativo transformador*. Río Piedras, PR: Palabra y Más, 2006.

Newton, Gary C. "Holy Spirit." In *Evangelical Dictionary of Christian Education*. Ed. Michael J. Anthony. Grand Rapids: Baker Academic, 2001.

Newton, Gary. "The Holy Spirit in the Educational Process." In *Christian Education: Foundations for the Twenty-first Century*. Ed. Michael J. Anthony. Grand Rapids: Baker Academic, 2001.

Pentecost, Dwight J. *The Divine Comforter: The Person and Work of the Holy Spirit*. Grand Rapids: Kregel, 1997.

Ryrie, Charles C. *Basic Theology: A Popular Systematic Guide to Understanding Biblical Truth*. Chicago: Moody, 1999.

Turner, M. M. "Holy Spirit." In *Dictionary of Jesus and the Gospels*. Ed. Joel B. Green, Scot McKnight, and I. Howard Marshall. Downers Grove, IL: InterVarsity, 1992.

Vanhoozer, Kevin J. "Truth." In *Dictionary for Theological Interpretation of the Bible*. Ed. Kevin J. Vanhoozer. Grand Rapids: Baker Academic, 2005.

Woodcock, Eldon. "The Filling of the Holy Spirit." In *Bibliotheca Sacra* 157. January-March 2000.

Zuck, Roy B. "The Role of the Holy Spirit in Christian Teaching." In *The Christian Educator's Handbook on Teaching: A Comprehensive Resource on the Distinctiveness of True Christian Teaching*. Grand Rapids: Baker, 1988.

Zuck, Roy B. *Spirit-Filled Teaching: The Power of the Holy Spirit in Your Ministry*. Nashville: Word, 1998.

Chapter 6

THE BIBLE AS CURRICULUM

Mike McGuire

The grass withers, the flowers fade,
but the word of our God remains forever.
(Isa 40:8)

The Church's Image in and Message to the Community

As the staff gathered around the church conference room, they were introduced to the church consultant. They faced two major issues: What had been the church's image in the community, and what image did they want to create?

The consultant pointed out that the church cannot *not* communicate an image to the community, so they needed to think carefully because their choice would influence everything about the church (for example, the proposed building remodel, promotional materials, scheduling, and literature). Some younger staff members pointed out the need for the church to be more relevant to younger people. Older staff pointed to the church's successful past, seeing little reason for changing. Others wanted the church to have a more upbeat and positive image. Still others argued that the church needed to get back to basics. There seemed to be little agreement concerning the needed image of the church.

The church consultant was right to say that the church cannot *not* communicate and, further, right to say that the church's chosen image should influence everything it does. One observation needed to be made and one question needed to be asked. The group needed to observe that the church's image is tied inextricably to its message, and the group needed to ask whether the church's message is up for discussion.

This chapter will suggest that, although different churches will accommodate their message to differing cultures and subcultures, the core message of the church to the community is not up for discussion. The church is required by its allegiance to God to present the biblical message. Thus, this chapter will ask two key questions: (1) Why does the Bible deserve this preeminent role? (2) Why must church staff members, the servants of God, give the Bible this preeminent role? The chapter will then turn to the practical implications of the answers provided to these questions.

Does the Bible Deserve the Preeminent Role?

In considering whether the Bible deserves the preeminent role in the church's educational mission, this section will examine how the Bible describes itself and then examine how evangelical theologians have described it.

A Biblical Self-Description

Old Testament (OT) writers repeatedly claimed to speak God's words. They recorded God speaking just as freely as they recorded humans speaking, and the OT is peppered with "thus says the Lord." Our Lord and the writers of the New Testament (NT) assumed that the OT was revelation from God and thus truthful, even in its details.

Matthew reported that Christ debated with His detractors using the tense of a word from the OT (Matt 22:29–32). Jesus' argument rested upon the tense of the OT quotation in verse 32, which reads, "I am the God of Abraham, the God of Isaac, and the God of Jacob." This passage was well-known to Jesus' audience, for in it God revealed Himself to Moses from the burning bush by revealing His name YHWH (I AM). In the context God declared Himself to be (our English present tense) not only the God of Moses (who was living) but to be the God of those who had died (i.e., Abraham, Isaac, and Jacob). Thus Jesus argued, based on the tense of the verb in the OT quotation, that God is the God of the both those then living and those living on after their death.

Similarly, Paul made a theological argument in which he depended on whether a word in an OT passage was singular or plural (Gal 3:16–17). Clearly, both Jesus and Paul believed in the truthfulness of

the details of the OT. Peter described how men were moved by the
Holy Spirit to write documents that were not their personal interpretations (2 Pet 1:21). Paul exhorted Timothy to study the OT, declaring that "all Scripture is inspired by God" (2 Tim 3:16).

The NT church, having received the OT as God's Word, viewed
the documents written by apostles as similarly inspired.[1] The author of the letter to the Hebrews wrote, "Long ago God spoke to
the fathers by the prophets at different times and in different ways.
In these last days, He has spoken to us by His Son, whom He has
appointed heir of all things and through whom He made the universe" (Heb 1:1–2). What was written in the OT and what Jesus said
were both seen as from God and truthful. By the time Peter wrote
his second letter, he was equating the writings of Paul with the OT
Scriptures (2 Pet 3:15–16).[2] This equation and comparison of the OT
prophets and the NT apostles also shows up in 1 Pet 1:10–12 and
2 Pet 3:2. The Jews had accepted the OT as inspired as did Jesus and
the authors of the NT. The church then recognized that God had
given them new revelation that was equally inspired and equally true
as the Scriptures that they accepted as inspired and true. The eternal
value of God's revelation was captured when Isaiah declared, "The
grass withers, the flowers fade, / but the word of our God remains
forever" (Isa 40:8) and when Peter reiterated this very truth (1 Pet
1:24–25). Both the OT and the NT affirm that the Word of God is
eternal, for it is the word of the true God and is of eternal value.

Theological Descriptions of the Bible

Theology represents an attempt to summarize the teachings of the
church. For those Christians who emphasize the Bible over church
tradition or philosophical speculation, these summaries attempt to
capture the essence of what the Bible teaches. Thus, theological statements about the Bible summarize what the Bible teaches about itself.
A brief summary of some of the key terms follow.

---

[1] J. N. D. Kelly, *Early Christian Doctrines*, rev. ed. (New York: Harper Collins, 1978;
   reprint, Peabody, MA: Prince, 2004), 56.
[2] Grudem points to 1 Tim 5:17–18 as another example of one NT document recognizing another NT document as Scripture. For the details see W. A. Grudem,
   Systematic Theology (Grand Rapids, MI: Zondervan, 1994), 61.

Theologians describe the Bible as revelation.[3] It is seen as reveal-ing who God is, who we are, what is wrong with us, and what we need to do to bring ourselves into harmony with God. They affirm that the Bible is inspired.[4] Although in everyday English we speak of authors being inspired, Paul wrote, "All Scripture is inspired by God" (2 Tim 3:16). That is, it is the document and not the author that is inspired. They affirm that the Bible is authoritative. If God, by defini-tion, is the highest of all authorities and if the Bible is His message to humans, then it follows that the Bible derives its authority from God.[5] Since the Bible is from God and carries His authority, then it is competent to accomplish His purposes.[6] Isaiah declared, "So My word that comes from My mouth will not return to Me empty, but it will accomplish what I please, and will prosper in what I send it to do" (Isa 55:11). They affirm that the Bible is true, for God is the God of truth and the source of all truth. God does not lie but speaks the truth. As Paul declared, "God must be true" (Rom 3:4). Thus, since the Bible is God's Word, it is the truth.[7]

Theologians refer to the Bible as the canon, an old term referring to a measuring stick.[8] In other words the Bible is the standard for authoritative teaching in the church.[9] Thus, the message of every teacher can be judged by comparing what the teacher says against this standard (see Acts 17:1–14). When the reformers declared their belief in *sola Scriptura*, they were affirming that "only Scripture" (and not church tradition) establishes the standard for the authorita-tive doctrines of the church.

The above doctrines are common conservative, evangelical, theo-logical descriptions of God's Word, but two more descriptions are pertinent to this discussion. These can be considered together by af-firming that the Bible is alien yet relevant. It is alien for it does not

---

[3] M. J. Erickson, *Christian Theology*, 2nd ed. (Grand Rapids, MI: Baker, 1998), 272; Grudem, *Systematic Theology*, 49.

[4] Grudem, *Systematic Theology*, 73–77.

[5] Erickson, *Christian Theology*, 271.

[6] Although this doctrine is assumed by conservative evangelical theologians, Grudem develops it in his *Systematic Theology*, 127–38.

[7] Ibid., 90–100.

[8] R. L. Saucy, "Which Books Belong in the Bible?" in *Understanding Christian Theology*, ed. C. R. Swindoll and R. B. Zuck (Nashville, TN: Thomas Nelson, 2003), 111.

[9] Erickson, *Christian Theology*, 259, 271.

come from our culture, and it is relevant because God has made it
so. First, it is alien to contemporary audiences because of its human
authors and context.[10] The books that compose the Bible were written
by people living in ancient times, composed in ancient languages, and
written to ancient peoples living in ancient cultures. Any attentive
reader will be aware of the cultural gap between this ancient world
and the contemporary one. Second, the Bible is alien to contemporary audiences because of its divine Author. Although humans were
coauthors and their personalities and backgrounds show in their
writings, the Bible did not come ultimately from humans and their
personal interpretations (2 Pet 1:20–21). The writers were moved
by God, and so this revelation came from above, from God, from the
kingdom of light. It came to those who live below, to humans, to
those in a sin-darkened world. Thus, the Bible is alien to contemporary audiences for exactly the same reason it was alien to its ancient
audiences: because its divine Author thinks differently about the
world than do humans. Yet, in spite of its alien qualities, the Bible is
profoundly relevant. It is relevant because God, who knows all, has
spoken to the deepest of human needs. He knows us and our needs
far better than we know ourselves, for He created us and shaped us.
He knows what sin and rebellion have done to us. He knows what we
need to know about our deliverance in this world and our ultimate
deliverance in the world to come. He chose the situations to which
His servants spoke, guided what they spoke, and preserved what He
desired to preserve. He fully intended these words to stand for all
time. Thus, the divine Author has designed the Bible to be relevant
to human audiences at every time and in all cultures. It is relevant
because, although the contemporary audience may differ in language,
culture, and technology with its original audiences, the contemporary
audience shares much in common (e.g., spiritually, physically, and
emotionally) with those original audiences. It is relevant to audiences
today because God had His servants in ages past write documents that
met the needs of their target audience—needs that God knew were
universal. His message is also relevant to contemporary audiences

---

[10] Almost all advocates of the verbal, plenary view of inspiration are careful to deny
the dictation theory of inspiration, recognizing that God worked though human authors and that the personality and writing styles of those human authors are clearly
observable in the biblical documents. See Erickson, *Christian Theology*, 232–33.

because they share those needs, whether felt or not. Thus, contemporary teachers and their audiences need to discover this relevance just as our spiritual forefathers have discovered it throughout history and just as our spiritual siblings do so around the world.

The Bible, God's special revelation, is crucial to a proper understanding of God, Christ, sin, salvation, and the church. It is crucial for one seeking to grow in the grace of the knowledge of Christ. With the Bible these concepts have particular meanings. Without the Bible one could assign any definitions one preferred, and a true Bible-based Christianity would cease to exist. As Lewis and Demarest have observed, "Clearly, special revelation is foundational to the entire Christian scheme of things."[11] So given what the Bible says of itself and what theologians have reasoned from its text, the Bible deserves the preeminent role in the educational mission of the church.[12] Now the question is this: Should God's servants give it this preeminent role?

Should God's Servants Give the Bible the Preeminent Role?

There are many ways to portray the believer's relationship to God and His Word. For example, God brings us forth by His Word so that we are His children (Jas 1:18). He sanctifies us by His Word so that we are a set-apart people, a holy priesthood (John 17:17; 1 Pet 2:5). Given, however, the brevity of this chapter, it will only consider one motif: the minister as servant. So, what is it about the servant of God motif that might profitably guide the attitude of God's servant concerning the Bible in the educational ministry of the church?

God's Servants Then

In the Bible those who were God's ministers were consistently referred to as His servants. These include Moses (Heb 3:5), David (Luke 1:69), and even our Lord, Jesus Christ (Matt 12:18). Similarly, many of the authors of the NT letters referred to themselves as slaves

---

[11] G. R. Lewis and B. A. Demarest, *Integrative Theology* (Grand Rapids, MI: Zondervan, 1996), 96.

[12] Responding to the possible objection that this is a circular argument (i.e., the Bible is important because it says that it is important) is beyond the scope of this chapter, but a succinct response is provided by Grudem, *Systematic Theology*, 78–79.

of God (Rom 1:1; Jas 1:1; 2 Pet 1:1; Jude 1; and Rev 1:1). In addition
to the words *servant* and *slave*, the word *steward* (or manager) is also
sometimes used to describe servants and ministers.[13] Relevant to our
topic, Paul identified his fellow ministers and himself as "managers
of God's mysteries" (1 Cor 4:1) linking the message of God and the
role of God's servant-managers (i.e., stewards). These men were all
servants in the sense of going about doing God's will, often including
speaking for God. As servants of God, they were to promote the message of God (Gal 1:10; 2 Pet 1:20).

God's Servants Now

God still calls those who believe in Him to serve Him. Thus, God
still calls men and women to be His servants and to promote His
message faithfully. The faithful servant is a student of God's Word
(see 2 Tim 2:15 and 4:13). Once the servant has understood the Bible
and obeyed it, the Bible then provides the subject matter for the servant's message. The faithful servant proclaims "the message of truth"
(Col 1:5), "sound teaching" (1 Tim 6:3, Titus 2:1), "the pattern of
sound teaching" (2 Tim 1:13), and "the faithful message" (Titus
1:9). This contrasts with those who promote "myths" (Titus 1:14),
"foolish and ignorant disputes" (2 Tim 2:23), and "irreverent and
silly myths" (1 Tim 4:7). As Paul wrote to Timothy, "If you point
these things out to the brothers, you will be a good servant of Christ
Jesus, nourished by the words of the faith and of the good teaching
that you have followed" (1 Tim 4:6). In the NT context, this clearly
means that the faithful servant of God is to point people to the Bible
and the truths taught there.

---

[13] The NT uses a variety of terms to refer to servants, including (1) *pais* meaning "one
who is committed to total obedience to another" (Walter Bauer, *A Greek-English
Lexicon of the New Testament*, ed. and trans. W. F. Arndt, F. W. Gingrich, and F. W.
Danker [BAGD], 2nd ed. [Chicago: University of Chicago Press, 1979], s.v. *pais*)
and often translated *servant* or *slave*, (2) *doulos* meaning "one who is solely committed to another" (BAGD, s.v. *doulos*) and often translated *bond servant* or *slave*, and
(3) *oikonomos* meaning "one who is entrusted with management . . . , [an] administrator" (BAGD, s.v. *oikonomos*) and often translated *manager* or *steward*. Louw and
Nida provide clarification, pointing out that *doulos* means a "slave in the sense of
becoming the property of an owner" (J. Louw and E. Nida, *Greek-English Lexicon
of the New Testament Based on Semantic Domains, vol 1* [New York: United Bible
Societies, 1989] domain 87.76). These three words provide some sense of what the
NT authors meant by being a servant of God.

Nevertheless, the wise servant knows that some will reject the message because the servant knows from the Bible that some even then heard the message as odd and alien and thus failed to embrace the message of God. It thus should not surprise the servant that some today do not see the importance of the Bible as curriculum. Therefore, the servant in educational ministry declares the Word of God as faithfully and winsomely as possible even if the audience rejects both the message and the servant-messenger.

This role of the servant crying boldly in the wilderness frightens some potential servants while appealing to others. It frightens those who value human approval too much and value God's approval too little. It appeals to some because God has called them to such a ministry, and it, unfortunately, appeals to others because they like the image of being God's servant and the servant of no man.

God, however, does not only call us to be His servants, but He calls us to be the servants of others. Jesus said to His disciples, "Whoever wants to become great among you must be your servant, and whoever wants to be first among you must be a slave to all" (Mark 10:43–44). Paul, similarly, asked the reader to embrace service to others, pointing to the examples found in Christ, Timothy, Epaphroditus, and himself, exhorting his audience not to look to their own interests but to the interests of others (Phil 2:6–8,17,19,25–29). Consequently, the servant of God is not only a messenger of God but is a self-sacrificial servant of others.

The servant of others will consider the other's point of view and seek ways to accommodate this biblical message so that it might be understandable and appealing (1 Cor 9:19–23). Being a servant of others requires one to be strategic in one's approach to serving people. As Paul wrote, "For although I am free from all people, I have made myself a slave to all, in order to win more people" (1 Cor 9:19).

Some who relish the idea of being the bold prophet crying in the wilderness, if they liked this image for mainly personal reasons and not for divine ones, are uncomfortable with the role of a servant to others. For to be a servant of others, one must give attention to those one serves, to their interests and their concerns (Phil 2:4). For just as one should know God well to serve Him, one should also understand people well in order to serve them. Thus, the servant of God in educational ministry must be a student of the Bible and of people.

Thus far we have seen how ministers are called to serve God. This leads to boldness and clarity of purpose in declaring God's Word as God's Word. We have also seen how ministers are called to serve others and how this insight leads to the need for understanding our audience and in packaging our message so that it might communicate the biblical message accurately and effectively to our contemporary audience.[14] Now we turn to the role of the steward, the servant who is over other servants, one who calls and enables others to serve.

The servant of God, who serves others, quickly becomes aware of the need for more servants in God's service and thus the need both to call others to become servants and then to enable them in various ministries. Accordingly, the wise servant of God must have plans for recruiting and incorporating more people into ministry.

Some servants are so faithful that God places them in charge of other servants. This servant has become an administrator (what the KJV referred to as a steward) and has become responsible for seeing that others serve the Master effectively. Christ recognized the value of this vital administrative role when He said, "Who then is the faithful and sensible manager his master will put in charge of his household servants . . . ? That slave whose master finds him working when he comes will be rewarded" (Luke 12:42–43). This faithful administrator is exceptionally valuable to our Lord's service, having the personal and interpersonal skills to plan, organize, motivate, and manage other servants for his Master.

The administrator is often required to reduce the amount of personal time given to frontline ministry. Nevertheless, the educational staff member with the skills of an administrator is exceptionally valuable to the church because this staff member acts as a "force multiplier," for the wise administrator is able to multiply the ministry by calling, organizing, and enabling others to serve. This administrator role is at the heart of effective educational ministry. In summary, the servant role includes faithful service to both God and others and may

---

[14] J. D. Charles has provided a particularly insightful analysis of Paul promoting the biblical message to a pagan culture in "Paul before the Areopagus: Reflections on the Apostle's Encounter with Cultured Paganism," *Philosophia Christi* 7 (2005): 125–40.

include faithful management of other servants. Yet in all these tasks, the servant is the servant to the Master and to the Master's message.

Given the nature of the Bible and the nature of the servants of God, the Bible deserves and should be given the preeminent role in the educational ministry of the church. For how can the servants of God tell God that His ideas should take second place to their own? Thus, educational ministers, as the servants of God, should give the Bible the preeminent place in the educational ministry of the church. The issue left is this: What are the implications of this role for the educational ministry of the church?

Implications for Educational Ministry

The above examination of both the nature of the Bible and the nature of the servants of God suggests that the educational ministry of the church should be God serving, biblically faithful, audience accommodating, servant building, and well managed. This section will now focus on implications for the broader educational mission of the church drawn from these observations. It will then consider the issue of what it means to be biblically faithful and will end with a consideration of how these insights potentially relate to the other chapters of this book.

Educational Mission and Educational Ministry

Every intentional ministry of the church has an educational component. The church worships, helps the poor, and comforts the hurting so that the church is not just preaching or teaching; however, all of these ministries send a message and thus are all part of a distinctively Christian educational process. Hence, the educational function of the church is larger than what the church might place under the oversight of an educational minister (the stewards described above), for the pastor and choir director, counselors and deacons, also fulfill an educational function.

As seen above, the revelation of God is the message of the entire church and thus includes the church's educational ministry. The church, in trying to reach more people, might consider what style of ministry is appropriate given their community or might consider how ministry styles may differ in reaching adolescents versus adults, but the church does not have a choice of messages. All groups within the church should be committed to the Bible as God's message.

This message will strike some as alien, for *it is* alien.[15] It comes from the kingdom of light into a darkened world. We should expect it to say things that do not fit our sense of what we need for it may address needs that God sees and we, in our finite and fallen state, do not. The message will also strike some as alien for these documents were originally written in ancient languages to people who lived in ancient cultures. The Bible, however, is relevant because God designed it to be so. God moved His servants of the past to write documents to address what was needed, and He superintended the writing so that these documents might be said to be authored by Him. It is the church's responsibility to communicate this importance and relevance to their contemporary audience. It is particularly important for the educational ministry to communicate this relevance to contemporary audiences because it is particularly prepared to work with small groups. Thus, the educational ministry can communicate the relevance of the biblical message to those particular groups. This involves not merely the training of teachers but also the choice of curriculum.

The Bible as Curriculum

If one understands the nature of the Bible and the nature of being a servant of God, then one must choose literature for the church that is faithful to the Bible and its message. This literature must have as its goal the communication of the Bible and its message to people. This communication is done in a way that accurately reflects the original text, that is understandable to the audience, and that challenges the audience in a way that is consistent with the original text.

What is meant by accurately reflecting the original text might be addressed through a thought experiment. As a teacher, picture yourself teaching a passage of Scripture and having the human author of that biblical passage sitting at the back of your class or on the back

---

[15] God's message appeared alien and thus served as a corrective to ancient culture, premodern culture, and modern culture. Now the biblical message may appear particularly alien to younger Christians who have grown up in a postmodern culture, but this is merely one more "culture" that God wishes to correct. See M. J. Erickson, *The Postmodern World: Discerning the Times and the Spirit of Our Age* (Wheaton, IL: Crossway, 2002), 59–86.

pew of your church. Assume, for example, that you are teaching
the fourth chapter of the Gospel of John concerning Jesus and the
woman at the well, and among the students you have the apostle
John. Further assume that God has provided him with a thorough
knowledge of your audience's culture. A biblically faithful message
would communicate John's message to a contemporary audience
and receive his approval. A pseudo-biblical message would leave the
apostle feeling his words had been taken out of context and twisted
to fit your preconceived notions. So as you teach, would John smile
approvingly or sit there with a confused look?

A similar standard would apply to entire books of the Bible. If one
is teaching the entire Gospel of John over some period of time, then
the standard would be whether the contemporary teacher's goal and
focus reflect the author's goal (see John 20:30–31). It is important to
reflect the entire book for two reasons. Many people in the church
may know a passage here or there but do not have any idea what any
entire book in the Bible says. Yet the books of the NT were written
to be read to the congregation, probably an entire book at a single
reading. In addition, not only passages have meaning, but these individual passages contribute to the meaning of the larger document. If
one does not understand the larger document, one may easily misunderstand the passages within it. It is crucial for people to understand
books as well as passages and verses.

A similar standard would work even for lessons that are drawn
from multiple passages (as was done in sections of this chapter). If
the lesson is pulled from passages written by OT prophet A and NT
apostles B and C, then the question becomes this: Would these three
approve of the way that you have chosen to use what God revealed
through them? Or would they suspect the message originated with
you, the contemporary teacher, and the passages quoted were merely
used to make the lesson appear as if it were from the Bible and thus
authoritative?

What is true of your teaching should also be true of the literature
chosen by the church. It should reflect the meaning in the original
context and at the same time state this meaning in a way that accom-
modates that message to the culture of a contemporary audience.
Thus, how the message is packaged varies. The literature for a lay

Bible doctrines class would differ in form from the literature used by
a support group, which, in turn, would differ in form from the literature used by a class for sixth graders. These differing purposes would
produce differing approaches to communication. Yet all would be
faithful to the Bible and thus to the God of the Bible.

The purpose of having a biblically faithful curriculum is not merely
an end in itself, but the purpose is to bring people to a saving faith in
Christ, to a trusting relationship with the Father, and to an empowering relationship with the Spirit. The purpose includes developing an
accurate view of who God is, learning to see the world from God's
perspective, developing a heart for evangelism, and encouraging biblically faithful relationships with those in and outside the church. The
goal of such literature should be to encourage a solidly Christian perspective of all of life and to help people avoid the errors that lead to
spiritual darkness. Its ultimate goal is to transform individuals, couples, families, and communities into conformity to what God desires.
The purpose of promoting a biblically faithful curriculum is to honor
God and to accomplish His goals for your community.

An Evaluative Checklist

There is a danger in thinking higher of oneself than one ought because it is difficult to be self-critical while it is easy to fall into criti-
cizing others.[16] With this in mind, the following set of questions are
offered to promote healthy self-critique.

1. Does your educational program communicate the Bible
   faithfully?
   a. Does it communicate passages accurately?
   b. Does it communicate the meaning of entire books
      accurately?
2. Does your program communicate the alien nature of the biblical message so that the audience truly understands the Bible's
   surprising message?

---

[16] Romans 12:3 warns against this tendency, which results in our being overly generous in evaluating our own programs while being overly critical of the programs
of others. S. K. Moroney convincingly argues from theological and psychological
sources that we humans tend to distort reality to our own advantage. See his *The
Noetic Effects of Sin: A Historical and Contemporary Exploration of How Sin Affects
Our Thinking* (Lanham, MD: Lexington, 2000).

3. Does your program communicate the relevance of the biblical message so that your contemporary audience grasps how this biblical message might apply to them and how they might change their lives in light of biblical truth?
4. Does your educational program accommodate to the culture of the audience without distorting the biblical message?
5. Is your educational program drawing people to a closer relationship with God and more biblical relationships with others?
6. Does your educational program communicate sound doctrine?
7. Is your educational program transforming how your church sees the world?
8. Is your program merely producing an audience, or is it producing more servants of God and others?
9. Is your educational ministry communicating to the broader community a clear image of a NT church that is committed to God and His ministry among people?
10. On a 1-to-10 scale, with 1 being exceptionally low and 10 being exceptionally high, how would you rate your church on how well your educational program is serving God? How do you think God would rate your church?

Other Implications for Educational Ministry

It is important for the reader not to miss the relationship between this chapter and other chapters in this volume. Those chapters will not take the time to reestablish the Bible as curriculum but will develop issues merely mentioned or hinted at here. For example, the chapter on the church (chap. 8) establishes the congregational context in which the biblical curriculum is taught. The chapters on organization and administration (chaps. 2 and 21) provide insight about being a steward in promoting effective ministry. The chapters on administration and volunteers (chaps. 21 and 22) address issues related to recruiting and working along with other servants. The chapter on studying the Bible (chap. 12) will help you know how to study the Bible and train volunteers how to teach others to study. Chapters on preschoolers, youth, adults, and families (chaps. 15, 16, 17, and 18) will help you accommodate the biblical message to those groups. The chapter on learning experiences (chap. 14) will help you understand how to communicate the biblical message effectively and creatively to a contemporary audience (another aspect of accommodation). The chapter on discipleship (chap. 7) will help you understand what should be produced if you have a biblically faithful curriculum. The chapter on curriculum (chap. 19) will help the reader understand what is meant by a well-developed curriculum (whereas, this chapter focused on the biblical content). The chapter on evaluation (chap. 23) will help the reader evaluate the ministry so that it can become more effective in delivering God's message. If we claim to have the greatest message on earth, we should pursue the most effective methodologies for promoting that message.

Clarifications and Qualifications

It is possible that one might read more into what is affirmed here than is intended, so a few clarifications and qualifications are in order. First, to say that the Bible is curriculum is not to say that one should have a curriculum that is only about content. It is because of the church's relationship to God that the Bible is emphasized. Thus, this approach is a God-centered approach, which secondarily and necessarily requires a focus on God's message.

Also, in theological terminology, God is a Person, and humans are persons in a derivative sense. Thus biblical teaching is about persons and for persons. Therefore, this approach, if executed properly, is also highly relational. If a so-called biblical curriculum is not relational, then it is not consistently biblical.

In addition, the goal of the Bible as curriculum is transformation. The Bible points people to a transformational relationship with God. These transformed people relate to their community in a transformative way. Thus, this approach, if executed properly, also has a community focus. Communicating content is absolutely crucial, but a biblical curriculum is far more than communicating content. It is communicating content while building biblical relationships so that it transforms people and reaches into the church's broader community.

Second and similarly, the goal of teaching the Bible is not mere knowledge. The Bible itself teaches that knowledge puffs up and love builds up (1 Cor 8:1). Thus, when teaching the Bible, one should aim at transforming the whole person through the power and message of God. The aim of biblical teaching is to produce Christians who are doers and not hearers only (Jas 1:22–27).

Third, although teaching the Bible is often associated with use of monologues (whether sermon or lecture), the servant of God should be creative in communicating the Bible. In the Bible we have far more examples of Jesus' dialogues than we do of His monologues. We also find the biblical authors using a variety of literary genres including dramatic narratives and extensive passages of poetry (the OT prophets wrote in Hebrew poetic form; the Psalms are all poetry as are most of Job and the Song of Songs). If one is consistent with the way the Bible teaches, then one will not restrict oneself to one approach to communicating the biblical message.

Fourth, one should not conclude that the slave motif, the motif that is emphasized here, is the only way to view one's relationship to God. This motif was chosen for this chapter because it is clearly biblical and because it emphasized duty, a concept that is in short supply in contemporary culture, even contemporary Christian culture.[17] In addition, it provides a valuable example of using a concept (that of slave) that is "alien" to contemporary culture in a way that is at the same time relevant to a contemporary audience. One should not conclude that the biblically faithful curriculum is only about duty and restrictions. As our Lord has said, "You will know the truth, and the truth will set you free" (John 8:32). The Bible calls us to be His servants, and in His service we find true freedom.

The Church's Message and Image—Revisited

This chapter has argued that the nature of Scripture (i.e., that it is the revelation of God), and the nature of God's servants (i.e., that servants of God have a duty to submit themselves to God and His message), when combined, lead one to the conclusion that the curriculum of the church should be faithfully biblical. This chapter also

---

[17] George Barna, in generalizing from findings from a nationwide survey of more than 4,000 people, stated, "It appears that most Americans like the security and the identity of the label 'Christian' but resist the biblical responsibilities that are associated with that identification." See "Commitment to Christianity Depends on How It Is Measured," *The Barna Update*, November 8, 2005 [online]. Accessed 23 July 2007. Available from http://www.barna.org; Internet.

considered the need for the church to accommodate the way it packages this message in order to be more winsome to the community, but it concludes that the message itself is not negotiable. The implications of these insights for educational ministry were then briefly explored. To state this in other terms, educational institutions are known for their particular approach to curriculum, and every church should be known by its focus on the Bible as curriculum.

In revisiting the beginning illustration, one might observe that the church consultant was right in saying that the church cannot *not* communicate, for everything the church does and says will create an image for the church before the watching community. The consultant was also right in saying that once the church's message is chosen, everything else follows. What the church consultant and the staff failed to say, or at least failed to say clearly, is that the church's message and core image had already been chosen by God.

There are only two choices left to the church and its staff. The first choice is, Will they choose to obey God or join the long history of people who have chosen to disobey Him? There are actions the pastor and leaders on the church staff can take to bring people along in their thinking and to clarify the issues, but ultimately some will choose to obey, and some will choose to disobey. Those who choose to obey do have a second choice (or even a series of choices) to make. The second choice has to do with how the church's assigned message might be accommodated to reach and minister to those in the community. The ancient message is relevant, but the church must faithfully seek to communicate this ancient message in an appealing way to its contemporary audience.

From this message flows a beautiful and appealing image for every church. It communicates to the watching world that we love God and His message. It communicates that we wish to live humbly and consistently with all that this entails. It communicates that we love the people in our churches, in our communities, and throughout the world. It communicates that we love them enough to minister to their hurts, present to them the good news of Christ, and train those who believe to follow in obedience. This message and image may result in aesthetically pleasing or plain buildings. It may result in a variety of musical styles. This commitment may be expressed in monologues, dialogues, poetry, or drama. It may produce a variety of ministries depending on the community in which God has placed the church. It may produce a homeless shelter, a school, a medical clinic, a support group ministry, a recreation ministry, a counseling center, a camp ministry, or a job fair. Yet whatever collection of ministries and ministry styles that are selected, the choices must first begin by embracing the Bible as the church's canon (i.e, measuring stick) for preaching, teaching, and ministry. Varied ministries may be developed, but they must flow from this core commitment.

The church has the authority to make these decisions, but it has no authority to change God's assigned message and thus to change its core image. Even if some wander from the message, they do not truly change it, for God's message is unchangeable. For as the prophet Isaiah declared, "The grass withers, the flowers fade, but the word of our God remains forever" (Isa 40:8; see also 1 Pet 1:24–25). In what more important and valuable message can one invest one's life?

Discussion Questions

1. What is meant by the statement that the church "cannot *not* communicate," and what exactly does this have to do with intentionally designing the educational ministry of the church?

2. How does one's view of the Bible influence how one thinks about the educational mission and ministry of the church?

3. How does one seeing oneself and other church members as "the servants of God" influence how one thinks about the educational ministry of the church?

4. How do you judge something as biblical or not biblical? Do you go with your intuitions? Do you look to your spiritual mentors? Do you judge whether it agrees with your theology? Do you look to your favorite authors? Are you skillful enough in understanding the Bible so that you can carefully discern for yourself? If so, how? What do you think of the thought experiment suggested by the author of this chapter?

5. How should Paul's reference to accommodation (1 Cor 9:19–23) influence how we see the educational ministry as it attempts to minister to various groups?

6. What can be learned about accommodation by studying the differences in how Jesus presented the gospel in John 3 and 4?
7. What can be learned about accommodation by studying the differences in how Paul addressed believers in his letters and the pagan philosophers in Acts 17:16–31?
8. How did Jesus and Paul stay faithful to God's message while packaging this message to different audiences?

Bibliography

Bauer, Walter. *A Greek-English Lexicon of the New Testament.* 2nd ed. Ed. and trans. William F. Arndt, F. Wilder Gingrich, and Frederick W. Danker. Chicago: University of Chicago Press, 1979.

Charles, Daryl J. "Paul before the Areopagus: Reflections on the Apostle's Encounter with Cultured Paganism." *Philosophia Christi* 7 (2005): 125–40.

"Commitment to Christianity Depends on How It Is Measured." *The Barna Update,* November 8, 2005 [online]. Accessed 23 July 2007. Available from http://www.barna.org; Internet.

Erickson, Millard J. *Christian Theology.* 2nd ed. Grand Rapids, MI: Baker, 1998.

_____. *The Postmodern World: Discerning the Times and the Spirit of Our Age.* Wheaton, IL: Crossway, 2002.

Grudem, Wayne A. *Systematic Theology.* Grand Rapids, MI: Zondervan, 1994.

Kelly, J. N. D. *Early Christian Doctrines.* Rev. ed. New York: Harper Collins, Inc., 1978; reprint, Peabody, MA: Prince, 2004.

Lewis, Gordon R., and Bruce A. Demarest. *Integrative Theology.* Grand Rapids, MI: Zondervan, 1996.

Louw, Johannes, and Eugene Nida. *Greek-English Lexicon of the New Testament Based on Semantic Domains.* Vol. 1. New York: United Bible Societies, 1989.

Moroney, Stephen K. *The Noetic Effects of Sin: A Historical and Contemporary Exploration of How Sin Affects Our Thinking.* Lanham, MD: Lexington, 2000.

Saucy, Robert L. "Which Books Belong in the Bible?" In *Understanding Christian Theology,* ed. Charles R. Swindoll and Roy B. Zuck. Nashville, TN: Thomas Nelson, 2003.

Chapter 7

THE DISCIPLE: CALLED TO LEARN

Margaret Lawson

We proclaim Him, warning and teaching everyone with all wisdom,
so that we may present everyone mature in Christ.
(Col 1:28)

What Is a Disciple?

I often begin my classes by posing a question to focus the students on the topic to follow. One such question is, What would be different in your church if every single person were living and operating according to the principles that Jesus taught His disciples? We always have such good discussion about a worshipping, serving, fellowshipping, baptizing, loving congregation where lost people are being won to Christ on a daily basis. Then I ask, "Is your church like that?" After the obvious silence, I ask them to suggest reasons why it is not. The answer inevitably comes back to the one word—*discipleship*. What about your church? Is it made up of converts or disciples? And is there a difference?

The difference is found in the challenge in the Great Commission to make disciples and teach them to obey all that Jesus commanded. It is not just the first part of the sentence that is important. Making disciples is sometimes seen as different from making converts, but that is not what Jesus taught. According to Jesus' teaching, there was no difference at all between disciples and converts because when He called men and women to follow Him, He called them to count the cost and abandon all else if they wanted to follow Him (Luke 9:23). He did not consider that becoming a fully committed follower was an option to be added to the salvation package. It is not like buying a car and making a choice about whether to add the extras like a spoiler or gold rims. It was an all-or-nothing decision. He made clear that it could cost them everything they had and it would cost some of them their lives. They were *obedient* to His teaching.

In reality, for many today the call to follow Christ is to repent and trust Him for salvation. The concept of lordship is left for some other time and some other place. According to Bonhoeffer, "Christianity without discipleship is always Christianity without Christ. It remains an abstract idea, a myth that has a place for the Fatherhood of God, but omits Christ as the living Son. . . . There is trust in God, but no following of Christ."[1] He further makes the distinction between *cheap grace* and *costly grace*. By cheap grace he means "the justification of sin without the justification of the sinner. Grace alone does everything they say, and so everything can remain as it was before." Costly grace in contrast recognizes that the ultimate reward of discipleship is to be like Jesus, conformed to His image (Rom 8:29). In the meantime we are exhorted to be imitators of Christ, in both attitude and action (Eph 5:1; 1 Cor 4:16–17).[2]

Several definitions follow, all of which embody the same principles expressed in a variety of words. One description is a guiding statement for discipleship materials produced by LifeWay publishers. It states, "Discipleship is a lifelong journey of obedience to Christ which transforms a person's values and behavior, and results in ministry in one's home, church, and in the world."[3] So a disciple is one whose life has been radically changed, and whose lifestyle makes that evident. The idea of transformation is reiterated by Barna who says:

> We might define discipleship as becoming a complete and competent follower of Jesus Christ. It is about the intentional training of people who voluntarily submit to the lordship of Jesus Christ and who want to become imitators of Christ in every thought, word, and deed. On the basis of teaching, training, experiences, relationships and account-

---

[1] D. Bonhoeffer, *Life Together: A Discussion of Christian Fellowship* (New York: HarperCollins, 1954), 64.

[2] Ibid.

[3] B. Sneed and R. Edgemon, *Transformational Discipleship* (Nashville: LifeWay, 1999), 3.

> ability, we become transformed into the likeness of Jesus
> Christ.[4]

Through the process of discipleship, the individual becomes transformed or changed into the likeness of Jesus Christ. This change is
described in terms that are akin to metamorphosis in nature. The
verb in Rom 12:2 is *metamorphoō*,[5] and Paul uses this same word
when he urges the believers in Rome to be transformed by the renewing of their minds (Rom 12:2). According to the dictionary this
metamorphosis is "a change in the form and the habits of an animal
during normal development after the embryonic stage—from the
Latin *metamorphōsis*, from the Greek *metamorphoun*, to transform."[6]
It describes the way a caterpillar is transformed into a butterfly.

A second dictionary meaning is a "marked change in appearance,
character, condition, or function." This provides an excellent descriptive analogy of the new believer in Christ. The apostle Paul says,
"Therefore if anyone is in Christ, there is a new creation; old things
have passed away, and look, new things have come" (2 Cor 5:17).

Dallas Willard prefers the term *spiritual formation* and explains
the change and growth in Christ as "the process of shaping our spirit
and giving it definite character. It means the formation of our spirit
in conformity with the Spirit of Christ. . . . The focus of spiritual
formation is the formation of our spirit."[7] Just as the change from
chrysalis to butterfly is gradual, so is the making of a disciple. Paul
says, "For we all, with unveiled faces, are reflecting the glory of the
Lord and are *being* transformed into the same image from glory to
glory" (2 Cor 3:17–18, emphasis mine).

Sometimes new believers are mistakenly led to believe that all
their problems will be over if they make the decision to follow
Christ. Disillusionment follows when this proves not to be the case.
On other occasions new believers are not encouraged to move beyond that immediate life-changing decision and simply told that all
they have to do is accept Christ as Savior. As important as it is, the

---

[4] Barna, *Growing True Disciples* (Ventura: Issachar Resources, 2000), 20.
[5] Thayer and Smith, Greek Lexicon entry for Metamorphoo, *The New Testament Greek
Lexicon*, http://www.studylight.org/lex/grk/view.cgi?number=3339.
[6] http://www.thefreedictionary.com/metamorphosis.
[7] D. Willard, *The Great Omission: Reclaiming Jesus's Essential Teachings on Discipleship*
(New York: HarperCollins, 2006), 53.

decision is not the final destination. It is the beginning of an exciting journey through hills and valleys, twists and turns toward a glorious end that is always in view.

The Disciple's Journey

No one knows exactly when the journey will end, but the journey itself is the immediate challenge. Jesus said clearly and decisively, "If anyone wants to come with Me, he must deny himself, take up his cross daily, and follow Me" (Luke 9:23). He did not sugarcoat the seriousness of the cost. He also told the rich young ruler that if he was not willing to turn his back on all his earthly wealth, he could not be a follower of Jesus (Luke 18:22). Jesus made even more radical demands for the disciple in determining priorities: "If anyone comes to Me and does not hate his own father and mother, wife and children, brothers and sisters—yes, and even his own life—he cannot be My disciple" (Luke 14:26). The disciple must be prepared to make a total commitment of all he is and all he possesses. Jesus was not trying to discourage His followers, but He wanted them to make the decision for the right reason. He gave them His word that however great the demands or difficult the journey, the disciple would not be alone. In the final analysis Jesus promised, "And remember, I am with you always, to the end of the age" (Matt 28:20).

An academic discussion of the disciple life is easy. It is actually much easier to talk about than it is to practice the life of holiness. Jesus both taught and modeled for His disciples what He expected of them, and He did it over a period of time. It was not through a lecture or a six-week course. It was lived out in the nitty-gritty of life with all of its challenges. Nowhere in the New Testament is the idea found that the Christian life is easy. Somewhere the message has been twisted into what Dallas Willard terms "The Great Omission." He says, "The missing note in evangelical life today is not in the first instance spirituality but rather obedience. We have generated a variety of religion to which obedience is not regarded as an essential."[8]

If we know the beginning and we know the end, a description of the journey of obedience is also important. If our churches are to be

---

[8] Willard, *The Great Omission*, 44.

nurturing fully devoted followers of Christ, there must be some instructions to follow.

Jesus' Pattern for Discipling

Jesus had a great deal to say about what it takes to be a disciple. Sometimes His followers understood and sometimes they did not, but He did not lower the standard. From the first Sermon on the Mount to His final dramatic teaching in the form of a living sermon on servanthood, as He washed His disciples' feet, He explained it to them. He raised the bar high. Sometimes His followers succeeded and sometimes they failed, but always He lifted them up and taught them again. Some Christians today would prefer to lower the standard to fit their busy and complicated lifestyles rather than changing their living to achieve the goal. Jesus explains how to reach the goal of Christlikeness.

Lessons from the Vine

One memorable metaphor that Jesus used to express the relationship of the disciple to the Master was that of abiding in the vine. Following the last supper and His announcement that He was going back to the Father, they all left the upper room. Jesus and His disciples passed through vineyards, and here He gave what we know as the "Vine Discourse." Through this metaphor, He explained the relationship of the branch to the vine. He spoke of the advantages of remaining connected to the vine and the consequences for those who did not. He also introduced the idea of pruning and trimming the branches to encourage increased production of fruit.

Jesus explained the concept of abiding or remaining attached to the vine in terms that His disciples would understand and indicated that the result of this relationship would allow them to be recognized as disciples. He described several ways this relationship could be maintained. Some have described these as the marks, the characteristics, or the disciplines of the disciple. Whatever you choose to call them, they ought to be present in the life of the maturing disciple. However, these disciplines will not by themselves produce spiritual growth. There is no magic formula that implies that if I do these things I will mature. It is the connectedness to the vine that produces these disciplines. Through practicing the disciplines, we enjoy a rich relationship with Christ, the living vine. Christ lives His life through us; we do not mold ourselves to be like Him. We focus on Him, and He produces growth and fruit in us.

The Marks of a Disciple

The characteristics Jesus requires of disciples are not those gifts that we bring to the table with us. Jesus demonstrated that by calling unlearned and seemingly insignificant men to be His disciples. He chose them "warts and all." He did not pick them because of what they were when He found them, but He saw their potential. He selected them because of what they could become when they allowed Him to transform their lives. What were the characteristics they were to learn as they developed into His likeness? Following are some characteristics from Jesus' analogy that provide a basis for the new life in Christ.[9]

Stay Connected to the Vine

The main characteristic of a devoted follower of Christ, according to Jesus' words in John 15, is that they "remain" in the vine. The King James Version uses the word *abide*. Jesus used several forms of the Greek word *menō*. It means "to stay, stand fast, stay where you are, not stir, or to remain as before."[10] A disciple who wishes to grow in his relationship with the Lord should stay connected to Him, the vine. Jesus expanded His explanation to the disciples as if to make certain they understood His meaning, by saying, "I am the vine; you are the branches. The one who remains in Me and I in him produces much fruit, because you can do nothing without Me" (John 15:5). At this time, so close to His death, He wanted His disciples to be sure of both the requirement and the result of remaining connected to Him. If they stayed properly connected to Him, they would bear fruit. The evidence of abiding or remaining in the vine is fruitfulness. The branch that is in Christ has all that is necessary to become fruitful.[11] Fruit is not limited to soul-winning. In this context love and

---

[9] Additional sources are listed in the bibliography with particular reference to this topic in R. Foster, D. Willard, T. W. Hunt, and G. Barna.

[10] Sneed and Edgemon, *Transformed Discipleship*, 8.

[11] Ibid., 7.

joy and answered prayer are mentioned too (John 15:7,11,12). Other passages, such as Gal 5:22–24 and 1 Pet 1:5–8, describe additional fruit.[12]

Pruning the Branches

There are also consequences for the branch that does not bear fruit. Jesus refers to two types of pruning, separating and cutting back branches. Fruit-bearing branches are sometimes cut back to promote growth and more fruit. Branches that do not bear fruit are cut off and burned and no longer enjoy the life-giving sustenance from the vine. The branches that bear fruit bring glory to the Father.

Jesus' emphasis on the life of sacrifice and pruning might give the impression to some that the Christian life is a series of hardships and pain. Although difficulties may be encountered along the way, there are also the joy and peace that come from living the new life in Christ in the present. Jesus said, "I have come that they may have life and have it in abundance" (John 10:10). The abundant life is found in living in a daily relationship to Jesus.

Now we will turn our attention to some marks of obedient disciples that help in developing in the believer the life of fruitfulness and abundance.

Prayer with Purpose

Remaining attached to the vine indicates a relationship. A connecting link in the vertical relationship between the believer and the Father is the discipline of prayer, and it defines a Christian's walk with God. The prayer life that characterizes the Christian is what Paul describes as "praying without ceasing" or praying constantly (1 Thess 5:17). We cannot spend all our time on our knees, but we can have a prayerful attitude at all times. The disciples asked Jesus to teach them how to pray, and He taught them. More than that, He showed them. He modeled the life of prayer Himself when He drew aside regularly in the midst of the busyness of everyday life to spend time with His Father. He modeled it in His life and taught the principles to His disciples. Prayer is foundational to all other spiritual disciplines and is much more than a religious ritual. As the disciple

---

[12] Notes on John 15:5, *NIV Life Application Study Bible* (Grand Rapids: Zondervan, 1997), 1775.

responds to Him in prayer, Jesus molds and shapes him into His image.

A Love for the Word

A vital component of a growing relationship with the Lord is time spent in Bible study, both corporately and individually. Jesus said, "If you continue in My word, you really are My disciples" (John 8:31). The Bible study hour or small-group time ought to provide opportunities for the disciple to hear God speak from His Word. In our churches today sometimes the tendency is to leave the "study" part to the expert, the pastor, and allow him to tell listeners what it says. Listening actively and learning from appropriate preaching and teaching are important, but so is personal study. Developing an intimate relationship with others involves spending time with them and learning how they think, feel, and act. A love for Christ is indicated by a love for His Word and by developing habits of reading, studying, meditating on it, and committing it to memory. Most of all it involves living it out and acting according to the principles learned and internalized. Just as Jesus applied the Word in His daily living, as when He responded to Satan in the desert, so we ought to follow His example. We are not to be a forgetful hearer but a doer who acts—this person will be blessed in what he does (Jas 1:25).

Fellowship with Other Believers

Horizontal relationships flow naturally from the vertical relationship with the Father. Discipleship that does not evidence itself in relationships with other believers is limited in its scope. Some would even consider that it is not true discipleship at all. Jesus said it eloquently: "By this all people will know that you are My disciples, if you have love for one another" (John 13:35).

In *Kingdom Principles for Church Growth*, Dr. Gene Mims asserts that fellowship is a companion to evangelism, discipleship, and ministry. He says, "Fellowship is more than just a feeling of goodwill in a congregation. Fellowship is the intimate spiritual relationship that Christians share with God and other believers through their relationship with Jesus Christ."[13] The love the disciples shared with one an-

---

[13] G. Mims, *Kingdom Principles for Church Growth* (Nashville: LifeWay, 2001), 45.

other is part of what made Christ's message so attractive and fruitful and provides an example for us to follow.

Witness to the Lost

Relationships with others are not limited to association with other believers. Witnessing Christians are those who have experienced an event with such impact that they have to tell others about it. Too often witnessing or evangelism is perceived as a requirement or a duty and it becomes a burden. In Acts 2:42 believers spread the word of the gospel with joy. The Great Commission requires that believers are all to be involved in the disciple-making process. Acts 1:8 explains how it is to be done. Part of equipping believers as disciples is to provide them with the skills and the opportunities to practice telling the story so others may be won to Christ.

Ministry and Service

The last act that Jesus carried out before His return to the Father was to wash the disciples' feet. This was not to institute foot-washing as a practice in the church but to teach a principle. He was introducing the most difficult of all concepts to the disciples, and perhaps that is why He left it to the last. What He modeled for them was servanthood, and He said it was to show them the full extent of His love. As He commissioned them to go to all nations with the message of the gospel, He modeled for them the means by which the mission would be accomplished.

Ministry and service are for all believers, not just for the paid staff. It is also important for church leaders to recognize the need for each person to participate in the ministry of the church early on. Some churches have introduced an assimilation process for new members that helps them identify their gifts and matches them up with appropriate ministries in the church. Jesus said the Son of Man did not come to be served but to serve others (Mark 10:45).

Obedience

A growing involvement in these disciplines characterizes a fully devoted follower of Christ. The thread that runs through them all is the mark of obedience. Jesus said, "If you love Me, you will keep My commands" (John 14:15). Obedience is not a visible mark, but it is

exhibited in such disciplines as those noted above. Obedience is not
a suggestion; it is a command for the disciple. The necessary ingredient for abiding in the vine is obedience (John 15:10).

Robert Mulholland stresses that obedience to the disciplines is not
something we do to assist in our being conformed to the likeness
of Christ. They are the result of our *being* and not our *doing*.[14] He
says, "Spiritual formation is relational or being oriented rather than
functional or doing oriented. Spiritual formation is a loving relationship with God that shapes our being rather than being a technique
or method or program for self-improvement."[15] Obedience to Christ
and abiding in Him is to allow Him to work in us. He set the example for us by going to the cross in obedience, and His call is to follow
Him.

The Disciples Carried the Flame

After Pentecost the disciples increased in number and spread out
carrying the message that reflected Jesus' teaching. Paul particularly,
and other New Testament writers as well, used several analogies to
explain to the people of the day what it meant to be a disciple in
the fullest sense of the word. Jesus told them that He would return,
and the early Christians highly anticipated His coming. They were
exhorted to live their lives daily in the expectation that Jesus would
soon return, and Paul wanted them to know how to live. Many of
these pictures paint for us the requirements for "followship" or discipleship, and they related closely to the audience of the culture. The
message is also clear for readers today.

In 1 Cor 3–4 Paul used three images: First he described some of
the believers as "mere infants" (1 Cor 3:1), whose immaturity had
led to divisions and quarreling within the church. He urged them on
to more mature behavior that required solid food and not milk. He
also described a building being built up out of stone. The foundation
stone is all important, and the materials must be of the best quality.
Anything else would not have lasting value or stand the test of fire
in the final day. The third image is that of a seed's being planted,
watered, and cultivated to grow up to bear fruit. Paul also asserts

---

[14] M. R. Mulholland Jr., *Shaped by the Word* (Nashville: Upper Room, 2000), 114.
[15] Ibid.

that many people may be involved in the process of growing the seed to maturity, and the application follows that God may use whom He chooses to assist in the maturing of the believer. Through each picture he described the growth of the disciple toward maturity in Christ.

On another occasion Paul used three different images: the soldier, the athlete, and the farmer (2 Tim 2:4–6). He frequently alluded to the process of disciplined training for the future ahead. He said, "I *press toward* the *goal* for the prize of the upward call of God in Christ Jesus" (Phil 3:14, emphasis mine).

Each of these analogies illustrates progress in Christian living. Becoming a disciple is not an event that can be documented and written on a calendar although that is where the process begins with the new birth. It is clear from Scripture that discipleship is initiated when a person accepts Christ but continues throughout life as the individual grows and matures. T.W. Hunt described it as developing the mind of Christ,[16] and Paul says, "Make your own attitude that of Christ Jesus" (Phil 2:5). We are not merely to resemble Christ; we are to think His very thoughts.[17]

Developing disciples is not a solo effort. Paul describes the purpose of growing in Christ within the context of the church when he writes that the task is "to build up the body of Christ" (Eph 4:12).[18] He expresses a similar idea in Col 1:28–29 where he says our purpose in teaching is "so that we may present everyone mature in Christ." It is our responsibility to grow toward maturity ourselves, as disciples and leaders; but we, as leaders, are also responsible for the spiritual growth of others. The church can plan specific learning experiences to assist the process. As educators we are given the unique opportunity of partnering with the Holy Spirit in His supernatural work of making disciples. Therefore, leaders in the church who are to assist in the process of developing disciples ought to have a plan in place.

Planning for Discipleship in the Local Church

Although a great deal of the responsibility for spiritual formation is the task of the individual, the church provides the community

---

[16] T. W. Hunt, *The Mind of Christ* (Nashville: LifeWay, 1994).

[17] Ibid., 12.

[18] For more on training in the context of the church, see chapter 18.

context as the arena in which the believer finds and participates in
body life. Chapter 8, "The Church's Role in Teaching," elaborates on
this concept. The local church is able to plan and provide discipleship experiences that facilitate the journey of the individual.

A number of patterns exist for equipping church members
through discipleship. Many church Web sites present a successful
strategy that works for their church, and while many of these may
suggest ideas, there is no "one size fits all" approach.[19] Among the
varied approaches to engaging disciples in growth-oriented learning, the best approach is one you design for your own location and
situation. Some common elements may be found in all effective discipleship systems, and these may be helpful as a starting point. The
university model works well for some churches, with courses offered
along tracks for different levels of spiritual maturity. Members are
guided through a series of courses or classes that help them move
on to the next level. Mentoring is another process, where an individual is matched with a more mature Christian and they arrange to
study and pray together. The well-known proponent of this method
is Waylon Moore,[20] and he bases his plan on 2 Tim 2:2. Other
church leaders frequently prefer a small-group approach, such as the
MasterLife series authored by Avery Willis, or *Experiencing God* by
Henry Blackaby. Yet another common approach is to offer a "smor-
gasbord" of courses based on popular interest. Sometimes these
groups choose to study the most recently released product on the
market, but this approach does not always offer a "balanced diet."

Church leaders who desire to involve a large number of members
in the discipling experience would do well to consider a variety of
approaches to reach the most people. Some people respond well
to one-on-one mentoring while others flourish in the small group
as they interact with others. The ingredient common to all the approaches is "accountability." As disciples, we are accountable first to
God and then to one another. The goal of accountability is to provide
honest feedback, affirmation, and support in an atmosphere of mutual respect, trust, and acceptance. Each church decides what type of
discipleship approach is best for their people. The important factor

---

[19] Willow Creek, Saddleback, FBC Springdale, AR, and Pantego Bible Church are a
few examples of churches with intentional discipleship courses.

[20] W. Moore, see www.mentoring-disciples.org.

is that the approach to discipling individuals ought to be intentional and should keep in mind the ultimate goal of producing mature followers of Jesus Christ.

Steps to Planning Intentional Discipleship Experiences

A simple plan follows to provide opportunities for Christians to grow in their faith, and many variations exist. The following are steps for leaders to consider:

1. Understand the purpose of discipleship.
2. Recognize your church possibilities.
3. Determine needs and interests of the people.
4. Provide qualified leaders.
5. Plan and offer discipleship experiences.
6. Evaluate the process.

Step 1. Understand the Purpose of Discipleship

The first consideration is recognition of the goal to be achieved by discipling believers. Some years ago the goal was to have a training program, but churches have moved away from this to a more purpose-driven approach. Two questions are crucial: What is the desired outcome in the life of the individual and in the life of the church? At what level of maturity are they currently? When the goal is clarified, it is easier to provide experiences that will help each individual move in that direction. The pastor and staff or leaders who are excited about personal spiritual growth and model it in their daily living will be able to motivate their church members by example.

Step 2. Recognize the Church's Potential for Developing Disciples

Important concerns are such items as the ages of the church members, the potential for leaders, space available, and times for meetings. To have a finger on the pulse of the church and a concept of the "spiritual temperature" will guide concerning when to introduce activities and encourage people to become involved. Some churches would respond well to a program and a specified time of meeting. The varied lifestyles and life patterns of the members may lead to a variety of times and venues for meeting. The leaders need to determine the potential for interest before moving forward. A small church, with the pastor as the only staff person, might begin by working with one or two individuals.

Step 3. Determine the Spiritual Growth Needs and Interests of the People

Everyone needs to be discipled, so let's begin a program for everyone. The truth is that not all believers know they ought to continue to grow toward maturity. A survey is one way to gauge the interest of the members; perhaps another is to talk with Sunday school teachers and members. Jesus began with the needs of people in His ministry, and the same approach is appropriate for churches today. Based on the needs in the church, the areas for growth may be determined and training offered. Some churches now require all new members to go through a period of training, and continuing discipleship groups would be the natural follow up to that. Ready-made target groups are new believers (and new church members), regular members, and leaders (and potential leaders).

Step 4. Provide Qualified Leaders

A first stage in turning disciples into leaders may consist of a few selected potential leaders who would be able to lead groups after a period of training. Sometimes another church, an association, or a state agency is able to provide initial training for leaders. Those who lead small groups for the purposes of discipleship should be trained in the necessary skills. Preferably, they should have participated in groups themselves, to gain experience, so as to provide positive experiences for the participants.

Step 5. Plan and Offer Discipleship Experiences

It is impossible to disciple everyone during the short time people are in Sunday school classes, and yet we live in an age when people have less and less time to spend at church. In small closed groups people can study and learn together how to be disciples. Learning experiences should be made available at times people are able to attend. Sometimes a group is enlisted for a study, and the members then decide on a time of meeting. New Christians might be involved in a study of basic Christian disciplines and doctrine. Others may study and discover their spiritual gifts. More mature believers might be directed to a group study like *The Mind of Christ*[21] or *Spirit of the Disciplines.*[22] Leaders might engage in a study of *Jesus on Leadership* as they grow in their understanding of servant leadership.[23] Many courses are available to engage people at a variety of levels of maturity. Web sites such as Navigators[24] and LifeWay Discipleship,[25] among others, provide introductions to resources and offer planning guides[26] for implementing discipleship in the local church. Among the plethora of discipleship materials readily available, the choices that church leaders make intentionally will help to challenge believers to new levels of maturity.

Step 6. Evaluate

Chapter 23 is devoted entirely to evaluation of the total church program, but evaluation is also essential for individual programs. The purposes outlined and the goals set at the outset of the program provide the guidelines for evaluation. Annual planning and evaluation will enable the church leaders to provide ongoing discipleship experiences that spur people on. In the words of the apostle Paul, "Therefore encourage one another and build each other up as you are already doing" (1 Thess 5:11).

Return to the Class

Do you remember the question I ask my students at the beginning of class? We envisage a church filled with believers who worship with joy, study the Bible, evangelize, serve, and contribute selflessly to building up the church body. Does this church really exist anywhere? No, unfortunately not, in its completed and perfect form. As each disciple is always "being transformed," so it is with a body of believers. Spiritual transformation is a continuing process and each disciple plays a part in the whole. A church that is alive and vibrant is one in which the believers understand and are excited about being in a process of change. Paul said it well: "We are God's children now,

---

[21] T.W. Hunt, *The Mind of Christ* (Nashville: B&H, 1994).

[22] D. Willard, *The Spirit of the Disciplines* (San Francisco: HarperCollins, 1991).

[23] C. Gene Wilkes, *Jesus on Leadership* (Wheaton: Tyndale House, 1998).

[24] Navigators, www.navigators.org.

[25] LifeWay Discipleship, www.lifeway.com.

[26] "Discipleship, Administrative Planning Guide" is available as a download on www.lifeway.com.

and what we will be has not yet been revealed. We know that when He appears, we will be like Him because we will see Him as He is" (1 John 3:2).

Questions for Further Discussion

1. How would you motivate church members to increase their interest in spiritual growth?
2. How does the personal spiritual walk of the pastor or other leaders influence the spiritual maturity of church members?
3. What suggestions would you make to a pastor who asked you how to develop members of the church in practical spiritual disciplines, such as prayer and personal Bible study?
4. Evaluate your church bulletin and newsletter on its promotion of spiritual development among members. Does this means of promotion assist in motivating people to spiritual growth? What other methods could you use?
5. Describe your image of a maturing Christian.

Bibliography

Barna, George. *Growing True Disciples.* Ventura, CA: Issachar Resources, 2000.

Bonhoeffer, Dietrich. *Life Together: A Discussion of Christian Fellowship.* New York: HarperCollins, 1954.

Foster, Richard. *Celebration of Discipline: The Path to Spiritual Growth.* New York: HarperCollins, 1988.

_____. *Prayer: Finding the Heart's True Home.* New York: HarperCollins, 1992.

Gangel, Kenneth O., and James C. Wilhoit, eds. *The Christian Educator's Handbook of Spiritual Formation.* Grand Rapids: Baker, 1994.

Hanks, Billie, and William A. Shell, eds. *Discipleship.* Grand Rapids: Zondervan, 1981.

Hunt, T. W. *The Mind of Christ.* Nashville: B&H, 1994.

Mulholland, M. Robert, Jr. *Invitation to a Journey: A Road Map to Spiritual Formation.* Downers Grove: InterVarsity, 1993.

_____. *Shaped by the Word.* Nashville: Upper Room, 2000.

Sneed, Barry, and Roy Edgemon. *Transformational Discipleship.*
   Nashville: LifeWay, 1999.
Willard, Dallas. *The Great Omission: Reclaiming Jesus' Essential
   Teachings on Discipleship.* New York: HarperCollins, 2006.
_____. *Renovation of the Heart.* Colorado Springs: NavPress,
   2002.
Williams, Steve, and Craig Beall. *Discipleship That Makes a Difference.*
   SBTC, www.sbtexas.com., 2005.

Chapter 8

THE CHURCH'S ROLE
IN TEACHING

Margaret Lawson

"I pray not only for these, but also for those who
believe in Me through their message.
May they all be one, as You, Father, are in Me and I am in You.
May they also be one in Us, so the world may believe You sent Me."
(John 17:20–21)

An Introduction to Pictures of the Church

Often in sermons or songs, we hear the church spoken of as the body of Christ. We sing, "I'm so glad I'm a part of the family of God," or sometimes we use a term such as the *bride of Christ*. What exactly do we mean by these concepts? In my teaching ministry classes, I usually ask the students to draw a diagram of what they understand by the concept *the church*. What would you draw? If we were to compare the drawings, it is unlikely that any two would be exactly the same. If a child drew a picture, it would probably be a building, perhaps with a steeple. When the students explain their "artwork," we see a variety of interpretations. Some draw people of all ages holding hands, and some illustrate the concept with a cross in a circle, and some draw a complicated theological concept. If I have 30 students, 30 different conceptions are portrayed. Usually all are correct. Each one is a different aspect of the same idea, and it would take a combination of all of them to give a representative picture.

How different from the concepts presented in my class would be the picture that is painted in Scripture? There is variety there too, and the New Testament portrays many analogies. Think for a moment of the vivid metaphor of the church as the bride of Christ, ready for her bridegroom and eagerly awaiting His coming (Eph 5:22–31). The church is also seen as God's new creation (2 Cor 5:17) or is described as a fellowship of faith with its members described as the saints (1 Cor 1:2), the faithful (Col 1:2), the witnesses (John 15:26–27), or the household of God (1 Pet 4:17).[1] Each of these images suggests plurality and indicates relationships. The bride, or fellowship, or saints, or household of faith points to the relationships within the church. Just as we respond in faith to the gospel as individuals, we work out our faith in the context of relationships in the church and in the world. Jesus explains what those relationships should look like when He says, "May they all be one, as You, Father, are in Me and I am in You. May they also be one in Us" (John 17:21).

The Church Finds Identity in Community: A Picture of the Godhead

One formal definition of the local church is found in a document produced by the Great Commission Council of the Southern Baptist Convention. It reads:

> A church is a community of called-out believers. The word for church in the New Testament is *ekklesia*. This Greek term was also used in the Septuagint to translate the Hebrew word in the Old Testament that referred to the nation of Israel assembled before God. The picture is of the people of God under His divine rule and called out for God's mission.[2]

This same term *church* in the New Testament most frequently refers to a fellowship of baptized believers. They are characterized as those who have willingly associated with one another in the faith and fellowship (*koinonia*) of the gospel. They are committed to Christ's

---

[1] "Church," *Holman Christian Standard Bible Dictionary*, online http://.lifeway.com/crossmain.asp.

[2] M. Maynard, comp., *We're Here for the Churches* (Nashville: Great Commission Council of the Southern Baptist Convention, LifeWay Christian Resources, 1999), 10.

teachings and are seeking to extend the gospel to the ends of the earth.[3]

Scripture also speaks of the church as the body of Christ, which includes the redeemed of all the ages.[4] The *Holman Bible Dictionary* states:

> The Greek term was used more than one hundred times in the Greek translation of the Old Testament in common use in the time of Jesus. The Hebrew term (*qahal*) meant simply "assembly" and could be used in a variety of ways, referring for example to an assembling of prophets (1 Sam 19:20), soldiers (Num 22:4), or the people of God (Deut 9:10).[5]

The reference to the church as the people of God in the Old Testament holds significance for understanding the term in the New Testament. The early Christians were Jews who used the Septuagint, a Greek translation of the Old Testament. The use of the term *people of God* indicated their understanding of the continuity linking the Old and New Testaments. These Christians understood themselves as the people of the God who had revealed Himself in the Old Testament (Heb 1:1–2), as the true children of Israel (Rom 2:28–29), and as the people of the new covenant prophesied in the Old Testament (Heb 8:1–13). They undoubtedly recognized themselves as constituting a church, and they perceived themselves as called out by God in Jesus Christ for a special purpose (Eph 2:19).[6]

From the beginning, the church understood that they were a people of community. The concept of community and family was common to the culture of the time, as it is in many contexts still today. The church was born out of the community of relationships that began before the beginning of time, taking her identity from the triune God.

In *Community 101*, Gilbert Bilezikian points out that community finds its essence and definition deep within the being of God. The first three verses in Genesis reveal that God is a community of three

---

[3] Ibid.
[4] Ibid.
[5] Harold S. Songer, "Church," *Holman Bible Dictionary*, online.
[6] Ibid.

persons in one being.[7] He further asserts that "God, although one being, is eternally three persons within oneness. He values community supremely because he experiences the dynamics and the synergy of three in one. Thus when he creates in his image, he creates community."[8]

The church exists within the context of community and grows and ministers through relationship with the community. The church

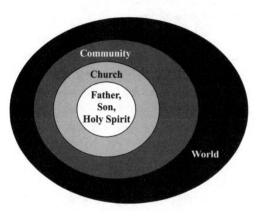

looks inward to find its identity and looks outward to exert its influence. This could be depicted by the ever-increasing circles in the diagram at left.

John 17 is often called the high priestly prayer or the prayer for the church. Here Jesus prays for the disciples whom He is soon to leave and prays also for those who will come after them. Just before His crucifixion, He prayed: "May they all be one, as You, Father, are in Me and I am in You. May they also be one in Us, so that the world may believe that You sent Me" (John 17:21). Jesus described His relationship with the Father in terms of oneness (John 10:30) and offered us the same kind of relationship with Him and with one another. Christ's pattern for unity with the Father is a pattern for us to display and enjoy in the church. Without Christian unity, the world will have little respect for our witness. "By this all people will know that you are My disciples, if you have love for one another" (John 13:35).

From the beginning of the Bible, God teaches us that community and family are the ideal. The concept is amplified in the creation of man.

---

[7] G. Bilezikian, *Community 101* (Grand Rapids: Zondervan, 1997), 16.
[8] Ibid., 18.

> God created a being in his own image and then he astound-
> ingly declared his creation to be "not good" because it was
> solitary. God was displeased with the fact that the man was
> alone (Gen 2:18). There was one solitary individual but he
> had no oneness because there was no one else with whom
> he could be together in oneness. Therefore, the creation in
> his image required the creation of a plurality of persons.
> God's supreme achievement was not the creation of a soli-
> tary man, but the creation of human community.[9]

The only reason given in the text for the creation of the woman was to help the man not to be alone. The woman was to be the necessary counterpart of the man for the making of community. Bilezikian continues, "Complete parity and mutuality are the irreducible conditions for the integrity of biblically defined community."[10] God the Father teaches us not only by what He is but also by what He does. In summary, he says:

> As noted above, community as God ordained it was not an
> incidental concern of his nor did it happen haphazardly
> as the serendipitously creative result of a transcendental
> cosmic brainstorm. Community is deeply grounded in the
> nature of God. It flows from who God is. Because he is
> community, he creates community. It is his gift of himself
> to humans.[11]

The church looks inward to the Godhead to find the model for community and teaches by example. As members experience oneness and community in the life of the church, so they begin to live in community themselves and, in turn, model community for others.

According to the New Testament, the servant relationship that was lost in the garden at the fall is recovered in the new community. It becomes the hallmark of the way Christians relate to one another. In both church and family, the two communities of oneness generated by the redemptive ministry of Christ, the mode of interaction between its members is reciprocal servanthood and, therefore, mutual submission (Matt 20:25–28; Gal 5:13; Phil 2:3–8).[12]

---

[9] Ibid., 19.
[10] Ibid., 24.
[11] Ibid., 24.
[12] Ibid., 25.

Therefore, the making of community is not to be regarded as an optional decision for Christians. It is a compelling and irrevocable necessity, a binding divine mandate for all believers at all times. It is possible for humans to reject or alter God's commission for them to build community and to betray His image in us; this cost is enormous since His image in us is the essential attribute that defines our own humanity.[13] The survival and welfare of authentic community are dependent on the members of community being in communion with God since He is the Creator of community. Therefore, the quality and the viability of human communities vary in response to the members' willingness to accept their own dependency on God.[14]

Abram was the first to accept God's plan for him to spearhead the establishment of the new community that would eventually bring together, in the church, believers from all the peoples of the earth. When Christ the Redeemer came, through His ministry on earth He established an unshakable foundation for the building of God's new community.[15]

The Church Exists through Community: A Picture of Fellowship

The operation of the church is founded on the concept of unity and is demonstrated through fellowship. The phrase "more caught than taught" is certainly applicable in this context. Members of the fellowship of saints experience fellowship, and then they contribute to it themselves. Many have reduced the word *fellowship* to mean little more than cookies and punch after the service. This idea is a *distortion* of biblical fellowship, which means mutual support and ministry to one another within the community.

The New Testament term for "fellowship," *koinonia*, appears in Acts 2:42. The believers "devoted themselves to the apostles' teaching, to fellowship, to the breaking of bread, and to prayers." The word means "to share in, to come into communion, to come into fellowship." It appears in our words communion and community.[16] It is

---

[13] Ibid., 27.

[14] Ibid., 27.

[15] Ibid., 33.

[16] G. Mims, *Kingdom Principles for Church Growth* (Nashville: LifeWay Church Resources, 1994), 45.

a concept not to be taken lightly or for granted or held up as an ideal
that we cannot attain. It is rather a reality created by God in Christ
and a privilege in which we are invited to participate.[17]

Dietrich Bonhoeffer, who was martyred for his faith in Christ,
spoke out of personal pain when, before his death, he wrote:

> It is easily forgotten that the fellowship of Christian breth-
> ren is a gift of grace, a gift of the Kingdom of God that any
> day may be taken from us, that the time that still separates
> us from utter loneliness may be brief indeed. Therefore
> let him who until now has had the privilege of living a
> common Christian life with other Christians praise God's
> grace from the bottom of his heart. Let him thank God
> on his knees and declare: It is grace, nothing but grace,
> that we are allowed to live in community with Christian
> brethren.[18]

The church is bound together not with creeds or confessions, not
with programs and ministries, but with a unity produced by the Holy
Spirit. Our communal bond is driven by God's love for us and our
love for Him and one another. Jesus declared, "I give you a new com-
mandment: that you love one another. Just as I have loved you, you
should also love one another" (John 13:34). The fulfillment of the
Great Commission hinges on our fellowship as well as on our evangelistic efforts, our discipleship commitments, and our ministries.
Paul urged his Ephesian readers to maintain fellowship "with all humility and gentleness, with patience, accepting one another in love,
diligently keeping the unity of the Spirit with the peace that binds
us" (Eph 4:2–3).

Church: The Fellowship That Teaches

It is important to understand what the church is to be and to do
but equally important to be aware of the *teaching role* that emerges
from these concepts. What does it mean to be a teaching church? In
curriculum design we talk of the overt and the covert curriculum.
Some activities are taught intentionally, but much of teaching is what
is caught, not taught. We teach through our example as we live out

---

[17] D. Bonhoeffer, *Life Together: A Discussion of Christian Fellowship* (New York:
HarperCollins, 1954), 30.
[18] Ibid., 20.

our convictions daily. If I ask my students to reflect on a teacher who had an impact on their lives, they seldom remember anything the teacher taught, but they remember who the teacher was. Most often they remember the way he or she related to the students. It is not just what we know that counts but how we live it out in the context of daily life. On a larger scale this is what we need to see for the church, a collection of individuals, to live out the concept of "church" in the context of the world in which we live. It is a cliché, but true nonetheless, that people will never care how much we know until they know how much we care.

Fellowship defines and validates our identity as believers. Jesus said the world will know how much we love Him by the way we love one another. The conduct of members in society activates the witness of the church in the world.

That world is constantly undergoing change and forms the backdrop for the teaching church. Without the principle of fellowship in operation, churches find it difficult, if not impossible, to practice other essential functions of the church. Where the fellowship is fractured and tensions run high, churches will do little in evangelism, discipleship, ministry, or worship.[19]

The church also teaches through the activities that symbolize the unity of fellowship in the church, such as the Lord's Supper. The challenge to "examine oneself" is an opportunity to restore any rift in relationships that may exist. Immediately after Paul spoke of "fellowship" with Christ through participation in the Lord's Supper (1 Cor 10:16), he said, "Because there is one bread, we who are many are one body, for all of us share that one bread" (1 Cor 10:17). The Lord's Supper is a family fellowship event that we observe in remembrance of Him. It is a reminder of His eternal presence with the fellowship of believers until He comes. Mims says, "The church is blessed with the ministry of the Holy Spirit. The Spirit convicts us of sins and makes us alive forever in Jesus. He gifts us to do ministry. He produces spiritual fruit to bind our lives together. He thus creates a church that is supernatural. If unity is absent from a local church,

---

[19] Mims, *Kingdom Principles*, 51.

the Holy Spirit is not in charge."[20] See chapter 5, "The Holy Spirit as Teacher," for more on this theme.

Fellowship is more than just a feeling of goodwill in a congregation. Fellowship is the intimate spiritual relationship that Christians share with God and other believers through their relationship with Jesus Christ. Fellowship is expressed in all activities in which church members are together. These include social occasions such as eating together and enjoying one another's company. Hospitality is an expression of Christian love and fellowship. So are business meetings in which the church together seeks the mind of Christ.[21]

Values are more caught than taught. This phrase is used so often that no one remembers who said it first, but it is certainly applicable in this context. The value placed on community and fellowship and the attitudes demonstrated through fellowship activities become the loudest teaching tools. Many of us cannot remember where we encountered reverence for the Lord and His church, but we certainly learned it, and we hold it dear still today. We learn to worship by being present in worship. We learn to pray by listening to others and joining in ourselves. We grow in maturity by working and worshipping alongside others who are on the same journey. Mims says the fellowship of the church provides an atmosphere in which believers can mature and be nourished. Without this fellowship and our accountability to the Lord and other believers, we might be tempted to live our lives apart from Him and apart from other believers.[22]

A church that practices NT fellowship cares for its members and watches to see if they are drifting away from their commitments to Christ. The love of Christ moves us to help those in our number who struggle with needs of one kind or another. Fellowship is also expressed through acts of loving ministry and support to hurting members of the body. A good church fellowship watches over its members and ministers to them when needs arise. "Building relationships of interdependence, evangelizing the lost, and caring for one another are the hallmarks of the kingdom principle of fellowship."[23] *Koinonia* is expressed whenever the church is together as a family of faith and

---

[20] Ibid, 48.
[21] Maynard, *We're Here for the Churches*, 16.
[22] Mims, *Kingdom Principles*, 51.
[23] Ibid.

love. Thus, the church expresses its fellowship as an integral part of other functions.

As believers direct their worship to God, they do so not only as individuals but as a body. Evangelizing either the community or the world is not done by one person but by partners in the gospel who call out the called, pray, and give. Discipleship is successful only as believers accept responsibility for discipling one another.[24]

The Church Operates through Community: A Picture of the Body

The nature and purpose of the church form a necessary structure for ministry. While there are many models of how the church should be organized to do its work, all of them include the concept of relationships and groups. Just as Jesus conducted His ministry of training the disciples at times in smaller groupings of two or three and at other times in the larger group of 12, so the church is organized to do the same. There are times, such as worship, when we meet together "in large group" as a faith community. On other occasions we meet in small groups for Bible study or discipleship. Still other occasions call for meeting one on one. Just as it is impossible to be Christian outside the context of others, so it is impossible for the church to function without the interaction of relationships. While these groupings differ, performing different tasks, through these groupings intentional teaching takes place.

Total participation of all through the stewardship of each one's spiritual gifting is an essential trait of the community of oneness. The imposition of restrictions and exclusions to ministry on the basis of role structures inhibits the expansion of authentic community. From the very beginning, God ordained that the making and the growth of community be the shared responsibility of all members of the community.[25]

The Church as Body

The picture painted by Paul in Romans 12 and 1 Corinthians 12 provides the biblical background for these small community groups

---

[24] Maynard, *We're Here for the Churches,* 16.
[25] Ibid., 27.

called "local churches." He presents the fellowship of these local groups through an analogy of the body in which every part has a purpose and none is to be regarded any more highly than another. "Instead, God has put the body together, giving greater honor to the less honorable, so that there would be no division in the body, but that the members would have the same concern for each other" (1 Cor 12:24–25). Also, in Rom 12:5–6 Paul asserts, "In the same way we who are many are one body in Christ and individually members of one another. According to the grace given to us, we have different gifts." These gifts are employed through the ministry in open and closed groups and ministry teams.

All believers are gifted for some responsibility in the ministry of the church. Helping them find their places of service helps the church and the kingdom. God gives each person gifts, talents, natural abilities, and interests for His glory. Involving each individual enables churches to build the body of Christ and reach out to a dying world.[26]

In *The Purpose Driven Church*, Rick Warren poses four questions: Why does the church exist? What are we to be as a church? What are we to do as a church? How are we to do it? Some believe the answer lies in innovation as the key to what the church should do, but Warren disagrees, saying, "It isn't our job to create the purposes of the church but to discover them."[27] The functions of the church are found in Scripture and generally include worship, evangelism, discipleship, ministry, and fellowship. Maria Harris in *Fashion Me a People* refers to the functions as *koinonia* (community), *leiturgia* (prayer), *didache* (teaching), *kerygma* (proclamation), and *diaconia* (ministry or service).[28] The well-known Saddleback model develops the functions of the church in the form of a baseball diamond titled the Life Development Process.[29] A visit to church Web sites provides interesting insights into how many models have been created to communicate the process.

As if to answer Warren's fourth question—How are we going to do it?—Gene Mims produced an administrative model that itself

---

[26] Mims, *Kingdom Principles*, 154.

[27] R. Warren, *The Purpose Driven Church* (Grand Rapids: Zondervan, 1995), 7.

[28] M. Harris, *Fashion Me a People*, 64.

[29] Warren, 144.

is anchored in the concept of relationships. The model is called the "1–5–4 Principle"[30] and has as its goal a return to the Great Commission. At the heart of his model lie several kinds of groups: open groups, closed groups, and ministry teams. It is to those groups within the body that we now turn our attention.

A Kingdom-Focused Church Model and Process

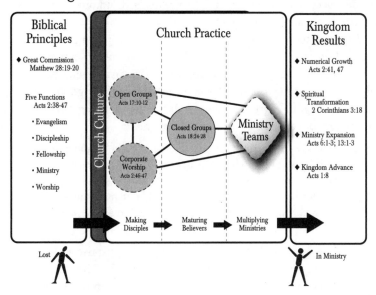

The Church as Small Groups

Jeffery Arnold defines a "small group" in this context as "an intentional gathering of three to 12 people who commit themselves to work together to become better disciples of Jesus Christ."[31] The author continues, "People can only learn and grow in an atmosphere of love and acceptance. That atmosphere is Christian community. Community is not one aspect of group life, it is the very structure within which the group operates."[32]

---

[30] Gene Mims, *The Kingdom Focused Church* (Nashville: B&H, 2003), 150.

[31] J. Arnold, *The Big Book on Small Groups* (Downers Grove, IL: InterVarsity, 1992), 9.

[32] Ibid., 11.

Mims's model for maturing a believer in Christ is shown above. It expresses the implementation of the functions of the church through groups. He suggests that in most churches unsaved individuals come into the church either through the worship service or through the Bible study or Sunday school. In these arenas they encounter the Word of God and experience the warmth of Christian fellowship. Such *open groups* are effective in drawing in new members because they feel accepted, welcome, and, in a real sense, at home.

Open groups exist to reach people, leading them to faith in the Lord Jesus Christ and growth into Christlikeness. Open groups accomplish these eternal ends by developing relationships among their members and by engaging them in evangelism, discipleship, fellowship, ministry, and worship. Open groups are small kingdom communities designed to bring believers and unbelievers together in an atmosphere of compassion to share the gospel.[33]

> *Closed groups*, on the other hand, exist to build kingdom leaders and to equip believers to serve. Closed groups engage learners in a way that moves them toward spiritual transformation through short-term, self-contained training in an atmosphere of accountability to God and to one another.[34]

They exist for a period of time and for a specific purpose and are designed to equip leaders for maturity and ministry. The focus is training, its context is discipling, and its intent is to move its members on to the next level of Christian experience and commitment.[35] The maturing process for the believer is focused in the closed groups through a sense of intimacy and accountability. Examples of these would be such studies as *Experiencing God*[36] or a grief support group. Through these small groups they are deployed in ministry and service to others. Equipping and training for service and ministry ought to be the natural outcome of the discipleship process.

The third small group is the *ministry team* that ministers to people in the church and out in the community.

---

[33] Mims, *The Kingdom Focused Church*, 130.
[34] Ibid., 141.
[35] Ibid., 143.
[36] H. Blackaby and C. V. King, *Experiencing God* (Nashville: B&H, 1994).

> Ministry teams exist to build up the body of Christ to ac-
> complish the work of service within the church and advance
> the kingdom of God throughout the world. The work of
> kingdom advance is a work of beginning new kingdom com-
> munities with an urgency to reach those without Christ.[37]

Ministry teams provide the tangible means for members to extend their reach and magnify their impact on the culture and the church.

The Church *One Anothering*

Jesus specifically commanded us to teach other believers the things He had commanded us. Teaching one another is the process by which the church builds itself up through its members.[38]

The New Testament is replete with admonitions and instructions about how Christians are to relate to one another in the body. Relationships are central. In light of this, it is significant that among the top 10 reasons ministers leave churches today is a failure in relationships.[39] Counselors are kept in business because of failures in relationships.

Ian Jones calls our attention to the fact that the Bible stresses the importance of relationships in the church by using the phrase "one another" approximately 160 times, 125 of those in the New Testament. The term occurs over 80 percent of the time in the New Testament to reflect the meaning of positive support and affirmation. Christians have a responsibility to develop, support, and maintain *koinonia* relationships with one another.[40] One example will suffice from 1 Thess 5:11: "Therefore encourage one another and build each other up as you are already doing."

The Church Reaches Out through Community: A Picture of the Family

You have all heard the old joke: "I love the church; it's the people I find difficult!" But the picture Jesus left with His disciples was

---

[37] Mims, *Kingdom Focused Church*, 150.

[38] Ibid., 29

[39] C. Turner, "Terminations," in *Facts and Trends*, LifeWay Church Resources, January/February 2007.

[40] I. Jones, *The Counsel of Heaven on Earth* (Nashville: B&H, 2006). Dr. Jones is professor of counseling and director of the counseling center at Southwestern Baptist Theological Seminary, Fort Worth, TX, 210.

no mere sentiment. In His final prayer for the disciples, He prayed, "Holy Father, protect them by Your name that You have given Me, so that they may be one as We are one" (John 17:11b). Paul reinforced this writing: "Show family affection to one another with brotherly love. Outdo one another in showing honor" (Rom 12:10). A picture of the church would not be complete without reference to the family of God. The American emphasis on individualism, so prevalent today, cuts right across the church community culture of mutuality, relationships, and servanthood. More will be said about this in chapter 9, but allow me to offer just one positive illustration.

On a recent trip to Honolulu, I met Pua, a student in our childhood ministry program.[41] She is a genuine Hawaiian from the forbidden island of Niihau where no visitors are allowed. She told us about growing up on the island and how her grandfather would gather the family at the end of the day for a time of Bible reading and prayer. She said no matter where she had been on the island, or how scattered the family was, devotions did not begin until she and the others were all there. After a time of singing, praying, and Bible reading, a time followed of confession and making things right with the others in the group. She told us her grandfather would seem to know when there had been harsh words or dissension among the smallest of them. He would give opportunities for family members to confess, and then he would wait. Only when every person was in right relationship with all the others would he close the prayer time, and they were allowed to go to bed.

What a wonderful heritage to grow up in a family where biblical principles were practiced in the family. This is the picture of the church as God's family. When Jesus prayed that His disciples would be one, just as He and the Father were one, that prayer was for the individual, the family, and the church. Mims says that when we receive Christ we become part of a living fellowship with others who, like us, have been called out. We are members of one another and part of a great family of believers across the world, across time, and for eternity. Believers share a bond in Christ that is unique and distinguishes our relationships from any other group in the world.[42]

---

[41] Anecdote is used with Pua's permission, January 8, 2007.
[42] Mims, *Kingdom Principles*, 47.

Mims calls this "familyship." Fellowship in the Spirit allows us to be part of God's family. We all belong to one another and to the Father.[43] As the family reaches out to the extended family and to the worldwide family, it projects a microcosm of the church.

A Personal Reflection

When I think back about what I learned from my personal church experience, one thing stands out above the others. I am frequently reminded how much theology I learned from singing the great hymns of the faith. As a child, I probably did not understand the significance of all the words I sang, but later in life those words are still etched in my memory. Although I may not remember where I put my keys down, I have not forgotten some of the truths in this chapter that I heard and learned as a child. For instance, these words by Samuel Stone penned in 1886:

> The Church's one foundation is Jesus Christ her Lord
>   She is his new creation, by water and the word:
> From heaven he came and sought her to be his holy bride;
>   With his own blood he bought her, and for her life he
>   died.[44]

The Church is Christ's most precious possession, and He has entrusted us with its care. Paul wrote to the believers in Ephesus, "Just as Christ also loved the church and gave Himself for her" (Eph 5:25b). Through our relationships with one another in the church, we teach, the means by which the world will come to know Jesus as Savior and Lord.

Discussion Questions

1. How does your church incorporate new members into the fellowship?
2. Discuss ways your church helps members grow into mature believers.
3. What church activities provide opportunities for making family memories?

---

[43] Ibid., 49.
[44] The Gospel Music Archive, www.gospelmusic.org.uk/a-g/churchs_one_**foundation**. htm, accessed September 14, 2007.

4. Create a model of your own to picture "relationships within the church."

Bibliography

Arnold, Jeffery. *The Big Book on Small Groups*. Downers Grove, IL: InterVarsity, 1992.

Bilezikian, Gilbert. *Community 101: Reclaiming the Local Church as Community of Oneness*. Grand Rapids, Michigan: Zondervan, 1997.

Blackaby, Henry, and Claude V. King. *Experiencing God: How to Live the Full Adventure of Knowing and Doing the Will of God*. Nashville: B&H, 1994.

Bonhoeffer, Dietrich. *Life Together: A Discussion of Christian Fellowship*. New York: HarperCollins, 1954.

Harris, Maria. *Fashion Me a People: Curriculum in the Church*. Louisville, Kentucky: Westminster/John Knox, 1989.

Jones, Ian F. *The Counsel of Heaven on Earth: Foundations for Biblical Christian Counseling*. Nashville, Tennessee: B&H, 2006.

Maynard, Morlee, comp. *We're Here for the Churches*. Nashville: LifeWay Christian Resources, 1999.

Mims, Gene. *The Kingdom Focused Church*. Nashville: B&H, 2003.

_____. *Kingdom Principles for Church Growth*. Nashville: LifeWay Church Resources, 1994.

Turner, Chris. "Terminations." In *Facts and Trends*. LifeWay Church Resources, January/February 2007.

Warren, Rick. *The Purpose Driven Church*. Grand Rapids: Zondervan, 1995.

Chapter 9

THE FAMILY'S ROLE
IN TEACHING

Scott Floyd

Only be on your guard and diligently watch yourselves,
so that you don't forget the things your eyes have seen
and so that they don't slip from your mind
as long as you live.
Teach them to your children and your grandchildren.
(Deut 4:9)

I just wish my family had been more like the Huxtables," Dave
said to me as we sat in the counseling room. I thought of
how many times as a counselor I had heard similar phrases.
Depending on the age of the client, it could just as well have been
Ozzie and Harriet, the Cleavers, or the Bradies. Many clients express
a desire for a family quite different from the one they had—support-
ive families who paid attention, communicated love and affection,
and taught about God and His ways. Dave's family was like so many
that clients have described to me—busy father and tired mother finally divorced, leaving Dave and his siblings to be shuffled between
houses and stepfamilies. Now Dave, a father himself, struggled with
hurt, anger, and sadness over the absence of a template of how to
be a good parent to his own children. We spent the next several sessions talking about how a parent can help a family grow into one
that honors God and reflects His love and care.

How can the church assist individuals like Dave to build strong
families? How can churches equip and support parents to rear
children "in the training and instruction of the Lord" (Eph 6:4)?
What role does teaching play in families that are vital and resilient?

141

Perhaps the most appropriate starting point in discussing the family's role in teaching is defining *family* and considering it from a theological, scriptural perspective. Next we'll address how teaching should take place in families, and specifically, what is necessary for parents to transmit to children regarding matters of faith. Last, how can the church assist families in teaching their children the things of God?

Defining Family

A universally accepted definition of *family* remains elusive even among those who study family. Efforts to define family often produce disagreement based on the motivation of those attempting to create the definition and whether they are coming from a legal, sociological, political, or biblical perspective.

In his book *The Future of the American Family*, George Barna was one of the first to identify the difficulty in defining family. He noted that American society was moving in the direction of having two definitions of family—traditional and nouveau. Barna defined the term *traditional family* as people "related to each other by marriage, birth or adoption." He also described what he called the *nouveau family*, or "two or more people who care about each other."[1] Barna believed that society was increasingly shifting in the direction of adopting a nouveau definition of family. Garland observed that struggles to define family also include whether the definition identifies how a family "is" or how the family "ought to be."[2]

Families: Ideal Versus Real

The biblical ideal is one man and one woman in a one-flesh, covenant relationship. As God allows, the couple bears children. The family relationship is to be marked by closeness, care, support, and commitment. Family is not an end in itself but a channel through which God works in the lives of those around the family.

Although the Bible presents an ideal for families, the Bible also portrays the reality of family life. Problems of family life as presented in Scripture include divorce, adultery, sibling rivalry, incest, single

---

[1] G. Barna, *The Future of the American Family* (Chicago: Moody, 1993), 26.

[2] D. Garland, *Family Ministry: A Comprehensive Guide* (Downers Grove, IL: InterVarsity, 1999), 22.

parenthood, pregnancy outside of marriage, blended families, co-habitation, jealousy, deceit between members, and in-law conflict. Many biblical characters struggled with family problems, including Abraham, Lot, Isaac, Jacob, Eli, Samuel, and David. While the Bible presents the ideal for family, it also notes the difficulties in achieving this level of functioning.

Similarly, family life in modern society is fraught with difficulties. While most adults marry, around one-third of all marriages end in divorce[3] with around 1.2 million divorces occurring in the U.S. each year.[4] Whitehead and Popenoe, experts in family-life trends, observe that a couple who marries now has a 40–50 percent lifetime probability of separation or divorce.[5] Two-parent families, where parents are married to each other, are increasingly less common. According to the 2000 census, the number of single mothers increased from three million in 1970 to ten million in 2000, and two million fathers are single parents.[6] Whitehead and Popenoe note that cohabitation is becoming progressively more common in American society: "Most people now live together before they marry for the first time. An even higher percentage of those divorced who subsequently remarry live together first. And a growing number of persons, both young and old, are living together with no plans for eventual marriage."[7] In 2003, one-third of all births and two-thirds of births of African-American children were out of wedlock.[8] Clearly, in modern-day America, the family faces numerous challenges. This, however, should not stop individuals from striving for the ideal. T. B. Maston states:

---

[3] Barna Update, "Born Again Christians Are as Likely to Divorce as Non-Christians" (Sept. 8, 2004), accessed 29 March 2007 at http://www.barna.org/FlexPage.aspx?Page=BarnaUpdate&BarnaUpdateID=170.

[4] Center for Disease Control, *National Vital Statistics Report—Births, Marriages, Divorces, and Deaths: Provisional Data for 2005*, vol. 54 no. 20, accessed 29 March 2007 at http://www.cdc.gov/nchs/data/nvsr/nvsr54/nvsr54_20.pdf.

[5] B. D. Whitehead and D. Popenoe, "The State of Our Unions: The Social Health of Marriage in America (2005)," http://marriage.rutgers.edu/Publications/Print/PrintSOOU2005.htm (accessed 7 February 2007), 18.

[6] P. Fraenkel, "Contemporary Two-Parent Families: Navigating Work and Family Challenges," *Normal Family Processes*, 3rd ed., ed. Froma Walsh (New York: Guilford, 2003), 64.

[7] Whitehead and Popenoe, 11.

[8] Ibid., 29.

> We need very much in the contemporary period to redis-
> cover and take seriously the biblical ideal for the family
> and family relations: one man and one woman joined to-
> gether as husband and wife for life, fulfilling the purposes
> of God for their home and sending out into the world
> individuals—husband, wife, and children—who will put
> first in their lives the kingdom or reign of God and who
> will be channels for God's love and compassion as he seeks
> to reach out to those in need.[9]

Such an ideal is not easy to obtain. A biblical understanding of family provides us with a clearer idea of family life and of God's design for families.

Theology of Family

An investigation into a scriptural/theological perspective of family pays rich dividends in our understanding of family. The Bible contains an extensive amount of information about family.

Family Created from the Beginning and Valued by God

We find family presented in the very first pages of Scripture. Genesis 2 provides a picture of the first couple. God created Adam, then fashioned Eve for him as a helper. Adam could hardly contain his excitement when he first saw Eve, saying, "This one, at last, is bone of my bone, and flesh of my flesh" (Gen 2:23). God instructed the couple to "be fruitful and multiply." From the beginning the Bible offers a picture of the first couple and the first family. Family was created before any other institution, including government, schools, social organizations, or even church.

Not only was family created from the beginning, but family is valued by God. Although Adam had the entire garden to himself, which included intimate fellowship with God, God observed, "It is not good for the man to be alone" (Gen 2:18). Similarly, King Lemuel noted that a wife of noble character was "far more precious than jewels" (Prov 31:10). Psalm 127:3–5 says, "Sons are indeed a heritage from the Lord, children, a reward. Like arrows in the hand of a warrior are the sons born in one's youth. Happy is the man who has filled his

---

[9] T. B. Maston, *The Bible and Family Relations* (Nashville: Broadman, 1983), 56.

quiver with them." Not only did God create family from the beginning, He places a great value on family.

God Came to Live with Us through Family

When God came to live among humankind, He chose to do so through a family. The family He chose was not wealthy, not especially educated, and lived in a town that was so small that it was the object of jokes. When God came to live with us in Christ, He entered the world as an infant and grew up experiencing all the things families go through. Jesus had siblings, surely had chores, and even once was left in the temple. Jesus, our great high priest, encountered things common to all families.

While Jesus experienced life as a part of a family, He also came to restore families. Malachi 4:6, the last verse in the Old Testament, speaks of the coming Messiah, stating, "And he will turn the hearts of fathers to their children and the hearts of children to their fathers." Luke 1:17 also acknowledges this purpose of the coming Messiah: "to turn the hearts of fathers to their children." God came to live with humans through a family with a purpose of restoring relationships between family members that can become so fragmented by the pressures of life.

The Bible Teaches about Family

The Bible contains many passages that provide direct information about families. Ephesians 5–6 instruct husbands, wives, parents, and children how to behave in relationship to one another. The book of Proverbs includes numerous passages teaching family members how to have healthy, God-honoring relationships. Some of the key family-related issues in the book of Proverbs are marital faithfulness (5:15–23), the wife of noble character (31:10–31), the value of a good wife (12:4; 14:1; 18:22), nagging (21:9), adultery (6:24–35; 7:6–27), obeying parents (1:8–9; 23:22–25), learning from parents (4:1–9; 6:20–22), parental discipline (13:24; 23:13–14; 29:15,17), the shameful son (19:26), and the value of passing along one's inheritance (13:22).

In addition to passages that provide direct information about families, many other stories and Bible figures offer indirect information regarding family life. God's Word relates narratives about marriages, childbirth, parenting, and sibling relationships. The Bible conveys both positive and negative pictures of family life in many of its stories. We can learn from both the good examples and from the problems faced by many family members presented in the pages of Scripture.

Indirect teachings in Scripture include God as Father, Jesus as the Son, fellow believers as brothers and sisters in Christ, and the collection of believers as the family of God. T. B. Maston states, "The importance of family is underscored by its symbolic or figurative use in the Scriptures. The family and family relations are frequently used to describe God's relation to his people and their relations to him."[10] From both direct and indirect perspectives, the Bible is a treasure trove of information about family life.

Family as Transmitter of the Faith

In Scripture one indisputable task of families is to be transmitters of faith. Deuteronomy 6:4–9 conveys this idea in an unambiguous, forthright manner. Moses gave the children of Israel the commandments of God and told them to

> "repeat them to your children. Talk about them when you
> sit in your house and when you walk along the road, when
> you lie down and when you get up. Bind them as a sign
> on your hand and let them be a symbol on your forehead.
> Write them on the doorposts of your house and on your
> gates."

Christianson states, "Having understood these commandments in depth, they [parents] were to *teach them diligently to their* children. The commandments were to be the focus of constant discussion inside and outside the home. In short, they were to *permeate every sphere of human life*."[11] Knowledge of God and of His commands was to be so woven into the lives of the Israelites that they would naturally convey the stories of God to their children.

The psalmist Asaph also communicated a similar message in Psalm 78. He spoke of not only being aware of God's mighty deeds,

---

[10] Maston, *Bible and Family Relations*, 53.

[11] D. Christianson, *Deuteronomy 1–11*, Word Biblical Commentary, vol. 6A, ed. David Hubbard and Glenn Baker (Dallas: Word, 1991), 144 (italics his).

but making sure future generations knew of these as well. In verses
2b–7, he states:

> I will speak mysteries from the past—
> things we have heard and known
> and that our fathers have passed down to us.
> We must not hide them from their children,
> but must tell a future generation the praises of the LORD,
> His might, and the wonderful works He has performed.
> He established a testimony in Jacob and set up a law in
>   Israel,
> which He commanded our fathers to teach to their children
> so that a future generation—
> children yet to be born—might know.
> They were to rise and tell their children
> so that they might put their confidence in God
> and not forget God's works, but keep His commands.

This passage imparts a method for transmission of the faith.
Individuals are to notice and remember the things God does. They
tell their children these things, communicating what God is like and
what God has accomplished. In turn, these children grow up and tell
the stories to their children, encouraging them to keep God's commands. In this manner faith is transmitted generation to generation.

Timothy's family provides a specific example of this generational
transmission of faith. In the opening of his second letter to Timothy,
Paul brings to mind Timothy's "sincere faith that first lived in your
grandmother Lois, then in your mother Eunice, and that I am convinced is in you also" (2 Tim 1:5). Timothy, the preacher and evangelist so loved by Paul, was a recipient of this generational transmission of faith, passed along by his grandmother and mother.

Family in Perspective

Without question family is important. Designed by God, families
are to provide a haven for members, offer support and encouragement, and help little ones grow up in a safe, protected environment.
However, devotion to family must be kept in perspective. While family is important, one's ultimate loyalty must be to God.

Jesus clearly emphasized this principle on at least a couple of occasions. Early in His ministry Jesus was teaching, and a large crowd

gathered around Him, filling the house where He was speaking.
His mother and brothers came to get Jesus, perhaps concerned that
He was embarrassing the family or making a fool of Himself (Mark
3:20–21). When Jesus was alerted that His family had come to get
Him, Mark 3:33–35 gives Jesus' response: "'Who are My mother
and My brothers?' And looking about at those who were sitting in a
circle around Him, He said, 'Here are My mother and My brothers!
Whoever does the will of God is My brother and sister and mother.'"

On another occasion, as He conversed with His disciples, Jesus
made a statement about family life that, on the surface, sounds harsh:

> "For I came to turn a man against his father, a daughter
> against her mother, a daughter-in-law against her mother-
> in-law; and a man's enemies will be the members of his
> household. The person who loves father or mother more
> than Me is not worthy of Me; the person who loves son
> or daughter more than Me is not worthy of Me." (Matt
> 10:35–37)

Both of these passages seem to contradict the idea that family is
important. However, Jesus was not saying that family is unimport-
ant but rather that family must never become an idol, a place where
one's affections are located instead of in God. Jesus was not saying
that He desired to divide families but rather that when a person truly
follows Him it might hinder or even damage family relationships,
turning family members against the one who is attempting to follow
God. While family is important, each individual's ultimate loyalty
must be to God. Nothing, not even the closest of family relationships, should supplant God.

Teaching through Families

The Bible clearly instructs parents to teach children about God.
Parents are responsible for passing along the things of God to the
next generation. But this task, educating children about God, is not
a simple one. Accomplishing this undertaking entails teaching as a
priority in family life, an intentional approach to teaching, and requires a level of dedication and commitment to the task of teaching
children.

Teaching Is a Priority, Not an Option

In Bible times, parents were the primary teachers of children, and this task was a priority of family life. We have already examined Moses commanding the Israelites to teach their children in Deuteronomy 6, but we find numerous other similar instructions as well (Deut 4:9–10; 11:18–19; 6:20–25; 32:46). Likewise, in his letter to the Ephesians, Paul exhorted fathers, "Don't stir up anger in your children, but bring them up in the training and instruction of the Lord" (Eph 6:4). The parents' role in instructing children is crucial to overall family development. While others may have aided them, the bulk of the responsibility in Bible times fell to the parents for the training of the child. Synagogues were meant to supplement what was done in families, not replace the teaching role of parents.

Teaching should also be a priority in family life because parents are a child's most important and influential educators. Parents spend far more time around children in their most formative developmental years, more time than schoolteachers or teachers in religious settings such as Sunday school. Similarly, family life affords many teaching opportunities, and parents do not have to create simulated environments for many lessons they may want to teach children. Maston states:

> Furthermore, parents can be opportunistic teachers, relating the teaching to immediate situations that arise in the daily life at home. Other teachers, school and particularly Sunday School teachers, have to imagine or erect more or less artificial situations. They can hope or trust that the child will succeed in carrying over into real life the truths they have sought to teach.[12]

Because parents exert such a strong and lasting influence, teaching must be a family priority.

Making Teaching Intentional

Effective parent-teachers are intentional about what they convey to children. Such parents make decisions about what they want to convey to children; then they work to do so. Often teaching takes place whether or not a parent intends to provide a child with

---

[12] Maston, *Bible and Family Relations*, 231–32.

information. Children often learn by observing parents and seeing how parents act in a variety of situations. Because children can learn in such a manner, parents have to be aware of what they are communicating and should be intentional about messages sent to children. On some occasions parents will say one thing and do another. Parents may say church is important but regularly sleep in when tired. In such circumstances the conflict between word and action confuses children who tend to imitate actions more than words.

Unfortunately, parents can teach both good and bad. One evening this past year, a local news station reported the story of a young teenager and her mother arrested for shoplifting. The mother had taught the child how to steal, and they were working together to take items from a store. Because children can learn bad as well as good, wrong as well as right, and immoral as well as moral, effective parent-teachers are intentionally positive in what they impart.

Teaching Involves Dedication and Commitment

Effective teaching in families requires dedication and commitment from parents, both to God and to the task of teaching. At the most basic level this means parents having a vital, growing relationship with Christ. Deuteronomy 6:4–9, discussed earlier, presupposes that a parent loves God with all his or her heart, soul, and strength. Slaughter notes that "if parents are to teach their children the truth about a relationship with God, they themselves must have hearts burning with passion for Him. They must love God with all their heart, soul, and strength; in other words, with every aspect of their being."[13] If parents are not seeking personal spiritual growth, teaching children the things of God becomes a much more difficult proposition.

Dedication and commitment also involves parents working together to teach children. Individuals who study family dynamics have long recognized the value of spouses being unified in their parenting, seeking parental accord in every aspect of family life, including attempts to help children learn and grow. Effective parent-teachers communicate with each other, work through couple con-

---

[13] J. Slaughter, "Toward a Biblical Theology of Family," in *The Christian Educator's Handbook on Family Life Education*, ed. Kenneth Gangel and James Wilhoit (Grand Rapids: Baker, 1996), 26–27.

flict, and work toward agreement in how best to teach children. True parental unity requires a great deal of commitment.

Single parents often do not have the luxury of support from other individuals in parenting tasks. In such instances successful single parents are consistent in how they relate to their children, including when teaching children. Grandparents can also be an important part of the teaching process. Both Deut 4:9 and Exod 10:2 encourage teaching both sons and grandsons the things of God. Grandparents can serve an important role in supporting parents as they attempt to achieve unity in marital and parenting tasks.

Yet another element of parent dedication to the teaching task is knowing each child and fashioning the educational process in a manner that most effectively helps a child learn and grow. Proverbs 22:6 says, "Train up a child in the way he should go, and when he is old he will not depart from it" (NKJV). Not only are parents commanded to train or teach, but effective parent-teachers develop an understanding of how a child grows and learns. Regarding this passage, Keil and Delitzsch state, "The instruction of youth, the education of youth, ought to be conformed to the nature of youth; the matter of instruction, the manner of instruction ought to regulate itself according to the stage of life, and its peculiarities."[14] Parents who have an understanding of a child's developmental level are more likely to be successful in the overall teaching process.

Effective parent-teachers not only have knowledge about stages of growth and development but understand each child's personality, temperament, and the unique manner in which the child tends to learn. Because children learn differently, parents need to know how best to convey information so a child can learn and grow. Several methods for accomplishing this task are identified later in this chapter.

Why Parents Don't Teach

If intentionally teaching children the things of God is such a vital part of a family's responsibility, why are so many parents reticent or

---

[14] C. F. Keil and F. Delitzsch, *Proverbs, Ecclesiastes, and Song of Songs*, vol. 6 of *Commentary on the Old Testament*, trans. M. G. Easton (Grand Rapids, Eerdmans, 1984), 86–87.

lax about doing so? Parents may have a variety of reasons for failing to teach children.

1. I don't know how; I don't know enough. Some parents fail to teach due to feeling inadequate to accomplish the task. Parents may be aware of personal shortcomings in knowledge of Scripture, or they may feel uncertain in making statements about God's nature and character. Other parents are unsure about how to pass along information about God. In some instances a parent may not have grown up in a Christian home or had parents that modeled how to convey the things of God. Like Dave in the story at the start of the chapter, many parents lack a template, model, or framework of how to teach children.

2. I'm too tired or too busy. Busyness often contributes to parents' lack of a systematic attempt to teach children. In today's society, families often function at a frantic pace, investing time and energy not only in a wide array of kid-oriented activities but in transporting children from one activity to the next. Such a pace of life leaves both parents and children fatigued, even exhausted. When families operate in such a manner, teaching is often relegated to school systems, coaches, instrument teachers, and church personnel. Parents may have good intentions to teach their children, but these are often shortchanged by the frantic pace of life.

3. My spouse will do it. Some parents fail to teach children, believing or hoping that their spouse will do it. Fathers may be most prone to this excuse as mothers are often considered the main nurturers of children. The Bible makes clear the father's responsibility in numerous passages, including Eph 6:4; Pss 44:1; 78:3; 38:19; and Gen 18:19. As was mentioned earlier, it is ideal when parents work together and support each other in teaching children. Such teamwork produces an effect far greater than either parent alone can accomplish in carrying out this function of the family.

4. My kids are too old; I missed my opportunity. Parents may believe that they have missed their opportunity and that children are too old to be taught. While teaching older children, especially teenagers, is markedly different from teaching young children, it is never too late to pass along to children the things of God. If a parent has failed one way or another, it might be appropriate to apologize sincerely to children, confessing not doing a better job at this important responsibility. Parents can then begin the teaching process again, even if children are older. If children are grown, parents may get another opportunity with grandchildren. Interestingly, the Bible never indicates an age at which parents are free to stop teaching. The generational transmission of faith appears to be a lifelong task.

5. **I'm trusting the church to do it**—This, unfortunately, is a common reason that many parents refrain from teaching children matters of faith. Because churches have resources and trained personnel, even committed Christian parents find themselves relying on the church to provide religious education to their children. At times the church may even cooperate in this matter, conveying to parents that "we," not parents, can do a better job of teaching children. The outcome is that parents become passive bystanders, sending children to Sunday school, discipleship, mission programs, and a myriad of church-based activities, relying on the church to do the bulk of spiritual education and training. When churches fail to train and support parents in education tasks, the result is parent passivity, church over-responsibility, and a method of educating children that is divergent from the model provided in Scripture.

Ways Parents Can Teach Children

How, then, should parents teach children? Are there approaches that will help parents transmit faith to the next generation? Such teaching can be formal or informal, planned or spontaneous, and can be accomplished through a variety of channels.

Formal or Informal, Planned or Spontaneous

A parent has available a range of ways to teach children. Teaching may be formal, where parents intentionally structure what they convey. Parents may make use of literature or specific activities to help teach. Teaching can be informal, where, in a relaxed and casual atmosphere, parents talk about religious stories, themes, or concepts. Teaching may be planned, where parents are systematic and deliberate in what they try to accomplish, or teaching may be spontaneous, where parents use natural opportunities to communicate abut God's world. Ideally, parents will be open to all these possibilities, having an overall plan but being attentive to a variety of opportunities to teach children. Parents have different ways they may accomplish both formal and informal training. Here we focus on seven specific ways parents can teach their children: modeling, discipline, the natural world, stories, special occasions, worship, and the child's successes and failures.

Teaching through Modeling. Children learn vicariously, that is, by watching and observing behavior of others, especially parents. When a child sees a parent praying, attending church regularly, talking with others about his or her faith, ministering to those in need, and living a consistent, God-honoring life, the child is in a position to learn efficiently and effectively. Both Jesus and Paul understood this principle. Jesus gathered around Him 12 followers and allowed them to observe Him over His three years of ministry. Similarly, Paul told believers, "Follow my example, as I follow the example of Christ" (1 Cor 11:1 NIV). Paul lived his life openly before fellow believers and urged them to watch and emulate him. When a parent models an active, growing relationship with Christ, it communicates more than many Sunday school lessons.

Teaching through Discipline. Discipline is often equated with punishment, but it is much more than that. One meaning of discipline is "to learn," and it is the word from which we get our word *disciple*, or "one who learns." Slaughter notes that discipline is an essential parental duty: "The Proverbs frequently address the parental responsibility of discipline in the child training process."[15] Proverbs, in fact, was written "for learning what wisdom and discipline are; for understanding insightful sayings; for receiving wise instruction in righteousness, justice, and integrity" (Prov 1:2–3).

When a parent wants a child to learn to brush his or her teeth, the parent must work with the child, over and over again, until dental hygiene is a part of the child's routine. In spiritual matters parents should assist children to develop habits of healthy spiritual functioning. This includes regular Scripture reading, prayer, worship attendance, tithing, and service to others.

Discipline requires parental consistency, persistence, and repetition. Parents labor with a child repeatedly in order for the child to

---

[15] Slaughter, "Toward a Biblical Theology of Family," 27.

learn a new repertoire of behaviors such as brushing teeth, riding a bike, or cleaning a room. Proverbs 13:24 states, "The one who will not use the rod hates his son, but the one who loves him disciplines him diligently." That is, loving parents are diligent about training their children through discipline. Moreover, the most effective parents discipline themselves even as they discipline their children.

Teaching through the Natural World. Romans 1:20 says that one way we learn about God is from the world around us: "For His invisible attributes, that is, His eternal power and divine nature, have been clearly seen since the creation of the world, being understood through what He has made. As a result, people are without excuse." Similarly David says, "The heavens declare the glory of God, and the sky proclaims the work of His hands. Day after day they pour out speech; night after night they communicate knowledge" (Ps 19:1–2). Parents can teach children about God by pointing to God's creation and making children aware of the intricacy of God's handiwork.

Parents can easily link things seen in nature to God as Creator. Taking a child for a walk, a parent can draw the child's attention to the detail of a leaf, the pattern of clouds overhead, or the number of stars in the nighttime sky. Parents can connect things seen in nature to Scripture. When looking at the stars, for instance, a parent could tell the child about Ps 147:4: "He counts the number of the stars; He gives names to all of them." Imagine knowing the names of all the stars! When viewing nature, parents have a wonderful opportunity of helping children express thanks to God for His creation. Children learn to be attentive to God's world and appreciative for it.

Teaching through Stories. One of the most effective methods of teaching children is through stories. Parents can both tell and read Bible stories to children, talking about what took place in these stories, about the characters and events presented. Parents can read to children from age-appropriate literature that teaches about God. Especially when they are young, story time is formative in children, establishing lifelong habits of loving to learn.

Stories may also involve parents telling children accounts of family history and events, of what life was like when parents were young, and of a child's own past. Parents can be intentional in communicating stories of how God has worked in their own lives and in the lives of grandparents, as well as stories of how God has cared for and provided for the family.

The Old Testament especially emphasizes storytelling as a method of communicating about God. Deuteronomy 6:20–21 says, "When your son asks you in the future, 'What is the meaning of the decrees, statutes, and ordinances, which the LORD our God has commanded you?' tell him, 'We were slaves of Pharaoh in Egypt, but the LORD brought us out of Egypt with a strong hand.'" When the child asked, the parent was to tell the story of the exodus from slavery.

Teaching through Special Occasions. Special occasions are wonderful opportunities for communicating messages about God, creation, and the need for thankfulness to God. Throughout the Old Testament, God established numerous feasts and festivals, memorials, and ways of remembering how God cared for His children. Special events and holidays are important in family and community life and serve as opportunities to help children learn traditions of a family or culture. In the book of Exodus, Moses instructed the Israelites in how to celebrate the Passover both initially and in the years to come. In Exod 12:26, Moses established a teaching ritual regarding the Passover observance: "When your children ask you, 'What does this ritual mean to you?'" the parents are to tell the children of God's deliverance.

Parents have the opportunity to shape holidays and special occasions to convey specific messages to children. Parents can talk about God, God's work, and God's care, as well as about how God wants people to celebrate and remember Him. Shaping holidays around God and His Word counteracts the damaging effects of commercialism that have become so commonplace in most holiday seasons.

Teaching through Worship. Children learn about God through worship, whether at church or in a family setting. In corporate worship children participate with the family of God as they express gratitude to God. In recent times many churches have opted to separate small children from worship, leaving them in nurseries. Other churches have children's church or even services for teens. While these may be attempts to help children and teens learn at age-appropriate levels, there is much for children to absorb in adult worship services. Parents still bear the responsibility for helping children know how to participate in worship in a corporate setting. Even when children are small, parents can help them with words to songs and looking up Scripture passages in the Bible. Following services, parents can dialogue with older children and teens about messages conveyed in the sermon. Simply watching parents and other respected adults sing, pray, and listen attentively prepares them to worship as well.

At home families can develop simple worship times for children. This may include singing, Bible verses, or family members identifying things for which they are grateful. Worship time may be structured around special occasions (Easter, Thanksgiving, and Christmas, for instance) or may be a regular occurrence throughout the year. Parents should help children know how to worship and can assist children in making this a regular part of life.

Teaching through a Child's Successes and Failures. Yet another avenue of teaching a child is through the child's own accomplishments and disappointments. When a child achieves success in some task, parents can encourage the child to express gratitude to God for His guidance, His help, and the abilities and talents given a child. Similarly, however, when a child undergoes disappointments, parents have wonderful opportunities to provide comfort and support, and to help the child face and cope with disappointment. In Rom 5:3–5, Paul says,

> And not only that, but we also rejoice in our afflictions, because we know that affliction produces endurance, endurance produces proven character, and proven character produces hope. This hope will not disappoint us, because God's love has been poured out in our hearts through the Holy Spirit who was given to us.

Struggles in life also provide a chance for children to learn that contentment is not based on outward circumstances or events. In Philippians, writing while imprisoned, Paul states, "I know both how to have a little, and I know how to have a lot. In any and all circumstances I have learned the secret of being content—whether well-fed or hungry, whether in abundance or in need" (4:12). Paul recognized that happiness is not based on circumstances and that contentment is a choice. Similarly, children can learn through difficult times as well as when things go well.

Thus, parents have numerous means available for teaching children about God. While the list above is certainly not exhaustive, it represents a wide range of ways—formal and informal, planned and spontaneous—whereby parents are able to help children learn.

How Can the Church Assist Families in Teaching Children?

Dr. Lawson's chapter on "The Role of the Church in Teaching" describes ways a community of believers fulfills a teaching function. But here we focus on the church's role and responsibility in helping families teach children. How can the church best assist families? There are a number of things churches can do to help equip parents as teachers of their own children.

Church leaders can understand and then foster the idea that they are colaborers with parents in the task of teaching children. Providing families with support, encouragement, and guidance in the teaching process increases the likelihood that parents can be effective in teaching children. Church leaders can point out theologically sound, developmentally appropriate curriculum or materials that parents may find beneficial. Leaders can provide parents information about stages of growth and development, including information about how children learn at each stage of development.

Leaders can train parents in actual methods and skills for teaching children, demonstrating how parents can accomplish the tasks described above. Churches can allow parents time to teach children. Many churches create and demand so much member busyness that parents are left little time for family activities. In order to avoid a church driven by programming and tradition, perhaps a critical beginning point for church leaders is to examine programming to see if the church is contributing unnecessarily to family stress and exhaustion. Perhaps leaders need to help some members learn how to say no to excessive church involvement since it is possible for members to become compulsive about religious busyness.

Last, churches may offer some form of parent support group where parents can exchange ideas about teaching and encourage other parents in their teaching endeavors. Support and encouragement are vital to success, and the knowledge that other parents share similar challenges and victories can hearten parent-teachers. The partnership between parents and churches is vital to successful generational transmission of the knowledge of God.

Dave Revisited

Though Dave lamented not having a relationship with his parents in which he received a model of how to relate in a healthy manner, he decided to become active in teaching his children the things of God. He committed to take seriously his own spiritual growth, including focused Bible study and daily prayer. Dave and his wife began reading Bible stories to their six- and four-year-old daughters and became more intentional in pointing out God's handiwork in the world around them. The couple decided to take both their children to Sunday worship services, even though the younger daughter was eligible to remain in child care during these services. Dave and his wife wanted to be more active in helping the daughters understand and participate in worship. The couple asked three other families to meet one Friday each month to fellowship, to share ideas for teaching children, and to pray for one another's families. In our final counseling session, Dave told me that he and his wife would regularly evaluate how they were doing as parent-teachers and would be open to making adjustments as necessary. Dave was not only enthusiastic about his plans, but he seemed to have a sense of purpose accompanied by a type of peace produced by his ability to provide his daughters some of those vital elements he had not received in his childhood years.

Conclusion

Family is important to God. God values family and family life. Family is the most natural and potentially most effective means of teaching young ones about God, His creation, and His plan for humankind. Churches and ministry individuals have the critical task of assisting and supporting families as they teach children about God. Churches and families who work together in providing for the needs of children in this manner become a powerful force in promoting, and ultimately proclaiming, the kingdom of God.

Bibliography

Barna, George. *Barna Update*, "Born Again Christians Are as Likely to Divorce as Non-Christians (Sept. 8, 2004)," accessed 29 March 2007 at http://www.barna.org/FlexPage.aspx?Page=BarnaUpdate& BarnaUpdateID=170.

_____. *The Future of the American Family*. Chicago: Moody.

Center for Disease Control. *National Vital Statistics Report—Births, Marriages, Divorces, and Deaths: Provisional Data for 2005*, vol. 54 no. 20. Accessed 29 March 2007 at http://www.cdc.gov/nchs/data/ nvsr/nvsr54/nvsr54_20.pdf.

Christianson, Duane. *Deuteronomy 1–11*. Word Biblical Commentary, vol. 6A. Ed. David Hubbard and Glenn Baker. Dallas: Word, 1991.

Fraenkel, Peter. "Contemporary Two-Parent Families: Navigating Work and Family Challenges." *Normal Family Processes*. 3rd ed. Ed. Froma Walsh. New York: Guilford, 2003.

Garland, Diana. *Family Ministry: A Comprehensive Guide*. Downers Grove, IL: InterVarsity, 1999.

Keil, C. F., and F. Delitzsch. *Proverbs, Ecclesiastes, and Song of Songs*. Commentary on the Old Testament. Trans. M. G. Easton. Grand Rapids, Eerdmans, 1984.

Maston, T. B. *The Bible and Family Relations*. Nashville: Broadman, 1983.

Slaughter, James. "Toward a Biblical Theology of Family." In *The Christian Educator's Handbook on Family Life Education*. Ed. Kenneth Gangel and James Wilhoit. Grand Rapids: Baker, 1996.

Whitehead, Barbara, and David Popenoe. "The State of Our Unions: The Social Health of Marriage in America (2005)." http://marriage. rutgers.edu/Publications/Print/PrintSOOU2005.htm (accessed 7 February 2007), 18.

Chapter 10

THE PASTOR AS TEACHER

Rick Yount

And He personally gave some to be apostles, some prophets,
some evangelists, some pastors and teachers,
for the training of the saints in the work of
ministry, to build up the body of Christ,
until we all reach unity in the faith and in the
knowledge of God's Son, growing into a mature man
with a stature measured by Christ's fullness.
(Eph 4:11–13)

W hat is the role of the pastor?[1] Some say the pastor is primarily a *prophet*, proclaiming the Word of God. Others say a *shepherd*, nurturing and protecting the church. Still others say a *leader*, managing and administrating the work of the church. Each has its importance, but congregations grow in the most healthy way when leaders are able to balance all three.[2]

Underlying all three roles is the fundamental calling of the pastor: "the training of the saints in the work of ministry" (Eph 4:12). This was, as we saw in chapter 2, Jesus' primary ministry role while on earth; and it remains His continuing task through the Holy Spirit.

---

[1] In February 1992, I taught a doctor of ministry seminar in educational psychology. My aim was to help students apply principles of the teaching-learning process to the pastor's role as teacher in a local church. The class consisted of pastors Robert Carter, John Brady, David Hixon, Steve Washburn, Dennis Suhling, and Rick Atkinson, and missionaries David Borgan, Alvin Gary, and Virgil Stuttles. Their final assignment was to write an exegesis of Eph 4:11–16 in light of educational principles discussed in the course. While the outline of this chapter is mine, their insights concerning the "pastor as teacher" were invaluable and are referenced throughout.

[2] This threefold perspective is expanded in chapter 11, "The Goal of Christian Education: Christlikeness," in which we define the Christian Teachers' Triad. The prophet, shepherd, and leader mentioned above tie into the three spheres of thinking, feeling, and doing described there.

161

The random noise of secular success models threatens to drown out the steady heartbeat of teaching. John Brady[3] stated the problem this way:

> The church is sick. This results from what Dallas Willard calls the "Great Omission from the Great Commission."[4] The third command of the Great Commission "teaching them all things whatsoever I have commanded you" has been omitted from serious application by the modern church. There are grand plans for evangelization and stewardship, but rarely is anything but lip service paid to discipleship.
>
> In recent years the church has done what it seems to do best—follow the world's lead. The pastor may be more directed by a business suit than a shepherd's heart. The CEO's power more the goal than the teacher's vision of changed lives. The models we are following seem drastically out of balance with the biblical model for church life. In Ephesians 4:11–16, we find a clear statement of the biblical model for church life.[5]

It is this biblical model of the pastor-teacher that we seek to develop in this chapter.

Even so, this chapter is not for senior pastors only. Any minister who teaches in a Christian context also serves as pastor (shepherd) to those he teaches. God calls every staff member to be pastor-teacher—every Sunday school teacher, deacon, organization leader, committee chair. Christ has gifted the church with many pastor-teachers to prepare others for kingdom service. And teaching is at the heart of this process.

Paul as Teacher

Paul was a teacher at heart. The great teacher Gamaliel thoroughly trained Paul in rabbinic law (Acts 22:3).[6] After Paul was converted,

---

[3] Dr. John Brady is now regional leader for NAME (North Africa, Middle East), International Mission Board, Southern Baptist Convention.

[4] D. Willard, *The Spirit of the Disciplines: Understanding How God Changes Lives* (San Francisco: Harper and Row, 1988), 15.

[5] J. Brady, "The Pastor as Teacher," D.Min. Seminar in Educational Psychology, April 5, 1992.

[6] Not only did Paul know the Old Testament as a devout Jew might know it, but he was also a trained rabbi, and he knew the Old Testament as a rabbi knew it. He

but while he was still a virtual unknown, Barnabas personally brought him to Antioch from Tarsus. There they "met with the church and taught great numbers of people" (Acts 11:26).

Paul's emphasis was on "living in Christ." We find the key to Paul's teaching in his thoughts concerning Jesus Christ, aptly expressed by his frequently repeated phrase "in Christ."[7] Jesus taught that true life grows from living in union with Him (John 15:1–8). Paul expressed the same truth: "Christ in you, the hope of glory" (Col 1:27). Thus, teaching that is Christian must have Christ at its center.

Though Paul taught large crowds (Acts 13:42–45; 17:12–13), he was personally interested in converts. The personal notes at the end of his letter to the Romans show the concern and care that Paul had for those whom he brought to the Lord: Prisca and Aquila, Epaenetus, Mary, Andronicus and Junia, Ampliatus, Urbanus, Stachys, Apelles, Aristobulus, Herodion, Narcissus, Tryphaena and Tryphosa, Persis, Rufus, Asyncritus, Phlegon, Hermes, Patrobas, Hermas, Philologus, Julia, Nereus, and Olympas (Rom 16:3–15). "[I warn] each of you night and day with tears" (Acts 20:31). His missionary journeys were much more than traveling gospel shows. As F. B. Meyer wrote, "All the fruit [Paul] gathered was hand-picked. He was more fond of the hand-net than the sieve."[8] His aim was to draw, to win, to establish, to equip, and to mature converts one by one.[9]

Paul discipled new converts and selected a few men, just as Jesus had, to train more extensively for the ministry. John Mark, Silas, Titus, and Timothy are all prominent examples of Paul's personal touch. Other coworkers with Paul include Tychicus, Onesimus, Aristarchus, Justus, Epaphras, Luke, and Demas (Col 4:7–14).[10]

---

knew not only the Old Testament; he also knew the special traditions of the rabbis. W. Barclay, *The Mind of St. Paul* (London: Collins Clear-Type, 1958), 13–14.

[7] R. Longenecker, *The Ministry and Message of Paul* (Grand Rapids: Zondervan, 1971), 89.

[8] F. B. Meyer, *Paul: Servant of Jesus Christ* (London: Lakeland, 1968), 131.

[9] How different is this mind-set from the modern desire to perform on stage before thousands. My own pastor, Al Meredith, demonstrates Paul's heart as he meets weekly with a small group of men for breakfast. He shares his studies and elements of future sermons, listens to their experiences, encourages their faithfulness, challenges them to greater faith, and learns from their questions and problems. This is only one of several small groups he engages week by week. In this he fulfils his role as pastor-discipler, even as he preaches before large crowds.

[10] "Brother Al" takes special joy in mentoring seminary students and has his own personal "graduates" serving all around the world. He maintains contact with them and continues to teach them, even years following their graduations. My pastor at

By teaching through personal example, Paul did far more than tell converts how to live. He showed them how to live a Christ-centered life and encouraged them to imitate him. To the Corinthians he said, "I urge you, be imitators of me" (1 Cor 4:16). To the Philippians, "Join in imitating me, brothers, and observe those who live according to the example you have in us" (Phil 3:17).

Paul taught in a variety of situations: in the synagogue, by the riverside, in prisons, in the marketplace, on a hilltop, in a school, from a staircase, in a council chamber, in the courtroom, on shipboard, and in a public dwelling in Rome. He taught in public and private and from house to house. In the groups he taught were Hebrews, Greeks, Romans, barbarians, friends, enemies, and strangers. There were philosophers, soothsayers, orators, jailers, prisoners, slaves, the sick, soldiers and sailors, women, devout, honorable, and industrious, rulers, magistrates, governors, a king, and a queen. His life was one teaching experience.[11]

Paul established churches as teaching stations. He expected believers to reach and teach others. Paul wrote to Timothy, "And what you have heard from me in the presence of many witnesses, commit to faithful men who will be able to teach others also" (2 Tim 2:2).

Paul sent "teaching letters" to churches in which he discussed the current situations in the churches and gave specific advice in dealing with them. Particularly, his last letters contained specific directions for organization, government, and worship.[12]

Paul was a deep thinker and philosopher. Before being trained by Gamaliel in rabbinical law, Paul probably attended the University of Tarsus in his hometown (Acts 9:11). This school surpassed all other universities of its day in the study of philosophy and educational literature.[13] His writings certainly reflect his depth of thought, so much so that even the apostle Peter admits that some of Paul's writing is "hard to understand," which the "untaught and unstable twist . . . to their own destruction" (2 Pet 3:15–16).

Columbia Baptist Church, Falls Church, Virginia, in the early 1970s, though long retired from full-time ministry, still writes me encouraging notes and continues to teach me. Such is the spirit of Paul concerning pastoral teaching and equipping.

[11] C. Collins Jr., *Paul as Leader* (New York: Exposition, 1955), 104.

[12] A. Leacock, *Studies in the Life of St. Paul* (New York: International Committee, 1964), 6–12.

[13] R. E. Speer, *Studies of the Man Paul* (New York: Fleming H. Revell, 1947), 19–20.

Paul was a practical problem solver. Though he was a philosopher and deep thinker, Paul was no abstract theoretician, weaving some obscure intangible systematic theology or religious philosophy. His teaching and his writings provided specific, practical, realistic, and functional advice for living "in Christ." His topics covered a large number of subjects: unity in the church, reliance on the Spirit, serving Christ, renouncing immorality, guidance on marriage and family relationships, the proper use of liberty and spiritual gifts, bearing one another's burdens, Christian stewardship, living like Christ, deacons, widows, apostasy, and discipline.

Paul emphasized the work and power of the Holy Spirit. He wrote that the Holy Spirit sets us free from sin and death (Rom 8:2); gives us righteousness, peace, and joy (14:17); sets us apart for God's use (15:16); justifies us before God in the name of Jesus (1 Cor 6:11); brands us as God's own (Eph 1:3); helps us know God better (1:17); reveals the mystery of Christ (3:4–6; Col 1:27); gives joy (1 Thess 1:6), helps to guard sound teaching (1 Tim 1:13–14); and is the agent by which the Father washes and renews us (Titus 3:3–6). As such, any work in Christian education that succeeds in helping people grow spiritually must be empowered by the Holy Spirit. This empowerment comes by way of personal surrender (Matt 16:24), humility before God (1 Pet 5:6) and with others (Rom 12:10,16), and prayer. Paul emphasized prayer. Because of his conviction concerning the power and work of the Holy Spirit, he believed any training program would be incomplete without prayer. Paul prayed faithfully for his trainees (Phil 1:3–8; 1 Thess 3:9–10).[14]

Finally, Paul stressed spiritual growth. He was more interested in the spiritual growth and maturity of churches than he was in mere numbers. This chapter's focal passage reinforces repeatedly the importance of maturity over mere size. This is the essence of Paul's Ephesian treatise on church growth. The remainder of the chapter analyzes the role of pastor-teachers in promoting spiritual growth in congregations.

The Pastor-Teacher: Qualifications

Paul expected believers to "walk (lead a life) worthy of the [divine] calling to which you have been called" (Eph 4:1 *Amplified*

---

[14] See chapter 5, "The Holy Spirit as Teacher," for more details

Bible; see also Col 1:10). Their faith was not some appendage to add
to their own system of values and lifestyle. "You are not your own,
for you were bought at a price; therefore glorify God in your body"
(1 Cor 6:19–20). Believers are to live "with all humility and gentleness, with patience, accepting one another in love" (Eph 4:2), not
arrogant, not mean-spirited, not hot tempered. We are to bear with,
or in today's language, "put up with" other believers, in love.

Believers are to "diligently [keep] the unity of the Spirit with the
peace that binds us" (Eph 4:3). Struggle to keep peace. Wrestle with
the forces that would divide believers into camps. Warfare among
believers never comes from the Holy Spirit but is always of the flesh
(Gal 5:19–23). This unity belongs to the body or the community
of believers (Eph 4:4) and is based on our unified hope in Christ:
"one Lord, one faith, one baptism, one God and Father of all, who is
above all and through all and in all" (Eph 4:5–6).

What is the purpose of our unity? To use our personal ("to each
one of us," v. 7) gifts ("grace") together, so that we will no longer
live like "Gentiles" (hard-hearted, sensuous, ignorant pagans; see vv.
17–19).

Since *believers* are expected to live in a way that is worthy of the
Lord—to be humble, gentle, patient, forbearing, loving, peaceful,
and united—their *leaders* should reflect these characteristics even
more: "shepherd God's flock . . . not lording it over those entrusted
to you, but being examples to the flock" (1 Pet 5:2–3).

The Pastor-Teacher Is a Member of a Team

Paul says that Christ gave four kinds of gifted leaders to the
church: apostles, prophets, evangelists, and pastors and teachers.
Missionary David Borgan gives an excellent description of each of
these leaders.[15]

> Apostle means "one sent out." Originally, Jesus sent out
> the Twelve—eleven of whom were eye-witnesses of the
> resurrection. But the New Testament records others who
> were also sent out into pioneer work. He first gives "some
> apostles"—not the Twelve, but men like "the apostles
> Barnabas and Paul (Acts 14:14) who are sent forth to plant

---

[15] D. Borgan, "The Pastor as Teacher," April 5, 1992.

the Gospel for the first time in a place."[16] The modern term
from the Latin translation of *apostolos* is "missionaries,"
ones who are sent out with the specific purpose of establishing new churches.

Prophet means "Speaker for God and Christ." [This
involves] not only foretelling but forthtelling the truth of
the Gospel. Robertson writes, "Prophets are needed today if
men will let God's Spirit use them, men moved to utter the
deep things of God."[17]

Evangelist means "Bearer of the Good News." Those
who have the gift of calling others to Christ. "These men
traveled from place to place to preach the Gospel and win
the lost (Acts 8:26–40; 21:28). . . . The apostles and prophets laid the foundation of the church, and the evangelists
built upon it by winning the lost to Christ."[18]

The term "pastors and teachers," our focus in this chapter, requires more analysis. Are "pastors and teachers" one
group or two? Guthrie and Motyer write, "The construction of the phrase pastors and teachers with one definite
article covering both words suggests that there were *two*
functions shared by the same individuals whose chief
task is described in Acts 20:28. These men would be local
congregational leaders in charge of established churches
brought into existence by the preaching of the apostles and
others."[19]

Curtis Vaughan writes that "pastors and teachers" constitute
one office with a dual function. The two functions are combined
in one person.[20] Marcus Barth notes that "often the word *and* has
the meaning 'that is' or 'in particular' and indicates that the 'shepherds' and 'teachers' are viewed as one common group, i.e., 'teaching
shepherds."[21] Pastor John Brady continues:

---

[16] D. Moody, *Christ and the Church* (Grand Rapids: Eerdmans, 1963), 93.

[17] A. T. Robertson, *Word Pictures in the New Testament,* vol. 5 (Nashville: Broadman 1931), 174.

[18] W. W. Wiersbe, *Be Rich: Are You Losing the Things That Money Can't Buy?* (Wheaton, IL.: SF Publications), 101.

[19] D. Guthrie and J. A. Motyer, *The New Bible Commentary: Revised* (Grand Rapids: Eerdmans, 1970), 116.

[20] W. C. Vaughan, *The Letter to the Ephesians* (Nashville: Convention, 1963), 91.

[21] F. Rienecker, *Linguistic Key to the New Testament,* trans. and ed. Cleon L. Rogers Jr. (Grand Rapids: Zondervan, 1980), 531.

This connects Paul's teaching with the instructive God of
the Old Testament whom David called "my Shepherd." Our
Lord's example gave Paul a key to the health of the church,
a teaching shepherd. Therefore the biblical model for leadership in each congregation is the pastor/teacher.[22]

Pastor Steve Washburn notes that the term *pastor* (*polmen*, "to
protect")[23] refers to the shepherding role of the minister. Jesus is
the model (John 10:11). "As shepherds of Jesus' flocks, pastors are
to love and nurture and meet the needs of their congregations."[24]
Also, pastors are to be "able to teach" (1 Tim 3:2). Again, Jesus is the
model. Washburn further writes, "It is enormously significant that
the only time the term *pastor* is used to describe the spiritual gifts
given to undershepherds of the churches, it is directly connected to
the gift of teaching: 'pastors and teachers.' "[25]

Pastor David Hixon reflects his understanding of Paul:

The pastor's primary role according to Ephesians 4 is not to
be preacher, or an evangelist, or a counselor. His primary
responsibility is to equip or to prepare God's people to do
the work. The church needs to grow and mature through
the ministry of the laity and not primarily through the
works of the paid staff.[26]

Such ministry is enhanced through the teaching (discipling, equipping) ministries of pastor and staff.

Pastor Richard Atkinson writes, " 'Feeding the sheep' means teaching them, nurturing them, equipping them. The very nature of the
pastor's role is that of a teacher."[27] Missionary Alvin Gary summarizes the role of the minister, the pastor-teacher, as one who "protects and instructs" the flock under his care.[28]

A. T. Robertson underscores the importance of the teaching function of the pastor-teacher: "It is a calamity when the preacher is no

---

[22] Brady, "The Pastor as Teacher," April 5, 1992.

[23] Robertson, *Word Pictures,* 537.

[24] S. Washburn, "The Pastor as Teacher," April 5, 1992.

[25] Ibid.

[26] D. Hixon, "The Pastor as Teacher," April 5, 1992.

[27] R. Atkinson, "The Pastor as Teacher," April 5, 1992.

[28] A. Gary, "The Pastor as Teacher," April 5, 1992.

longer a teacher, but only an exhorter."[29] Borgan emphasizes the importance of this truth for new pastors:

> New preachers tend to identify themselves more with the
> first three ministries (apostle, prophet, evangelist) than
> they do with the title of teacher. The most significant bibli-
> cal insight in this passage for new pastors is how it clearly
> identifies the pastoral ministry as a teaching ministry. In
> fact, in small churches a pastor has almost total responsibil-
> ity for Christian teaching in areas of salvation, baptism, and
> classes for new Christians and new members. . . .
>
> American Christianity has compartmentalized church
> work into pastoral ministry and religious education depart-
> ments. Pastors should not look down upon their biblical
> title of "teacher." Jesus called Himself a teacher (John
> 13:13). Pastors need to become more like Christ in devel-
> oping their teaching expertise as well as their pastoral tal-
> ents. The practical application of this should include learn-
> ing principles and methods of expert teaching throughout a
> pastor's career.[30]

The Goal of the Pastor-Teacher: The Primary Work

What do pastor-teachers do? What is their primary task? Why does Jesus "gift" churches with pastor-teachers? Paul says pastor-teachers are given "for the training of the saints in the work of ministry" (Eph 4:12a). To "equip the saints" (KJV). To "train Christians in skilled servant work" (*The Message*). The word *train* or *equip* means "to mend, to complete, to fit out, to make one what he ought to be."[31] It is used in Matt 4:21 to refer to mending nets. Pastor Robert Carter writes, "The pastor-teacher sees the goal of his ministry to be, not teaching a great lesson to people, but teaching people to be great."[32]

Teaching people to be great in what way? The focus of equipping is "works of service" (*diakonia*). Basically, the word means "wait-ing at tables." The term came to mean any discharge of service in

---

[29] Robertson, *Word Pictures*, 174.
[30] Borgan, "The Pastor as Teacher," April 5, 1992.
[31] E. Y. Mullins, *Studies in Ephesians* (Nashville: Sunday School Board of the Southern Baptist Convention, 1935), 96.
[32] R. Carter, "The Pastor as Teacher," April 5, 1992.

genuine love for the benefit of the Christian community.[33] The Lord's call to every believer is to serve Him and others. Each believer has gifts given by the Lord to enhance the work of the church. Human nature's call, however, is to personal convenience and personal comfort. The pastor-teacher lives in the gulf between the Lord's will and individual human wills in the church. He calls out the called and equips them to use their gifts effectively. As James Smart says, "The pastor who refuses to get involved in the personal aspects of teaching is like a farmer who simply scatters seed and refuses to do anything else to encourage a successful harvest."[34] Unfortunately this task has many obstacles, as we'll discuss later.

Equipping God's people for works of service is required "to build up the body of Christ" (Eph 4:12b). The body of Christ is the church (Col 1:18,24). What exactly does "build up" mean? Does this mean numerical growth, helping the church to get bigger? Despite the fact that the highest praise, the best opportunities, and the largest headlines are reserved for pastors who produce the best "growth" numbers, this is not Paul's emphasis. "Build up" has the meaning of edifying (Rom 14:19; 1 Cor 14:5) or strengthening (Rom 15:2; 1 Cor 14:26) or benefiting (Eph 4:29). The result of this may certainly include numerical growth, but the emphasis is on strengthening, benefiting, and edifying the existing church body. Washburn writes passionately on this point:

> We are asked to consider the effectiveness and efficiency of a body that develops and grows proportionately (1 Cor 12). Such a body is able handily and happily to do everything it is asked to do. Conversely, we are asked to consider the effects of a body where some parts do not develop, or where they are underdeveloped. The picture in our mind is that of a sadly deformed body that is unable to perform even the simplest of tasks, no matter how often or how passionately we may plead with it to do so.
>
> Any pastor who devotes himself primarily to church growth or new buildings or increasing budgets or improved administration or even to sermonizing, to the neglect of

---

[33] *Theological Dictionary of the New Testament*, ed. G. Kittel and G. Friedrich, vol. 2, trans. and ed. G. W. Bromiley (Grand Rapids: Eerdmans, 1964), 87.

[34] J. Smart, *Teaching Ministry of the Church* (Philadelphia: Westminster, 1954), 83.

preparing God's people to do their works of service, will soon find himself in a sadly deformed church body that is unable to perform even the simplest of church tasks, no matter how often or how passionately he may plead with them to do so.

But as a pastor-teacher focuses on preparing God's people through instructive and applicable preaching, through teaching and discipling that develop member gifts, and through one-on-one counseling that encourages members and helps them become what God intended them to be, then the marvelous revelation that unfolds before his eyes is that of a strong, proportionate, evenly developed, beautiful body of Christ growing and building itself up, able to hear and respond to pastoral leadership, handily and happily doing the work of the ministry.

What is a pastor supposed to do? He is to prepare God's people for works of service. If this one simple truth were embraced by many struggling pastors, it would transform their ministries.[35]

One major stumbling block for contemporary pastors is the fear of losing control over the congregation. As one young pastor told me in the middle of a conversation on leadership, "Someone has to be in charge. It might as well be me!" Following society's values, pastors may seek, like powerful corporate executives, to pull to themselves all the power they can in order to impose their own wills over their congregations. Brady writes, "The model of the teaching shepherd seeks to empower the disciple to follow Christ and to be involved in discipling others. Often power has been carefully guarded as something that cannot be shared. 'If you share, then you have less.' This is a false assumption. Empowering another enhances the one who empowers."[36]

How long? How long do we focus on church maturity? Do we focus on equipping God's people in ministry at the beginning and then use our equipped members to do what's really important: create big crowds, budgets, staffs, and prestige? The apostle Paul says we are to focus on equipping the saints "until *we all reach unity* in the faith and in the knowledge of God's Son" (Eph 4:13a, emphasis

---

[35] Washburn, "The Pastor as Teacher," April 5, 1992.

[36] Brady, "The Pastor as Teacher," April 5, 1992.

mine). Pastor Suhling writes that the pastor-teacher's goal is for "the whole congregation [to] believe the same thing in and about the Son of God."[37] Paul's term "knowledge" *(epignosis)* does not refer to mere information about Him. It stresses the experiential knowledge of knowing Christ by being yoked with Him (Matt 11:29) and living in union with Him (John 15:4–5). This was Paul's passion for himself (Phil 3:12–14) and, as we see here, the church at large.

Notice that a significant part of this experiential knowledge comes to individuals by participating in the body, living in community with one another. The focus of this entire passage is the unity and community of the church. Believers will not develop fully as long as individuals hold to a "me and Jesus" piety. Jesus taught us to pray, "Our Father," not "My Father."[38]

The focus of this development is, Paul says, spiritual maturity: "into a mature man" (v. 13). Paul uses this same term to mean "full-grown" in his letter to the Colossians: "We proclaim Him, warning and teaching everyone with all wisdom, so that we may present everyone mature [*teleios*] in Christ" (Col 1:28). Paul had no thought of church size or numerical growth rate in his plea for the Ephesian church to grow. His emphasis was the maturity of the body, developed as believers are equipped in ministry and united in their faith and knowledge of Christ by effective pastor-teachers.

How mature? How mature must the church become? How long do pastor-teachers teach and equip? When can pastor-teachers move on to other matters? Paul's goal for the church was nothing short of the maturity of Jesus Christ—"with a stature measured by Christ's fullness" (Eph 4:13b). When the body is united and as mature as the Lord Jesus, then the work of pastor-teachers is complete. Pastor Atkinson reflects that the pastor is to "so nurture and equip the members that [the church] grows as a unified body until it measures up to Christ's standard. This is a continuing process since the church cannot achieve perfection here on earth."[39]

Our present obsession with numerical growth rates and "ten more next Sunday" has dangerous implications for church maturity. When

---

[37] Suhling, "The Pastor as Teacher," April 5, 1992.

[38] See chapter 8, "The Church's Role in Teaching," for more details on this social dimension of teaching.

[39] Atkinson, "The Pastor as Teacher," April 5, 1992.

evangelism outruns discipleship, converts' growth in the Lord is stunted. A church filled with carnal Christians cannot fulfill its mission. The church entered the Dark Ages when Emperor Constantine made Christianity the state religion of Rome. As thousands of soldiers marched along a riverbank, priests baptized them into the church by using trees, bent into the river with ropes and released, to fling water over them. This provided rapid numerical growth for the church but had nothing to do with biblical faith or spiritual maturity. Numerical growth does not necessarily equate with spiritual growth. Spiritual growth is the result of members of the body of Christ serving God through their spiritual gifts. As Atkinson points out, "It is the pastor's responsibility to lead church members to discover their service gift or gifts in order for the church to carry out her ministry."[40] This is not to denigrate evangelism ("do the work of an evangelist," 2 Tim 4:5) or to retreat from the task of reaching the whole world for Christ ("Go . . . and make disciples of all nations," Matt 28:19). The fact is, though, that the world will be reached only by equipped and mature churches, by equipped and mature believers.

Paul's emphasis was maturity, not numerical growth. The result of Paul's personal teaching in Ephesus was missionary activity throughout the region, which established churches in Hierapolis, Colossae, and Laodecia.[41] Further, Paul's emphasis on maturity so changed Asia Minor that some 200 years later the pagan temples were largely empty because the majority of pagans had become Christians. The *emphasis* is growing up in Christ. The *effect* is healthy numerical growth. To reverse this order, to place emphasis more on numerical

---

[40] Ibid.

[41] "[In the synagogue in Ephesus], in the cool and shadowed interior, [Paul's] congregation sits on little stone benches. Timotheus and Titus and Priscilla have brought them hither. Most of the listeners are Jews, such as have not been frightened away by his strange doctrine, but have, on the contrary, found in it consolation and strength and hope. Some of them have already accepted baptism. There are Ephesians among the listeners, but there are also visitors from towns nearby, merchants who, having heard strange reports of a wonderful message, have come to hear for themselves. They come from Colossae, from Laodicea, and from Hierapolis. What they have heard they will carry forth from Ephesus, even as they carry their merchandise; and as they sell the latter, they will distribute the former. They will found new congregations and churches of believers, which will grow into one great organization with the church of Ephesus as its center." S. Asch, *The Apostle* (New York: G. P. Putnam's Sons, 1943), 515–16.

growth than on the maturing of the church, is to open the church to strife, division, and ruin. Today's emphasis on giving baby boomer worship consumers whatever they want would invite a rebuke from Paul, who wrote to Timothy to

> proclaim the message; persist in it whether convenient or not; rebuke, correct, and encourage with great patience and teaching. For the time will come when they will not tolerate sound doctrine, but according to their own desires, will accumulate teachers for themselves because they have an itch to hear something new. They will turn away from hearing the truth and will turn aside to myths. But as for you, keep a clear head about everything, endure hardship, do the work of an evangelist, fulfill your ministry. (2 Tim 4:2–5)

Pastor Washburn drives the point home:

> [There is a] popular new approach to churchmanship that strives to appeal to the baby boomer church-shoppers by offering the most exciting and joyous worship product in the community market. Laboring to tickle the fancy of the worship experience consumer may fill a pastor's church with warm bodies, but it does little to foster commitment, involvement, and true discipleship.[42]

The Results of the Work of the Pastor-Teacher

What happens in a congregation that grows according to Paul's pattern? "Then we will no longer be little children, tossed by the waves and blown around by every wind of teaching, by human cunning with cleverness in the techniques of deceit" (Eph 4:14). Believers will put away the instability, fickleness, and gullibility that mark the immature. When Paul says we will "no longer be infants," he is attacking the "fickleness of children's volatile moods, shifting like a kaleidoscope, dazzled by the first glittering bauble or flimsy distraction that catches their eye."[43] Such infants are "tossed back and forth by the waves," unstable in their thinking and believing.

---

[42] Washburn, "The Pastor as Teacher," April 5, 1992.
[43] E. K. Simpson, "Commentary on the Epistle of the Ephesians," in *Ephesians and Colossians* (Grand Rapids: Eerdmans, 1980), 98.

They are "blown here and there by every wind of teaching," fickle in their convictions and confused by false teaching They are gullible, swallowing fraudulent claims and deceptive promises by the "cunning and craftiness of men in deceitful scheming." The term "cunning" (*kubia*) refers to playing with dice, trickery, or fraud. This deception is intentional and designed by evil men.[44] "Craftiness" (*panougria*) literally means "readiness to do anything"[45] and implies a trap ("unable to trap him," Luke 20:26, NIV) or being "led astray" (2 Cor 11:3). "Deceitful scheming" (*methodeia*) has the positive meaning of "handling according to plan," but came to mean "handling craftily, overreaching, deceiving."[46] Paul uses the same term in chapter 6 when he writes, "Put on the full armor of God so that you can take your stand against the devil's schemes" (Eph 6:11). Missionary Gary writes, "Pastors who use their gift for instructing the flock in truth and who emphasize discipleship in their ministries will provide protection from heretical teaching. They will help church members examine truth, become settled in the truth, and hold fast to the truth."[47]

Pastor Hixon writes, "Many of our people are seduced by false teachers because we, as pastors, have not done our job in growing them up in Christ Jesus. Discipleship is the key to avoiding an infantile ministry."[48] Pastor Suhling believes "the goal of the teacher is spiritual maturity in the believer. If this is not achieved, then the result will be that the believer will be like one who is foolish and inexperienced when it comes to doctrine and practice. Indeed, the immature believer will be like a cork tossed about on rough water[49] or a weathervane at the mercy of a hard uncertain wind[50] when it comes to believing the right teaching." [51]

---

[44] Hixon, "The Pastor as Teacher," April 5, 1992.

[45] *Greek-English Lexicon of the New Testament and Other Early Christian Literature*, 2nd English ed., revised and augmented by E. Wilbur Gingrich and Frederick W. Danker from Walter Bauer's 5th ed. (Chicago: University of Chicago Press), 613.

[46] TDNT, 5:102.

[47] Gary, "The Pastor as Teacher," April 5, 1992.

[48] Hixon, "The Pastor as Teacher," April 5, 1992.

[49] J. Moulton and G. Milligan, *The Vocabulary of the Greek New Testament Illustrated from the Papyri and Other Non-Literary Sources* (Grand Rapids: Eerdmans, 1974), 332.

[50] *Greek-English Lexicon*, 659.

[51] Suhling, "The Pastor as Teacher," April 5, 1992.

So what alternative does Paul offer? What is the option? "But speaking the truth in love, let us grow in every way into Him who is the head—Christ" (Eph 4:15). Here's the clincher, Paul's definitive word on church growth: "to grow *up* into him" (KJV, emphasis added). Leonard Griffith considers the distinction between merely growing, and growing up. "Academic learning leads to knowledge, but not necessarily to maturity. Some adults with high IQ's remain psychologically children. This is the difference between 'growing' and 'growing up.' Is the church seeking only to grow or is it growing up?"[52]

Pastor Atkinson notes that this may seem idealistic since so few churches have attained such maturity. What may be implied is that *too few pastors function as teachers.*

> Whether by misguided expectations of church members
> or his own misinterpretation of his pastoral role, pastors
> are not fulfilling their calling as equippers of the saints. By
> directing qualitative attention to discipleship, a pastor's
> teaching ministry in the church can lead the church to at-
> tain the Lord's intended purpose for his Body, that is, unity
> and spiritual maturity. Spiritual maturity is the natural
> result of a biblical understanding of the role of the pastor as
> teacher.[53]

Missionary Gary warns that spiritual growth in the church is hindered if the pastor-teacher is too crowd-oriented. "The pastor should follow Jesus' example of focusing on small groups, and giving in-depth training. Jesus never took pride in huge crowds that followed him. He emphasized quality over numbers."[54]

Churches grow up into Christ by "speaking the truth in love" (Eph 4:15a). The *truth* Paul refers to is the gospel, but "speaking the truth" involves more than saying religious words. Believers cannot *speak* the truth until they *experientially know* the truth.[55] Believers cannot speak the truth effectively until they exercise the truth in

---

[52] L. G., *Ephesians: A Positive Affirmation* (Waco: Word, 1975), 87.

[53] Atkinson, "The Pastor as Teacher," April 5, 1992.

[54] Gary, "The Pastor as Teacher," April 5, 1992.

[55] This is the basic distinction between head knowledge, *gnosis*, of religious information, which "puffs up," "makes proud" (1 Cor 8:1), and heart knowledge, *epignosis*,
of life and Life-Giver, which gives wisdom.

daily living, solving problems biblically. The writer of Hebrews chided his readers on this very point:

> We have a great deal to say about this, and it's difficult to explain, since you have become slow to understand. For though by this time you ought to be teachers, you need someone to teach you again the basic principles of God's revelation. You need milk, not solid food. Now everyone who lives on milk is inexperienced with the message about righteousness, because he is an infant. But solid food is for the mature—for those whose senses have been trained to distinguish between good and evil. (Heb 5:11–14)

Those who personally know the Lord and have applied His Word to their lives are well qualified to speak the truth. But how should the truth be spoken? What shall be the manner of our speaking? Paul says believers are to "speak the truth *in love.*" Pastor Suhling comments, "Teaching the believer is not a matter of teaching facts in a cold manner. The truth must be modeled and bathed in the warm embrace of Christlike love."[56]

Some speak the truth but have no love. They tend to be mean-spirited, dogmatic, angry people who use "the truth" like a weapon to intimidate others. They have confused personal arrogance with confidence in the Lord. Others love but have little appreciation for or experience with "the truth" as objective reality. They tend to be happy-go-lucky, compliant people who just want everyone to be happy and contented. They cannot understand why anyone would want to fight over something as cold and inflexible as "objective truth." They have confused cheerful compromise with the Lord's harmony.

Paul says the truly mature in the Lord speak the truth in love. They speak the truth warmly, carefully, patiently, kindly. They love with integrity, honesty, and sincerity. Warm, not harsh. Caring, not hurting. Lifting, not condemning. This was the manner of Jesus' teaching, fulfilling the prophecy of Isaiah: "He will not break a bruised reed, and He will not put out a smoldering wick; He will faithfully bring justice" (Isa 42:3; cf. Matt 12:20). Jesus spoke the truth with love and so should all of us who carry His name. Albert Barnes underscored the importance of the balance between truth and love. "[One] has

---

[56] Suhling, "The Pastor as Teacher," April 5, 1992.

done about half his work in convincing another of error who has first convinced him that he loves him; and if he does not do that he may argue to the hour of his death and make no progress in convincing him."[57] The result, as we have already noted, is that we will "grow in every way into Him who is the head—Christ" (Eph 4:15).

And finally, Paul concludes, "From Him the whole body, fitted and knit together by every supporting ligament, promotes the growth of the body for building up itself in love by the proper working of each individual part" (Eph 4:16). The body grows because of Christ ("From Him"). The body strengthens itself ("grows and builds itself up," NIV) by being held together, unified. This is an ongoing process. How is this accomplished? By having "each part of the body function properly in its own sphere."[58]

The equipping pastor-teacher builds relationships among the members of his congregation. These relationships, says missionary Brady, "must be genuine relationships built on honest loving communication that builds a team that works together."[59] Pastor Washburn writes, "As the pastor-teacher focuses himself on preparing God's people individually, lovingly, encouragingly, the body of Christ that he serves will build 'itself' up into the fullness of Christ our Lord."[60]

The Challenge of the Pastor-Teacher

Paul finally described the challenge that pastor-teachers face as they endeavor to fulfill their task: hardened Gentiles. These pagans had hardened their hearts toward God, separating them from life in Him. They could not fathom what life in the Lord might mean, because they had been "darkened in their understanding" (Eph 4:18). Because they had lost all sensitivity for spiritual things, they indulged themselves in every kind of sensual impurity. Yet their indulging did not satisfy them, so they became lost in an ever-increasing cycle of continual lust for more (Eph 4:19). "Therefore, I say this and testify

---

[57] A. Barnes, *Barnes on the New Testament: Ephesians, Philippians and Colossians* (Grand Rapids: Baker, 1949), 82.

[58] Robertson, *Word Pictures,* 539.

[59] Brady, "The Pastor as Teacher," April 5, 1992.

[60] S. Washburn, "The Pastor as Teacher," April 5, 1992.

in the Lord: You should no longer walk as the Gentiles walk, in the futility of their thoughts" (Eph 4:17).

The community where you serve or will serve as pastor-teacher is populated with the same kind of sensual, self-serving Gentiles that lived in Ephesus. American culture is Greek in that Americans tend to compartmentalize their lives into separate areas: home and family, work, school, recreation, friends. American Christians add the compartment of "church," but many fail to see the connection between what they say and do at church and the other compartments of life. These carnal Christians have not yet grown into a biblical mind-set in which the Lord is at the center of life, so that all of life, every compartment, revolves around Him. So, just as in Corinth and Ephesus, sexual perversion, violence, abuse, and petty power plays face pastor-teachers at every turn. False teachers, magicians, and demagogues feed on the church, often from within the body itself. Greek compartmentalization is common in churches, dividing the body into self-serving blocks of power: Sunday school, missions, music, age groups, deacons, committees, and special interests. Pastor-teachers who emphasize unity of the whole body can be perceived as self-serving. The logic of "turf protectors"[61] goes like this: "Leaders who won't promote my interests over the interests of other groups are really acting against me." If several lay leaders fall prey to this line of reasoning and find themselves at cross purposes with one another, there is no way pastor-teachers can succeed. They are always seen as "self-serving" by one group or another. This fragmentation truly pulls pastor-teachers to pieces as each part demands attention and promotion over the others and attacks them when their demands are not satisfied. Churches grow increasingly unteachable as Satan builds wedges between pastor-teachers and their congregations. This is why the writer of Hebrews cautioned church members, "Obey your leaders and submit to them, for they keep watch over your souls as those who will give an account, so

---

[61] "Turf protectors" are leaders who use whatever power they have to promote their agenda, their organization, their committee, their class—to the detriment of others and the fragmentation of the church. Some do this unintentionally and may consider themselves nothing more than committed workers. Others use their organizations as a means of promoting their own ego and widening their influence.

that they can do this with joy and not with grief, for that would be unprofitable for you" (Heb 13:17).

This is in no way a license for pastor-teachers to lord it over their congregations. Jesus' directive stands: "You know that the rulers of the Gentiles dominate them, and the men of high position exercise power over them. It must not be like that among you. On the contrary, whoever wants to become great among you must be your servant, and whoever wants to be first among you must be your slave" (Matt 20:25–27).

The apostle Peter further underscores this principle: "*Shepherd* God's flock among you, not overseeing out of compulsion but freely, according to God's will . . . *not lording it over* those entrusted to you, but *being examples* to the flock" (1 Pet 5:2–3, emphasis added). When leaders function as true pastor-teachers rather than self-serving tyrants, and when the congregation submits to the leadership of the pastor-teacher rather than assuming ill motives behind every move, then the body is free to progress. But such an ideal state is seldom achieved for very long. Satan prowls "around like a roaring lion, looking for anyone he can devour" (1 Pet 5:8b). Misunderstandings, rumors, and malicious perceptions persist even under the best pastor-teachers. Therefore, Peter warns us to "keep a cool head" and to "stay alert" (1 Pet 5:8a *The Message*).

As with the Ephesians, Paul tells us to "take up the full armor of God, so that you may be able to resist in the evil day, and having prepared everything, to take your stand" (Eph 6:13). Equipping the saints to conduct effective ministry operations is not safe work. Satan follows the adage, "Strike the shepherd, and the sheep will be scattered" (Zech 13:7). He is not so much concerned with our large crowds and fancy buildings—so long, that is, as the crowds are self-satisfied and passive. But begin to equip believers for spiritually empowered ministry, and he will attack. Fortunately, you are not alone.

Are All Ministers Pastor-Teachers?

This chapter has focused on those called by God to be undershepherd, or pastor, of a local congregation. Yet there are lessons here for any who are called to lead or teach in the church, whether they be vocational or lay ministers, ordained or not.

Ministers of education are called to oversee the various educational programs of churches. *Effective* ministers of education will serve churches as pastor-teachers, protecting their educational flocks and teaching workers at all levels of leadership how to use their gifts more effectively. Ministers of music, youth, children, counseling, or recreation can all benefit from Paul's view of the pastor-teacher. Our first calling is to minister: to protect (pastor) and instruct (teacher). Our secondary calling is to an area of specialization.

All leaders in the church—deacons, Sunday school teachers, committee chairmen, or program directors—would serve more effectively if they saw themselves as *pastor-teachers* of the groups they lead. The church grows stronger as lay pastor-teachers learn how to give and take with other leaders in the church. As each leader emphasizes the whole above his or her own small area, he or she becomes a "supporting ligament" that helps the whole to be built up (Eph 4:16). Turf protectors care only for their own areas and use whatever means to build them up, even to the detriment of other areas and the whole. This is the work of the flesh ("selfish ambition, dissensions, factions," Gal 5:20) born in the heart of Satan to hinder the Lord's work through His churches.

In light of the rampant "me first" philosophy in our society, the greatest challenges facing pastor-teachers today are in helping lay leaders understand the destructiveness of self-serving turf wars and in leading believers to love one another in the practical day-to-day life of the church.

Summary

Paul laid out the character, the work, and the fruit of the pastor-teacher: as to character, becoming like Christ; as to work, enabling believers to minister by winning them, protecting them, and instructing them; as to fruit, promoting spiritual maturity in learners particularly and in the church at large.

We complete Paul's treatise on healthy church growth, the goal of the pastor-teacher, with these observations. Healthy church growth can be defined as believers, equipped to work together in the ministry, carrying out the Great Commission, reaching our world for Christ, and "teaching them to observe everything" Jesus commanded (Matt 28:20). It requires churches that live out the truth of the gospel in loving ministry, devoid of petty strife or division, because leaders and those being led are growing together into Christ.

When I fly to Moscow, Russia, a navigator guides the aircraft on our first leg from Fort Worth to London by taking bearings from the North Star. We never reach the North Star, but we have, so far, always reached London, and eventually home again. So Paul has given us a North Star for pastor-teachers to navigate congregations toward healthy church growth. We may never reach the ideal he has given us. But by properly charting our course, we can overcome the turbulence of immaturity, the storms of sensuality, and the lightning bolts of conflict and division. Thus, we can make our way safely home, becoming congregations that possess the qualities of Jesus, sharing those qualities in ministry with one another, the local community, and the world at large. Oh, Lord Jesus, make it so!

Discussion Questions

1. What is your reaction to the description of the pastor-teacher given in this chapter? How does Paul's model of the pastor-teacher compare to "secular" models of leadership?
2. Discuss the importance of perseverance in the ministry of the pastor-teacher. How is perseverance related to the pastor-teacher's goal?
3. Compare your view of teaching to Paul's view of teaching. How would others describe your teaching?
4. What will your ministry look like in 10 years if you follow your current pattern of leadership? What suggestions from the pastors quoted in this chapter speak to your need to grow as a pastor-teacher?

Bibliography[62]

Barclay, William. *The Mind of St. Paul*. London: Collins Clear-Type Press, 1958.

---

[62] The older publication dates reflect both the libraries of pastors in 1992 as well as classical writings on the subject.

Barnes, Albert. *Barnes on the New Testament: Ephesians, Philippians and Colossians.* Grand Rapids: Baker, 1949.

Greek-English Lexicon of the New Testament and Other Early Christian Literature. 2nd English ed. Revised and augmented by E. Wilbur Gingrich and Frederick W. Danker from Walter Bauer's 5th ed. Chicago: University of Chicago Press, 1968.

Guthrie, D., and J. A. Motyer, *The New Bible Commentary: Revised.* Grand Rapids: Eerdmans, 1970.

Longenecker, Richard. *The Ministry and Message of Paul.* Grand Rapids: Zondervan, 1971.

Meyer, F. B. *Paul: Servant of Jesus Christ.* London: Lakeland, 1968.

Moody, Dale. *Christ and the Church.* Grand Rapids: Eerdmans, 1963.

Mullins, E. Y. *Studies in Ephesians.* Nashville: Sunday School Board of the Southern Baptist Convention, 1935.

Rienecker, Fritz. *Linguistic Key to the New Testament.* Trans. and ed. Cleon L. Rogers Jr. Grand Rapids: Zondervan, 1980.

Robertson, A. T. *Word Pictures in the New Testament.* Vol. 5. Nashville: Broadman, 1931.

Simpson, E. K. "Commentary on the Epistle of the Ephesians." *Ephesians and Colossians. NICNT,* vol. 9. Grand Rapids: Eerdmans, 1980.

Smart, James. *Teaching Ministry of the Church.* Philadelphia: Westminster, 1954.

Theological Dictionary of the New Testament. Vol. 2. Ed. Gerhard Kittel and Gerhard Friedrich, trans. and ed. Geoffrey W. Bromiley. Grand Rapids: Eerdmans, 1964.

Vaughan, W. Curtis. *The Letter to the Ephesians.* Nashville: Convention, 1963.

Wiersbe, Warren W. *Be Rich: Are You Losing the Things That Money Can't Buy?* Wheaton, IL: SP Publications, 1980.

Willard, Dallas. *The Spirit of the Disciplines: Understanding How God Changes Lives.* San Francisco: Harper and Row, 1988.

Suggested Reading

Browning, R. L. *The Pastor as Religious Educator.* Birmingham: Religious Education Press, 1989.

Hull, Bill. *The Disciple Making Pastor.* Baker, 2004.

Sheip, Earl E., and Ronald H. Sunderland. *The Pastor as Teacher*. New York: Pilgrim, 1988.

Zuck, Roy B. *Teaching as Paul Taught*. Eugene, OR: Wipf & Stock, 2003.

Chapter 11

THE GOAL OF CHRISTIAN EDUCATION: CHRISTLIKENESS

Rick Yount

Christ in you, the hope of glory
(Col 1:27)

To Be like Christ

To be like Christ. What a goal! Strong *and* gentle. Just *and* loving. Truthful *and* merciful. Demanding *and* accepting. No one but Jesus has blended the rod and the staff so well. Even Paul, given to religious devotion as much as any man of his time, fully committed to the exalted Christ who saved him and called him as an apostle to the Gentiles, strained to grow toward Christlikeness. We are in a journey, says Paul. More like the Lord today than yesterday. Press on to be more like Him tomorrow. But in the process, Paul says, live up to what you've attained.

To lead others to be like Christ. What a calling! Christian teachers are far more than transmitters of lessons from quarterly to class. Our calling is to help learners grow toward Christlikeness. Paul writes of Christ, "We proclaim Him, warning and teaching everyone with all wisdom, so that we may present everyone mature in Christ. I labor for this, striving with His strength that works powerfully in me" (Col 1:28–29).

There will be plenty of time spent with commentaries, notes, illustrations, stories, and examples. But the goal of our teaching in Christ is nothing short of Christlikeness in our learners. How do we begin? How do we proceed? How do we know if we're making progress?

The Christian Teachers' Triad: Then and Now

This chapter uses the Christian Teachers' Triad to frame a synergistic perspective on teaching toward Christlikeness. I developed the triad for the original edition of this text, drawing from both lectures and experiences in principles of teaching and educational psychology classes. My intent was to move away from educational systems that focus solely on knowing and thinking (cognitive theories), or personal valuing (humanistic theories), or competent doing (behavioral theories). Rather, I sought a way to bring all three systems together, simultaneously, in a single perspective. My first formal attempt at the synergism was the original chapter, written in 1994.

During 1995, I used the triad to pull together disparate chapters on learning theories—Skinner's behaviorism, Bandura's observational learning, Bruner's discovery learning, information processing, and Maslow's humanistic learning—into harmony for *Created to Learn*. It was about that time, in class and conference settings, I began defining profiles for thinkers, feelers, and doers. While leading a teachers' conference at Glorieta Conference Center, I described the three profiles. Without a clue about what might happen, I decided to ask participants to group themselves physically in three areas of the room by these labels. Slowly the 60 participants began moving in three directions, the whole breaking down into single participants, and then reforming into three different groups. The groups were roughly equal in size, approximately 20 per group. Most husbands found themselves in a group different from their wives. Over the next hour, as I asked questions about teaching preferences, each group displayed distinct—*and often vocal*—attitudes about the nature of learning, teaching, and spiritual growth.

I have experimented with many groups since that early conference: classes here at Southwestern, seminars at professional meetings, and many conferences. Specific groups included a seminar with 30 Fort Worth public school music teachers, a conference of 25 Deaf pastors and missionaries at IMB headquarters in Richmond, and still another conference of 300 African-American Sunday school teachers in Oklahoma City. I began annual teaching trips to the former Soviet Union in 1996 and conducted similar experiments with classes of Ukrainian, Russian, and Kyrgyz pastors. Regardless of the group, people gathered themselves in roughly the same way, reflecting the same three perspectives.

Wherever I find a group of students, whenever I define thinker, feeler, and doer characteristics, the groupings they themselves form always share the same common characteristics, the same likes and dislikes, the same desires for meaningful Bible study. But the three disagree sharply across spheres.

The groups are generally the same size—the larger the class or conference, the more equal the groups. The thinkers group commonly contains more men than women, but there are always women in the group. The feelers group commonly contains more women than men, but there are always men in the group. The doers group contains men and women in roughly equal numbers.

Whenever we lead a group of learners, we can be sure that all three spheres of learning are present. Since each sphere learns differently from the others, this presents a problem. Worse yet, we teachers tend to teach out of our own preferred sphere, and so—and this was the most startling discovery—even when we teach perfectly well in our preferred sphere, we can still fail to engage two-thirds of our class or congregation *every time we teach.*

What do we do to stretch ourselves into better balance? How do we engage all three spheres of learners sitting in our classrooms? This aching passion drove the writing of *Called to Teach* (1999), which used the triad as its beginning point and foundation. Ten years of teaching Russian and Ukrainian students, four to six weeks each year, confirmed the three spheres were as volatile there as here. I found the same on a teaching trip to Sao Paulo and Brazilia, Brazil. These discoveries led to *Called to Reach: Equipping Cross-Cultural Disciplers* (2007), in which both Disciplers' Model and Christian Teachers' Triad carry readers through principles for connecting with students of a language and culture not our own.

For those of you familiar with these three books or the first edition of our text, this updated chapter will be review. But it was here the triad first got its start. And for those of you unfamiliar with educational psychology, the updated chapter will introduce you to the breadth, depth, height, and complexity of helping learners grow toward Christlikeness.

The Triad of Life

The three intersecting circles at left represent four areas of human life—three psychological spheres, and, at center, the spiritual. Each sphere is connected to the other two but develops in its own way.

Each sphere can be any size and can overlap the others in an infinite number of combinations. The figure represents an ideal: all three circles are the same size, and all three intersect equally.[1] The three psychological spheres represented by this triad reflect processes of thinking, valuing, and doing skillfully. Let's look at each of these.

Thinking

The first circle represents the rational—what educational psychologists call the *cognitive*—sphere of life: knowing, conceptualizing, problem-solving, analyzing, synthesizing, evaluating. Without a clear focus on "correctly teaching the word of truth" (2 Tim 2:15), we open our learners to deception and delusion. The rational confronts John 3:16 with *conceptual* (objective) questions: What did God do when He *loved* the world? What is the *world* that He loved? What does it mean to *believe* in His Son? What kind of *life* do we obtain through this belief? What does *eternal* add to this life?

Jesus said, "Do not judge, so that you won't be judged" (Matt 7:1). What did Jesus mean by *judge*? Are we not to have an opinion? Are we to go through life without evaluating ideas, priorities, and actions? The apostle John writes, "Test the spirits to see whether they

---

[1] Were we to draw the triad depicting Jesus, we would see all three spheres perfectly overlapped, forming a seamless, single whole.

are from God, because many false prophets have gone out into the world" (1 John 4:1). Is this testing not a judgment? Did Jesus and John disagree? Is this a contradiction? Just what did Jesus mean by "[Do not] judge"? These are rational questions, which we will delve into a little later.

The classic hymn "Come Thou Fount of Every Blessing" introduces the second verse with the words: "Here I raise my Ebenezer." *What is an Ebenezer?*[2] I seldom asked the question until I began interpreting for Deaf worshippers. The second phrase of the second verse helps clarify the meaning: "Hither by Thy help I'm come." The sense of the verse is, "Here I raise my praise to the Lord, for, right up to now, He has always been my source of help." The hymn was a favorite for years, but until I studied the meaning of the words, I didn't understand what I was singing.

If learners grow rationally in the Lord, it is because they move beyond mere words to clear meanings, beyond pat answers to cogent principles. None of us can grow "in every way into Him who is the head—Christ" (Eph 4:15) without a clear understanding of what God's Word means.

Feeling and Valuing

The second circle represents the emotional—what educational psychologists call the *affective*—sphere of life: listening, sharing, loving, valuing, prioritizing, and reflecting spiritual truths in daily life. Scripture uses the word *heart* to refer to both "mind"[3] and "emotion." But the Bible often uses the term to refer specifically to the affective elements of life. "A glad heart makes a cheerful countenance, but by sorrow of heart the spirit is broken" (Prov 15:13). Here "heart" refers to feeling happy or depressed.

---

[2] "Afterwards, Samuel took a stone and set it upright between Mizpah and Shen. He named it *Ebenezer* [Rock of Help], explaining, 'The LORD has helped us to this point'" (1 Sam 7:12).

[3] "With the heart one believes, resulting in righteousness" (Rom 10:10). Strong's number 2588 *kardia* (kar-dee'-ah); "the heart, i.e. (figuratively) the *thoughts* or *feelings* (*mind*)."

The emotional confronts John 3:16 with *personal* (subjective) questions: How has God loved *you*? How have *you* learned to believe in Jesus Christ? What has been the result in *your own life*? How has *your life changed* through your relationship with Jesus? How have *you experienced* "God's kind of life" since you gave your life to Him?

King David writes, "I have treasured Your word in my heart so that I may not sin against You" (Ps. 119:11). This was David's way of reflecting his heartfelt commitment to live by God's Word. While he seriously failed to live up to it, he passionately desired to do so. He displayed this passion in his excessive dance before the Lord (2 Sam 6:16–22) and in his deep grief when confronted by his sin (2 Sam 12:13–20). His heart-centered response was to repent and to embrace his Lord. It may be due to these qualities that Samuel declared this future adulterer and murderer "a man after his [God's] own heart" (1 Sam 13:14 KJV).

If learners grow emotionally in the Lord, it is because they move beyond historical facts to present experiences, from cold doctrine to warm lifestyle. Further, learners will grow as they move from surface feelings to unrestrained devotion to the Lord, from self-centered agendas to God's priorities for us. None of us can grow "in every way into Him who is the head—Christ" (Eph 4:15) without a humble, loving embrace of the Lord and His ways.

Doing

The third circle represents the doing or skill sphere of life—what educational psychologists call the *behavioral*. Here we convert ideas and values into tangible actions. Without a willingness to obey Jesus' declaration—"hears these words of Mine and acts on them" (Matt 7:24)—we open ourselves and our learners to great danger. Those who only hear Jesus' words and fail to act on them will be swept away by life's storms (vv. 26–27). Hearing alone is not enough.

The behavioral confronts John 3:16 with competent *ministry outcomes*: How can I love people in my world this next week? How well will I depend on the Lord this week as I face problems, frustrations, disappointments, and temptations? What are ways I can exercise my love skillfully, exercising my dependence on God at work and at home? What evidence of God's tangible actions in our lives do we provide one another week by week as we report on our faithful actions and God's faithful blessing?

We may clearly understand "biblical love," but *do we love?* We may love missions, but *do we support missions* with personal time, talent, and money? We can believe in forgiveness with all our hearts, but *do we forgive?* What we do with our lives, what we do in our lives, is a window on who we are. Jesus said, "Beware of false prophets. . . . You'll recognize them by their fruit. Are grapes gathered from thornbushes or figs from thistles? In the same way, every good tree produces good fruit, but a bad tree produces bad fruit . . . for a tree is known by its fruit" (Matt 7:15–17; 12:33).

If learners grow behaviorally, skillfully, in the Lord, it is because they move beyond words and feelings to ministry actions, from high-sounding word magic[4] and superficial feelings to disciplined behavior. Further, learners will grow as they eliminate old bad habits and practice new good habits. None of us can grow "in every way into Him who is the head—Christ" (Eph 4:15) without a dedicated, action-oriented obedience to put Jesus' words into practice.

In chapter 10, we established the apostle Paul's view of the work of the pastor-teacher: "for the *training of the saints in the work of ministry*, to build up the body of Christ" (Eph 4:12, emphasis added). Such training includes teaching learners and followers to know and think correctly (rational, cognitive sphere) and to embrace joyfully the attitudes and values set before us (emotional, affective sphere). But the proof, the verification, the witness, the confirmation that true preparation has been accomplished is found in service itself, in ministry, in doing what God has called us to do.

The Distortion of Imbalance

The problem, of course, is that God calls us to prepare *people*. People do not come to us prepackaged and preequipped to learn

---

[4] *Word magic* refers to statements that sound important but are actually empty: "If we truly believe, then we will walk forever in His steps!" "We must see people with God's eyes!" Statements like these draw hearty amens, but what do they mean?

and serve. They do not come spin-balanced and ready to roll. Every person tends toward one of the three spheres of the triad. Some emphasize the rational, others the emotional, and still others the behavioral. But imbalance in life, just as in automobiles, causes vibration and eventual breakdown.

While I want to be careful about making broad generalizations, I am bound to tell you what I find in class and conference groupings. Whether in Fort Worth, Texas, or Bishkek, Kyrgyzstan, I find adult learners—pastors, missionaries, seminary students—repeating the same kinds of perspectives and attitudes again and again.

Thinkers

Learners who emphasize the rational over emotional or behavioral elements are thinkers. Thinkers generally prefer theologically sound hymns over foot-tappin' choruses. They prefer factual and conceptual questions over personal ones. They like well-organized lectures more than group discussions—particularly if the discussion "slogs through" people's feelings and personal experiences more than the Scripture. Thinkers like studies that are deep, profound, and challenging. They actually enjoy grappling with Greek and Hebrew. Context is important, both historical and theological. They thrive on conducting word studies or making comparisons and contrasts among biblical concepts. Distilling biblical principles. Considering various (theoretical) applications. They enjoy creating relationships among ideas in the passage more than others in the class. Cold, analytical classrooms are welcome and safe; warm, superficial classrooms can be dangerous—one never knows when a rabbit will be chased[5] or an overly personal story shared. Thinkers keep their focus on "thus saith the Lord" and tend to define learning itself as primarily conceptual and rich in content. The classrooms of thinkers reflect the ambiance of an old library, lined with great books and furnished with overstuffed chairs, where scholars engage inquiring minds with great truths.

---

[5] "Chasing rabbits" refers to leaving the main point of the study to venture off in tangential pursuits. The term *rabbit trails* is also used. For thinkers, rabbits are usually a waste of time because they seldom support the points being made in the study.

Cold Intellectualism

Such an approach, *taken to extreme*, produces a purely academic Bible study process that focuses on the rational while dismissing the emotional and behavioral. In this environment we find ourselves immersed in cold, rather dry, impersonal abstraction. While such learning may change our thinking, it can make little or no difference in the way we live (which, by the way, rarely bothers thinkers at all).

It is one thing to understand honesty but quite another to value honesty or actually to be honest. It is one thing to understand the plan of salvation, quite another to be saved. One thing to understand Matt 28:19–20, quite another to support and engage in missions. Bible knowledge, doctrinal understanding, Christian principles, and spiritual concepts will lead to spiritual pride unless we integrate them into personal attitudes and actions (1 Cor 8:1–3).

Feelers

Learners who emphasize the emotional over rational or behavioral elements are feelers. They focus on feelings, attitudes, values, and personal experiences. Feelers prefer freewheeling discussions over structured lectures, especially if the discussions engage the lives of learners and touch the heart. Feelers enjoy giving testimonies and hearing the testimonies of others. They want learning to be fun and spontaneous, not heavily structured with explanations of terms or historical background. Feelers want their classroom to be friendly, warm, accepting, and never threatening. Feelers care more about people than principles. More about experiences than teaching points. More passion and less analysis, please. And they consider their relationships with other learners far more important than relations among ideas. And if teachers do not "finish the lessons," it is no problem so long as "we've shared our lives in meaningful ways." Feelers define learning itself as emotional, celebrative, liberating, and warm. The classrooms of feelers reflect the ambiance of evening campfires, hand-holding, and "Kumbaya," where counselors love the campers unconditionally, hoping they will understand and practice what they've so deeply enjoyed.

Superficial Emotionalism

Such an approach, *taken to extreme*, produces a purely personal Bible study process that focuses on the emotional while dismissing the rational and behavioral. In this environment we find ourselves immersed in warm, interactive, lighthearted feel-good. Subjective relevance trumps objective meaning. The Bible means *what it means to me*. Learning is superficial and self-centered. While such learning produces a momentary emotional high ("fun and excitement"), it can make little or no difference in the way we live (which, by the way, may not bother feelers at all). Worse, such an extremely subjective process, over time, may well lead to deception and delusion.

It is one thing to get excited about a mission trip but quite another to understand its purpose or develop the skills to help others. It is one thing to "share an experience" about faith, quite another to differentiate between "faith" and "presumption." One thing to volunteer freely to mow a widow's lawn, quite another to complete the task and do it well. Joining a group, sharing experiences, having fun, getting excited, letting go, and opening up will lead to spiritual pride unless we graft these emotions into biblical meanings and Christian actions.

Doers

Learners who emphasize the behavioral over rational or emotional elements are doers. Doers focus on practical, tangible outcomes for learning: What are we going to do with this? How can we use it? How can we live and work more effectively? As such, doers are passionately utilitarian. They eschew the paralysis of analysis of thinkers—preferring one clear application that learners can actually make during the week to five "possible applications" that never seem to be done. Likewise, they dislike the superficial wandering of feelers as woefully inefficient. While sessions may begin with a concept or personal experience, doers push toward realistic competence, the mastery of life, and ministry skills.

Doers keep their focus on "What doth hinder thee?" and tend to define learning itself as practical, efficient, and focused. The classrooms of doers reflect the ambiance of busy laboratories and workshops, where engineers convert theory and passion into life practice through ongoing action-oriented projects.

Burnout

Such an approach, *taken to extreme*, produces an action-oriented Bible study process that focuses on the behavioral while dismissing the emotional and rational. In this environment we find ourselves immersed in mindless, unfeeling busyness—one ministry project after another, which can lead eventually to ritual and exhaustion. While such learning may engage us in practical ministry, at least for a moment, it can make little or no difference in the way we live (which, by the way,  Exhausting Busyness rarely bothers doers at all). Without understanding the why of ministry, without personally owning the ministry, we simply go through the motions until we burn out and give up.

Striking a Balance

So here is our dilemma as teachers and teacher-trainers: an effective teaching ministry requires thinking, but too much focus on thinking leads to a cold, idealistic intellectualism. An effective teaching ministry requires positive feelings toward the class, the content, and the teacher, but too much focus on feelings leads to mindless, sentimental, impractical fluff. An effective teaching ministry requires skillful doing, but too much focus on doing leads to mindless, unfeeling ritual.

The answer to this dilemma is to balance the rational, emotional, and behavioral elements of our own Christian growth as teachers as well as our teaching. Develop biblical concepts, embrace Christian values, engage in spiritual activities. Proper understanding provides the foundation for biblical values and ministry. Personally embraced biblical values inject life into biblical exegesis and ministry practice. Christ-centered ministry builds the bridge between Bible study (concepts and values) and the world of people in need.

Making this move toward balance is both frightening and difficult, and it requires intentional effort: for thinkers—to embrace personal emotion and practical action; for feelers—to embrace scholarly analysis and practical action; and for doers—to embrace scholarly analysis and personal emotion. And yet this intentional pain is necessary if any of us would succeed at engaging every learner in our classrooms. It should be no surprise, then, that the Master Teacher reflected the triad in His own teaching ministry.

The Triad of Jesus the Teacher

Jesus reflected this triad of rational, emotional, and behavioral elements in His ministry. Jesus was **a prophet** (Matt 13:57; 21:11; Luke 24:19; John 6:14), proclaiming the kingdom of God. He used stories and illustrations to explain the kingdom of heaven. He represented God the Father to the people and proclaimed the Word of God. As prophet, Jesus focused on the objective element of faith.

Jesus was a **priest** (Heb 3:1; 4:14). He loved people and gave His life for others. He healed their sicknesses and calmed their fears. He ministered to them. He moved among the people and lifted them to the Father. As priest, Jesus focused on the subjective element of faith.

Jesus was **king** (Mark 15:2; Luke 23:3; John 18:37; Acts 17:7). He chose 12 apprentices and trained them for action (Matt 10). He sent His followers into the whole world to "make disciples of all nations, baptizing them . . . and teaching them to obey everything I have commanded you" (Matt 28:19–20). He is our Leader, our Lord. He called us to action (Matt 5–7; John 17:20) and taught that our fruit (actions) exhibits our roots (concepts, values) (Matt 7:16–17). Our spiritual wisdom is shown in how we practice His words—not by how well we understand them or value them (Matt 7:24–27).

Jesus demonstrated in His teaching ministry and life the balance we raise as our standard. He is our Model, our Guide, and our Helper as we seek to emulate this balance in our own life and ministry.

The External Influence of the Teacher

How do we provide a learning environment that permits balanced growth in the rational, emotional, and behavioral spheres of life? How do we help learners think clearly, or appreciate warmly, or put into practice skillfully? Here are some practical suggestions.

Helping Learners Think Clearly

A little boy sat in his Sunday school class listening to his teacher intently. She asked, "What is gray, has a furry tail, and stores nuts for the winter?" The little boy thought for a moment and then said, "Well, it sounds like a squirrel, but I'll say Jesus Christ." He was not being irreverent. He was doing his best to answer the teacher's question. And it seemed to him that "Jesus Christ" was the answer to most of her questions. How can we help our learners to think clearly? We will do well if we focus on the meaning of concepts, ask conceptual questions, pose problems, and provide meaningful examples. Let's look more closely at each of these.

Concepts versus Words. What does the word *run* mean? Here are some sentences that use various meanings of the word *run:*

- Johnny runs (moves swiftly) to second base.
- Judy runs (manages) her business well.
- Tim runs (operates) a printing press.
- The congressman ran (campaigned) for office.
- Water always runs (flows) downhill.
- Jane has a run (defect) in her hose.
- Peter's team scored a run (score) in the second inning.
- Fido was kept in a nice dog run (an outdoor enclosure).

There is *one word*—run—with *several meanings*. Earlier in this chapter I asked you *several* questions about Jesus' statement, "Do not judge, or you too will be judged" (Matt 7:1). Jesus was condemning the nagging, carping, censorious spirit of the Pharisees and religious leaders of His time. He was saying that when we live with a judgmental spirit, we will be criticized by others. Citizens of the kingdom are to avoid the hypercritical, judgmental spirit of religious bigotry. It is not enough to say, "Jesus said, 'Don't judge.'" Unless we *explain what Jesus meant* by *judge*, we leave our learners to define the word for Him, and their definition of *judge* may not agree with Jesus' definition.

One day a student of mine led the class in a Bible study on "joy" (Gal 5:22). "Joy is one of the fruit of the Spirit. Joy is the kind of joy that only God can give. It's the kind of joy we'll experience in heaven. Ohhhh. The joy of the Lord is wonderful!" These words show that he had no clue about the meaning of *joy*. He talked about it, said nice words about it, and even expressed deep feeling. But his words were empty. He might have said something like this:

> Joy is similar to the concepts of fun, pleasure, and happiness. In fact, some Christians mistakenly believe that biblical joy means fun or happiness. Notice that all of these terms are emotional. The distinction is that inward joy is detached from life circumstances, while circumstances control fun, pleasure, and happiness. We discover joy in the dark times when we depend on the Lord rather than on circumstances. As we lean on Him, despite our surroundings, He produces a sense of overwhelming joy by his Spirit.

Go beyond words to meanings. Help learners avoid *eisegesis* (reading personal meanings into a passage, which produces heresy). Lead them to embrace *exegesis* (reading God's meaning out of a passage, which changes their perceptions).

Questions versus Answers. We help learners think clearly by asking more questions and giving fewer answers. When we give an answer, it may be little more than noise in the air because learners haven't invested in it. In one ear and out the other. Forgotten by Monday lunch. But when we ask a question, we drive learners into the Bible for answers. We confront them with a dilemma, and as a result, they process facts, define concepts, relate those concepts to the question, and formulate an answer. Along the way they may develop questions of their own—a sure sign that thinking is taking place. Evaluate their answers. Mold their responses into clear understanding. Help them discover God's answers to your questions.

Posing Problems versus Giving Reasons. We help learners think more by posing problems than by giving reasons. Giving five reasons "why Christians ought to forgive" leaves them with little more than sound bites. An understanding of "forgiveness" will better grow from a confrontation with a problem learners solve. "Based on our study this morning, how would you handle this situation?" Listen to their answers. Correct misunderstandings. Suggest alternatives. Lead the class to see the relevance of "biblical forgiveness" in a contemporary situation.

Examples versus Facts. Love is patient, kind; it does not envy, boast; it is not proud, rude, self-seeking, easily angered; it keeps no record of wrongs, does not delight in evil but rejoices with the truth (see 1 Cor 13:4–6). These are the facts of love. What do these facts mean? What is an *example* of patient? How do you *describe* kind? *Illustrate* envy and boasting. *Explain* proud, rude, self-seeking, and easily angered. *How* might I keep a record of wrongs? *Why* would anyone delight in evil, and *what is the truth* with which I am to rejoice?

The popular King James Version of Scripture uses 1611 English that is unfamiliar to most people today. "Charity suffereth long, and is kind; charity envieth not; charity vaunteth not itself, is not puffed up" (1 Cor 13:4 KJV). Unchurched learners will choke on the "eth" endings, and words like "suffereth," "vaunteth," and "puffed up." The New King James helps, bringing the beauty of the classic text into the twentieth century. It reads, "Love suffers long and is kind; love does not envy; love does not parade itself, is not puffed up." Even here, unchurched folks may strain at "suffers" and wonder why the Bible is talking about parades. The Holman Christian Study Bible reads, "Love is patient; love is kind. Love does not envy; is not boastful; is not conceited." *The Message* paraphrases the verse this way: "Love never gives up. Love cares more for others than for self. Love doesn't want what it doesn't have. Love doesn't strut, doesn't have a swelled head." While biblical purists wince at the casual feel of *The Message*, there is no argument that it conveys contemporary meaning much better than the old King James.

Still, even when using contemporary versions, we give attention to clear explanations of biblical meanings. Whatever translation of Scripture is used, focus on correctly translating the words on the page so that the Word, the message, comes through clearly. Paul said it this way: "Be diligent to present yourself approved to God, a worker who doesn't need to be ashamed, *correctly teaching the word of truth*" (2 Tim 2:15, emphasis added). This demands rational engagement with the text.

Helping Learners Feel, Respond, and Value

One day, years ago, I was having a cup of coffee with a pastor acquaintance. He told me of a boy who had come forward during the invitation. His parents were getting a divorce, he had no friends at school, his grades were bad—he just didn't know what to do. The pastor reported his response this way: "Son, I really don't care to hear about your problems. Do you know that you are a lost sinner? Do you know that if you die tonight without Jesus, you'll spend eternity in hell?" The boy looked at him with wide eyes, brimming with tears. His mouth fell open, and for a moment time stopped. Then he turned and ran out of the church. I was heartsick. The pastor was proud. "So I guess I put the fear of God in him!"

I never think of that boy without praying that the Lord will send someone to share the love of Jesus with him. The pastor was doctrinally correct, but he had not one ounce of care, concern, or compassion for the heartfelt needs of this 10-year-old boy.

Hearts are touched when learners inhabit an atmosphere of openness, warmth, and trust. So how do we create such a climate? We will make good progress toward emotional warmth in the classroom if we focus on sharing ourselves, sharing the experiences of class members, accepting them as they are (while helping them grow), using humor appropriately, and building trust. Let's look at each of these more closely.

Personal Experiences versus Wooden Stories. A good way to begin a session is to tell a story related to the subject. Curriculum materials provide suggestions for doing this: "Joan is a single mother, working two jobs" and the like. These are good suggestions but not necessarily the best material for any particular class. Fictitious testimonies, contrived case studies, and artificial anecdotes may do little to warm up your class. No matter how good they are, they are wooden, stilted, often forced because they do not relate to the life experiences of you or your class. Far better are stories that come from our own experiences or the experiences of learners. All of us have experiences of success and growth and victory in the Lord. As these experiences are shared, to the glory of God, the class is warmed by His presence and our praise of Him.

The Right versus the Spot. Teachers do not have the right to call on learners to confess their sins in front of the group—to put them on the spot—but some do so anyway. A seminary student of mine began his session this way: "How many of you haven't had a daily devotional this week?" There was a silent pause. "Just lift your hands." A long uncomfortable pause and some frowns. "Well now, I know there's someone in a class this size who hasn't had a regular time of Bible study and prayer this week. Remember, God is watching, and He knows who you are." The only response to the student's whip was several groans. Then, a young man in the back of the room bowed his head and slowly lifted his hand. The student teacher had no right to do this. It humiliated the learner. It angered the class. It certainly killed any sense of openness toward the student teacher. It is not for us to tear down our learners through guilt but to handle God's Word correctly (2 Tim 2:15). The Holy Spirit convicts people of sin (John 16:8), not teachers.

If the student had "earned the right" to ask that question—sharing his own struggles with having a daily quiet time—there would have been no problem. Look at the difference: "This past week I've not spent time in prayer and Bible study as I normally do. Things have gotten so busy and hectic, and I've let them push my devotional time aside. Are any of you struggling with this problem?" I know for a fact that several students would have nodded in agreement. "Let's see what we can discover that will help us give top priority to the Lord."

Such an approach increases openness. It warms the class because "we have a common struggle" and "we're working together" to find answers from God's Word. When we share ourselves, others are more likely to share as well. Earn the right.

Acceptance versus Judgment. We discussed Jesus' command "Do not judge, so that you won't be judged" earlier in the chapter. Jesus was condemning the carping, nagging, nit-picking, censorious spirit of the Pharisees. We will drift in this same direction, unless we pray through negative attitudes toward learners. "My people never want to pray." Or, "I can't get anyone to answer a question." Or, "Projects? I can't get anyone to do anything in my class!" I can only hope these teachers keep these opinions to themselves.

The disciples failed in many ways, but Jesus forgave them, loved them, and continued to teach them. Accept learners as they are. Love them, teach them, and encourage them to grow in the Lord. Some grow more slowly than others. Commitment level of some may never please us. But when our focus is accepting rather than judging, openness and warmth will blossom and bear fruit in spiritual growth.

Humor versus Solemnity. Humor opens up the emotions of a class. Gravity shuts them down. Paul was a great Christian philosopher. His letters are deep and often hard to understand.[6] Yet philosophical reasoning and theological expertise were not, for Paul, the evidence of Christ in our lives. It was rather the joy and peace we experience from the indwelling Christ.

- "Rejoice in hope; be patient in affliction; be persistent in prayer" (Rom 12:12).
- "For the kingdom of God is not eating and drinking, but righteousness, peace, and joy in the Holy Spirit" (Rom 14:17).
- "Now may the God of hope fill you with all joy and peace in believing, so that you may overflow with hope by the power of the Holy Spirit" (Rom 15:13).

---

[6] Even Peter had trouble understanding him (2 Pet 3:16)!

- "May you be strengthened with all power, according to His glorious might, for all endurance and patience, with joy giving thanks to the Father" (Col 1:11–12).

The Bible is a solemn book with a solemn message. We are wise to approach Scripture study with absolute reverence. But this reverence differs from the stoic, stern, dispassionate logic of the false teachers Paul opposed. Where the Spirit is free to produce fruit, there is joy (Gal 5:22).

The superserious has little warmth. The supersilly has little depth. While biblical joy is much more than good humor, the proper use of humor can both warm up and settle down a class. Humor can enhance the openness of class members, not just to one another but to God's Word as well. People who honestly laugh together can also honestly share together or pray together or weep together (see Rom 12:15). The natural use of humor enhances openness in the classroom.

Be sure the humor is positive and uplifting. Avoid crude or vulgar jokes, stories with double meanings, and even lighthearted pranks or gags. Humor misfires when it denigrates others or demeans the sacred task at hand. "Coarse and foolish talking or crude joking are not suitable, but rather giving thanks" (Eph 5:4).

Trust versus Guilt. Guilt is a strong motivator. Perhaps that is why so many immature leaders use it. It produces quick results but undermines trust, the glue that holds human relationships together. B. F. Skinner conducted many experiments in which he taught rats to run mazes. In some cases he used a positive reinforcer, food. In others he used punishment, electric shock. He found that electric shock motivated the rats to learn the maze faster than food. But the shock also taught the rats to fear the maze. Eventually, the rats refused to move, regardless of the degree of shock applied, even to the point of death.

Guilt is like an electric shock to the personality. It produces quick results but leads to fear in a class or congregation. Guilt is toxic to learners.

Where do we find Jesus, the Lord of lords, teaching this way? "For God did not send His Son into the world that He might condemn the world, but that the world might be saved through Him" (John 3:17).

Where do you find Paul, strong personality that he was, teaching this way? Paul's enemies in Corinth claimed he was strong in
his letters but weak in person (2 Cor 10:10). Paul responded by
pointing out his weakness: "You put up with it if someone enslaves
you, if someone devours you, if someone captures you, if someone
dominates you, or if someone hits you in the face. I say this to [our]
shame: we have been weak" (2 Cor 11:20–21). Rather, Paul loved
the church at Corinth and grieved over their problems: "For out of
an extremely troubled and anguished heart I wrote to you with many
tears—not that you should be hurt, but that you should know the
abundant love I have for you" (2 Cor 2:4). By his clear teaching and
firm but loving exhortation, Paul led the church at Corinth away
from her problems and into a more focused relationship with Christ.

Trust grows among people as they live, work, and pray together,
as they share needs together, as they forgive one another. Paul underscored this social element of the Christian faith:

> But now you must also put away all the following: anger
> [fury **toward others**], wrath [settled hatred **toward oth-
> ers**], malice [**wishing harm on others**], slander [demean-
> ing the character of **others**], and filthy language [abusive
> talk **toward others**] from your mouth. Therefore, God's
> chosen ones, holy and loved, put on heartfelt compassion
> [soft-heartedness **toward others**], kindness [helpful actions
> **toward others**], humility [right thinking **toward others**],
> gentleness [tenderness **toward others**], and patience [long-
> suffering **with others**], accepting **one another** and forgiving
> **one another** if anyone has a complaint **against another**.
> Just as the Lord has forgiven you, so also you must forgive.
> Above all, put on love—the **perfect bond of unity**. (Col
> 3:8,12–14)[7]

Paul's words are relational marching orders for pastors and teachers. When we keep in step with them, we find the level of trust
among members—and beyond this, openness of heart—dramatically
increased.

---

[7] All bracketed words and bold-face emphasis were added by the author.

Helping Learners Do Skillfully

Years ago I taught a Sunday school class for Deaf college students. One day I ran into Keith, a member of the class and a student at Gallaudet College, where he studied and I worked. During our conversation I asked him what he discovered during our study the previous Sunday. He shrugged his shoulders. "That was a long time ago." Yes, I agreed. It had been a few days since class. I asked again what he had learned. "We studied something in the Old Testament, right?" Actually, we studied a passage in Ephesians. "Ephesians! Right! I remember now!" So what did he discover? What did he learn? "I don't remember. That was a long time ago!" I had spent five or six hours preparing to teach. I had given the presentation all I had. Now, on Wednesday, he couldn't remember the first thing about what we'd studied. And since he did not remember the study, it was clear he was not living it out.

A Rational Approach to Doing. Facts cannot be "done." They just are. Further, learners cannot "do" biblical concepts where they live unless they understand them. We discussed this at length under "Helping Learners Think Clearly."

I had failed Keith in my teaching because I filled our time with 45 minutes of facts, with explanation. Asking questions and solving real-life problems during class time anchor Scripture in the minds of learners and build bridges into their lives. This seminal event, a chance meeting on campus, changed my view of teaching forever.

King

An Emotional Approach to Doing. Learners will more likely practice biblical concepts and values *outside the class* when they share personal "life experiences" with others *inside the class*. We discussed this sharing process at length under "Helping Learners Feel, Respond, and Value." Hearing tangible testimonies of day-to-day applications from *some* makes it more likely that *many* will "do" them as well. These two general approaches to learning—understanding concepts and appreciating values—lay a firm foundation for Christian action.

But there is a far more direct way to provoke Christian action outside of class.

An Action Approach to Doing: Assignments. The most direct way to encourage learners to do their lessons during the week is to make specific assignments. Assignments can vary in their intensity and scope: selected verses to read, specific questions to answer, a simple project, making entries in a journal, words to analyze, and the list goes on. Assignments can be done individually, in pairs, or in groups of various kinds. By giving learners things to do during the week, you give them the opportunity to learn from the Lord on their own. For details of how to plan various approaches to making assignments, see the end of chapter 13, "Planning to Teach."

Christ, the Center of the Triad

Teachers who model a thoughtful, passionate, skillful approach to life create the best environment for learning. This environment of thoughtful, passionate, skillful action is a veritable greenhouse for human growth. We have taken a Christian view of thinking-feeling-doing in this chapter, but the triadic balance need not be Christian. In the early days of the Russian revolution, Vladimir Ilyich Ulyanov, better known as Lenin, set up a state security agency known as the Cheka. The motto of the Cheka was triadic: "The Chekist is a man with a 'warm heart, a cool head, and clean hands.' "[8] The Cheka later morphed into the more familiar KGB, which carried on the triadic formula, as well as the twin symbols of shield—to defend the Revolution—and sword—to defeat its enemies. The first time I read these lines, a cold chill swept over me. I had been using the Christian Teachers' Triad in conferences for nearly 10 years, and now I read that its essential *head, heart, and hand* reflected the essence of the Soviet Secret Police? I could not form words to pray, so I simply groaned to God: What had I done? Then I saw it differently: the triad did not reflect the Chekist motto; the Chekist motto reflected God's fundamental design of man: *head, heart, hand.*

Notice that the triad forms a small triangle in the center where the three circles overlap. This is the seat of the will, the ego, the "I" of

---

[8] A. Christofer and V. Mitrokhin, *The Sword and the Shield: The Mitrokhin Archive and the Secret History of the K.G.B.* (New York: Basic, 1999), 23.

the personality. Those without Christ determine the course of life for themselves: what *I* think, what *I* value, what *I* choose to do. The nineteenth-century Russian Christian Dostoyevsky once wrote, "If God did not exist, everything would be permitted." This was the beginning point of existential philosophers like Nietzsche and Sartre: "God does not exist, so everything is permitted. Make your choices." By contrast Paul wrote, "But the natural man does not welcome what comes from God's Spirit, because it is foolishness to him; he is not able to know it since it is evaluated spiritually" (1 Cor 2:14).

After we accept Christ as Lord and Savior, He lives in us (Col 1:27). If 'I' continue to reign, determining for myself what 'I' think, what 'I' value, and what 'I' do, there will be little perceptible difference between us and the unredeemed around us. Jesus said, "If anyone wants to come with Me, he must deny himself, take up his cross daily, and follow Me" (Luke 9:23). Deny self. Follow Christ. This makes all the difference, for it engages Christ as Internal Teacher. Spiritual growth is learning how to let Jesus be Teacher and Lord, both learning from Him and obeying Him. Paul knew this: "I have been crucified with Christ; and I no longer live, but Christ lives in me. The life I now live in the flesh, I live by faith in the Son of God, who loved me and gave Himself for me" (Gal 2:19b–20). We provoke our learners to grow in the Lord as we teach them to depend on Him. "Christ in you" makes all the difference. Let's see how.

Earlier we looked at psychological elements of thinking-valuing-doing. Now we turn to the spiritual elements, energized by the Christ within. He does not force His way into our life spheres, nor does He dominate them. He gives us freedom to invite Him in or lock Him out. As we invite Him to lead us, to teach us, to mold us into what He desires, He helps us to think, to value, and to do—according to His will. "I stand at the door and knock. If anyone hears My voice and opens the door, I will come in to him and have dinner with him, and he with Me" (Rev 3:20).

CHRISTian Thinking

> We haven't stopped praying for you. We are asking that you may be filled with the *knowledge* of His will in all *wisdom* and spiritual *understanding*, so that you may walk worthy of the Lord, fully pleasing to Him, bearing fruit in every good work and growing in the knowledge of God. (Col 1:9b–10, emphasis added)

The knowledge Paul prays for the Colossians to have is not the head knowledge *(gnosis)*, which inflates with pride (1 Cor 8:1), but an intimate knowledge *(epignosis)* that comes through devotion to Christ. What Scripture *says* is more than words printed on a page because we could read into the text our own definitions. The Spirit illumines the Word so that we correctly know God's message. He does not speak for Himself but illumines what He hears from the Son (John 16:13–14).

But not knowledge only. The Lord leads us into spiritual understanding— that is, what Scripture *means*. As we walk with the Lord, He explains, just as He did with the two disciples on the road to Emmaus. "Weren't our hearts ablaze within us while He was talking with us on the road and explaining the Scriptures to us?" (Luke 24:32).

But not understanding only. The Lord leads us beyond understanding into "wisdom." Paul, a philosopher by training, rejects human philosophy and rational thought, emphasizing rather the ability "to judge correctly and follow the best course of action."[9] This harmonizes well with Jesus' own words: "Therefore whoever hears these sayings of Mine, and *does them*, I will liken him to a wise man" (Matt 7:24 NKJV, emphasis mine).

Doing in the Lord begets broader knowledge of His Word, which begets deeper understanding, which begets more effective doing.

---

[9] "Wisdom," *Nelson's Bible Dictionary, PC Study Bible*, Ver. 2 (Seattle: Biblesoft, July 1995).

The cycle of rational development proceeds *under the direction of the Lord* who lives within and teaches us. The means: knowing what the Bible says, understanding what the Bible means, and putting it into practice—as Jesus leads. The result: learners being "transformed by the renewing of your mind" (Rom 12:2).

CHRISTian Valuing

> Rejoice in hope; be patient in affliction; be persistent in prayer. Share with the saints in their needs; pursue hospitality. Bless those who persecute you; bless and do not curse. Rejoice with those who rejoice; weep with those who weep. Be in agreement with one another. Do not be proud; instead, associate with the humble. Do not be wise in your own estimation. (Rom 12:12–16)

Jesus declared kingdom beatitudes and behaviors in the Sermon of the Mount (Matt 5) that are impossible to develop in our own strength. The Lord within helps develop these kingdom elements into action. Many Christians have emotional problems and defects in values just like unbelievers: hatred, anger, instability, harshness, insecurity, bitterness, selfishness, and the like. Scripture underscores the importance of progression in removing the negative and growing in the positive. Paul emphasized several positive values in the above passage: joy, hope, patience, persistence, benevolence, hospitality, blessing, empathy, agreement, relationships. Each affective quality is developed out of the tangible fabric of everyday situations—conflicts, misunderstandings, disappointments, and loss—and requires a humble heart and a denial of self.

All believers experience affective challenges as they move from pagan to believer to teacher to missionary to leader: Love, not hate. Forgiveness, not anger. Steadfastness, not instability. Gentleness, not harshness. Courage, not insecurity. Sweetness, not bitterness. Generosity, not selfishness. The affective component of spiritual growth revolves around openness, values, priorities, and commitments in classroom and congregation. As we walk with the Lord, He teaches us within each day's struggle how to put off the negative and put on the positive. Seeking His values produces dramatic positive results not only in our own lives but also in the lives of those around us. His priorities, not ours. His values, not our culture's.

CHRISTian Doing

> "All of you, *take up My yoke* and learn from Me, because I am gentle and humble in heart, and you will find rest for yourselves. For My yoke is easy and My burden is light." (Matt 11:29–30, emphasis added)

As our understanding of God's Word and commitment to the Lord deepen, our actions change. Old habits die; new habits grow. How do we refine those habits? How do we learn the skills of spiritual living as Jesus lives within us and teaches us?

Jesus shows us the way. He says, "Take up My yoke." "Take up" denotes a voluntary action. I can take the yoke, or I can leave the yoke. "Yoke" refers to a wooden beam that ties two oxen together. Two can pull a load more easily than one, and the yoke ties them together. "My" refers to whose yoke it is. Jesus invites us to accept His yoke—not our parents', nor our pastors', nor our friends' yokes. The yoke of the Lord is my ministry—that which the Lord wants me to do. All believers are gifted (Eph 4:7) in order to help edify—strengthen— the church (Eph 4:12). Where should we serve? What should we do? "Take up my yoke," Jesus says.

Why should we give up what we want to do in order to do what the Lord wants? The answer strikes at the heart of natural self-centeredness: The yoke of Jesus is the only place where we find "rest"—"relief and ease and refreshment and recreation and blessed quiet" (*Amplified*).

The invitation of Jesus is not to learn more *about* Him but to "learn *from* Him." My grandfather once trained young horses to pull a plow by hitching one alongside a steady plow horse. After a time of fighting the traces, the colt learned to cooperate in the pull because it meant getting back to the oats with much less effort. In the same way the Lord invites us to hitch ourselves to Him in order to learn from Him how to minister. This does not diminish the importance of books, conferences, or seminary classes, since the most effective writers, leaders, and professors share what they have experienced in the Lord's yoke—that is, what they have already learned from Him.

His yoke is "easy"—*comfortable*—and his burden is "light"—*easy to be carried.* Rough wooden beams would irritate, chafe, and even cut the shoulders of oxen. The Carpenter had shaped many beams for a custom fit—an "easy" fit—to the shoulders of the animals. The yoke distributed the load across the oxen and so made the burden lighter. Jesus custom-fits our ministry to who we are, making even our sacrificial service comfortable, making our burdens light. In His will, pulling with Him, going His direction, there is restoration and renewal, even in the work. Ministry burnout grows out of work done in our own will, when we pull alone, going our own direction.

The Lord has invited me to take on several yokes over my life. The first was His call into Deaf ministry. The Lord helped my wife and me learn sign language and understand Deaf culture. We had no one in our families who was deaf, but He gave us a heart for Deaf people. Through years of working with Deaf people, Jesus taught me things about teaching and listening and communicating that permeate my efforts. My second call was to education ministry. He gave a 28-year-old seminary graduate the ability to learn—from the pastor and older staff, experienced lay leaders, and from the Lord Himself—how to lead the educational program of a church of 3,500. My third yoke was a call to the faculty of Southwestern Seminary. Every time I step into the classroom, I sense the preparation I received from the Lord through Deaf and education ministries. After 15 years in the seminary classroom, the Lord invited me into yet another yoke—to carry what I had learned over the previous 20 years to the former Soviet Union. For 11 years now I have taught four to six weeks each summer. To teach, equip, shape, challenge, mold, and learn from young ministers from around the world is an indescribable joy. The Lord's yoke leads to fulfillment and joy for us and for those we teach.

Final Words

The goal of Christian teaching is Christlikeness in our learners. The teacher helps by provoking clear thinking, passionate valuing, skillful doing, and humble submission to the Lord day by day. We, of course, cannot produce Christlikeness in our learners, but we are instruments in the Master's hand. We can cooperate with Him in the process.

In the end, when we honor Jesus as Teacher and Lord, when we teach others as He teaches us, when we love others as He loves us, we will influence them toward Christlikeness. May God richly bless you as you spend your life pursuing this wondrous task. "In any case, we should live up to whatever truth we have attained" (Phil 3:16).

Discussion Questions

1. Are you predominately a thinker, a feeler, or a doer? What evidence supports your evaluation? What dangers do you risk in focusing only on this "natural" emphasis?
2. Think of persons you know who fit the areas other than your own. How do you relate to them? What conflicts have you had?
3. Where do you need more emphasis: helping people think, feel, or do? What specifically will you do to strengthen these areas?
4. How are you allowing the Lord to shape your thoughts? Your values? Your actions?
5. What was your greatest discovery in this chapter? Why? What will you do differently as a result?

Suggested Reading

Downs, Perry G. *Teaching for Spiritual Growth*. Grand Rapids: Zondervan, 1994.

MacArthur, John F. *The Pillars of Christian Character*. Wheaton: Crossway, 1998.

Willard, Dallas. *Renovation of the Heart: Putting on the Character of Christ*. Colorado Springs: Navpress, 2002.

Yount, William R. *Created to Learn: A Christian Teacher's Introduction to Educational Psychology*. Nashville: B&H, 1996.

Yount, William R., and Mike Barnett. *Called to Reach: Equipping Cross-Cultural Disciplers*. Nashville: B&H, 2007.

Part Three

PREPARATION FOR TEACHING

Chapter 12

HOW TO STUDY THE BIBLE

Octavio J. Esqueda

The instruction of the LORD is perfect, renewing one's life;
the testimony of the LORD is trustworthy,
making the inexperienced wise.
The precepts of the LORD are right, making the heart glad;
the command of the LORD is radiant, making the eyes light up.
The fear of the LORD is pure, enduring forever;
the ordinances of the LORD are reliable and altogether righteous.
They are more desirable than gold—
than an abundance of pure gold;
and sweeter than honey, which comes from the honeycomb.
(Ps 19:7–10)

The Importance of Bible Study

I magine this scenario. A person is given the responsibility of teaching a Bible class but without any guidance about what exactly to teach. Obviously this teacher now faces the dilemma of what content is essential to convey to the students.

Unfortunately, this situation is common for many teachers who want to serve their churches even though they lack the training they need to communicate God's Word effectively to the learners. In many cases teachers look for popular books or Bible curricula to serve as their teaching notes. Although these materials may be helpful, these teachers tend to teach *about* the Bible, not necessarily *the* Bible itself. Since God's written revelation is the central content of Christian education, we need to know how to study the Bible by ourselves before we attempt to teach it. Further, since we teach Bible-centered content to people, it is imperative that we appropriately understand our audience. Other chapters in this book deal with the

217

nature of Scripture and how to understand our students. This chapter focuses on how to study the Bible.

Pause for a moment and think about your favorite food. Imagine someone offers you the most delicious meal you can dream of. You can eat whatever you desire and as much as you want. Are you hungry now? The conditions are that you can only eat this meal twice a week and you are forbidden to eat anything else. Now the offer does not sound attractive, does it? If you only eat two wonderful meals a week, you will probably develop anemia. To eat only twice a week is not enough to satisfy the needs of our bodies, regardless of the food quality.

Many Christians encounter a similar situation. They listen to a great sermon and, hopefully, a profound Bible study. The pastor and teacher spent countless hours preparing to preach and teach. However, people will not grow in the Lord if they only "eat" two excellent spiritual meals a week. We need daily the spiritual nourishment of the Word of God. Therefore, we are to study the Bible regularly and help others study the Bible on their own. The purpose of personal Bible study is nothing less than to become better disciples of Jesus by understanding the Word and applying its message to our lives.

The Need for Biblical Hermeneutics

As another chapter has discussed ("The Bible as Curriculum"), the biblical authors were inspired by the Holy Spirit. Thus, we call this collection of books the Word of God. As a divine book the Bible is inerrant, without any error in the original writings. It is authoritative, the guide for our faith and behavior. It has complete unity. Although the Bible was written by approximately 40 writers, it presents one theme, without contradiction. Finally, its mystery sometimes goes beyond our human comprehension because in some occasions we need to acknowledge that some passages are hard to understand.[1]

However, the Bible is also a human book that needs to be read and interpreted like any other. The Bible uses human language for the purpose of communicating information to its readers. Regarding the

---

[1] R. Zuck, *Basic Bible Interpretation: A Practical Guide to Discovering Biblical Truth* (Colorado Springs: Victor, 1991), 70–75.

human aspect of the biblical text, Roy Zuck provides six corollaries that help us in our study efforts:

1. Each biblical writing—that is, each word, sentence, and book—was recorded in a written language and followed normal, grammatical meanings, including figurative language.
2. Each biblical writing was written by someone to specific hearers or readers in a specific historical, geographical situation for a specific purpose.
3. The Bible is affected and influenced by the cultural environment from which each human writer wrote.
4. Each biblical writing was accepted or understood in the light of its context.
5. Each biblical writing took on the nature of a specific literary form.
6. Each biblical writing was understood by its initial readers in accord with the basic principles of logic and communication.[2]

Hermeneutics, exegesis, and *exposition* are key terms essential for studying, understanding, and teaching the Bible. All three are important and should work together when one prepares to teach or preach the Word of God. The word *hermeneutics* comes "from the Greek verb *hermeneuein* that means 'to explain, interpret or to translate,' while the noun *hermeneia* means 'interpretation' or 'translation'."[3] Through exegesis, we determine the meaning of Bible passages in their literary and historical contexts. Through exposition we communicate the "meaning of the text along with its relevance to present day hearers."[4] Therefore, the science of hermeneutics (interpretation) provides guidelines to Bible teachers to help them determine the meaning of the text as the original author intended it (exegesis) so they and their students can apply the text in modern-day situations (exposition).

During their time in seminary, students learn how to write exegetical papers. The objective of these projects is to discuss a Bible passage considering its structure and original context. Although

---

[2] Ibid., 61–66.
[3] W. W. Klein, C. L. Blomberg, and R. L. Hubbard Jr., *Introduction to Biblical Interpretation* (Nashville: Thomas Nelson, 1993), 4.
[4] Zuck, *Basic Bible Interpretation,* 20.

Christian teachers do not need to write formal research papers, the following steps used in such papers will help any teacher study the Bible better:

1. Read the passage several times in various translations.
2. Map the boundaries of the passage by observing format markers (headings, paragraphing, and punctuation) in the translations.
3. Construct a structural analysis of the passage and display it in graphic form (a diagram showing how sentences relate to one another).
4. Create an outline from the structural analysis of the passage.
5. Focus on syntax (main verbs and clauses), semantics (key words and repeated themes), and summation (trace the argument from one paragraph to another).
6. Conclude with a focus on significance (application).[5]

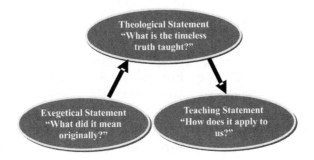

As we have said, finding the original meaning of the text (exegesis) is the first task of a Bible student.[6] Warren proposes the following paradigm for sermon preparation: exegesis, theological process, and homiletical product.[7] Bible teaching follows the same process during its preparation and delivery. Bible study allows us to state the original meaning of the text (exegesis) and to state the universal principles

---

[5] B. Corley, "A Student's Primer for Exegesis," in *Biblical Hermeneutics: A Comprehensive Introduction to Interpreting Scripture*, ed. Bruce Corley, Steve Lemke, and Grant Lovejoy (Nashville: B&H, 1996), 13–18.

[6] G. D. Fee and Douglas Stuart, *How to Read the Bible for All Its Worth: A Guide to Understanding the Bible*, 2nd ed. (Grand Rapids: Zondervan, 1993).

[7] T. S. Warren, "A Paradigm for Preaching" in *Bibliotheca Sacra* 148 (October–December 1991): 463–86.

that we can learn from the passage (theological process). Application,
however, is the ultimate goal of Bible study and teaching.

Inductive Bible Study Approach

There are several ways to study the Bible,[8] but I believe the
best way is to follow the inductive method, which will allow us
to obtain a more accurate understanding of a Bible passage. This
method includes three steps: observation, interpretation, and application. Observation answers the question, what does the text say?
Interpretation answers the question, what does it mean? Application
answers the crucial question, what shall we do?

Observation

Observation refers to reading a text to discover what it says in its
own context. Observation helps us see things the way they really are.
The temptation to move to interpretation and application without
sufficient observation leads to the distortion of both. For example,
Matt 2:1–12 records the story of the visit of the magi to Jesus after
He was born. Ask people to describe the scene, and many will describe three men named Caspar, Melchior, and Balthazar, kneeling
at the manger. However, the passage gives no names, nor does it say
how many wise men there were. We do find that the wise men came
from the east, first to Jerusalem and then to Bethlehem looking for
Jesus. They visited Him in a house, not in the stable, and offered Him
gold, frankincense, and myrrh. They gave Jesus three kinds of gifts,
but there were not necessarily three magi. These common miscon-
ceptions are quickly dispelled by cautious observation.

Cautious observation requires that we read the passage as if it
were the first time. While this is especially hard for people who are
familiar with the Bible, it is crucial that we let God speak to us in a
fresh way every time we read His Word.

Bible teachers need to be good observers. Competent journalists
model careful observation when they write their stories. I earned a
diploma in journalism in Guadalajara, Mexico, to help me with my

---

[8] For a complete discussion about the history of biblical hermeneutics and recent lit-
erary and social-scientific approaches for Bible study and interpretation, see W. W.
Klein, C. L. Blomberg, and R. L. Hubbard Jr., *Introduction to Biblical Interpretation*
(Nashville: Thomas Nelson, 1993).

writing and understanding of the field. One of the important rules I
learned was that competent journalists engage in careful observation
before they write their stories. Six questions guide the observation of
reporters: Who? What? Where? When? Why? How? Journalists are
not alone in the use of these questions. Good detectives also discover
basic information by using these same questions. Every time we read
a Bible passage, let's ask: "Who is talking or being talked about?
What is the subject being discussed? What comes before the passage,
and what follows after? When and where is the action taking place?
Why is the action taking place (purpose)? How are the people involved responding?[9]

During the observation step we take into consideration four elements in the passage: terms, grammatical structure, literary form,
and atmosphere.[10] Terms are key words, usually nouns and verbs,
that define the meaning of the text. Terms are often repeated
throughout the passage. For example, the word *Spirit* is a key term
that appears repeatedly in Romans 8.

Observe the gender and number of the nouns, as well as the verb
tenses. John writes, "The one who has the Son has life. The one who
doesn't have the Son of God does not have life" (1 John 5:12). There
are four nouns: one, Son, life, and God. One refers to any person.
Notice the direct connection between anyone having (or not having)
the Son and, therefore, having (or not having) life. The verb "has" is
in the present tense. The life that the Son gives starts the moment we
receive the Son.

Second, the grammatical structure of a passage helps us derive
meaning from it. Structure reveals how the elements of a passage are
put together and is created through the use of objects, verbs, prepo-
sitional phrases, modifiers, and connectives.[11]

For example, the connective "therefore" introduces a logical conclusion derived from previous statements. In each of the following
examples, writers use "therefore" to shift from doctrinal arguments
to life application for believers:

[9] D. J. Mock, *Bible Study Methods and Rules of Interpretation* (Atlanta: Bible Training
Centre for Pastors and Church Leaders, 1998). This book forms part of a curriculum
designed to train church leaders worldwide. More information at www.btcp.com.

[10] H. G. Hendricks and William D. Hendricks, *Living by the Book* (Chicago: Moody,
1991), 36–38.

[11] Ibid., 116–17.

> *Therefore* since we also have such a large cloud of witnesses
> surrounding us, let us lay aside every weight and the sin
> that so easily ensnares us, and run with endurance the race
> that lies before us. (Heb 12:1)
>
> *Therefore*, brothers, by the mercies of God, I urge you to
> present your bodies as a living sacrifice, holy and pleasing
> to God; this is your spiritual worship. (Rom 12:1)
>
> I, *therefore*, the prisoner in the Lord, urge you to walk wor-
> thy of the calling you have received. (Eph 4:1)

Therefore, it becomes imperative to be a good grammar student in
order to become a better Bible student.

Third, Bible passages also present a literary form that organizes
their argument. Books may present their arguments around people
(biographical outline in Genesis and Acts), places (geographical
outline in Exodus), events (historical outline in Joshua), ideas (theological outline in Romans), or times (chronological outline in 1 and
2 Kings).[12] Passages use the literary structures of comparison (Matt
6:28–30), contrast (Matt 6:25), repetition (Ps 136), cause and effect
(Rom 1:18–32), problem and solution (Rom 1–3 with 3–5), or questions (Matt 22:15–46).

Fourth, the atmosphere of a passage is the "underlying tone,
mood, or spirit of a passage and the emotional response which
it causes."[13] The biblical context provides the tone or mood by
which we can experience the emotions of the passage. Isaiah 6 and
Revelation 4 describe the magnificence and splendor of the God
of the universe. As we read these passages, our hearts are drawn
into their atmosphere, which evokes deep spiritual responses.
In Exod 18:18–20, the people's reaction after receiving the Ten
Commandments describes an atmosphere of fear and awe in the
presence of the Holy God. As we enter into that atmosphere, we taste
their awe of God.

The Bible is a literary work and as such displays various literary
genres. We will understand more clearly when we read any particular passage in light of the peculiarities of its literary genre. The
Bible includes works of narrative (Joshua), epistles or discourse

---

[12] D. J. Mock, *Bible Study Methods,* 37.
[13] Ibid., 41.

(Ephesians), poetry (Song of Songs), proverbs (Proverbs), parables (sections of Luke), and prophecy (Revelation). Since different hermeneutical principles are applied to the various genres, a careful analysis of a passage's genre will be extremely helpful during the process of interpretation.

Interpretation

Clear biblical interpretation builds on careful observation. The purpose of interpretation is to discover the meaning of the biblical passage as the author intended. Interpretation is commonly used as a synonym of hermeneutics and "the various methods used to examine texts."[14] John Stott in his classic book, *Understanding the Bible,* argues for three basic principles of biblical interpretation: simplicity, history, and harmony. First, one should look for the natural sense of the biblical passage. This is simplicity. Second, one should look for the original sense of the text. This is history. Finally, one should look for the general sense of the Bible. This is harmony.[15]

The principles of simplicity, history, and harmony help us build a bridge between our (modern) world and the biblical (ancient) world. The Bible was written, as we just noted, using different literary genres. Furthermore, it was written in different languages (Hebrew, Aramaic, and Greek), in different geographical contexts within various cultures, and with specific historical conditions. Consequently, the grammatical-historical method of interpretation that considers all these circumstances is the key approach for understanding the Bible.[16]

Mock proposes several rules to interpret the text. By following these rules, we gain clearer understanding of the grammatical and historical context of any Bible passage.[17]

1. Interpret the passage literally. We read the text considering its words and sentences in their usual and customary way. The literal meanings of words are determined in three ways: (1) by their basic definitions, (2) by the way the term is used elsewhere in the

---

[14] W. R. Tate, "Interpretation," in *Interpreting the Bible* (Peabody MA: Hendrickson, 2006), 180.

[15] J. Stott, *Understanding the Bible* (Grand Rapids: Baker, 2001).

[16] W. Tolar, "The Grammatical-Historical Method," in *Biblical Hermeneutics: A Comprehensive Introduction to Interpreting Scripture,* ed. Bruce Corley, Steve Lemke, and Grant Lovejoy (Nashville: B&H, 1996), 217.

[17] D. J. Mock, *Bible Study Methods,* 50–61.

Scripture and in other contemporary writings, and (3) by the context in which the word is used.

Literal interpretation includes figurative language like that in Psalm 1. These figures of speech (e.g., "tree planted beside streams of water," "chaff that the wind blows away") produce mental images to communicate concrete meaning. Lexicons and Bible dictionaries serve as helpful tools for interpretation because they explain the meaning of the biblical words. These tools "provide the reader with etymologies, an identification and discussion of irregular grammatical forms, possible meanings, and the usage of a word within a given context."[18]

2. Interpret the Bible passage considering its immediate context. The context of a passage determines the meaning of a particular text. To interpret a passage correctly, we need to consider the paragraph in which it is located, its chapter, its book, and the entire Bible. Some critics argue that the Bible is vague, that we can make the Bible say anything we want. This is true only when readers take verses out of their context. A text out of context becomes a pretext to present ideas contrary to what the Bible is really saying.

The meaning of Paul's expression in Phil 4:13, "I am able to do all things through Him who strengthens me," for example, could be used to say that in Christ Paul became a superhero with invincible powers. However, the immediate context tells us that the word "all" refers to Paul's economic and social situation. In Christ, Paul can face economical hardships because he had learned to be content in plenty and in want.

3. Interpret the passage in view of history and culture. Bible authors faced particular social and cultural conditions under particular historical settings that influence the content of their books. Culture affects everything human beings do because it is "a system of symbols, attitudes, behaviors, relationships, beliefs, and responses to the environment shared by a particular human group in contrast to others."[19] A proper biblical interpretation requires that we pay attention to the geographical, religious, topographical, social, and political

---

[18] W. R. Tate, "Lexicons," in *Interpreting the Bible* (Peabody, MA: Hendrickson, 2006), 192–93.

[19] J. L. González, "Culture," in *Essential Theological Terms* (Louisville: Westminster/ John Knox, 2005), 42.

factors surrounding the biblical text. The occasion and purpose of each biblical book is central for a proper understanding of the historical context.[20] Bible commentaries and books dealing with manners and customs of biblical times offer insights into the historical and cultural background of biblical passages. However, their use should follow a careful observation of the Bible passage.

4. Interpret the passage in view of literary form. As we have discussed, the literary genre of Bible books affects the interpretation of their meaning.[21] The Bible uses six major literary genres: epistles, narrative, poetry, proverbs, parables, and prophecy.

Epistles. The New Testament letters follow a logical flow of ideas with the goal of communicating a specific message to a specific audience. Since the epistles were intended to be read in public, it is important to read them in their entirety to discover their structure and how the argument develops. This kind of literature uses a straightforward language to develop an argument. The epistles follow a relatively fixed form containing conventional aspects of Hellenistic letters but with distinctive features:

- Opening (sender, addressee, greeting).
- Thanksgiving (prayer for spiritual welfare and remembrance or commendation of the spiritual riches of the addressee).
- Body.
- Paraenesis (exhortation).
- Closing (final greetings and benediction).[22]

Narrative. The Bible, especially the Old Testament, is full of stories. The plot is the key element of any story. In order to have a good story, something needs to happen to someone somewhere. Therefore, the plot (action), setting, and characters form the essential elements of biblical narrative. Bible stories are descriptive, not prescriptive because they share the lives of people, including their achievements and mistakes. We can learn from their experiences. They do not, however, provide a model of behavior in every instance. Several narrative elements guide the proper understanding of this genre:

---

[20] G. D. Fee and D. Stuart, *How to Read the Bible,* 23.
[21] L. Ryken, *How to Read the Bible as Literature* (Grand Rapids: Zondervan, 1984), 12.
[22] L. Ryken, *Words of Delight: A Literary Introduction to the Bible,* 2nd ed. (Grand Rapids: Baker, 1992), 434.

- Physical, temporal, and cultural settings of the story.
- Characters of the story, with special emphasis on the protagonist.
- Plot conflicts and their resolution.
- Aspects of narrative suspense (how the story arouses curiosity about outcome).
- The protagonist's experience in living as an implied comment about life.
- Narrative unity, coherence, an emphasis.
    - † Elements of testing and choice in the story.
    - † Character progress and transformation.
    - † Foils, dramatic irony, and poetic justice.
    - † The implied assertions about reality, morality, and values.
    - † Repetition and highlighting as clues to what the story is about.
    - † Point of view in the story—how the writer gets a reader to share his attitude toward the character and events.[23]

Poetry. Biblical poetry paints images with words to express human experiences. The New Testament includes several poetic sections, and many books in the Old Testament are poetry. The capacity of unfolding the possibilities of images, metaphors, and similes is essential for proper interpretation of the Psalter and other poetic books.[24] Poetry is an emotional and intimate way of communication. Therefore, we need to "feel" the text as we read it to grasp the author's experience.

Hebrew poetry uses parallelism as a structural technique to organize the verses. Parallelism consists of "two or more phrases that express an idea in different words but in similar grammatical form."[25] In most occasions the second line (or verse) relates to the first one in different ways. For example, it can restate the same truth expressed in the first line (synonymous parallelism); it can contrast the ideas

---

[23] Ryken, *How to Read the Bible as Literature*, 68–69.
[24] R. Jacobson, "Imagery and the Psalms," in *Teaching the Bible: Practical Strategies for Classroom Instruction*, ed. Mark Roncace and Patrick Gray (Atlanta: Society of Biblical Literature, 2005), 197.
[25] L. Ryken, *Words of Delight*, 442.

presented on the first line (antithetic parallelism); or it can comple-
ment the idea shared on the first line (synthetic parallelism).

Four key questions should guide our reading and interpretation
of biblical poetry: What is the overall effect of the poem? What is the
structure of the poem? What are the figures of speech of the poem?
What are the themes and theology of the poem?[26]

Proverbs. The Bible contains many aphorisms or proverbs, including a complete book that bears that name. Proverbs "are moments
of epiphany—high points of human insight."[27] The biblical wisdom
literature includes the book of Proverbs. Wisdom in biblical perspective refers to godly living because correct behavior is a manifestation
of an accurate understanding of God. Although proverbs are statements of truth, they should be considered as principles, not promises. Consequently, a proverb presents a general statement of the way
life *should* be, not necessarily the way it *will* be. "A gentle answer
turns away anger, but a harsh word stirs up wrath" (Prov 15:1). This
statement reflects a desired outcome, not a promise that our kind
answers will always turn away anger.

Parables. Our Lord Jesus Christ made parables an active ingredient
of His teaching. A parable is a short story based on real-life events
with the purpose of teaching a central truth. A parable develops
only one key truth. Thus we need to concentrate on the main focus
of the parable instead of spending time on the details of the story.
Robertson McQuilkin suggests six basic guidelines for understanding parables: "Begin with the immediate context, identify the central
point of emphasis, identify irrelevant details, compare parallel and
contrasting passages, and base doctrine on clear literal passages."[28]

Prophetic literature. Fully one-fourth of the biblical text deals with
prophetic literature. Although a common aspect of this genre is the
prediction of future events, prophetic books also focus on God's
messages of judgment, warning, and calling to repentance. The Lord
called biblical prophets to proclaim His messages, to "forth-tell" His
truths more than just merely foretell the future. Prophetic material is
filled with symbols and figurative language. Thus we need to be care-

---

[26] M. E. Travers, "Poetry," in *Dictionary for Theological Interpretation of the Bible,* ed.
Kevin J. Vanhoozer (Grand Rapids: Baker Academic, 2005), 596.

[27] L. Ryken, *Words of Delight,* 315.

[28] R. McQuilkin, *Understanding and Applying the Bible* (Chicago: Moody, 1992), 186.

ful not to make conclusions about the meaning of the passage before
we consider the context and structure of the book. Use the following
principles when interpreting biblical prophecy:

> Compare all related and parallel passages, realize that
> there may be a long time (hundreds or thousands of years)
> between the announcement of the prophecy and its fulfill-
> ment, distinguish between already fulfilled and yet to be
> fulfilled prophecy, identify figures of speech and symbolic
> language and interpret accordingly, and make certain the
> interpretation does not conflict with other Scripture.[29]

5. Interpret the passage in view of other parts of Scripture. The
Bible always interprets itself (*Scriptura sui ipsius interpres*). Thus we
need to pay attention to similar or related passages as we interpret a
biblical text. Also we need to interpret some passages, especially in
the Old Testament, according to progressive revelation. God revealed
Himself to the biblical authors "progressively throughout history.
The most obvious proof is to compare incomplete Jewish theology
with the fuller revelation of Christian theology in respect, for example, to such doctrines as the Trinity, Christology, the Holy Spirit,
resurrection, and eschatology."[30]

Even though the Bible was written by many authors in different
times and places, it presents a thematic unity that brings together all
books. The three main Bible themes are creation, fall, and redemption.[31] The first two chapters of the book of Genesis explain the story
of God's good creation. However, in Genesis 3 the first human beings
sinned against the Creator, and consequently all humanity became
alienated from the Lord. From Gen 3:15 to Revelation 22 the Bible
tells the story of redemption. The Old Testament, especially through
the covenants that represent the backbone of biblical narrative, deals
with the promise of redemption. In the New Testament, Jesus Christ
consummates the redemption of humanity. The Bible ends with the
promise of the second coming of Christ and the new heavens and
new earth.

As Bible teachers, our goal is to apply the text and proclaim its
truths. However, this can only be done as we understand the text's

---

[29] D. Mock, *Bible Study Methods*, 72–73.
[30] C. C. Ryrie, *Basic Theology* (Chicago: Moody, 1999), 28.
[31] D. K. Naugle, *Worldview: The History of a Concept* (Grand Rapids: Eerdmans, 2002).

original intended meaning. Dockery and Guthrie suggest seven steps that summarize biblical interpretation for Bible teachers:

1. Choose a text and prepare spiritually.
2. Study the backdrop for the text.
3. Work on translations and general observation.
4. Perform word and concept analysis.
5. Study the broader biblical and theological contexts.
6. Apply the text.
7. Proclaim its truths.[32]

God has the goal of transforming us to be more like Jesus Christ (Rom 8:29). Application helps us to change our behavior, attitude, and way of thinking so that we please God and live according to His will. In the Bible we find the parameters for our renovation. The key question we need to ask ourselves when we read a text is, How does God want me to change in light of this passage? Observation and interpretation prepare the way to application, which is the most important aspect of Bible study (Matt 7:24; Jas 1:22).

An accurate application of the biblical text has to be practical, personal, and precise. Application is more than good desires and general principles. The dedicated practice of biblical truths in daily experiences, every day, all the time, is a central desire of every serious believer. God speaks to us through His Word, and we should individually respond to His message. We are effective as Bible teachers when we live out what we teach and then lead our students to do the same. Good applications are concrete, attainable, and measurable. For example, the statement, "We studied today about the importance of Bible study; now let's go and spend more time in the Word," only conveys good intentions. It lacks the three characteristics of application. A better application would be able to answer the following: When should I read the Bible? How much? Where do I start? How long? Where? At what time?

Hendricks suggests nine questions to ask during the application process of a particular biblical text: Is there an example for me to follow? Is there a sin to avoid? Is there a promise to claim? Is there a prayer to repeat? Is there a command to obey? Is there a condition

---

[32] D. S. Dockery and G. H. Guthrie, *The Holman Guide to Interpreting the Bible* (Nashville: B&H, 2004), 47.

to meet? Is there a verse to memorize? Is there an error to mark? Is there a challenge to face?[33]

Conclusion

A popular maxim says, "You can only give what you possess." This saying also applies to Christian teaching. By carefully observing the Word, interpreting its meaning, and applying its message to our lives, we raise a solid platform from which to teach it to others. As Christian teachers, we should follow Ezra's example:

> *The gracious hand of his God was on him,*
> because *Ezra* had *determined in his heart*
> to *study the law* of the LORD, *obey it,*
> and *teach* its statutes and ordinances in Israel.
> (Ezra 7:9b–10, emphasis mine)

Discussion Questions

1. Why is it important to study the Bible?
2. What is the connection between exegesis, hermeneutics, and teaching or exposition?
3. Explain in your own words the inductive Bible study approach.
4. Describe the general rules of biblical interpretation.
5. What can we learn from Ezra's example of studying and obeying the Word before teaching it to others?

Bibliography

Corley, Bruce, Steve Lemke, and Grant Lovejoy, eds. *Biblical Hermeneutics: A Comprehensive Introduction to Interpreting Scripture.* Nashville: B&H, 1996.

Dockery, David S., and George H. Guthrie. *The Holman Guide to Interpreting the Bible.* Nashville: B&H, 2004.

Fee, Gordon D., and Douglas Stuart. *How to Read the Bible for All Its Worth: A Guide to Understanding the Bible.* 2nd ed. Grand Rapids: Zondervan, 1993.

González, Justo L. *Essential Theological Terms.* Louisville: Westminster/John Knox, 2005.

---

[33] H. G. Hendricks and W. D. Hendricks, *Living by the Book*, 304–9.

Hendricks, Howard G., and William D. Hendricks. *Living by the Book*. Chicago: Moody, 1991.

Klein, William W., Craig L. Blomberg, and Robert L. Hubbard Jr. *Introduction to Biblical Interpretation*. Nashville: Thomas Nelson, 1993.

McQuilkin, Robertson. *Understanding and Applying the Bible*. Chicago: Moody, 1992.

Mock, Dennis J. *Bible Study Methods and Rules of Interpretation*. Atlanta: Bible Training Centre for Pastors and Church Leaders, 1998.

Naugle, David K. *Worldview: The History of a Concept*. Grand Rapids: Eerdmans, 2002.

Roncace, Mark, and Patrick Gray, eds. *Teaching the Bible: Practical Strategies for Classroom Instruction*. Atlanta, Society of Biblical Literature, 2005.

Ryken, Leland. *How to Read the Bible as Literature*. Grand Rapids: Zondervan, 1984.

——————. *Words of Delight: A Literary Introduction to the Bible*. Grand Rapids: Baker, 2nd ed., 1992.

Ryrie, Charles C. *Basic Theology*. Chicago: Moody, 1999.

Stott, John. *Understanding the Bible*. Grand Rapids: Baker, 2001.

Tate, Randolph W. *Interpreting the Bible*. Peabody, MA: Hendrickson, 2006.

Vanhoozer, Kevin J., ed. *Dictionary for Theological Interpretation of the Bible*. Grand Rapids: Baker Academic, 2005.

Warren, Timothy S. "A Paradigm for Preaching." *Bibliotheca Sacra* 148 (October-December 1991): 463–86.

Zuck, Roy. *Basic Bible Interpretation: A Practical Guide to Discovering Biblical Truth*. Colorado Springs: Victor, 1991.

Chapter 13

PLANNING TO TEACH

Rick Yount

Pay careful attention, then, to how you walk—
not as unwise people but as wise—
making the most of the time, because the days are evil.
(Eph 5:15–16)

I n the previous chapter Octavio Esqueda discussed ways to
study a Bible passage in preparation for teaching. "So what's left
to be done?" we may ask. We have analyzed the text. We have
defined key concepts and outlined the verses. What more should
teachers do—*could* teachers do—than walk into their classrooms and
talk through their notes?

The simple answer is "plenty." Analysis of a text is the beginning
point of preparation, but effective teaching is far more than talking
through one's study notes. What are the needs of our learners? How
does this passage speak to them? What do we want to result from the
study? How will we prepare hearts and minds to receive a word from
the Lord? What kinds of activities will we use to establish knowledge, deepen understanding, change attitude, or stimulate Christian
action? How will we know if we have achieved what we planned?
How will we bring the session to an effective conclusion? How will
we prepare learners for next week's study? How will we evaluate
what we did or didn't do, in order to become more effective as a
Christian teacher?

I like the old King James phrase "redeeming the time." The
Holman Christian Standard Bible renders it "making the most of the
time," and the *Amplified* adds "buying up each opportunity." There
is so much to do and so little time. How do we make the most of our

teaching time? How do we buy up each opportunity to transform the lives of learners? The key to this puzzle is found in the lesson-planning process. A lesson plan reflects the care and thought a teacher has made, in cooperation with the Holy Spirit, for what will happen in a particular Bible study session. Without a plan teachers and their classes may well end up . . . who knows where? Worse, teachers waste a lot of time getting there. Let's examine five key ingredients to an effective lesson plan.

The Instructional Objective: "Set Up a Target"

When I was 10, my folks gave me a bow and arrow set for Christmas. Living in El Paso, Texas, at the time, I was able to head out to the backyard—it was a balmy 65 degrees—and shoot my arrows. I set up a target on a box in front of a stone wall and shot my first arrow. I missed the target and the box, hit the fence, and split the arrow down the middle. I didn't want to break any more arrows, so I made up a new game. I shot an arrow straight up in the air, and watched it fly upward, slow, and fall back toward me. I kept myself directly under the arrow until the last moment and then leaned back, moving my foot as close to the impact point as possible—without being hit, of course. It was a great game and provided hours of enjoyment without splitting any more arrows. Of course, I never learned how to put arrows in a target.

When I began teaching Sunday school, I found myself doing the same thing. I "shot" the Bible up into the air, and anywhere we landed by the end of the class was the Lord's will. While God can bless even these misguided efforts, I did not develop skill as a teacher because I had no target to hit, no way to evaluate what I had accomplished. Skill development requires targets. Shoot at the target, miss the target, adjust your aim. Shoot, miss, adjust. Eventually we master the skill.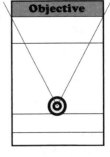

A properly prepared instructional objective provides a target for teaching. This target is something concrete to aim for—an intended place to end—at the conclusion of the session.

Importance of the Learner

An instructional target underscores the importance of the learner, who is the most important ingredient in the Bible teaching-learning process. The Pharisees of Jesus' day put the observance of the Sabbath above the people who observed it. They criticized Jesus for healing on the Sabbath because "healing is work," and work was forbidden on the Sabbath. Jesus, on the other hand, put the observer above the observance: "The Sabbath was made on account and for the sake of man, not man for the Sabbath" (Mark 2:27, *Amplified*).

The learner is the key ingredient in the learning experience. What will the learner be able to do at the end of our teaching that he could not do before? What impact will we make on the individuals sitting in our class? How have they been changed? In writing an instructional objective, we plan ahead of time, with prayerful dependence on the Lord, what our learners should be able to do as a result of our teaching.

Type of Learning Desired

Instructional targets differ according to the emphasis we desire in a given lesson. We can identify four major emphases in teaching: knowledge, understanding, appreciation, and purposeful action.

Knowledge. Knowledge refers to the learner's ability to identify or recall information given to him. Learners will demonstrate knowledge of

- John 3:16 by quoting it from memory.
- Paul's first missionary journey by identifying from a list of Asian cities the names of the cities he visited.

Understanding. Understanding refers to a "domain" of learning that includes five levels: comprehension, application, analysis, synthesis, and evaluation. Space does not permit a detailed analysis of each level,[1] but we can define "comprehension" as the learners' ability to explain, paraphrase, or illustrate biblical concepts or principles. Examples of *comprehension* objectives include the following:

---

[1] The six levels of learning—knowledge through evaluation—were first developed by Benjamin Bloom and his committee of educators in the 1950s. They remain an effective means of structuring cognitive learning.

Learners will demonstrate understanding[2] of

- John 3:16 by explaining in their own words the terms *loved the world, believes in him,* and *eternal life.*
- The armor of God (Ephesians 6) by explaining how truth is a "belt," salvation is a "helmet," faith is a "shield," and the Word of God is a "sword."

Application refers to (learners) using concepts (comprehension) to solve problems and answer questions. *Analysis* refers to (learners) discerning relationships among concepts in a passage and is found in comparison and contrast, exegesis, and outlining. *Synthesis* refers to (learners) reassembling analytic components into complex definitions or narratives: a short-answer essay, a letter, a lesson plan, a sermon. *Evaluation* refers to (learners) making judgments based on clearly defined criteria, synthesized from Scripture. I emphasize learners here to counter the common mistake of focusing learning on what teachers do. Objectives target what learners are able to do as a result of teaching.

Appreciation. Appreciation refers to a "domain" of learning that includes five levels: receiving, responding, valuing, organizing, and characterization. Space does not permit a detailed analysis of each level,[3] but we can generally define "appreciation" as the learners' willingness to share personal experiences with others, defend personal values, and reorder personal priorities. We will define these more specifically in a moment, but examples of commonly used *responding* objectives include the following:

Learners will demonstrate appreciation for

- John 3:16 by giving a personal testimony in class about life before and after being saved.
- Paul's first missionary journey by sharing an experience in missions.

Receiving refers to (learners) attending to teaching by listening and watching. *Responding* refers to (learners) answering questions, sharing experiences, and asking questions of their own. *Valuing*

---

[2] The domain is understanding; the measurable outcome reflects the individual level, e.g., comprehension.

[3] These five levels of learning were developed by David Krathwohl and his associates, based on Bloom's work in the cognitive domain.

refers to (learners) placing importance on topics or positions for themselves. Learners defend positions and share them with others. *Organizing* refers to (learners) reordering their values. Learners place higher priority on "loving enemies" and less on "seeking revenge." *Characterizing* refers to (learners) living out concepts and values as a part of their lives. Learners are known by others as prayer warriors. These last two levels usually happen over time rather than in a single Bible study session.

Purposeful Action. Purposeful action refers to the learners' ability to use what they have learned in class or during the week. Such action can flow out of either an understanding or appreciation focus. Here is an example of each.

- Learners will demonstrate an understanding of the armor of God (Eph 6) by developing appropriate responses to case studies involving spiritual warfare (problem-solving).
- Learners will demonstrate appreciation for Paul's first missionary journey by working in one of our church's mission projects over the next month (commitment).

By setting up targets, teachers focus the entire lesson planning process to a specific end. Lecture, discussion questions, and dialogue are all focused on hitting the target. This redeems the time.

Learning Readiness: "Priming the Pump"

I spent many childhood summers working on my grandfather's farm in Indiana. One of my responsibilities was to water the chickens every morning. Water was drawn from an outside well by means of an old hand pump. Before it could draw water out of the ground, I had to "prime" it by pouring water into the top of the pump. Then I could pump as much water as I needed. A bucket sat next to the pump to hold water for priming. The last responsibility of anyone drawing water was to fill that bucket because, without priming, the pump could not draw water out of the ground.

We make a dangerous assumption when we walk into a classroom thinking our students are ready to learn. Our learners have their hearts and minds on a hundred different things, and they may not be at all ready to focus on the subject at hand. Jesus said, "Don't give what is holy to dogs or toss your pearls before pigs" (Matt 7:6). Learners are seldom ready to study when they walk into the room. Their pumps need priming. And this is what the learning readiness section of a lesson plan does. Here are some guidelines to follow in designing learning readiness activities.

Remember the Objective

A discussion of last week's football game or the morning's headlines seldom prepares students for the day's session. The intention of pump priming is to focus hearts and minds on a central issue that will prepare the way for the learning activities that follow. Here are some examples of learning readiness drawn from the objectives we stated above.

1. *Objective*. Learners will demonstrate knowledge of Paul's first missionary journey by identifying the names of the cities he visited from a list of Asian cities.

Suggested learning readiness. Hang a large map of the Middle East and Asia Minor on the front wall. This can be drawn by hand on several sheets of newspaper. Identify each of the major cities Paul visited on his first missionary journey with a large dot and printed name. Introduce "Paul's first missionary journey" and ask learners to name the cities—dots—on the map. Point out the route Paul took on this first journey. "Let's open our Bibles to the book of Acts and see where Paul went, and what happened." (The Bible study will retrace the route and emphasize major events that took place on the journey.)

2. *Objective*. Learners will demonstrate understanding of John 3:16 by explaining in their own words ("comprehension") the terms *love, world, believe* and *everlasting life*.

Suggested learning readiness. Write the following words on the chalkboard before class: *love, world, believe, everlasting, life*. As the class begins, ask learners to define each of these terms. These definitions display learner comprehension prior to the study. (The Bible study will analyze these terms in light of John 3:16 and parallel passages.)

3. *Objective.* Learners will demonstrate appreciation for Paul's missionary journey by sharing an experience in missions ("responding") with the class.

Suggested learning readiness. Write the words *Experiences in Missions* on the chalkboard and share a personal experience you've had in a mission project or on a mission trip. Emphasize the positive impact the experience had on your life. (The study will look briefly at Paul's experiences but focus most of the time on the shared experiences of learners.)

4. *Objective.* Learners will demonstrate understanding of the armor of God (Eph 6) by developing appropriate responses to case studies ("application") involving spiritual warfare (problem-solving).

Suggested learning readiness. Write the following words on individual pieces of blue poster board: *belt, breastplate, shoes, shield, helmet,* and *sword.* Write these words on pieces of yellow poster board: *truth, righteousness, gospel, faith, salvation, Word of God.* Tape these words randomly on the front wall of the classroom. At the beginning of class, have learners match them up. (The Bible study will focus on the meanings of the pieces of spiritual armor, then present case studies to be solved.)

Avoid Gimmicks

Avoid gimmicks that might shock, frighten, or offend learners. Immature teachers certainly get attention by using sudden loud noises (firecrackers, air horns), "pretend" rude comments and abusive remarks, or embarrassing skits. Youth ministers seem to be particularly fond of such tactics because of the perceived need to "grab teenagers by the throat" at the beginning of the session. Teenagers gathering for a See You at the Pole Rally at Wedgwood Baptist Church on September 15, 1999 had no idea that, within moments, a lone gunman would shoot and kill three adults and six teenagers before taking his own life. When the shooting began, many teens assumed "it was just a skit to make us *really* think about death and heaven." Violent skits had numbed them. Shock will do more to disrupt learning than to enhance it.

On the other end of the spectrum lies mindless humor. "Revving up the crowd" with cheap shots and empty laughter may be appropriate fare for late-night television, but it does not enhance the atmosphere for hearing a word from the Lord. Avoid gimmicks. Rather, like John the Baptizer, let us "prepare for God's arrival! Make the road smooth and straight!" (Matt 3:3).

Build a Bridge to Bible Study

Plan carefully for the transition from learning readiness to Bible study. The best learning readiness exercise leads naturally into the study portion of the session. Notice these transition statements:

- *Knowledge of Paul's First Journey.* "We've traced Paul's first missionary journey on the map. Now let's open to Acts 13 and dig a little deeper into what happened along the way."
- *Understanding of John 3:16 Transition.* "We've written your definitions for *love, world, believe, everlasting,* and *life* on the board. Let's open our Bibles to John 3:16. We're going to use this verse and other passages to see what they say about these terms."
- *Appreciation for Paul's First Journey Transition.* "My experience taught me so many things about the Lord, but the apostle Paul had many such experiences. Let's look at some of them. Meanwhile, think of experiences you've had in missions that you'd like to share later."
- *Understanding the Armor of God Transition.* "We've matched up the pieces of armor and spiritual characteristics. Open your Bible to Ephesians 6 and check our work. Did we match them all correctly?" (After checking and making changes if needed:) "Let's look at each of these spiritual characteristics and see what they mean."

If the pump has been primed correctly, our learners will be eager to get into the Scripture to find answers, clarify meanings, or share the experiences of Bible personalities. In just a few moments, we have focused the attention of learners on the issues we've targeted in the objective. This is a major step toward "buying up the opportunity" we've been given to teach.

Bible Study: "Haul the Freight"

I had a friend in high school who spent a great deal of his time polishing his candy-apple red 1949 Ford pickup. It had chrome wheels and dual chrome exhaust pipes. He spent most of his time caring for that truck. One day I asked him what kind of load it would carry. "Carry? Carry?! I don't use this truck to carry anything! I carry it on a trailer when I take it to car shows." What good is a truck if it doesn't haul the freight? What good is a lesson plan—presenting a lecture or leading a discussion—if it doesn't convey the deep things of God in ways that learners can understand?

The Bible study section is the heart of the lesson plan. It is here that we analyze texts, explain concepts, make applications, share values, challenge attitudes, and discuss lifestyles. Yet from one end of the world to the other, I find pastors and teachers who consider teaching as nothing more than conveying information and learning as nothing more than receiving information. For these individuals, the more teachers know, the better teachers they are. Worse, these information transmitters hold that if learners experience confusion and failure, they have only themselves to blame. It is not surprising that such teachers give 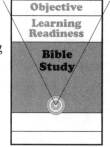 years to gathering information and mere minutes to planning a strategy for conveying it effectively, sometimes—as one professor shared with me—on the way to the classroom.

No, the essence of teaching is far more than information transmission. Teaching pushes learners into life change through shared experiences and new understandings. *Here* is where we haul the freight— we can't be satisfied merely to polish the truck! Let's consider how to organize the Bible study section and what teaching methods are most appropriate.

Organization

Organization of the Bible study section can take one of several general forms. Let's consider verse-by-verse study, group study, key concepts study, and personal response.

Verse-by-Verse Study. Teachers explain each verse, or key verses, in the assigned passage. Verse-by-verse is by far the most common approach in youth and adult Bible studies. Perhaps this is because commentaries provide information this way.

The greatest challenge is to maintain learner interest. Explain a verse or verse fragment. Ask a question about your explanation. Correct any misunderstandings. Enliven explanations with illustrations, personal examples, and practical applications.

> Example: Trace Paul's first missionary journey, verse by verse. Move from city to city, explaining key events and implications as you go.

Small Group Study. After learning readiness, give a brief background study of the passage and explain key terms. Divide the class into groups of three to five persons. Give members a question or list of questions and time to study the assigned passage to find answers. Plan to spend about half the session in group work and half for class discussion of discoveries. Take opportunity to clarify meanings and correct misunderstandings during the group discussion.

> Example: Answer the following questions from Acts 13–15: Who was the leader of the first missionary journey at the beginning? Who was the leader at the end? When did this change in leadership occur? Why? How did the older, established leader react to the new leader? Who deserted the team? What was the reaction of the two leaders to this "quitter"? Which of the two reacted more like you would? What key discoveries did you make in these three chapters?

Key Concepts Study. Organize your material around the key ideas in an assigned passage. In Revelation 1 we have the twin pictures of Jesus as Lord-judge and as friend. In Galatians 5 we have a contrast between flesh-works and Spirit-fruit. Separate the related key concepts in a given passage and help learners analyze them.

> Example: Focus on the key concepts in Eph 4:15. "But speaking the truth in love, let us grow in every way into Him who is the head—Christ." Organize the Bible study section around these four concepts:

- Speaking "the truth"—Christians should live lives of integrity.
- Speaking "in love"—Christians should live lives of mercy.
- Speaking "the truth in love"—A fusion of the two. Not callous conviction; not sentimental fuzziness; loving with integrity; speaking truth mercifully.
- Growing up into Christ—The result of balancing truth and mercy is spiritual growth. Compare with Prov 3:3–4.

Personal Response. Organize the Bible study around the personal experiences of class members. This approach is the most unstructured of any discussed so far. It is also the best way to involve the hearts of learners in class discussion. Call for positive experiences: When has someone been a good Samaritan to you? or What experiences have you had with answered prayer? or How have you been blessed by tithing? Avoid calling for confession of failure: When have you had an opportunity to share your faith and refused to do so? or Have you ever failed to pray for someone in need? What happened? or How have you failed the Lord in the area of tithes and offerings?

Sharing personal experiences can easily slide into emotional fluff unless we tie the process to biblical truths ("Jesus wept") or theological thoughts (the hymn "I Surrender All"). While there is danger in this approach to study, the positive sharing of Christian experiences can be a powerful motivator for living out the teachings of the Bible.

> Example: After learning readiness (Earn the right—share an experience in missions), briefly survey the first missionary journey of Paul and ask class members to share a meaningful missions experience they've had. How did you feel before you went? How did you prepare? What happened to you during the trip? How did the experience change your life?

There are definable principles of teaching tied to each of the four types of learning: knowledge, understanding, personal response, and Christian action. Some of the material here will seem vaguely familiar because it connects closely with discussion in chapter 11, "The Goal of Christian Education." Here is the distinction: There we focused on fundamental definitions and principles, such as "Examples versus Facts." Here we focus on the technical aspects of the planning process and focus on how to use "Examples and Nonexamples" in a lesson plan. In the following sections we discuss practical ways to put fundamentals of learning into practice. We turn to those now.

Teach so They'll Remember

When we desire learners to remember the essentials of what we teach, we should set up a target for knowledge, then plan a study process that establishes recall. We are more effective in achieving a knowledge outcome through the use of advance organizers, clear structure, proper sequence, and active recall.

Advance Organizers. An advance organizer tells learners, at the beginning of class, what material will be learned in the session. An example is the map of the cities of Asia Minor suggested earlier under the discussion of learning readiness.

For example, tell the learners, "At the end of the class today, you will be able to list the pieces of the armor of God from memory." Or give a short self-graded quiz over the major points of the session. Or write out an outline of the key points on poster board and tape it to the front wall of the class. Advance organizers provide learners with an overview of the key ideas in the session and help them focus on elements to be memorized.

Structure. Learners remember key elements much better when they are organized and presented in a clear manner. Emphasize major points as you go along. Use verbal markers to separate one topic from another: "OK, we've seen how the disciples avoided Paul when he came to Jerusalem. Now let's see how and why they eventually accepted him." Review the section on "organization" for specific suggestions.

Sequence. Learners do better when our material seems to be "going somewhere." Sequence the presentation logically from point to point. Help learners visualize the sequence much like a series of snapshots telling a story.

Active Review. The learner will remember key points better if we use active review throughout the Bible study section. Learners themselves conduct active review by repeating key items. Teachers conduct passive review by reminding learners of past sessions. Active review is far more effective in producing knowledge than passive review.

Recall of key ideas in the future requires some measure of repetition, often called drill and practice. In leading a session to memorize the nine fruit of the Spirit, we would list the nine (marker board, poster, chalkboard) in three groups of three. *All right, let's say the first three together.* (Learners repeat in unison "love, joy, peace.") *Again?* ("Love, joy, peace.") Explain the meaning of "love." (Learners repeat the three.) Explain "joy." (Learners repeat the three.) Explain "peace." (Learners repeat the three.) Erase all but the letters "L, J, and P." Again? (Learners repeat the three.) Move on to do the same process with the second set, the third, and finally the whole list.

As you can see above, we keep the drills short and alternate between drilling and explaining meanings of the terms. This reduces boredom, which is natural in drill and practice exercises.

Teach so They'll Understand

When we desire learners to understand the key concepts we teach, we should set up a target for one of the levels in the understanding domain, then plan a study process that leads learners to explain simple concepts, solve problems, analyze texts, synthesize complex concepts or principles, or evaluate perspectives. We are more effective in achieving an understanding outcome when we move from "simple to complex" and "concrete to abstract," provide examples, ask questions, and present problems. We turn to each of these.

Simple to Complex. Begin with simple, single concepts. Then move to more complex principles that meld these concepts. The "key concepts study" presented earlier follows this sequence. It is fairly easy to explain "speaking the truth." Few would misunderstand the idea. Explaining "Speaking . . . in love" is again fairly easy. Again, few would misunderstand.

But when we put the phrase together, "speaking the truth in love," we confront learners with a complex principle that will be new to many. People can speak truthfully (often losing their tempers). And they can speak lovingly (often ignoring the truth of wrongdoing).

But to do both at the same time is a complex concept to teach! *Loving with integrity; speaking truth mercifully.*

Concrete to Abstract. Begin the session discussing things that learners know: their experiences, opinions, or ideas. These are tangible, concrete elements. Then move to Bible words (knowledge), Bible meanings (concepts), and finally to eternal principles. Each stage moves learners beyond personal reality to greater levels of abstract thinking.

Jesus' parables are excellent examples of this sequence. He began with things tangible to His hearers: wind, sheep and goats, treasure. Then He moved them to consider how these concrete things reflected the (abstract) kingdom of God.

Examples and Nonexamples. Use examples to clarify what a concept means, and nonexamples to clarify what it does not. In a session on *agape* love, we want to distinguish *agape* love from other kinds of love. What *is agape* love? What kinds of love is it *not*? Both kinds of comparisons are important. Contrast *agape* (doing good to others, meeting another's need) with *eros* (lust) and *phileo* (brotherly affection) to remove romantic and family aspects of our English word *love*. Jesus did not command us to "like" our enemies, but to do what is best for them.

In a similar way contrast "Christian joy" (flows from within despite circumstances, a fruit of the Spirit), with concepts often confused with joy, such as happiness, pleasure, and fun (dependent on external circumstances).

Ask questions. Clarify the meaning of concepts by asking questions. By far the most important part of teaching for understanding is being able to ask the right question at the right time. The kind of question we ask is critical.

Avoid rhetorical questions. Do not ask a question and then answer it yourself. Rhetorical questions condition learners not to answer, reduce participation, and hinder thinking. Much of the lag time between teacher questions and learner responses is due to learner uncertainty: Do they want us to answer this time? My rule is simple: Never ask a rhetorical question in a teaching situation. Make a simple statement instead. When asking questions, always encourage answers from students. If we consistently apply this rule, answer lag time will dramatically decrease.

Avoid leading questions. Do not ask questions that have obvious answers. Such questions bore learners and stifle their interest in the study. "Do you see that Paul is saying that we should . . ." (Of course!) "Do you understand that Jesus is teaching us to . . ." (That's what you just said!) It is better to explain the meaning of the passage than to ask leading questions.

Avoid simplistic questions. Avoid yes/no questions. "Was Jesus Jewish?" "Was the apostle Peter married?" "Did Cain kill Abel?" "Was Barnabas the one who helped Paul in Jerusalem and Antioch?" These factual questions extinguish the thinking process.

Use conceptual questions. Focus learner attention on meaning. "John describes Jesus' eyes as 'like a blazing fire' (Rev 1:14). What does this mean?"

Or another: "In Colossians 3:8–15, Paul lists some characteristics that Christians should take off and others we should put on. How are these characteristics related?"

Or another: "Jesus says, 'Let your light shine before men, so that they may see your good works and give glory to your Father in heaven' (Matt 5:16). He also says, 'Be careful not to practice your righteousness in front of people, to be seen by them' (Matt 6:1). How do you explain this apparent contradiction?"

Use probing questions. Ask questions that carry learners deeper into meanings. Go beyond initial responses to get at the heart of what learners understand. Ask for more detail. For example,

> Teacher: How might we *agape* people this week?
> Learner: We can be kind to people.
> Probe: OK. How would you do that?
> Learner (*thinks a moment*): Well, I'd be nice to people.
> Probe: So *how* will you be nice to people? What will you do?"
> Learner (*thinks a little more*): I know! I could visit my friend who's in the infirmary!
> Teacher: Good! You've got the idea! Someone else have a suggestion?

Use redirection of questions. Probing questions can cause discomfort for some learners. We can make learners feel harassed if we continue to probe too long. Redirect the question by asking the entire class for an answer. Let's say that the learner in the example stammers, looks at the floor, pats his leg. He is showing that the probing is embarrassing. Redirect the question to the class: "Class, what specifically can we do to be nice?"

Clarify meanings through problem-solving. When we present a problem or dilemma related to our theme, we get a good picture of how well class members can use what has been explained. Problem-solving takes learners as close to real-life events as we can get inside a classroom. The dilemma can be as simple as a statement. The problem can be a situation learners may well face. It can be a case study involving several principles in a single problem. Learners discuss and respond to the problem before the Bible study and then return to their analysis after the study. Have they changed their thinking during the session? Do they respond differently now? Learners discover the values and ideals of others as they solve these problems. The process reveals blind spots. Learners gain experience in looking at the situation from perspectives other than their own. All these elements—statements, situations, case studies—make problem-solving an effective tool for learning to make specific applications of biblical concepts to contemporary situations.

Teach so They'll Personally Respond

Learners share their opinions and experiences when there is an atmosphere of freedom and openness in the classroom. As we have seen, learner ideas and experiences are essential to our goals of "redeeming time" and helping them grow. The more we can involve our learners in the session—the less detached and isolated they are—the better they learn and the more they change. How do we improve the openness of our classes? How do we help learners become personally involved? Let's look at these two vital aspects of Bible study.

Improve openness. We improve openness by using *subjective questions*. Subjective questions allow the learner to share personal opinions related to the passage. They do not require specific factual knowledge of the Bible passage, nor do they depend on the learner's ability to think clearly or logically. The intention of the question is to "open up the learner" to see how the learner is feeling or thinking within himself. Here are some examples of subjective questions.

- "Jesus forgave Peter for his betrayal during the trial (John 17). How would you have reacted if you had been in Peter's place?"
- "What experiences of forgiveness have you had?"
- "God gave Moses an 'impossible task.' Have you received God's call to what seemed an impossible task? How did you respond? What happened?"

Subjective questions move into the hearts of learners. Answers to these questions say little about the text itself, but they do far more to build a trusting, interactive environment than poorly worded, factual questions.

> "Can anyone name the twelve disciples?"
> "Someone tell me who Saul was. No, no, the other one."
> "What was David's wife's name? No, the second one."
> "Where was James when he wrote Revelation? Oh, I meant John!"

Teachers who use too many factual questions, even if worded well, will reduce the willingness to contribute in class.

Another way to improve openness is to *ask questions of the whole group*. Calling a learner's name before asking a question takes every other learner in the class out of the interaction. They do not need to think about the question. Asking questions of the whole group gives each member an opportunity to think and allows anyone to share. Furthermore, calling on a specific learner puts the "chosen one" on the spot and can lead to humiliation.[4]

We improve openness when we *earn the right* to ask personal questions by sharing one of our own first. Share an appropriate

---

[4] Teachers in public schools may be required by state law to "provide every child in the classroom an equal opportunity to succeed or fail." One implication is that teachers are required to ensure that questions are asked of every child in the room on a rotation basis. My wife uses a coffee can with popsicle sticks containing student names. She picks up the can and shakes it ("She's going to ask a question"), asks the question ("I'd better have an answer"), and then picks a stick at random and calls the name. The stick goes into another can. When all sticks have been used, the process starts again. An important advantage of this procedure is the prevention of a few energetic students answering all the questions.

experience in order to prepare the way for your learners to share their own.

We improve openness when we focus on *positive experiences*. A common mistake of inexperienced teachers is to ask students to share failures rather than successes. "When was the last time you had an opportunity to share your faith but didn't?" You will do more for class openness and mutual trust if you only call for positive experiences. "Who would share a time you told someone about the Lord?"

Learners sometimes volunteer times of failure if they feel comfortable and accepted in the class. This sharing can be a wonderful display of trust in a class. We want to be very sensitive in these times because the heart is wide open and the learner is vulnerable, even fragile.

That said, asking learners to share their failures is never appropriate: "How many of you have not had a devotional time this past week? C'mon. God is watching." Public confession of wrongdoing has long been an essential tenet of communistic brainwashing and should never be a part of a Christian classroom. But the sharing of personal, positive experiences in the class, over time, helps members learn from one another and develops an atmosphere of trust and acceptance.

Handle wrong answers. Give attention to how to respond to wrong answers. When learners answer our questions, it shows they have enough confidence to risk being wrong. What do we do when the answer is, indeed, wrong? If we react in a way that belittles or humiliates learners, they will immediately "mask up." It may take several weeks to win back trust, and we can lose the chance to teach them altogether.

How, then, do we respond when a person answers wrongly or shares an opinion that does not reflect clear biblical thinking? *Support the person* and deal with the answer. *Redirect the answer* to the class for analysis. *Defend the learner's willingness to share* if others criticize him, but guide the class to see what the Bible says. Or *respond yourself.* "I think I see what you mean, but it raises another question for me. It seems to me that Paul is saying (express the idea in other words). How does that fit with your thinking?"

When members begin to argue, *defend the right of all* to speak their minds. Keep the discussion *on the issues* involved. *Defuse negative emotions* as much as possible. "Beloved, tension is growing. We may not be able to agree on this point. But let's not become disagreeable. Let's see if we can find some common ground here."

We do not give up the truth of God's Word in order to placate the feelings of people (2 Tim 4:1–5). At the same time we do not condemn or ridicule God's people in the name of truth (John 3:17–18). We teach the truth by patiently leading them to compare their own conceptions with those of the Bible. This requires trust and openness. Nothing hampers openness in the classroom more than harsh, judgmental, humiliating responses to incorrect answers. By contrast, loving responses affirm the learner, correct the answers, and teach both biblical content and Christian behavior at the same time: "Speaking the truth in love, let us grow in every way into Him who is the head—Christ" (Eph 4:15).

Avoid a harsh or negative attitude. When teachers display a negative, dominating spirit, they build psychological walls between themselves and those who disagree with them. They hinder learner participation and quench any sense of openness in the class. Ultimately they destroy their opportunity to teach.

Model desired attitudes and behaviors. Subjective learning is more "caught from the teacher" than "taught by the teacher." We are effective in subjective teaching when we naturally model the truths we teach. On the other hand it is difficult to teach "patience" when we display impatience at every turn. We ask the Lord to show us how to live the principles we teach. We aspire to narrow the gap between biblical standards and the way we live; it is a matter of personal growth.

It is always dangerous to pretend to possess spiritual qualities that we lack. It is hypocritical for teachers to "preach tithing" when they do not tithe. But such hypocrisy is also self-defeating because learners are uncanny in their ability to see through religious masks. Our open and honest struggle toward Christlikeness can be a living example to our class members.

Work with small groups. Learners feel less threatened in a group of 4 than they do in a group of 14 or 40. We all have learners who seldom raise a question or make a comment. They lack the confidence to speak up, especially in a large group. But when placed in smaller groups, they may be less anxious and therefore more willing to share.

Further, large classes allow one person to speak at a time. When we divide the class into smaller groups, more learners can speak and in a safer setting. The result is greater freedom for sharing and participation by more learners.

Learners are worthwhile individuals. Whether our learners agree with us or not, whether they are pleasant or not, they are individuals for whom Christ died. They are worthy. They are valuable. We do well to treat them as precious jewels. We may lose the teaching battle today but ultimately win the learning war if we persevere in loving the individual. Consider Jesus' treatment of the Samaritan woman, the Roman centurion, tax collectors Matthew and Zacchaeus, and Nicodemus the Pharisee. May we treat our learners as Jesus did His. God brought our learners into our classes. We are stewards of those we teach. Teachers who love their students overcome many deficiencies in style or technique, for "love covers a multitude of sins" (1 Pet 4:8).

Teach so They'll Do the Word

Jesus made clear that learning and action go together. "Go and do the same" (Luke 10:37) accompanied His teaching. The problem-solving activities and removing-the-mask techniques already discussed are excellent ways to get learning out of the classroom. But how, specifically, can we coax learners into action? By assigning activities to be done during the week. These assignments can be given to individuals, to groups, or to the class at large. Here are some suggestions.

Individual Assignments. When learners show special interests or talents, suggest a project that will allow them to use these. They will learn more on their own. And they can share with the class as well. Let's say one of our members likes geography. Ask her to draw a map of the unfamiliar area the class is studying. Another might enjoy language study. Assign him a list of words from soon-to-be-studied passages. He can dig into commentaries and be prepared to share his findings in class. Others may have talents for drama or music or poetry. They can direct miniplays or write songs or poems to share in class. The variety created from learner contributions enhances the study. More importantly, the focused attention of learners on passages, places, words, and scripts deepens their commitment to God's Word.

Group Assignments. From time to time, we can ask a group of three or four learners to work together on an assignment. They teach one another in a relaxed setting outside of class. Their presentation to the class will add variety to the hour. It gives the group members a sense of belonging and usefulness in the class. It also is an ideal way to involve members who are hesitant to accept an individual assignment.

Class Assignments. We can make a general assignment for the whole class every week. This might be a question to answer. It might be a specific verse or two to read. It might be a short list of words to define for the next session, or a case study to analyze, or a spiritual diary to keep for the week. These kinds of assignments draw class members together in doing common tasks. Of course, we do the assignments ourselves! By doing so, we give the proper example, but more, we make ourselves part of the whole group.

At the end of a study on "love" (1 Cor 13), I found myself with 10 extra minutes. Not knowing what else to do, I asked my class of 12, "How can we love someone this week?" After the typical Sunday school answers along the lines of "Be kind to people," I became much more specific. "Whom do you know right now that you can help this week?" Sarah[5] said she had a friend in the infirmary. "I can go visit her!" Exactly. That is exactly what *agape* means! Meeting the needs of another. Sam spoke up and mentioned the struggle his roommate was having in math. "I can help him prepare for our exam on Friday." Every member of the class, including the teacher, thought of someone we could *agape* during the week. As they went back to their lives, they carried the Lord's message with them. They carried Him with them, and He was about to teach them Himself.

Use assignments in class. It is essential that we provide time, in the following session, for learners to share what they did and what the Lord taught them. Learners shine as we encourage them to share what happened to them during the week. By doing this, we reinforce

---

[5] Sam and Sarah are not their real names

future completion of assignments because it shows in a tangible way that we think doing the assignments is important. Failing to debrief assignments indicates the assignments are not important.

When my Gallaudet class gathered the following Sunday, I asked them to report what happened. Since this was the first time I had ever made an assignment, most of the students had forgotten. They had nothing to report. I did not fuss about their failure—doing so would have been counterproductive, I thought. Instead, I focused on the two who had reports. Sam sat in the classroom beaming. He told us about helping his roommate study, and the result was that he passed his exam on Friday—the first passing grade all semester. And then, to the surprise of us all, Sam pointed to another student in the class: "And there he is. He's visiting with us today."

Sarah visited her friend on Tuesday. She took along several magazines to leave with her and sat with her for an hour, catching her up on the campus news. As she prepared to leave, her friend asked, "Why did you come to see me? I've been here two weeks, and you are my first visitor." Sarah's answer wrapped itself around my heart. "Because Jesus loves you and I wanted to share some of His love with you. I'll come back tomorrow and bring another magazine."

Three weeks later Sarah's friend began attending our Bible study class. Within six weeks these two new members—brought into the class by the "doing" of Sam and Sarah—made professions of faith. That year, 32 of the 35 new members of our class made professions of faith. And much of this was the result of learners putting into practice what they learned in class. Assignments need not be difficult or complex. But the regular, intentional, and patient assignment of tasks to "put into practice" the words of Jesus pays rich dividends in Christian learning and growth.

Benefits of Outside Work

What are the rich dividends? We can list many. An assignment

- recognizes and develops the gifts of learners.
- increases interest in personal Bible study.
- increases enthusiasm for the Sunday school hour.
- reduces teacher study time as learners share in teaching.
- increases the variety of learning experiences.

- encourages learners to explore biblical topics in more detail.
- builds rapport between teacher and members through sharing.
- develops teaching skills in learners.
- helps shy members to become more involved with others.
- expands the Sunday school "hour" into the week.
- furnishes resources for future learning through increased sharing.
- reduces dependence on the teacher as it increases independent study.

Moving a group of teenagers or adults to engage in assignments during the week may take some time. Classes in their natural state normally come to sit and listen. Many teachers like it that way. To move the group away from "sit and listen" to "engage and act" is a major undertaking and is itself a central part of teaching ministry.

Choosing Bible Study Activities

We've concentrated on the complexities of the Bible study section of a lesson plan. From this mass of perspectives and procedures, how do we decide what specifically to do in a given Bible study? Here are some suggestions to help us determine which learning tools to use and when.

Class History. Consider a middle-aged man who wants to get into shape. He will be wise to go slow, making changes gradually, building up to exercises that are more strenuous. In the same way we begin with a class where they are and lead them into approaches that are more effective. What kinds of teaching experiences is the class used to? Classes accustomed to lecture (and little or no participation) will not like being asked questions and may rebel at the suggestion of group work. Classes accustomed to freewheeling discussion will not like to sit and listen to lectures and may resent that we are trying to (over-)structure the class by way of questions or comments. We start where they are, then move them gradually and gently into better methods of learning.

Class Preferences. What do class members respond to best? If the class enjoys group discussion, use this while integrating more explanation. If the class prefers lecture, use this while integrating more participatory activities.

Choose new approaches wisely. Consider new approaches that can be used without creating undue anxiety or resistance. Let's say the class is comfortable with listening to lecture-based explanations but resists open discussion—most see it as "shared ignorance." Many teachers accept this as reality and will not attempt to change it. But this class will not grow in affect and application unless we change their perspective. Begin the change by remaining the same: prepare and present well-structured lectures. After several sessions, ask a conceptual question or two about explanations. Then, session by session, gradually increase the number of conceptual questions. Along the way add a subjective question or two. If there is little or no resistance from the class, use a short small-group exercise. Moving from class to small groups is a large step, but we reduce the shock to learners by centering the small-group discussion on the lecture. After using small groups several times, add a subjective question for small groups to discuss.

Classes used to freewheeling discussion may have little appreciation for structured word studies, history, and deeper theological issues—most see these as "boring." We can accept this as reality, or we can commit ourselves to the Lord to move learners into a deeper understanding of His Word. Continue to lead discussions. Ask conceptual questions. Present explanations. Provide Bible study resources for in-class research. Present problems. Make Bible research assignments. Over time class members will deepen their appreciation for in-depth Bible study as they experience structure within the discussion.

The greatest obstacles to this process, I suppose, are teachers themselves. Those who are unable or unwilling to teach in a variety of ways discussed here will simply leave classes where they are.

Choose appropriate activities. Effective planners choose activities that support the process from learning readiness to target. If the objective is knowledge, then choose activities—overview, active recall, drills, structure—that establish knowledge. If we fear that a particular activity will be unacceptable to learners, then we can change the objective. Set up realistic targets for learners and then plan appropriate activities in line with those targets.

Watch for fire. In time one of our class members will "catch fire." A discovery made. An experience had. A lesson put into practice with positive results. Interest is ignited. Enthusiasm recharged. These events motivate continued change. Move the class in this learner's direction by emphasizing his experience.

Be patient and move gradually. As one and then another of our learners catch the excitement of life-changing Bible study, we are given greater freedom to do new things in class. Be cautious. Do not go too far too fast. Be patient with learners who aren't excited and don't seem to care. They may come around (think of the disciple Thomas), or they may not (think of the disciple Judas). As the old hymn encourages: "Keep telling the story, be faithful and true, / Let others see Jesus in you." And you will see God move among your learners, changing them, growing them, calling them, equipping them, and sending them.

Hit the Target?

The Bible study section ends when our learners (or at least some of them) hit the target we've set up. If our target is knowledge, we test whether learners (individually or as a class) can repeat from memory the elements we set before them. If our target is understanding, we test whether learners can explain or give examples of the concepts we've taught. We do this by asking a question or posing a problem. If personal response, have (at least some) learners shared experiences related to the study? If purposeful action, have learners reported actions taken during the week?

If not, why not? Was the target too small? Did we fail to plan teaching time correctly? Did we use inappropriate methods? Did we use methods correctly? Did something unexpected happen in class? Such evaluation provides tangible help for our next teaching plan.

The Conclusion: "Tie It Up in a Bow"

We have achieved our objective (or not). We now briefly conclude the session by summarizing, or leading the class to summarize, what has happened. The way we draw our session to a close is as important as anything we've done so far. It is our last chance to "redeem the time" for our learners. Remember, "all's well that ends well." Here are some suggestions for ending well.

Avoid Total Closure

People want to close discussions and end learning activities in a satisfactory way. They want to find solutions to problems we've raised. Educators call this psychological tendency *closure*. It is frustrating for learners to be left hanging in the middle of an unresolved problem or guessing at what the point of the study was supposed to be. On the other hand we create a sense of finality or ending to the session when we bring the class to total closure. This is not good because we want the learning and experiences to follow our learners into the week. Therefore, draw the session to a close without coming to total closure. Here's how to do it.

Review major points. Briefly review the key discoveries of the session. We can do this passively (teacher review) if time is short or lead the class actively to review what they've learned (learner review).

Involve learners. Ask learners to share their discoveries, feelings, and reactions to what they've learned from the session. If we listen carefully, we will notice the kinds of things that interest and satisfy our learners.

Lead to commitment. Ask learners to suggest ways they will act on what they've learned during the week. Write down these suggestions and review them at the beginning of the next class period (without names, of course!).

Prompt for the next session. Plant a seed! Disjointed sessions waste time. When sessions are linked Sunday by Sunday, we extend Bible study time into the week and buy back time for spiritual growth. Links are established between sessions by providing learners a brief but meaningful assignment that ties into the next study.

Raise a question, pose a problem, or provide a situation analysis for learners to work on during the week. This "advance organizer" for the next session helps learners focus on Sunday school study during the week and establishes a beginning point for learning readiness in the next session.

Make an Assignment: "Plant a Seed"

Finish the session by suggesting an assignment for learners to do during the week. See the earlier section in this chapter, "Teach so They'll Do the Word," for specific suggestions. By doing so, you plant seeds for learning during the week, under the Lord's direction. Follow up assignments with discussion the following Sunday to see what fruit was produced by the Spirit.

Close the session with prayer. Ask the Lord to seal the learning of the day and to prompt us during the week to remember and meditate on concepts and values we've discussed. Ask the Lord to bless every effort to put learning into practice.

Beyond Simple Parameters

The approach to planning suggested in this chapter is simple and straightforward. A single target (knowledge, understanding, personal response, Christian action), which sets up parameters for a single focus through the session, is the simplest path to meaningful, measurable learning. It is possible, of course, to add elements to make for a more complex session. Add affective elements to a Gain in Understanding plan to warm it up. Add understanding elements to a Personal Response plan to anchor it in Scripture. Once the basic building blocks are mastered, teachers can construct any size plan from cottage to ranch house to high-rise to mansion.

The simple approach presented here is most effective with youth and adult plans. Preschoolers and children learn better in environments filled with toys, games, songs, parallel learning centers, multiple teachers—connected together by age-appropriate outcomes. These approaches can be seen more fully in chapters 15, "Teaching Preschoolers," and 16, "Teaching Children," as well as teacher guides produced by children's curricula publishers.

In Summary

A basic lesson plan consists of the following **elements**:

An Instructional Objective (Set Up the Target)
Learning Readiness (Prime the Pump)
Bible Study (Haul the Freight)
Test of Learning (Hit the Target?)
Conclusion (Tie It Up with a Bow)
Make an Assignment (Plant a Seed)

Using this format to structure lesson plans will put more punch into teaching sessions. We accomplish much more with this approach than without it, and "redeem the time" in practical ways.

Discussion Questions

1. Evaluate a class at church or school. What kind of learning readiness was used? How did the teacher explain concepts? Encourage or discourage discussion? Express appreciation for members' contributions? Bring the lesson to a conclusion? Avoid closure? Review major points? Lead the class to commitment?
2. Select a Scripture passage. Write an objective and a learning readiness activity for the passage.
3. A class member responds to the teacher's question with a wrong answer. What are some appropriate ways for the teacher to respond?
4. How important is spiritual preparation to an effective lesson? Ask several teachers the process they use to prepare themselves for teaching a Bible study class.

Suggested Reading

Coleman, Lyman. *Basic Training for Leaders of Small Groups Video Series*. Littleton, CO: Serendipity House, 1993.

Edge, Finley B. *Teaching for Results*. Rev. ed. Nashville: B&H, 1995.

Hendricks, Howard. *Teaching to Change Lives: Seven Proven Ways to Make Your Teaching Come Alive*. Sisters, OR: Multnomah, 2003.

Pazmñio, Robert W. *Basics of Teaching for Christians: Preparation, Instruction, and Evaluation*. Grand Rapids: Baker, 1998.

Richards, Lawrence, and Gary Bredfeldt. *Creative Bible Teaching*. Chicago: Moody, 1998.

Wilkinson, Bruce. *The Seven Laws of the Learner: How to Teach Almost Anything to Practically Anyone*. Sisters, OR: Multnomah, 2005.

Yount, William R. *Called to Teach: An Introduction to the Ministry of Teaching*. Nashville: B&H, 1999.

Chapter 14

CREATING AN UNFORGETTABLE LEARNING EXPERIENCE

Robert DeVargas

They went to Capernaum, and when the Sabbath came,
Jesus went into the synagogue and began to teach.
The people were amazed at his teaching, because
he taught them as one who had authority,
not as the teachers of the law.
(Mark 1:21–22)

Students learn what they care about and
remember what they understand.
Stanford C. Ericksen

The film *Dead Poet's Society* (1989) tells the story of a handful of students at an all-male preparatory school steeped in academic tradition. Early in the film we see the young men burdened with the rigorous demands of their professors. They are held to unrealistic expectations of perfection and made to feel guilty, even threatened. Against this backdrop of what Yount terms "toxic teaching," we meet the new literature teacher, Mr. Keating, played by actor Robin Williams.

At their first meeting Mr. Keating leads his students out of the classroom and into a hallway filled with photographs of students from the past. The class reads the seventeenth-century Robert Herrick poem "To the Virgins, to Make Much of Time," a work that warns of the fleetingness of youth and beauty. Mr. Keating explains that the Latin phrase for the author's sentiment is *carpe diem,* meaning "seize the day." He then instructs his learners to step toward the photographs and study the faces of the young men who, like they, were full of life but have now grown old and died. Having set the stage, Mr. Keating dramatically echoes the legacy of the dead. In a ghostly voice he whispers, "Seize the day, boys. Make your lives extraordinary." The students sense, perhaps for the first time, their own mortality and a call to *carpe diem.* Mr. Keating has created an unforgettable learning experience.

How often have we sat through "learning experiences" that were, frankly, forgettable? How would our students or congregation answer that question? What makes the difference between a run-of-the-mill lesson and an unforgettable learning experience? Standford Eriksen, in his book *The Essence of Good Teaching,* makes this statement: "People learn what they care about and remember what they understand."[1] This powerful sentence holds the keys to creating an unforgettable learning experience. They are *motivation* and *understanding.* If we can tap into what motivates learners and provide a way for them to understand clearly, then our students will walk away with a learning experience that not only has meaning to them but also is one they remember.

In this chapter we will look at these two keys of unforgettable teaching. We will learn the secret of how to engage our students and motivate them to want to learn. Then we'll discuss creative ways in which we can foster greater understanding by reaching our students in the ways they learn best.

Mastering Motivation

You've heard the stories of the school principal or teacher who finds himself or herself in a scary, inner-city school rife with apathy and delinquency. Against all odds they manage to turn things around by somehow finding what motivates their students to learn. Based on real events, the film *Dangerous Minds* (1995) tells about LouAnne Johnson, an ex-marine turned teacher who struggles to connect with

[1] Standford C. Ericksen, *The Essence of Good Teaching* (San Francisco, CA: Jossey-Bass, 1984), 51.

her rebellious high school students. To fit in, Johnson changes her appearance and the way she talks. She reinforces participation by throwing candy bars to students who answer correctly. But what makes the biggest difference is the time she spends with her students outside of class. In fact, Johnson's role as a teacher in the classroom becomes secondary to her role as a friend and mentor. She provides emotional support for a pregnant student. She helps another student who is in debt. And she protects another who is caught in gang trouble. Through these ordeals Johnson not only builds trusting relationships with her students, she also learns their deepest needs. Herein lies the secret to motivating others: knowing and addressing their needs.

You've been there. Sunday morning, early. The youth show up one by one. Mostly for the donuts. That's why we bring doughnuts, isn't it? You go through the lesson plan, perhaps with passion and energy. Yet 50 minutes later you sense that few lights have come on. Their eyes tell you they don't want to be there. You wonder if you've given them a reason to come back.

Jesus dealt with these kinds of learners, too. Yet He shows us how He masterfully moved unmotivated people to become engaged in His teaching. Think, for instance, of the Samaritan woman at the well. She was coming for water to drink, and she left with water for her soul. How did this happen? In her own words the woman tells us that Jesus "told me everything I ever did!" (John 4:29).

Remember that rich, young man who came to hedge his bet on getting eternal life (Mark 10:17–22)? Jesus went right to the central issue in this man's life by telling him to stop relying on his possessions. Do you think that lesson was unforgettable? Sadly, for him, it was.

Felt Needs and Real Needs

Jesus' teaching is so powerful because He deals with the real needs of people. This is why people respond to Him. Christian educators often make a distinction between *felt needs* and *real needs*. Felt or "presenting" needs, as they're sometimes called, are the needs that a person knows or feels they have. These could be physical, emotional, or even spiritual. Since felt needs are—well—felt, people actively seek to have them met. This is an important point: *Felt needs moti-vate people to action.* The Samaritan woman was thirsty physically and emotionally. So she did what every other person would do in her place. She *actively* tried to quench her thirst. The rich man's felt need was for psychological security. Apparently nothing that he had done up to that point could give him the assurance he needed about the afterlife. So he *actively* sought to have that need met by talking to the person he saw as an authority on the subject.

Real needs, on the other hand, are often the deeper, more pro-found needs that lurk under the surface, unseen and unfelt. They are sometimes termed "perceived needs" because someone other than the person who has them, usually a teacher or counselor, may clearly see or perceive them in the learner even though the learner is unaware. Real needs are often the underlying deficiencies deep in a person's psyche or spirit that force felt needs to the surface. Consequently, real needs often hide below the shallower felt needs of an individual.

On a rafting trip down the Zambezi River in southern Africa, I remember that our guide was concerned about us keeping our feet and shoes dry. That made little sense to us. After all, this was a wild adventure through some of the most dangerous rapids in the world. Yet, at the end of the day, we understood his concern. To reach the vehicles that were to take us back to camp, we had to climb several hundred feet almost vertically up the side of a ravine. If our feet weren't dry, the climb would certainly have taken its toll on our ten-der, swollen skin. Our guide perceived our real need for dry feet long before we arrived at the ravine.

Although one's felt needs are the needs that a learner will actively try to address, the real needs are usually the ones of greater or even eternal importance. A junior high school student may *feel* the need to go along with her friends. Her wiser parents, though, perceive that the student's *real* need is to learn how to choose better friends. The business owner *feels* like he can't give generously in a down economy. But his mentor perceives that the businessman's *real* need of giving to charity during hard times will give him a better perspec-tive on life and business.

The trick for us as educators is to connect for the learners their felts needs to the real needs we know they have. When this happens, our learners transfer their motivation to satisfy their felt needs to their real ones as well. The Samaritan woman came for water. Jesus connected her felt needs—physical and social thirst—to her deeper, invisible real needs that He perceived she had—social and emotional isolation, spiritual confusion, and guilt. She was thirsty in many ways she didn't even realize. So Jesus offered her Living Water. The woman went away satisfied.

The rich young man came for assurance of salvation. Jesus lovingly connected for him this felt need to his lack of faith in God. "What must I do to inherit eternal life?" "Sell all your possessions and give the money to the poor, and you will have treasure in heaven. Then come, follow me." Boom. There it is. The connection. Felt need (assurance of salvation) tied to the deeper real need (trust on God rather than riches). Now that's an unforgettable learning experience.

Steps to Motivating Students

From these and other examples of Jesus' ministry, we see three steps we can take to motivate our learners. First, it is important that we spend time with our learners to build trusting relationships. This means spending significant time with our students *outside* of the class or worship service. We have to find ways to get into the lives of our learners so they know and trust us. It's unrealistic to give only one hour per week to a pastor or teacher and expect them to facilitate changed lives. It can happen by God's grace. But it's rare. God made us to live and learn in the context of authentic community. This kind of community cannot form in a couple of hours a week. It takes time—intentional, informal, and messy. And lot's of it. There's no way around it. Jesus poured His life into a handful of men and women for three solid years, night and day. He knew the need for that kind of community.

Second, we strive to discover the needs of our students. Without understanding their felt and real needs, what hope do we have to scratch where they itch? It will be difficult to draw them to learn biblical truth. They will only be motivated to the degree that our teaching addresses their needs. Let me say that again: *They will only be motivated to the degree that our teaching addresses their needs.* As we spend time with our learners, we begin to pick up the concerns they have and anxieties they carry. We learn of their dreams of the future. We begin to take on the mind-set of the people we are trying to teach. We understand them. Through casual conversations in a car, on a fishing boat, or during long hours in a waiting room, we learn their needs, interests, and motivations.

Third, we carefully and lovingly connect their (subjective) felt needs to their (objective) real needs. That is, we start with the things that concern or interest them and connect those to the deeper things of God. Remember, our learners are motivated to attend to and act on the things that relate to their felt needs. If we don't start with those, we forfeit our chance to tap into the powerful, built-in motivations of our students. By making this connection, we answer the "so" questions: "So what does this have to do with me?" and "So why should I learn this?"

A great way to tap into their inner motivations is actually to meet the felt needs of our students. I can't estimate the number of large pizzas I ordered as a youth minister trying to do just that. Don't be afraid to address the needs directly. Jesus did. He fed the crowds before He told them about the Bread of Life. He healed the sick before He told them about the forgiveness of sin. In fact, meeting felt needs builds trust and creates teachable moments.

Hierarchy of Needs

American psychologist Abraham Maslow is noted for his model of the "hierarchy of human needs." In it he establishes two general categories of human needs: *deficiency needs* and *growth needs*. Deficiency needs are the most basic of human experience and represent those conditions that healthy humans cannot live without. See diagram 1.

Maslow termed his model a "hierarchy" because he believed a person must experience some degree of satisfaction of a lower need before he or she is psychologically able to address a need at the next higher level. For instance, a person who hasn't eaten in days has a physiological need for food. Unless this need is met to some satisfactory degree, he won't be able to attend to the next higher needs of safety and security. Such a person may risk getting hurt or arrested for stealing food.

Here's another example: Until a child receives some degree of un-conditional love from a caregiver (love and belongingness need), she will be unable to develop a positive self-image (esteem need). The child will be stuck at the love and belongingness level, trying to find the unconditional love she needs. Until she does, she'll have trouble attending to the higher levels of needs in the hierarchy.

The second group of needs, growth needs, is made up of the top four levels. They are termed "growth" because they add quality to one's life. These needs emerge once the deficiency needs are met. Growth needs are also hierarchical, capped by self-transcendence. Maslow defined this highest need as one's spirituality.

As both deficiency and growth needs emerge to the conscious level in a person's life, they become felt needs—those that a person will be motivated to satisfy. The hemorrhaging woman reached out to Jesus because she had a safety need. So did blind Bartimaeus. The Samaritan woman came to the well to satisfy a physiological

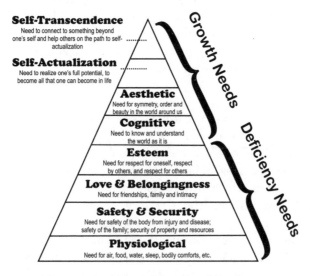

Diagram 1. Maslow's Hierarchy of Needs

need. The rich young man sought answers to his self-actualization needs. Each of these needed; then they acted.

Jesus was often quick to meet the deficiency and growth needs of His followers. He did this so He could take them to the deeper, transcendent issues. In the same moment He relieved a person from a deficiency need, He squarely addressed some higher transcendent need. He turned the corner from felt to real needs. From the temporal to the eternal.

This is where Maslow's model seems to break down. Jesus moved people from much lower needs to the highest of all (self-transcendence), skipping the hierarchical ranking of everything in between. Maslow saw this same inconsistency when he observed that people who where not yet at the self-actualizing stage could still experience self-transcendent experiences. That is to say, some people who shouldn't have concerned themselves with spirituality were, in fact, spiritually minded. Of course, as believers, we know that regardless of our level of need, we are spiritual beings with deep spiritual needs. So, instead of a two-dimensional model with self-transcendence at the top, perhaps we can adjust the model to a three-dimensional one

Diagram 2. Adjusted Hierarchy of Needs

as seen in diagram 2. Here, self-transcendence, renamed "spiritual-ity," becomes a third dimension of all human needs. Now, no matter where on the hierarchy a person falls, spirituality is right alongside.

With this model in mind, think of how Jesus ministers. He first deals with the felt deficiency or growth needs and then turns the corner to address the deeper spiritual needs behind them. The woman who had been hemorrhaging for 12 years was miraculously healed with the touch of Jesus' garment. Her safety need was finally met. She was whole. So what did Jesus say to her? "Daughter, *your faith has made you well*; go in peace and be healed of your affliction" (Mark 5:34). He didn't say, "My *power* has made you well," or "Your *persistence* has made you well." He could have. Yet He moved away from the surface issues and took her to the deep issues of her own spirituality and faith. "Your faith has made you well."

Zaccheus acted on the cognitive need to know and understand when he climbed that sycamore tree. As a despised tax collector, he probably had a few belongingness and esteem needs, too. Jesus could have passed by unseen. Instead, Jesus not only gives the man a front row seat; He also shows him respect by choosing to stay at *his* house. Can you imagine how that made Zaccheus feel? Immediately, we see the change in Zaccheus. He declares, "Half of my possessions I will give to the poor, and if I have defrauded anyone of anything, I will give back four times as much" (Luke 19:8). Then Jesus turns the corner to the deeper issues by stating, "Today salvation has come to this house, because he, too, is a son of Abraham." Jesus first addresses a number of Zaccheus's felt needs. Then He swiftly and wonderfully addresses the profound spiritual needs He perceives in Zaccheus's soul.

Turning the Corner

This idea of "turning the corner" in our teaching and preaching is a key to motivating our students to learn. Turning the corner means that we first address the felt needs of our learners and then skill-fully and lovingly connect those needs to the deeper real needs they have. Addressing both kinds of needs in this order is paramount. If we only address the felt needs of our learners, we risk losing our message. Sure, felt needs are being met, but who's teaching the deep things of God? Pizza only takes us so far.

Conversely, if we only address the real or deeper spiritual needs of our learners without regard to felt needs, we risk losing our audience. Our teaching will seem irrelevant to them. We may passionately preach or teach the profound truths of God's Word, but our voices are drowned out by their felt needs that clamor for attention.

However, when we address the felt needs of our learners, then carefully turn the corner to the deeper things they need, our voices will be heard. Our learners will eagerly hear our message because it becomes relevant and gives them hope. Creating this connection between felt needs and real needs is the secret to motivating our students and moving them beyond their own little worlds.

In the dangerous high school mentioned earlier, LouAnne Johnson spent a lot of time with her students. She learned about them and figured out how to meet their felt needs. She tapped into the things that inherently motivated them. As a result, her students learned to trust her. They allowed her slowly to cut through their thick resistance. Eventually, she was able to turn the corner with them, to focus on the deeper issues of their lives. By motivating and engaging her students in this way, LouAnne Johnson created learning experiences that were unforgettable.

Creating Understanding

The second key to creating an unforgettable learning experience is to facilitate clear *understanding* of the material you teach. Naturally, when a learner understands a concept, he is able to use and apply the concept in new ways. (This is called "transference of learning" and is a major goal for educators.) Yet Stanford Ericksen reminds us that understanding also has another important benefit. Understanding promotes retention.[2] A learner who grasps a concept not only can use it, but he or she won't soon forget it. It sticks.

The reason for this is that the mind is on a constant search for meaning. From its earliest days of development, the brain receives sensory data in the forms of sound, sight, touch, smell, and taste. Flooded with this input, the brain strives to make sense of these new

---

[2] Ericksen, *Essence of Good Teaching*, 53.

stimuli by creating neural networks. These networks are the raw brain material from which cognitive structures, called "schema," are created. Like sorting mail into a matrix of pigeonhole compartments, incoming data is sorted or *assimilated* into existing schema for later use. If data comes that does not seem to fit into existing compartments, then the brain expands the schema to *accommodate* the new information. Over time many bits of data are stored into large, interrelated, and complex schemas.

Imagine that a learner is being taught the meaning of the word *meek*. If she is given the right kinds of experiences related to the word—for instance, defining it, seeing examples of it, discovering its benefits, and so forth—her brain will integrate the concept of "meekness" into her schema in such a way that she will be able to remember and use the concept in the future. If, however, she is unable to grasp the meaning—perhaps she is given two incompatible definitions—her brain cannot easily integrate the concept, and she will have difficulty retrieving and using the idea later on.

Different Learners Learn Differently

In order for a concept to become successfully stored into one's mental schema, two things must be true: (1) the learner has to take the concept into his or her conscious brain *(perception)*, and (2) the learner has to unpack the concept to try to make meaning of it *(processing)*. Although these two steps are true for every person, there are significant variations of how each person does them most effectively. Over the years a variety of learning theorists have arrived at similar conclusions about how this happens. Their theories, particularly those of David Kolb, have been pulled together by Bernice McCarthy into a useful framework she calls the *4MAT System*.[3]

McCarthy's model answers the questions about how the functions of perception and processing happen best in the mind of the learner. Research shows that for each of these functions the individual learner falls somewhere along a continuum. For instance, Kolb believed that people take in information best through either *concrete experience* or *abstract conceptualization* (see diagram 3). Those who prefer to learn through concrete experience are those

---

[3] Bernice McCarthy, *The 4MAT System* (Barrington, IL: Excel, 1987), 34–35.

who prefer to use their senses. They are the "sensor/feelers" who want to be in the middle of things, experiencing life, getting their hands dirty. They love field trips and experiments and out-of-door experiences. Don't tell them about hang gliding. Let them do it. They need to feel the rush when the ground falls away and the wind beats against their faces.

Concrete Experience

Those on the other side of the continuum are the learners who prefer to take in new ideas and experiences abstractly. They are "thinkers" among us who tend to stay separate from the experience but who live through it in their minds. These are the people who sit through a three-hour lecture about an expedition to Antarctica and feel like they've been

Abstract Conceptualization

Diagram 3. How People Take in New Information.

there. No need to strap them to a dog sled. Just let them read about it, and they're happy.

Everyone falls somewhere on this continuum with a preference for one side or the other. In a study among more than 2,300 adults throughout North America, McCarthy found almost a 50-50 split between sensor/feelers and thinkers.[4] What does this mean? Half of the people sitting in our pews learn best by taking in new ideas and information through concrete, sensory experiences. The other half doesn't mind sitting and listening to the sermon.

Mr. Keating asked his students to read a poem about the fleeting nature of youth. They discussed the meaning of the abstract idea *carpe diem*. These two activities are perfectly suited for the thinkers in his class. But then he did something unusual. He asked his students to look into the faces of those now dead students. He made them listen to their collective voice from the grave. He uttered an eerie legacy that put an abstract idea into perspective. Mr. Keating created a concrete experience to which his sensor/feeler students could connect.

---

[4] Ibid., 80.

In answer to the second question about how people best integrate or own new ideas, Kolb found that people tend to fall across another continuum. On one end is *reflective observation*. At the other is *active experimentation* (see diagram 4). Those who tend toward reflective observation are those who process or make meaning of new ideas and experiences by stewing them over in their minds. They are "watchers" who create meaning by observing and reflecting on experiences and ideas. These watchers are the philosophers and poets of our world.

On the other end are the doers. Through active experimentation, these learners energetically work through the concept they are learning with their whole bodies. They have difficulty integrating a new idea by just thinking about it. They have to put the idea into practice to take hold of it. These learners are the builders, the movers, and the shakers among us.

Active Experimentation	Reflective Observation

Diagram 4. How People Process New Information.

Each of us tends toward one side or the other in how we process or make meaning of the things we take in. McCarthy found that 54 percent of her respondents tended toward reflective observation while 46 percent favored active experimentation. Still a fairly even split. What this means is that sitting in your Sunday school class are students who need to take the concepts you teach and immediately put them into practice in order to call them their own. And there are an almost equal amount of students who can simply reflect on your teaching and create the meaning and ownership they need.

When Kolb put both of these continuums together, he found that he could identify four distinct kinds of learners. Each is represented by a quadrant as seen in diagram 5. In the first quadrant are the learners who take in information best through concrete experiences (sensor/feelers) and who process those experiences through reflective observation (watchers). These learners love to experiment and experience life and then sit back and reflect on what they've done.

They are the social scientists, counselors, teachers and administrators among us. McCarthy calls them *imaginative learners*.[5] Their favorite questions to ask, and the ones we must answer to reach them, are "Why?" "Why learn this?" and "Why is this important to me?"

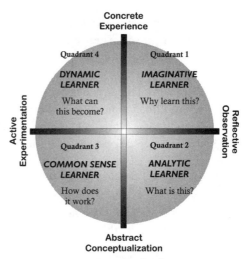

Diagram 5. Four Kinds of Learners

The second type of learner is one who takes in new ideas abstractly (thinker) then processes them reflectively (watcher). These learners are the Stephen Hawkings of our world—the mathematicians, natural scientists, and researchers. McCarthy calls them the *analytic learners*.[6] Their burning question revolves around "What?" "What is this?" "What does this mean?"

In the third quadrant we find the next type of learner who takes in information abstractly (thinker) but who needs immediately to work it out actively (doer). Unlike the imaginative and analytic learners, this type of learner won't sit back and simply reflect on what they've heard or read. They have to put the idea into action and work it out in real life. McCarthy calls these learners *common sense learners*.[7] These are the engineers, surgeons, and applied scientists. They learn well from lectures and books but have to put what they hear or read into action in order to integrate it into their thinking. The question these learners ask is, "How?" "How does this work?" "How can I take this idea and put it into practice?"

The last quadrant represents the type of learner who learns best by being immersed in an experience related to the lesson (sensor/feeler)

---

[5] Ibid., 37.
[6] Ibid., 39.
[7] Ibid., 41.

and then given a chance to work out the concepts actively to make them their own (doer). These energetic learners are the marketing and sales people, the entertainers, and the "people persons" who integrate their experiences into a plan for action. McCarthy terms them *dynamic learners.*[8] These visionary types ask the questions, "What if?" "What can this become?" and "What can I do with this?"

In her study McCarthy found that 23 percent of respondents were imaginative learners, 31 percent were analytic learners, 17 percent were commonsense learners, and 29 percent dynamic learners. These numbers indicate that our classes and congregations are filled with all four types of learners—each type asking a different question. If we are to reach them in ways they learn best, it seems we should figure out how to answer the different educational questions they ask.

Going around the Circle

If we start with the first type of learner—the imaginative learner—and move in clockwise sequence through the four quadrants, we hear, in order, these questions:

1. Why learn this?
2. What is this?
3. How does this work?
4. What can this become?

Look again at these four questions. Do you see the progression? They show us a natural learning sequence of *motivation, examination,* and *application.* First we motivate our students so they care about what is to come. We answer the question, Why learn this? in a way that makes them excited to learn. Next we help the students actually come face-to-face with the material by teaching them from the textbook and then letting them figure out how to use it on their own. At this examination stage we answer the two questions: What is this? and How does it work? The final stage, application, is where we help learners take their experiences outside the classroom. The goal is to help learners apply what they've learned to real life. We guide the learner into answering the question, What can this become?

If we go around the circle and answer these questions one by one, we have a greater chance of reaching each learner in the way he or

---

[8] Ibid., 43.

she learns best. Let's see how this is done with a lesson on ministry to prisoners based on the Matthew 25 parable of the king who rewarded the "sheep" because of their acts of kindness to those in prison.

Assume that the goal of our lesson or sermon is for the learner to understand the importance of ministry to inmates, as well as to become involved at some level in a prison ministry. By setting these goals at the beginning, we have already established where we want to go.

We begin with the first question, "Why learn this?" To appropriately answer this question for the imaginative learners, we need to *create a concrete experience.* Imaginative learners are experience seekers. This is how they (and the dynamic learners) best begin the learning process. Our job, then, is to brainstorm ways to create a sensory, real-life, emotional experience that hooks them. Such an experience will also set up why this lesson is important. If we had enough time and resources, we could take our class to a local prison-ministry event. We could lock them in a cell block with inmates whose lives have been touched by Christ. An easier approach may be to invite an ex-convict or parolee to speak in our class or worship service. A less powerful yet still effective activity is to view a video testimony or a movie clip that relates to the central idea of the lesson. Whatever we do, our aim is to place learners inside of some concrete experience that grabs their attention and sets the stage for the lesson.

Say we decide to invite the warden of a local correction facility into our Sunday school class. We ask him to address the class as if he were orienting new inmates. He'll lay out how life will be lived for the next five to ten years. To heighten the sensory experience, we decide to hold class in an empty maintenance room of the church, furnished only with aluminum chairs. We ask a friend, a police officer, to come dressed in uniform. He's instructed to stand like a prison guard and keep an eye on the class. Under each chair we place a small plastic bin in which students are told to place all of their belongings, including wallets, cell phones, purses, keys, and such. At the front of the room are regulation prison uniforms sorted and stacked by size.

The warden paints a clear picture of how difficult life will be. He talks about how isolated prisoners will be from the outside. He emphasizes that prison life is not meant to be enjoyed; it is punishment for serious crimes. After his address, the warden and the officer leave the room. Done properly, this could be quite an experience. Although everyone knows this is a Sunday school class, learners get a small taste of what prison life is like.

You can create an unlimited range of experiences—from showing videos to designing simulations games to going on real-life adventures. Whatever kind of experience you create, here are a few important guidelines:

- *Make the experience concrete.* The experience should invite the learner to use the senses of sight, sound, smell, taste, and touch. The more senses you use, the better.
- *Make the experience emotional.* By their nature sensory experiences are more emotional than abstract ones. We don't inappropriately or needlessly manipulate the emotions of our learners. Instead, we create experiences that stir or tap into the emotions that motivate learning.
- *Make the experience proportional.* Allow the importance and scope of the lesson to determine the scope, effort, and time given for the experience. A study of Christian charity at home would probably use a smaller experience than a study on world evangelism or Christian martyrdom. Don't allow the physical or emotional size of an experience to overshadow the central idea of the lesson.
- *Make the experience relevant.* The experience *must* relate directly to the main point of the lesson. Avoid the temptation to "kick things off" with some unrelated bit of nonsense. Seize the day with a powerful, concrete, and *relevant* experience.

Before we get to the second question, we first create a meaningful transition between the experience they've just had and the lesson to come. The best way to do this is to lead the learners through a series of questions that prompt them to *reflect* on the experience. Remember, quadrant one and two learners integrate information best through reflective observation. So we ask specific questions that help them to think through the experience.

In the case of the prison activity above, we may ask the students how this experience would make them feel if it were real. What would they miss the most if they went to prison? What one thing would help them not to lose hope? How do they think prisoners without hope deal with things? What difference would having people visit then in prison make?

If we ask the right questions and *listen carefully to the answers*, the learners themselves will bring to the surface ideas that naturally lead us to the main concept of the lesson. When they surface, identify these responses and use them to introduce the lesson. For example, you may say, "A few of you have said that your faith is the one thing that would give you the most hope if you were imprisoned. You also mentioned that having people on the outside care enough about you to visit would also give you something to look forward to. In today's lesson we'll learn the importance Jesus placed on ministering to those in prison, and how, when we care and give hope to them, we also minister to Him."

Once the learners reflect on the experience, and we introduce the learning goal based on their reflection, we are now ready to move to the second quadrant. In this quadrant our analytic learners are asking, "What is this?" Our task is to *teach it to them*. This is when we go to the Bible, the textbook, and the dictionary. Here is where we engage the learners in traditional learning activities like lecture, question and answer, and reading. Remember, analytic learners take in information best through abstract conceptualization, that is, words and ideas. So go to the commentaries and encyclopedias. Read the poets and the playwrights. Examine the Scriptures. Expose the learners to the objective ideas you want them to understand and help them ponder and make sense of them.

In our lesson we read the "Sheep and Goats" parable (Matt 25:31–46). Then, through question and answer, we'll identify the actors of the parable (Son of Man, king, sheep, goats, least of these my brothers, etc.). We may ask the students to study other Scripture passages that reinforce the use of these symbols. To help the students better understand the hardships of the day, we could also read from a commentary or a historical background text. A few notable quotes from early church fathers, or even contemporary prison ministers might also add light to the topic.

Once these activities are completed, each learner should have a book knowledge of the main ideas of the lesson, including definitions, precepts, Bible truths, examples, and contemporary perspectives. These kinds of academic learning activities are the domain of the analytic learner.

From here we move into the third quadrant where the common-sense learners ask, "How does this work?" To answer that question we have to *let them try it*. This quadrant (and the fourth quadrant, as well) is a bit tricky because we have to allow the learners actively to experiment with the new concepts on their own. In the third quadrant, we allow the learners to practice the concepts they just learned. We may hand out a modern-day case study and ask the learners to identify the "sheep" and the "goats" and state their reasons. We might ask them to share recent opportunities in which they could have given care and hope to someone in need but didn't. Then we have the class tell what a "sheep" would do in that situation. Maybe we ask the students to write a job description or want ad for a person who would visit prisoners and encourage inmates.

The point of these quadrant-three activities is to allow learners to practice their new understanding of the concepts taught earlier in quadrant two. This happens best when we guide learners into activities that allow them to play with the ideas and add a part of themselves.

The dynamic learners in the final quadrant are the sensor/feelers who thrive on concrete experience and are the doers who waste no time putting things into practice. To answer their question, "What can this become?" we must help them to *take it out of the classroom*. This is the last step of application we talked about earlier. Our job here is to guide and encourage our learners to create a plan of action that will help them live out what they've learned. To do this we can provide examples of what is possible and give real opportunities for action.

For instance, in our example, we might suggest two or three coming ministry opportunities that relate to prison outreach. If students are interested, they can put their name on a list after class. Perhaps our learners have specific ideas of how they could be involved in other ways. Encourage them to write them down and set goals for carrying them out. It is often beneficial to have the learners work together in small teams to brainstorm ideas. This also builds in a certain amount of accountability. The point here is to allow learners to create a plan of action or a project they can carry out once they leave the classroom. A few project guidelines include:

- *Make the project realistic.* Project ideas should be reasonable in size, scope, and cost. They should also be achievable.
- *Make the project voluntary.* Each learner must be given the freedom to carry out their project or ministry plan without compulsion. Voluntarily putting into practice a new attitude or behavior is a strong indication that real learning has taken place.
- *Make the project relevant.* What the learner does outside of the classroom should reflect the learning that has taken place inside the classroom.
- *Make time for reports.* Ask learners to be prepared to report back to the class about their project. Again, this should be voluntary. Sometimes, a student's report about his or her ministry project becomes a quadrant-one experience that sets off a meaningful impromptu lesson.

Now that we've gone around the circle, we have answered the four educational questions our learners are asking. An easy way to remember how to answer them is the words *hook, book, look,* and *took*.[9] *Hook* means that we create an experience that will hook the learner, giving them a reason to learn. *Book* refers to us going to the Bible or the textbook and teaching the concepts to them. Then the learners are given a chance to *look* deeper for themselves, to figure out how to use the concepts they're learning. Finally, *took* reminds us that the real learning is what happens out of the classroom when learners take and apply what they learn.

This approach to teaching is proven and powerful. Its benefits stem from the way it reaches different kinds of learners in the mode by which they learn best. It also stretches learners to learn in ways they may not naturally prefer. This format is also flexible and can be applied to any teaching-learning situation including sermons, dis-

---

[9] Lawrence O. Richards and Gary J Bredfeldt, *Creative Bible Teaching* (Chicago: Moody, 1998), 156–59.

cipleship training, missions education, music and skill training, and academic education.

The 4MAT cycle can also span different teaching time frames. It can be used for a single 50-minute lesson, for a unit of study that may cover several weeks, or for an entire semester of classes. For a unit of study of, say, five weekly lessons, the first lesson could be the quadrant-one motivational experience and reflection exercise. The second week's lesson follows with the quadrant-two examination activities. The third week would continue with the quadrant-three examination activities. Then, on the fourth lesson, learners plan their quadrant-four project. They then carry out their project that same week. The fifth week could be used for reporting back to the class how the projects turned out.

The Essence of Unforgettable Teaching

Eriksen got it right when he claimed that "people learn what they care about and remember what they understand." Our task as pastor-teachers is to find ways to help people *care about* and *understand* the life-changing truths of Scripture. By tapping into the needs and natural curiosities of our learners, we find fertile ground in which ideas grow. Fueled by their intrinsic motivations, we move our students to consider ideas and concepts about which they've never dreamed. By introducing and teaching these things in ways that leverage each person's style of learning, we enable our learners to grab onto and own the truths we teach.

At the end of the story, when Mr. Keating is abruptly forced to leave his teaching position at the preparatory school, his students demonstrate the depth and sincerity of their learning experiences. As their beloved mentor slowly leaves their classroom for the last time, Mr. Keating's literature students boldly defy the crusty establishment. One by one, his students stand up on their desks and address their mentor as "Captain, oh, Captain!" It's a moving display that not only shows the depth of care these young men have for their teacher, but also reveals the outworking of their newfound belief to seize the day and live extraordinary lives. Like Mr. Keating, the challenge before us in the short time we have is to do all we can to lead our students into this kind, unforgettable learning.

Discussion Questions

1. Think about the teachers or coaches who made the biggest difference in your life. What makes them so memorable? Which impresses you more today: the content of their teaching or the way in which they taught? Why?

2. What are some ways that you could get to know what motivates your learners? How much time would it take to learn their needs and understand how they tick?

3. Describe a time in your life when you were focused on your felts needs while a caring adult or friend was trying to get you to see a deeper, hidden need that they perceived you had.

4. Recall a time when a teacher, parent, or minister effectively "turned the corner" with you.

5. Imagine that your students learn the biblical meaning of the word *forgive* (Gk. *aphiēmi*) through study of the Lord's Model Prayer found in Matthew 6. What are some ways they might demonstrate "transference of learning" of this concept?

6. Consider the four quadrants of McCarthy's 4MAT model. Which quadrant(s) best represents your preferred style of learning?

7. Which quadrant is most *unlike* the way you like to learn? Describe a time when you were made to learn in this way. How did it hinder you or help you?

8. In quadrants three and four we find the analytical and common sense learners. McCarthy points out that traditional academic education tends to swing between these two learning styles. What does this say about the success imaginative and dynamic learners have in our academic settings?

9. It is natural for a person to teach in the way he or she learns best. Think about your own quadrant. How does the way you teach reflect the kind of learner you are?

10. What changes might you make in your teaching to "go around the circle" so that all of your learners benefit?

Bibliography

Ericksen, Stanford C. *The Essence of Good Teaching*. San Francisco, CA: Jossey-Bass, 1994.

Gregory, John Milton. *The Seven Laws of Teaching*. Grand Rapids, MI: Baker, 1997.

Hendricks, Howard G. *Teaching to Change Lives*. Portland, OR: Multnomah, 1987.

LeFever, Marlene D. *Creative Teaching Methods: Be an Effective Christian Teacher*. Colorado Springs, CO: Cook Ministry Resources, 1985.

————. *Learning Styles: Reaching Everyone God Gave You to Teach*. Colorado Springs, CO: David C. Cook, 1995.

McCarthy, Bernice. *The 4MAT System*. Barrington, IL: Excel, 1987.

————. *About Teaching: 4MAT in the Classroom*. Wauconda, IL: About Learning, Inc., 2000.

McCarthy, Bernice, and Dennis McCarthy. *Teaching Around the 4MAT Cycle*. Thousand Oaks, CA: Corwin, 2006.

Richards, Lawrence O., and Gary J. Bredfeldt. *Creative Bible Teaching*. Chicago, IL: Moody, 1998.

Chapter 15

TEACHING PRESCHOOLERS

Marcia McQuitty

[The young boy[1]] Samuel
was lying down in the tabernacle of the LORD
where the ark of God was located.
Then the LORD called Samuel.
(1 Sam 3:3–4)

R eflecting on the story of Samuel, I wonder what kind of
teachers and learning environments Hannah would find if
she brought Samuel to some of our churches in the United
States? When I ask my students to share with me what comes to
their mind when I speak of teaching preschoolers, someone in the
class will always say, "Babysitting!" This attitude can be found in
many churches. Some nominating committees will find teachers for
the children, youth, and adult classes before looking for teachers for
preschoolers. "After all, *anyone* can babysit!"

But preschoolers can learn spiritual truths from trained teachers
who develop relationships with them in the classroom. Preschoolers
can certainly learn Bible stories, but they can also learn how to pray.
The first step in providing a sound education program in the church
for preschoolers is to recognize in them the potential for spiritual
growth.

Preschoolers Growing Spiritually

Samuel's mother had been barren for several years, and out of her
anguish she prayed and asked God to give her a son. She promised

---

[1] The Bible does not tell us Samuel's exact age. But many Old Testament professors
would suggest that Samuel was around four or five years of age.

to give him back to the Lord "all the days of his life" (1 Sam 1:11). Henry Blackaby says, "Hannah's faith in her Lord, expressed in her prayer, set a tone to develop a solid character of faith in Samuel. Samuel knew God in boyhood and he knew God in manhood."[2]

Remembering her promise to the Lord, Hannah took Samuel to the temple to serve. Eli, the priest, taught Samuel the rudiments of caring for the temple. But Eli failed to listen to the heart and mind of the Lord and failed to discipline his own sons, who were also serving the people of God in the temple. Because Eli would not listen, God chose to speak to him *through a young child*. While Samuel lay sleeping, the Lord called out to him. Not recognizing the voice of the Lord, Samuel went to Eli thinking that he had called. After three attempts, Eli finally realized that the Lord was the one calling Samuel. Eli instructed the child to acknowledge the Lord and wait for the words of the Lord to be given to him. Samuel returned to his mat and listened.

> The Lord said to Samuel, "I am about to do something in Israel that everyone who hears about it will shudder. On that day, I will carry out against Eli everything I said about his family, from beginning to end. I told him that I am going to judge his family forever because of the iniquity he knows about: his sons are defiling the sanctuary and he has not stopped them. Therefore, I have sworn to Eli's family: The iniquity of Eli's family will never be wiped out by either sacrifice or offering." (1 Sam 3:11–14)

Samuel heard the words of the Lord and was afraid to share them with Eli. But Eli insisted that Samuel repeat every word that came from the Lord, and Samuel obeyed. God entrusted a small child with a powerful message to give to a religious leader who was serving God's people in the house of the Lord. E. M. Bounds writes, "If more children were born of praying parents, brought up in direct contact with the house of prayer, and reared in prayer environments, more children would hear the voice of God's Spirit speaking to them."[3] Preschoolers are spiritually sensitive and can learn spiritual truths

---

[2] H. Blackaby and K. L. Skinner, *Chosen to Be God's Prophet Workbook: Lessons from the Life of Samuel* (Nashville: Thomas Nelson, 2003), 41.

[3] E. M. Bounds, *E. M. Bounds on Prayer* (Kensington, PA: Whitaker House, 1997),419.

when they are modeled and intentionally taught by significant adults in their lives.

I often ask seminary students what they remember about their preschool years at church and at home. Did their parents teach them spiritual truths? What did they learn about God and Jesus from their teachers? Their responses help me understand how preschoolers absorb and process spiritual truths. Here are some examples of their memories.

- Sitting in church and sharing a hymnal with my father
- Lying to my father and having the worst feeling as I did it
- Learning that Jesus was good and that we could pray to Him
- Praying as a family
- Learning the songs "Amazing Grace" and "Jesus Is Lord"
- At the age of four asking Mom and Dad how to go to heaven while waiting in the parking lot of a restaurant
- Singing praise songs with my dad at the ages of three and four
- Praying for my mom when she went to the hospital to have my brother

Very young children, not yet influenced by the world at large, are spiritually sensitive. Godly parents can nurture the spiritual domain of their children by the intentional teaching of spiritual truths. The second step in a church's ministry to preschoolers is to teach parents how to be the spiritual teachers of their children.

Parents Are Spiritual Teachers

Listen, Israel: The Lord our God, the Lord is One. Love the Lord your God with all your heart, with all your soul, and with all your strength. These words that I am giving you today are to be in your heart. Repeat them to your children. Talk about them when you sit in your house and when you walk along the road, when you lie down and when you get up. Bind them as a sign on your hand and let them be a symbol on your forehead. Write them on the doorposts of your house and on your gates. (Deut 6:4–9)

The defining event in the life of the Israelites of the Old Testament was their deliverance as a people from slavery in Egypt. God performed amazing miracles as He led them to the land of promise where they were to be a peculiar people. In the Deuteronomy passage known as the Shema, God instructed the Israelites to teach their children about the wonders and ways of the Lord, never forgetting the miracles performed on their behalf. This instruction was to be done during the everyday walk and events of life, sometimes intentionally and sometimes through modeling.

George Barna says, on the basis of recent research, that "four out of five parents (85 percent) believe they have the primary responsibility for the moral and spiritual development of their children but more than two-thirds of them abdicate that responsibility to the church."[4] Two D.Ed.Min. students at Southwestern Seminary decided to develop a training program for parents as their final project.[5] When these students talked with the parents in their respective churches, they found that parents did not know *how* to teach their children spiritual truths. An effective ministry of churches today, whether they are large or small, would be to provide seminars, books, and other training programs to help parents learn *how* to teach their preschoolers spiritual truths.

Parents can teach their preschoolers to love the Bible as a special book. Bud Fray, retired missionary and seminary professor, tells of a friend who remembers his father being so disciplined in Bible reading that, each month, he would read the four Gospels. He continued this practice for 25 years. The son remembered a dad who not only knew the details of Jesus' life, but he "talked like Jesus, ministered like Jesus, and became angry over the things that angered Jesus."[6] This parent modeled for his son the discipline of reading the Bible on a daily basis.

Parents can teach their preschoolers to pray. Another professor at Southwestern Seminary told me that when he was five his mother gave him money and a short grocery list to take to the nearby store.

---

[4] G. Barna, *Transforming Children into Spiritual Champions* (Ventura, CA: Issachar Resources, 2003), 109.

[5] Doctor of educational ministry degree, a terminal practitioner's degree, similar to the Doctor of Ministry (D.Min).

[6] W. (Bud) Fray, *It Is Enough* (Columbus, GA: Brentwood Christian, 2000), 15–16.

They were so poor that he did not have any shoes to wear, so he asked his mother if he could have money for shoes. The mother gently explained that there was no money for shoes but they could pray and ask God to provide the shoes. They knelt in prayer, and then he went to the store. As the clerk took the list, he noticed that he was not wearing shoes. When the clerk asked him why, he told him that his mother did not have any money for him to buy shoes. After filling the list, the clerk gave him a note to take to his mother, along with enough money for shoes. With gratitude to God, his mother purchased the shoes. When people asked him where they came from, he would proudly say, "God gave me the shoes!" This young boy will never forget the intentional teaching that God answers prayer.

Parents can teach their preschoolers how to give money to the Lord. Parents have intentionally taught their children to take one dime out of every dollar they earn or receive as an allowance and give it to the ministry of the church. Parents can also teach their preschoolers how to share their possessions with the poor and learn about missionaries who serve around the world.

Anna Mow, former professor of Christian education at Bethany Biblical Seminary, believes that preschoolers and children are more able to learn spiritual truths than many think.

> The condition of the child's responsiveness during the vital years from *birth to rebirth* is in the hands of the adults who people his world. Every minute of every hour of every day counts in a child's life, until he is old enough to put his own will into receiving the Lord of Life.[7]

Ken Hemphill and Richard Ross firmly believe that our children should be raised by godly parents for the kingdom of God. This requires that parents live a holy life before their children. "God is looking for a family(ies) who will dare to embody his character, embrace his mission, and obey his Word. This will be the most exciting family adventure you have ever shared."[8]

> I will honor the holiness of My great name which has been profaned among the nations—the name you have profaned

---

[7] A. Mow, *Preparing Your Child to Love God* (Grand Rapids: Zondervan, 1983), 22.

[8] K. Hemphill and R. Ross, *Parenting with Kingdom Purpose* (Nashville: B&H, 2005), 15.

among them. The nations will know that I am Yahweh—
the declaration of the Lord God—when I demonstrate my
holiness through you in their sight. (Ezek 36:23)

Pastors and church staff can encourage parents to make reading their Bible a daily priority. They can encourage parents to pray,
tithe, and participate in mission activities. As parents grow in their
relationship to God, perhaps they will understand God's clear command to teach biblical truths to their children. When parents bring
their preschoolers to church, trained preschool teachers will add
support to the teaching already done in the home. Providing training
for preschool teachers is the third step in a church's ministry with
preschoolers.

Training Teachers in the Church

Training persons to teach preschoolers biblical truths is important! According to Anna Mow, preschoolers need to know that

> Bible stories are about real people who lived in a land
> far away. If it is only a "happy experience" that is being
> planned for the child, then the day may come when he
> will decide that he is "happier elsewhere." On this basis
> the church now will lose out in the competition with those
> who make a business of entertainment.[9]

Frank Page, current president of the Southern Baptist Convention,
expressed the desire for churches to become "relevant and transforming without clever gimmicks."[10] What does this mean?

When preschoolers come to church, they need to hear God's
word clearly presented by teachers who love them and know how to
teach them. Preschoolers are active learners and will learn best when
teachers use a variety of methods to teach Bible stories and spiritual
truths. Since teaching preschoolers requires skill, spiritual sensitivity, and a dependence on the Holy Spirit, we can help teachers by
taking them to associational training meetings, providing training
sessions in the church, and giving them books to read about how
to teach their particular age group. Some churches can ask a skilled

---

[9] Mow, *Preparing Your Child,* 33.
[10] T. L. Goodrich, "Southern Baptist Leader Heard God's Call as a Boy," *Fort Worth Star Telegram,* 21 October 2006.

teacher to work with a new teacher for a year, forming a mentoring relationship. The experienced teacher can model and explain to the new teacher the the art of teaching preschoolers.

Catherine Stonehouse, Asbury Theological Seminary professor, says that leaders and teachers working with preschoolers and children need a philosophy of education, an understanding of human development, and a theology that are in harmony, each area supporting the others.[11] By philosophy of education, Stonehouse means a way of looking at the teaching-learning process. Who is the teacher? Who is the learner? What is the process? The outcome? Human development refers to the "pattern of change that begins at conception and continues through the life span."[12] She says that teachers "must be students of the Scripture to help us as we utilize our understanding of the secular disciplines to provide developmentally appropriate activities and learning environments to maximize the effectiveness in teaching the Bible stories and truths to preschoolers."[13]

Preschoolers grow rapidly in at least five dimensions. The most effective teachers are those who understand how these five dimensions work together.

Growing Five Ways

Luke described the growth of Jesus in five dimensions. He wrote, "Jesus increased in wisdom [mental development] in stature [physical development] and in favor with God [spiritual development] and with people [social and emotional development]" (Luke 2:52). While spiritual development is the chief concern for teachers of preschoolers, the other four areas come into play. These supporting areas of development have been studied for years by people who have given their lives to understanding the human mechanism of physical, mental, emotional, and social development. We can learn a great deal from their work, including age-appropriate methods, classroom arrangement, and the teaching-learning process as a whole.

---

[11] C. Stonehouse, *Joining Children on the Spiritual Journey* (Grand Rapids: Baker, 1998), 16.

[12] J. W. Santrock, ed., *Life Span Development*, 11th ed. (New York: McGraw Hill, 2007), G-3.

[13] Stonehouse, *Joining Children*, 21.

Mental Development

Jean Piaget, a physician who spent his life studying the process of mental development, discovered that children process information through specific stages. The first stage of mental development is the *sensorimotor period*, a term that emphasizes learning through the senses (sight, hearing, touch, taste, smell) and through movement (stretching, pulling up, crawling, walking). With this stage in mind, we select toys for babies, ones, and twos that have smooth, round edges, have no detachable parts, are easy to clean, and are free of cartoon and fantasy characters.[14]

The second stage of mental development is the *preoperational period*. This period will last from approximately two to seven years. During this period the young preschooler uses symbolic forms such as language, mental images, drawings, and make-believe to imitate those in their world.

One little three year old had an imaginary bear named Smokey. Whenever he would get into trouble, he would tell his mother, "Smokey made me do it!" Preschool teachers can use the developing imagination of preschoolers to help them understand that Jesus lived many years ago; we cannot see Him, but we can learn that He loves us.

Piaget has helped us understand that the preschooler has difficulty seeing from another person's point of view. Being *egocentric,* the preschooler believes that if someone has a toy and he wants it, then he should have it. As the preschooler grows older and learns to be more social, he can and should be taught to share.[15]

Physical Development

Babies depend on caregivers to meet their every need. By the time they reach the age of five years, preschoolers can walk, run, climb, write their name, use a paintbrush, and build with blocks. Babies need small items to hold in order to strengthen small muscles in their hands. One and two year olds need lots of floor space for crawling and walking. Four and five year olds need sturdy objects for

---

[14] T. Sanders and M. A. Bradbury, *Teaching Preschoolers: First Steps toward Faith,* (Nashville: Lifeway, 2000), 61.

[15] N. Hedin, "Teaching Preschoolers," in *Teaching Ministry of the Church,* ed. Daryl Eldridge (Nashville: B&H, 1995), 216.

climbing and tables and chairs the right size on which they can work puzzles, play with Play Doh, and participate in other appropriate learning activities.

Another aspect of physical growth involves brain development. The brain begins to develop at conception and continues after birth, with physical changes taking place throughout the preschool years and beyond. "At birth, the brain is still in a relatively undeveloped state."[16] Dr. Bruce Perry, physician and researcher, says that touching, talking, singing, cuddling, comforting, and reading to the infant and young child can produce dramatic increases in brain development. Children who have been neglected in infancy have been known to have brains that are smaller than the well-cared-for child.[17] Even the consistent presence of familiar teachers in each classroom fosters healthy brain development in preschoolers.

Social and Emotional Development

Erik Erikson helps us understand how preschoolers develop in the psychological (self) and social (others) areas. Preschoolers pass through three separate stages. Stage one, *Basic Trust versus Mistrust,* lasts from birth to approximately age two. During this stage the baby/one year old depends on primary caregivers/teachers in life to meet basic needs such as changing the diaper when wet and providing food when hungry. If the preschooler is abused and neglected, he develops fear and suspicion. As the child grows to trust parents and teachers at church, people he can see, he will be better prepared later on to trust the words of Jesus, a person he cannot see. The child moves from total dependence to gradual independence when he learns from adults he can trust.

Stage two, *Autonomy versus Shame and Doubt,* lasts from approximately age two to age three. During this stage of growth the preschooler takes a major step toward independence. During this "I can do it myself" stage preschoolers want to do many things on their own, in their own way, and in their own time. Preschoolers need teachers who will encourage them to try new art materials and work puzzles that are a little more challenging, and who will provide

---

[16] D. Bergen and J. Coscia, *Brain Research and Childhood Education* (Olney, MD: ASCI, 2001), 27.

[17] S. Morganthaler, *Right from the Start* (St. Louis, MO: Concordia, 2001), 93–94.

adequate supervision and direction. If teachers criticize them for
their failures, preschoolers may withdraw. The greatest challenges
at this stage can involve feeding, dressing themselves, toilet training,
and learning to share personal possessions and toys. The favorite
word of many two year olds is no!

Gabrielle was almost three years old, and her parents wanted her to
move from using diapers to using training pants. The more the mother
pleaded, the more Gabrielle refused. One Sunday the mother confided
in Gabrielle's Sunday school teacher and told her about the struggle.
This wise teacher helped the mother understand that Gabrielle was ex-
erting her growing independence and would eventually do away with
the diapers when she realized that other children in her class were
wearing training pants. The mother listened and relaxed, and within
weeks Gabrielle told her mother that she did not need to wear diapers
any more. Gabrielle wanted to make *this* decision on her own!

Stage three, *Initiative versus Guilt*, describes four and five year
olds. At this stage preschoolers may appear to adults to be "into
everything!" They want to expand their world of experiences, explore, and try out new things. Four year olds are known to have
many questions. One little fellow asked his Sunday school teacher
if Superman was real. "No," she replied, "he is make-believe." After
her reply, he asked her if Jesus was real. "Yes, of course, Jesus is
real. And we can read about Him in the Bible." Teachers need to
encourage older preschoolers to ask questions and try new things in
appropriate ways. "If fours and fives are rejected or punished for ini-
tiating activities, they can experience guilt and become afraid to try
new things on their own."[18] Helping teachers understand these three
stages of social emotional development will greatly enhance their
ability to teach the growing preschooler.

Another skill needed by preschool teachers involves knowing how
to prepare the learning environment for each age group.

Preparing the Learning Environment

When Mike and Sharon moved to Rochester, New York, to become pastor and wife at an old-established church, they found a
congregation with few young families. In fact, there were no pre-

---

[18] Hedin, "Teaching Preschoolers," 216–217.

schoolers attending Sunday school. Mike and Sharon knew that preschoolers learn best when their learning environment—the classroom in which they learn—is arranged specifically for them. They first located two rooms close to adult classrooms and the sanctuary. By setting up these rooms for preschoolers, they were preparing for the day when more young families would come to the church.

Room Set-up

Every learner needs an environment that is safe and secure. Pictures of *real* animals, *real* children, and families can be placed around the room at eye level for babies who might be crawling. These pictures can be found in curriculum resource kits or made from outdated calendars. Cover pictures with plastic so that they can be wiped clean throughout the session. The room should be free of unnecessary furniture and clutter. A Bible should be placed in every preschool room for the teacher to use when talking with the preschoolers and telling the Bible story for the session. All toys in the room should be washable and large enough to prevent choking when the preschooler puts one in his mouth.

Three, four, and five year olds will learn best in a room that provides *learning centers* and a corner of the room set up for *large group time*. *Learning centers* are designated portions of a room set up for home-living activities, puzzles, books, music, art, blocks, and nature. Even if preschool funds are limited, say, in smaller churches, learning centers can still be equipped. Blocks of various kinds can be made with stuffed milk cartons or other throw-away boxes. Artwork can be done on plastic cloths that are placed on the floor. Puzzles can be made from real-life pictures, mounted on heavy cardboard, and covered with clear contact paper. When preschool rooms are set up appropriately, teachers can teach through the use of activities in both the learning centers and large group time.

Activity Learning

In advance of the session, preschool teachers gather the materials to be used in each of the centers. Usually the director of the department prepares to tell the Bible story in the large group time. Preschoolers learn best when they have the same teachers in the room Sunday after Sunday. Preschoolers are curious, active, creative, self-focused, and have short attention spans. They learn best when they can have hands-on experiences. Therefore, preparing the learning centers for preschoolers will enhance their learning experiences.

When older preschoolers enter the room, they should be directed to one of the centers to do the activity set up for the session. In some centers teachers will be available to give instructions if needed, talk about the Bible story, sing songs, and share Bible thoughts. Other centers, such as the block center, may not have a teacher available to guide the child's learning. If preschoolers hear the Bible story told in several of the centers, they will be better prepared to participate in the large-group time. Preschoolers learn through repetition. Preschoolers, after working for a while in one center, may choose to move to another center.

Toward the end of the time spent in the learning centers, the teacher preparing for large-group time will ask the preschoolers to put away all of the materials being used. Blocks are placed on the shelves, and books are returned to the book rack. Puzzles are completed and placed in the puzzle rack. Art materials are put away and/or cleaned. Preschoolers learn to work together, finish a task, and prepare for the large-group Bible story time as they help clean up the learning centers.

Large-Group Learning

Teachers preparing for large-group learning should consider the age and attention span of the children involved. Use the following suggestions as guidelines for the length of group time:

Three year olds	five to ten minutes
Four year olds	ten to fifteen minutes
Five year olds	fifteen to twenty minutes[19]

A variety of activities should be planned for this Bible story time in a group setting. Learning activities include singing, praying, and sharing experiences, playing games, looking at Bible pictures, reading Bible thoughts, and hearing the Bible story. When actually telling the Bible story, teachers hold the Bible in their hands. Teachers can ask older preschools to pray in the large group. Sometimes, we will be amazed at what preschoolers can learn!

---

[19] Sanders and Bradbury, *Teaching Preschoolers,* 119.

In my son's church one senior adult lady greets the preschoolers and children every Sunday as they come to the worship service. She loves to let them choose a piece of candy from her basket. The children have affectionately named her Granny Chocolate. One Sunday morning the pastor told the congregation about Granny's illness and asked them to remember to pray for her throughout the day. Breanna, age four, turned to her mother and quietly said, "I'm going to pray for Granny Chocolate right now!" She bowed her head and silently prayed. Breanna had learned from her parents and her Sunday school teachers the importance of praying for others in need.

Choosing a Curriculum

A preschool minister came to me with the following question: Is it OK to tell a three year old that "God is a big leader and Jesus is a little leader"? As a rule we do not tell preschoolers anything that has to be altered or unlearned later. Teachers need to teach Bible truths that are true to the text. Choosing a Bible-based, child-centered and doctrinally sound curriculum for preschoolers can be a challenge. Some popular curriculum on the market today will look attractive, will have little or no advance preparation requirements for teachers, and are developed around a theme that engages and entertains. Spiritually sensitive preschoolers need to learn age-appropriate Bible stories when they come to church. When choosing preschool curriculum, one author asks the following questions: [20]

Are the Bible stories doctrinally accurate and consistent with your church's teachings? Teachers will usually teach what is written in the curriculum, regardless of their church's doctrinal stance.

Do the Bible stories contain appropriate content for preschoolers? Three year olds might have difficulty understanding the story of the fig tree that did not produce fruit. They would be able to understand the story of the good Samaritan.

Are sound educational approaches used, or are the teaching methods primarily busywork? Quality preschool curriculum will suggest learning activities for the learning centers, which will allow preschoolers to explore key components of the story. While studying the story of the good Samaritan, ace bandages could be used in the home-living

---

[20] J. Haywood, *Enduring Connections* (St. Louis: Chalice, 2007), 103–6.

center to enable the preschoolers to pretend to wrap the broken arm
or leg of a friend.

Preschoolers need to learn from a curriculum that focuses on
learning basic attitudes about the following concept areas: God,
Jesus, Bible, Church, Self, Others, Family, and the Natural World.[21]
Preschoolers, because of their developing cognitive abilities, cannot
understand abstract concepts, nor can they handle large amounts
of historical data. As they move into the school-age years, they can
learn from curricula that will teach them the names of the patriarchs,
the Ten Commandments, and the names of the twelve apostles. As
teenagers, they will begin to learn the meanings of the parables, the
spread of the gospel through the missionary journeys of Paul, and
the implications for God's call on their life. When preschoolers learn
basic biblical attitudes about the eight concept areas, they are building a foundation that will last a lifetime. Let's look at these eight content areas and what attitudes preschoolers can learn.

GOD—Babies and ones can learn that God loves people. God wants
    people to love Him. Older preschoolers can learn that God is
    special and He made everything. God wants people to pray to
    Him. People can worship God.

JESUS—Babies and ones can learn that Jesus loves them. Jesus wants
    people to learn about Him. Older preschoolers can learn that
    Jesus performed miracles and healed the sick.

BIBLE—Babies and ones can learn that the Bible is a special book.
    Stories in the Bible teach us about Jesus and what He did. Older
    preschoolers can learn that the Bible helps them know what God
    wants them to do.

CREATION—Babies and ones can learn that God made day, night,
    plants, and animals. Older preschoolers can learn that God
    planned for people to care for the things He made.

SELF—Babies and ones can learn that God made them. Older pre-
    schoolers can learn that God wants them to pray. God has a plan
    for each person.

---

[21] C. Davis, *Breakthrough Preschool Sunday School Work* (Nashville: Convention,
1990), 153.

FAMILY—Babies and ones can learn that God made their family. Older preschoolers can learn that God plans for mothers and fathers to teach their children.

CHURCH—Babies and ones can learn that people at church love and teach them about Jesus. Older preschoolers learn that a person is baptized after becoming a Christian.

NATURAL WORLD—Babies and ones learn that God cares about other people. Older preschoolers learn how they can be a part of God's work in the world.

Curriculum specialists prepare materials for teachers of preschoolers that directly connect with their age-appropriate abilities. Selecting the right curriculum is important and calls for a well-trained teaching staff.

Administrative Issues

A successful preschool ministry in the local church requires a large number of teachers. Babies and one year olds need one teacher for every three children on the roll. Two and three year olds need one teacher for every four children on the roll. Four and five year olds need one teacher for every five children on the roll. At least two nonrelated adult teachers should be in each preschool room during the session. Churches often struggle to find enough preschool teachers.

During my first church experience as minister of preschool education, I learned that prayer is the key to enlisting teachers. The first Sunday at First Church, I learned that the Mission Friends teachers for the kindergarten class would not be returning in the fall. I remember specifically praying for two teachers to teach in this class. The next Sunday a couple who were on a one-year furlough from the mission field asked me if I would *consider* letting them teach in Mission Friends. Would I *consider*? The Lord showed me in this one incident *that He wanted me to depend on Him to help me* find teachers for the preschoolers in our church. Enlisting teachers involves constantly looking, asking, and praying.

A second important administrative area in preschool ministry involves providing a safe environment. Persons who work with preschoolers must have a criminal background check. Persons who have previously been accused and/or convicted of committing either sexual or physical abuses of children should not be allowed to serve in any program in the church where preschoolers and children will be found. Two adult teachers are to be in every preschool room. Churches with only a few preschoolers should combine ages in one room with two workers rather than divide the preschoolers into two rooms with one teacher in each room. The church cannot be too cautious in protecting preschoolers and children from persons who would look for opportunities to inflict harm.

Conclusion

How seriously does your church take its ministry to preschoolers and their families? Preschoolers can learn biblical truths that become a foundation for the rest of their lives. Preschoolers learn through relationships with preschool teachers who love them and who model and intentionally teach biblical truths. God intended for parents to be the primary teachers of spiritual truths to their children.

Preschoolers can learn about God and Jesus by going to church with their families and seeing people of all ages singing, praying, giving, and listening to Bible reading and sermons. What a privilege for parents to be able to model and intentionally teach their preschoolers how to worship!

Will your church accept the challenge of equipping parents of preschoolers to teach their little ones spiritual truths? Because "the fear of the LORD is the beginning of wisdom, and the knowledge of the Holy One is understanding" (Prov 9:10).

Will your church enlist and train teachers who will commit to being in the classroom Sunday after Sunday, prepared to "teach a youth about the way he should go; even when he is old he will not depart from it" (Prov 22:6)?[22]

Will your church provide a learning environment appropriate for the preschooler and safe from anyone who would seek to harm the child? Will your church do whatever it takes to major on preschoolers "learning the Scripture . . . and being enlightened by the Holy Spirit, apart from whom the Scriptures will not be understood"?[23]

---

[22] See chapter 22, "Ministering alongside Volunteers."
[23] A.W. Tozer quote from Jim Gallery, *Prayers of a Dedicated Teacher* (Nashville: Brighton, 2001), 29.

Samuel, a young boy, heard the voice of the Lord. So may our preschoolers heed His voice through parents, teachers, and church leaders as we pray for them and serve them in Jesus' name.

Questions for Discussion

1. What are your earliest memories about learning Bible stories and learning to pray?
2. Why do churches have a difficult time enlisting teachers for the preschool ministries?
3. What will it take to get parents to become the teachers of spiritual truths to their children?

Bibliography

Barna, George. *Transforming Children into Spiritual Champions.* Ventura, CA: Issachar Resources, 2003.

Bergen, Doris, and Juliet Coscia. *Brain Research and Childhood Education.* Olney, MD: Association for Childhood International, 2001.

Blackaby, Henry, and Kerry L. Skinner. *Chosen to Be God's Prophet: Lessons from the Life of Samuel.* Nashville: Thomas Nelson, 2003.

Bounds, E. M. *E. M. Bounds on Prayer.* Kensington, PA: Whitaker House, 1997.

Davis, Cos. *Breakthrough Preschool Sunday School Work.* Nashville: Convention, 1990.

Fray, William (Bud). *It Is Enough.* Columbus, GA: Brentwood Christian, 2000.

Gallery, Jim. *Prayers of a Dedicated Teacher.* Nashville: Brighten, 2001.

Goodrich, Terry Lee. "Southern Baptist Leader Heard God's Call as a Boy." *Fort Worth Star Telegram,* 21 October 2006.

Haywood, Janice. *Enduring Connections.* St. Louis, MO: Chalice, 2007.

Hedin, Norma. "Teaching Preschoolers." In Daryl Eldridge, ed. *Teaching Ministry of the Church.* Nashville: B&H, 1995.

Hemphill, Ken, and Richard Ross. *Parenting with Kingdom Purpose.* Nashville: B&H, 2005.

Morganthaler, Shirley. *Right from the Start*. St. Louis, MO: Concordia, 2001.

Mow, Anna. *Preparing Your Child to Love God*. Grand Rapids: Zondervan, 1983.

Rainer, Thom. *Simple Church*. Nashville: B&H, 2006.

Sanders, Thomas, and Mary Ann Bradbury. *Teaching Preschoolers: First Steps toward Faith*. Nashville: Lifeway, 2000.

Santorck, John W., ed. *Life Span Development*. 11th ed. New York: McGraw Hill, 2007.

Stonehouse, Catherine. *Joining Children on Their Spiritual Journey*. Grand Rapids: Baker, 1998.

Suggested Reading

Barna, George. *Transforming Children into Spiritual Champions*. Ventura, CA: Issachar Resources, 2003.

Haywood, Janice. *Enduring Connections*. St. Louis, MO: Chalice, 2007.

Stonehouse, Catherine. *Joining Children on Their Spiritual Journey*. Grand Rapids: Baker, 1998.

Chapter 16

TEACHING CHILDREN

Karen Kennemur

Some people were bringing little children to Him
so He might touch them, but His disciples rebuked them.
When Jesus saw it, He was indignant and said to them,
"Let the little children come to Me. Don't stop them,
for the kingdom of God belongs to such as these."
(Mark 10:13–14)

H ave you ever encountered silence on a Sunday morning
in the preschool or children's area of a church due to the
absence of children? My dad, a retired pastor, once encountered such a silence. He found it in a dying church. On the first
Sunday of a new interim, he was walking through the church during
the Bible study hour. He entered the preschool area, and he realized
no babies were crying, no children were laughing, and no teachers
were teaching. It was quiet. He said:

> The sad scene was heart-breaking. However, it became sad-
> der when I walked through the wing of the church and saw
> four or five workers eager for children, but none came. The
> final result was the church no longer exists. They merged
> with another congregation. Without babies and children a
> church simply cannot exist very long.[1]

Children are critical to the life and growth of the local church.
Church growth specialists and pastors agree that "most growing
churches have one thing in common: children."[2] Young families with

---

[1] Dr. J. Poteet, interview by Karen Kennemur, June 14, 2007, live interview,
Southwestern Baptist Theological Seminary, Ft. Worth, Texas.
[2] B. Campbell, "Connection with Pastor Important for Successful Children's
Ministry," *Lifeway*, 2002, http://www.lifeway.com/lwc/article_main_page/ (ac-

children attract other young families with children, resulting in numerical growth. Thom Rainer discovered through his own research
that "focused efforts to assimilate young people often resulted in
entire families becoming involved in a church."[3] Therefore, churches
that intentionally reach children and their families are more effective
in assimilating them into the church body where they will experience true Christian community.[4] They do this through superior programs and ministry opportunities.

Jesus expressed the importance of children in Mark 10:13–16. In
this Gospel passage, parents were bringing their little ones to see the
Savior. The disciples began turning away the children. Perhaps they
were merely reacting as adults often do toward younger generations.
They had not been with Jesus long enough to know His love for children. Jesus' reaction was one of displeasure toward His disciples. "Let
the children come to me. Don't stop them! For the Kingdom of God
belongs to such as these. I assure you, anyone who doesn't have their
kind of faith will never get into the Kingdom of God."[5] In this one act
Jesus was telling us that children are important to man and to God.
Not only do they deserve the attention, guidance, and assistance of
adults; children exemplify the faith required of all Christians.[6]

Leaders who understand the importance of children in the church
are committed to providing quality Christian educational experiences for them. We know today's parents are looking for quality in
programs for their children. Such standards may seem overwhelming
to the average church. However, as congregations assess their goals
for children's ministries, perhaps they might consider building on
their strengths rather than maintaining all programs whether strong
or weak.[7] Most churches "have a limited amount of resources, and
if they funnel their energies to weakest areas, the strong areas often
begin struggling."[8] Strong, successful programs energize parents,

---

cessed February 9, 2007); Kevin Doughterty, "Instituional Influences on Growth
in Southern Baptist Congregations," *Review of Religious Research* 42:2 (2004): 119;
and Reginald Biddy, *Restless Gods: The Renaissance of Religion in Canada* (Toronto:
Stoddart, 2002), 12.

[3] T. Rainer, *High Expectations* (Nashville: B&H, 1999), 19.

[4] S. May et al., *Children Matter* (Grand Rapid: Eerdmans, 2005), 132; and John
Westerhoff, *Will Our Children Have Faith?* (New York: Seabury, 1976), 53.

[5] Mark 10:13–16 NLT.

[6] R. Zuck, *Precious in His Sight* (Grand Rapids: Baker, 1996), 12.

[7] J. Haywood, *Enduring Connections* (St. Louis: Chalice, 2007), 9.

[8] Ibid.

children, and leaders to work as a team to provide quality and to strengthen weak areas. The partnership of the church with parents offers excellence in ministry for all concerned.

In the first edition of this book, Daryl Eldridge tells a personal childhood story about one of his missions education teachers.

> Mr. Bailey was late again for our boys' mission education class. He gave his typical apology for not having prepared a lesson. "But," he said, "on the way to church the Holy Spirit spoke to me and told me what to say." I was curious. I knew God spoke to Saul on the road to Damascus. I'd been told that God sometimes spoke in a loud voice. Did God speak to Mr. Bailey in that same way? Did his sons in the back seat hear God, too? There wasn't anything spectacular about the lesson. In fact, it was similar to last week's lesson. It was one of his favorites, the eleventh commandment. Maybe you've heard it: "Women shall not wear pants in church." As a nine-year-old boy, I didn't mean to be disrespectful to God, but it seemed to me he could have given Mr. Bailey a better lesson.[9]

Excellence in ministry involves much more than planning the lesson on the way to church. We turn now to some basic ingredients in children's ministry necessary for equipping children with a firm biblical foundation. Ministers who focus on the following ingredients provide support for teachers and workers as they effectively minister to children and their families.

How Children Learn

In order to teach children effectively we must understand how children learn, keeping in mind that not every child learns the same way. Paula Stringer and James Hargrave of LifeWay Church Resources identify eight ways to encourage learning. Learning for children is most effective when:

- The learner perceives the material being presented as meaningful. Children see the relevance *for themselves* in the learning experiences.

---

[9] D. Eldridge et al., "The Role of the Holy Spirit in Teaching," in *The Teaching Ministry of the Church* (Nashville: B&H, 1995), 43.

- The learner is comfortable in the classroom setting. Children experience a classroom free from fear, humiliation, and condemnation.
- Learning addresses the way a child learns. The teachers provide a variety of learning experiences so that each child can learn in his or her way.
- The learner is actively involved in the lesson. The child participates at some level rather than simply sitting and listening while someone tells them a story.
- The learner is given the opportunity to make choices, which requires teachers to prepare multiple experiences.
- The learner is ready to learn. Teachers intentionally engage children personally and provide readiness experiences to prepare them to hear the Lord speak through His Word.
- The information is repeated during class time through various activities because repetition helps reinforce learning, translating information into knowledge.
- The learners develop relationships with their teachers and classmates with the ultimate goal of developing a stronger relationship with Christ, which means teachers provide learning activities that encourage teamwork and interaction among teachers and learners.[10]

As boys and girls enter the church doors, the congregation has a great responsibility to help them learn about God and His plan for their lives. Teachers play a significant role in the lives of children. By keeping in mind how children learn, teachers can bring the Scriptures alive for children.

Foundational Teaching Components of a Children's Ministry

Conversion

George Barna reported in 2004 that "nearly half (43 percent) of all Americans who accept Jesus Christ as their Savior do so before

---

[10] P. Stringer and J. Hargrave, *Crayons, Computers and Kids* (Nashville: Convention, 1996), 15.

reaching the age of 13."[11] These statistics help us realize the importance of sharing the gospel with children. Parents, children's ministers, pastors, and children's workers need to present the gospel clearly. They should provide many and varied opportunities for boys and girls to accept Christ into their lives.

The North American Mission Board has an excellent resource for training workers, teachers, and parents to share the gospel with children. *Sharing God's Special Plan* teaches adults to recognize the signs indicating when a child is ready to become a Christian. This literature also guides the adults through the process of sharing the gospel with a child.

Church Membership

In many denominations church membership begins with a conversion experience. According to the statistics cited above, most people become Christians during their early childhood years. Children need to understand the role of church members. They are not always aware of the responsibilities of church membership. If children are taught that commitment to Christ also involves a commitment to His kingdom's work through the church, they will more likely become lifelong supporters of the church's ministries.

LifeWay has a resource for children who are new Christians, *I'm a Christian Now*. This curriculum promotes church membership. When using this material with teachers, I suggest that you spend additional time describing the structure of your individual church. Explain how decisions are made, the role of each minister, the roles of the deacons, as well as other specifics of church business.

Bible Study and Bible Literacy

James Emery White wrote, "We are always one generation away from being biblically illiterate."[12] Sunday school is the most consistent and important means of helping children study the Bible within the confines of the church. Teachers who promote Bible study within their classrooms provide powerful influences in the lives of children.

---

[11] G. Barna, "Evangelism," *The Barna Group*, 2004, http://www.barna.org/ (accessed June 21, 2007).
[12] J. E. White, *A Mind for God* (Downers Grove, IL: InterVarsity, 2006), 57.

LifeWay has developed excellent tools for teachers to use with children. One is a guide of biblical skills. This guide is a list of age-appropriate skills that children can accomplish during the elementary years. The tool can be downloaded from www.lifeway.com, the LifeWay Web site. While skills like locating books of the Bible, memorizing Scripture, finding Bible verses, and others are important, children's leaders should keep in mind that the ultimate goal is for children to "understand God's love for us . . . [in responding] to His redemptive work in Jesus Christ."[13]

Prayer

Is prayer intentionally taught in your children's ministry? How well do children understand the concept of prayer? A recent study found evidence that five-year-old children have a clear understanding of prayer. [14] We can see this in a prayer given by a five-year-old named Rachel. "Dear God, Thank-you for this wonderful day we have got and thank-you for answering our prayers. In Jesus' name, Amen."[15] Rachel's prayer shows she understood that God is the Creator and He answers prayers.

By six years of age, children believe their own conversations with God alter life circumstances. Seven and eight year olds show development in their understanding of prayer. They realize that the cognitive element outweighs the importance of bowing their heads, closing their eyes, and folding their hands.

NavPress has developed a resource for teaching children how to pray. The curriculum is a hands-on approach to teaching children the components of prayer. This resource provides a year's worth of lessons.[16] While LifeWay does not have this type of curriculum, the writers continually mention the importance of prayer in the Sunday school curriculum, as well as in the discipleship curriculum. There is an old adage that good attitudes are better caught than taught. While this may be true with regard to prayer, it is too important to leave

---

[13] G. Davis and F. Heifner, *Teaching Children the Bible* (Nashville: Convention, 1991), 17.

[14] J. Woolley and K. Phelps, "The Development of Children's Beliefs about Prayer," *Journal of Cognition and Culture,* no. 1.2 (2001): 142.

[15] Ibid., 155.

[16] It can be ordered from www.navpress.com.

to chance. Intentional teaching will produce tangible growth in the prayer lives of children.

Discipleship

Discipleship training begins as early as the preschool years. For older boys and girls discipleship is a program designed to teach:

- How to become a Christian.
- How to live as a Christian.
- How to minister to others in Christ's name.
- How to be a church member.
- What we believe and why we believe the way we do.[17]

Missions Education

Evangelical churches are committed to sharing the gospel. Most participate in mission efforts to spread Christianity throughout the world. Southern Baptist churches began teaching children about missions in 1888 under the leadership of the Woman's Missionary Union.[18] WMU leaders designed missions education programs to help children integrate missions activities into their daily lives. Children need to understand the importance of spreading the gospel throughout the world and how their lives can impact the world. Missions organizations are designed to help children understand the functions of both international and national missions programs, how to pray for missionaries, how to give toward missions causes, and how to get personally involved in mission activities. Missions organizations provide learning experiences that lead some to incorporate missions into their lifestyle while others may surrender their lives to full-time missions.

Two Southern Baptist organizations offer several choices of programs for teaching children about missions. The North American Mission Board, the Southern Baptist national missions organization, publishes curricula for the Royal Ambassadors, an organization for elementary-aged boys. They also publish a curriculum for boys and girls titled MissionKids that focuses on the stories of missionary kids and the countries in which they live. The Woman's Missionary

---

[17] B. Couch et al., *The Ministry of Childhood Education* (Nashville: LifeWay, 1996), 88.
[18] Ibid., 103.

Union publishes curricula for Girls in Action, an organization for elementary-aged girls. The WMU also developed a program for boys and girls titled Children in Action. This missions organization is structured like RAs and GAs except the children are not separated by gender. CIA is a good organization for churches who cannot find enough male leaders for RAs or female leaders for GAs.

Stewardship

According to Christ, our attitudes toward finances are indicators of our desire for true discipleship. Jesus stated in Matt 6:21, "For where your treasure is, there your heart will be also." As Larry Burkett wrote:

> In Jesus' teachings and parables—whether the rich young ruler, the lost son, the widow's mite, the sheep and the goats, or many others—He taught that what we do with money and possessions is a direct reflection of what is in our hearts. A person's checkbook is like a thermometer, measuring the heat of his or her love and commitment to God and His principles.[19]

Children also need to understand the verse, "No household slave can be the slave of two masters, since either he will hate one and love the other, or he will be devoted to one and despise the other. You can't be slaves to both God and money" (Luke 16:13). Without intentional teaching about stewardship, children do not understand biblical financial principles. Therefore, if we teach children "God's way of handling finances, they'll learn His principles and be better equipped to govern their whole lives according to those principles."[20]

Worship

Many churches separate children from congregational worship in order to provide age-specific worship experiences. They believe that children learn to worship more quickly and completely if they are experiencing church with their peers. This allows them to sing songs they understand and hear messages they can more readily grasp.

---

[19] L. Burkett, "Teach the Next Generation," *LifeWay*, http://www.lifeway.com (accessed July 4, 2007).
[20] Ibid.

However, there are important reasons for including children in corporate worship:

- Children are avid observers and learn how to worship from watching the adults around them.
- Children will feel more a part of the congregation when they worship with the larger community.
- Children are able to hear the needs and desires of the ministers and other members who voice prayers during worship.
- Children will grow in their understanding of worship as they participate on a regular basis. As Cavalletti states, "Often children experience God in fleeting moments of their awareness and may not be fully conscious of the encounter. Such glimpses germinate within the child and someday may come into the full bloom of conscious love for God."[21]
- The church can be a parent's "greatest ally and key partner" in helping pass down the Christian faith to children.[22] Attending church as a family supports this partnership.

Children are a constant reminder of simple faith to all church members. The presence of children in worship helps adults to remember the childlike faith Jesus describes in Matt 18:3: "I assure you . . . unless you are converted and become like children, you will never enter the kingdom of heaven."

While age-graded worship may seem effective, is it really best for our children? Children need to feel a part of the Christian community. They also need to learn firsthand how to function within corporate worship. Church leaders who are considering children's worship should look at the benefits of both kinds of worship for children: age-graded and corporate worship. They should also consider the level of parental involvement. In other words, if there is a large number of children attending church without their parents, age-graded worship is probably the best option. However, if most parents attend church, corporate worship for the family provides many advantages for children.

---

[21] S. Cavalletti, *The Religious Potential of the Child: The Description of an Experience with Children from Ages Three to Six* (New York: Paulist, 1983), 56.

[22] J. Trent, R. Osborne, and K. Bruner, *The Spiritual Growth of Children* (Carol Stream, IL: Tyndale House, 2000), 144.

Psychological Foundations

Cognitive Development—Jean Piaget

Jean Piaget was the famous and well-respected Swiss developmental psychologist known for his theory of cognitive development. He stated that "children actively construct their understanding of the world and go through four stages of cognitive development."[23] These stages explain how children of different ages organize their experiences. Each one is "age-related and consists of a distinct way of thinking."[24] Piaget's stage for elementary children is called concrete-operational stage of cognitive development (first and second graders are preoperational). During this stage average children ages seven to eleven have the ability to reason logically about concrete events and can classify objects into different sets.[25] Thus, they think about existing objects, events, or "commands they could act out, but they are unable to process concepts that can be represented only in words."[26]

Psychosocial Development—Erik Erikson

Erik Erikson, a German developmental psychologist, believed that human beings develop in psychosocial stages throughout the life span.[27] In other words, we develop our personalities as we interact with others. Erikson's theory presents eight stages of development.

The elementary years form the stage labelled "industry versus inferiority." During this fourth stage, Erikson said that children direct their "energy toward mastering knowledge and intellectual skills. At no other time is the child more enthusiastic about learning than at the end of early childhood's period of expansive imagination. The danger is that the child can develop a sense of inferiority."[28] If a child acquires a sense of inferiority, this enthusiasm is squelched. Sunday school teachers, children's ministers, and other church leaders can encourage children through their teaching as well as by building re-

[23] John Santrock, *Life-Span Development* (New York: McGraw-Hill, 2008), 43.
[24] Ibid.
[25] Ibid.
[26] Catherine Stonehouse, *Joining Children on the Spiritual Journey* (Grand Rapids: Baker, 1998), 81.
[27] Santrock, *Life-Span Development*, 41.
[28] Ibid.

lationships with children and their families. All children need to feel a sense of accomplishment in religious education classes to ensure a desire for a lifetime of biblical learning.[29]

Sociocultural Theory—Lev Vygotsky

Lev Vygotsky developed the sociocultural cognitive theory, which emphasizes "how culture and social interaction guide cognitive development."[30] According to Vygotsky, a child's development is "inseparable from social and cultural activities.[31] Social interaction with others is essential because children learn how to adapt to their culture. Cultural activities help children function successfully in their community. In one culture children may need to learn computer skills, while in another culture farming knowledge is imperative. Vvgotsky believed that the interaction with "more-skilled adults and peers"[32] furthered a child's cognitive growth. For example, in Sunday school if a teacher continually uses the Bible throughout class time, a child will understand the importance of God's Word to the Christian culture or community. The result is that the child will be more likely to continue to read his/her Bible. Vygotsky believed social and cultural interaction are significant parts of a child's learning process.

The Implications for Teaching Children

What do the educational theories of Piaget, Erikson, and Vygotsky imply for the teaching of children? Norma Hedin identifies several implications:

- Use Bible stories that have one clear concept. Use visual aids to reinforce learning. Give concrete examples of concepts, such as how to show love for your neighbor or times when you can trust God.
- Provide opportunities for students to classify, categorize, and memorize. Utilize their strengthening mental abilities in their learning activities.

---

[29] For more information on the implications of Piaget's and Erikson's theories of children's learning in a Christian context, see Yount's *Created to Learn*.
[30] Ibid, 44.
[31] Ibid.
[32] Ibid.

- Use frequent questions to clarify their thinking. Do not assume that the right answer equals right understanding. Ask "why" questions.
- Use prayer even though its meaning may be vague. The ritual of prayer becomes important along with other rituals like the celebration of holidays. Each exposure to these rituals deepens the child's understanding of their meaning.
- Make sure teachers are comfortable living out their faith. Children are imitating adults and need teachers who model godly attitudes and actions.
- Use self-competition to encourage successful completion of learning activities without comparison to other children, which leads to feelings of inferiority.[33]

Choosing Curriculum

One of the responsibilities of the children's minister is to choose curriculum for Sunday school or Bible study, as well as discipleship, Vacation Bible School, and missions education programs. This responsibility has become more complex in recent years as literature choices have increased. Churches no longer simply buy denominational products. Margaret Lawson provides a checklist for evaluating literature in chapter 19. Use this helpful list, but customize it as you consider the learning needs of children.

In customizing the list, one should consider developmental appropriateness of the suggested activities, of the concepts presented, and of the Bible stories. Are the activities, concepts, and stories appropriate for your children's ministry?

The book *Crayons, Computers, and Kids* suggests a simple A, B, C formula when considering curriculum for children. The literature should be "Activity-oriented, Bible-based, and Child-centered."[34] *Activity-oriented* means that, because children are active learners, a "strong curriculum will be structured around teaching through activities."[35] *Bible-based* means the selected curriculum presents foundational biblical truths. *Child-centered* means the curriculum

---

[33] Norma Hedin, "Teaching Children," in Eldridge, *Teaching Ministry*, 233.
[34] Stringer, *Crayons, Computers, and Kids*, 58.
[35] Ibid.

is "designed to meet developmental needs and address the various learning styles of children."[36] LifeWay's Bible Skills document, referred to earlier in this chapter, provides guidelines for appropriate learning approaches for the average child. By using these guidelines, teachers provide a variety of activities that engage the various learning styles within a class. The result is that children learn more, learn better, and experience a greater sense of satisfaction in the process.

When children succeed at church, they increase their interest in coming. When children repeatedly fail to learn at church, they quickly lose interest and may stop coming altogether. Choosing children's curriculum is an important part of helping children succeed.

Methods for Teaching Children

Art

"Art enriches the lives of all children, not just a talented few."[37] Age-appropriate artistic experiences help children learn about themselves while learning about God's world. Children enjoy experimenting with an assortment of art materials and tools. When using art in church with children, boys and girls are able to participate in artistic experiences that help them reflect on God's Word.

In my first church as children's minister, we held an annual art show for parents. It took place on Sunday morning prior to Sunday school. Since it was winter, we served hot chocolate and doughnuts. Teachers displayed the children's artwork in the hallways of the children's division. This event provided a wonderful time of fellowship for teachers, parents, and children.

Drama

"Creative drama activities allow children to experiment, rehearse, and recreate actions and words in a social setting."[38] This multisensory activity lifts the stories out of the Bible and into the lives of children as they become the characters of long ago. They may have

---

[36] Stringer, *Crayons, Computers, and Kids*, 58.
[37] R. Isbell and S. Raines, *Creativity and the Arts with Young Children* (New York: Thomson Delmar Learning, 2007), 106.
[38] Ibid., 247.

heard the words of stories before, but drama may actually produce understanding for the first time.

In the book *Crazy Clothesline Characters* by Carol Mader, there is a drama script written about the story of Queen Esther. This is a creative activity in which children play the part of human puppets. Prior to the activity, the leader hangs costumes from a clothesline. The children stand behind the costumes and perform like puppets. It is an innovative and fun way to tell a story.

Edutainment

Edutainment is the combination of the two words, *education* and *entertainment*. It is "the process of purposefully designing and implementing a media message to both entertain and educate, in order to increase audience members' knowledge about an educational issue."[39] Much of edutainment is interactive with an emphasis on fun as the driving force of holding interest during the activity.

When using edutainment, the teacher should ask the following questions:

- Is this the best use of class time?
- Does this use of edutainment contribute to building relationships within the group?
- Is the format of the edutainment developmentally appropriate?
- Is the length of the edutainment age-appropriate?
- Is it biblically sound?
- Does this form of edutainment display an appropriate reverence to God?

Parents Night Out is a great time to utilize edutainment in a children's ministry. These evenings are usually four to five hours in length. Since most children enjoy watching movies, showing a Bible story movie is both educational and entertaining. *Nest* offers quality biblical stories on DVDs (www.NestFamily.com).

Music

Children enjoy music, which provides opportunities for interaction and participation. Musical activities include listening, singing, move-

---

[39] A. Singhal, M. Cody, E. Rogers, and M. Sabido, comps., *Entertainment-Education and Social Change* (Mahwah, NJ: Lawrence Erlbaum Associates, 2004), 5.

ment, and playing instruments. New research has found that music is essential in the brain development of young children.[40] Children remember Bible verses and spiritual truths when they are learned through songs. Older children can also research the history of hymns, giving them an appreciation of music used in corporate worship.

Creative Writing

Elementary-aged children are encouraged to express their ideas and feelings through the medium of creative writing. "Children should not write to please adults; but to express their feelings, ideas, and how they think."[41] There are many ways to use creative writing such as writing stories, poetry, litanies, newspaper articles, and letters.

I teach classes of seminary students who plan to become children's ministers. One of my assignments in "Teaching Creative Arts and Drama to Children" is writing poetry. Since writing poetry is not an easy task for most people, we use two ancient forms of poetry: cinquain and haiku. A cinquain poem follows a given pattern in a five-line stanza. Haiku contains 17 syllables. These two forms make writing poetry easier for children as well as seminary students.

Bible Games

Bible games are effective in helping children retain biblical facts. After hearing a Bible story or missions adventure, playing Bible games is a good way to reinforce truths through repetition. The teacher introduces the facts or Bible truths by telling the story. Then children repeat these by answering questions or solving problems while playing a game. Games do more than reinforce factual retention. They also help boys and girls learn social skills like negotiation, taking turns, sharing, and listening.

I distinctly remember the first time I saw Bible games used in Vacation Bible School. I was very impressed as I watched children repeat the Bible facts and truths they had learned. The games enhanced the learning process. Moreover, the children felt a sense of accomplishment by using the information they had learned earlier in the day.

---

[40] Isbell, *Creativity and the Arts,* 183.
[41] Chris Ward, David Morrow, and Anne Tonks, *Teaching Children: Laying Foundations for Faith* (Nashville: LifeWay, 2004), 96.

Storytelling

Boys and girls enjoy listening to storytellers dramatize Scriptures.
Storytelling has been used historically for passing information from
generation to generation as well as entertaining audiences. James
Fowler, a widely regarded figure in the field of developmental psychology, believes young children find comfort in stories "where
good prevails and, in the end, evil people must pay for their sins."[42]
Children have opportunities to see God prevailing over evil. Many
stories provide good role models for boys and girls. Other stories
prepare children for the ups and downs of life, as well as the joys and
problems of human relationships.[43]

Jesus used storytelling as a powerful teaching tool. One example
of Jesus' storytelling ability is the story of the prodigal son, found in
Luke's Gospel. Jesus' vivid description of the prodigal's actions helps
us see the story in our mind. He also describes the reactions of the
father and the older son in enough detail so that children can relate
to the story. Jesus was a master storyteller and used His storytelling
abilities throughout His ministry.

Research

"Research is a way of finding information to answer a question or
develop an activity or project."[44] Teachers can make research fun.
By looking in old books, using the church library, or surfing reliable
sources on the Internet, teachers can assist children in researching
projects. If teachers and leaders show excitement in these projects,
children will be more motivated to learn.

Several years ago the fourth-grade Sunday school class in our
church was made up of all boys. From time to time the class was
quite challenging. The male teacher decided the class would research
some of the battles described in the Old Testament. With small plastic soldiers the boys recreated the battles. As you might imagine,
these fourth-grade boys looked forward to Sunday school for an
entire month. They learned about biblical events and enjoyed their
research.

---

[42] Stonehouse, *Joining Children,* 157, and James Fowler, *Stages of Faith* (San Francisco:
HarperCollins, 1981), 130–31.

[43] Hedin, "Teaching Children," 237.

[44] Ward, *Teaching Children,* 73.

Ministry Experiences

"Involving children in ministry is a real experience that enables children to put the Bible truths they are learning into action."[45] Teachers and children's leaders can help children be involved in ministry within the church or outside the church. Within the church children can learn to minister by doing such things as helping preschoolers during an activity or picking up trash around the church building. Outside the church children might visit elderly people or work in a food pantry for a day. By participating in mission action, children will grow up understanding the importance of helping others.

I had the opportunity of growing up in a church with a strong children's missions program. Our missions class was involved in missions projects on a monthly basis. We were able to assist in the planning as well as the implementation of missions action. On Labor Day the boys' missions organization provided a rest stop on the major highway that went through our town. The boys gave free coffee, doughnuts, and tracts to all travelers who stopped.

Training Teachers

I remember seminary classes in which professors stressed the importance of training teachers. However, I do not recall that they defined areas of training. I found this frustrating as an inexperienced children's minister. Therefore, the following is a list of suggested areas for teacher training.

- *Developmental Characteristics of Children.* Children develop spiritually, emotionally, cognitively, socially, and physically in patterns and stages. Teachers need to understand how children develop in their assigned age-group.
- *Learning Style Theories.* There are many theories on learning styles. LifeWay uses Howard Gardner's learning theory in writing its Sunday school curriculum for preschoolers and children. An explanation of this theory helps teachers use the materials successfully.
- *Creative Arts and Drama.* At times teachers may not feel they are as creative as in other times. Providing training and

---

[45] Ibid., 66.

new ideas helps them continue to bring a freshness to the classroom.

- *Discipline.* Many teachers become frustrated over discipline problems at church. Training teachers in the area of discipline will ensure a lower frustration level for teachers and children.[46]
- *Spiritual Development of Children.* Teachers need to understand their role in helping children develop spiritually. A training session is a good reminder to teachers that we need to help children pray, memorize Scripture, and understand Scripture, among many other spiritual disciplines.
- *Parent Education Training.* The children's minister can learn to encourage parents in their role as the main spiritual leaders to their children.
- *Sharing the Gospel with Children.* An essential element of training is helping teachers learn how to share the gospel with children. As mentioned earlier, the North American Mission Board publishes curriculum for training adults to share the gospel with children. The curriculum is titled *Sharing God's Special Plan.*
- *Church Security.* Safety and security are areas that need to be addressed on a regular basis. Sometimes we become relaxed in our churches and forget that predators may be lurking around the corner or, unless we are careful, in our classrooms. Marcia McQuitty addressed this concern in the previous chapter.

This list may be a good beginning, but there are many other areas of concern. I am not implying that children's teachers must be experts in all areas, but the more well-rounded the training, the more effective the teacher will be. Christian publishers have done an excellent job in providing teacher-training materials. Also, Christian elementary principals and teachers make excellent teacher-training speakers. Local associations have seasoned experts who will come into the local church for training sessions. Seminary and Christian

---

[46] See Yount's book, *Called to Teach,* "Teacher as Classroom Manager" for a practical step-by-step approach to handling discipline problems in the classroom.

college professors are good speakers as well. Please remember, as the children's minister you are not alone in your ministry to children.

Conclusion

George Barna admits an unintentional disregard for children:

> Like most adults, I have been aware of children, fond of them and willing to invest some resources in them, but I have not really been fully devoted to their development. In my mind they were people en route to significance— i.e., adulthood—but were not yet deserving of the choice resources.[47]

As we have seen, children are spiritual beings and deserve their fair share of the "choice resources."

Research shows that spiritual training during the formative years produces lifelong results. The team of Thomas O'Connor, Dean Hoge, and Estrelda Alexander studied a group of young adults who grew up in three different denominations, Baptist, Catholic, and Methodist. They wanted to see if there was a correlation between involvement in church as children and youth and the level of church involvement as adults. The study revealed that church involvement as youth and children had a significant correlation with church involvement in adulthood. Persons who were involved in church as children were more likely to be involved in church as adults.

We have the most important story to share with children. As we grow in our understanding of children—how they learn, how they grow spiritually—we will become more effective as teachers and leaders, laying the foundation for the church of today and the leaders of tomorrow.

Discussion Questions

1. What role does a teacher play in the life of a child? Why is it important for the teacher to encourage biblical learning?
2. Parents many times are the driving force for a church to establish children's worship. Discuss the pros and cons of children's worship.

---

[47] G. Barna, *Transforming Children into Spiritual Champions* (Ventura: Regal, 2003), 11.

3. Discuss the foundational teaching components of a children's
   ministry. What component would you add to this list?
4. Explain why teachers need to vary their teaching methods.

Suggested Tools and Reading Materials

Levels of Biblical Learning and *Levels of Bible Skills*. These documents can be downloaded from www.LifeWay.com. They are found in the Children's Ministry section.

Parents' Guide to the Spiritual Growth of Children by John Trent, Rick Osborne, and Kurt Bruner.

Growing Up Prayerful. Available from www.NavPress.com.

I'm a Christian Now. Available from www.LifeWay.com.

Bibliography

Barna, George. "Evangelism." *The Barna Group*, 2004. http://www.barna.org/. Accessed June 21, 2007.

_____. *Transforming Children into Spiritual Champions*. Ventura: Regal, 2003.

Biddy, Reginald. *Restless Gods: The Renaissance of Religion in Canada*. Toronto: Stoddart, 2002.

Burkett, Larry. "Teach the Next Generation." *LifeWay*. http://www.lifeway.com. Accessed July 4, 2007.

Campbell, Brandy. "Connection with Pastor Important for Successful Children's Ministry." *Lifeway*, 2002. http://www.lifeway.com/lwc/article_main_page/. Accessed February 9, 2007.

Cavalletti, Sofia. *The Religious Potential of the Child: The Description of an Experience with Children from Ages Three to Six*. New York: Paulist, 1983.

Couch, Bob, et al. *The Ministry of Childhood Education*. Nashville: LifeWay Press, 1996.

Davis, Ginny, and Fred Heifner. *Teaching Children the Bible*. Nashville: Convention, 1991.

Doughterty, Kevin. "Institutional Influences on Growth in Southern Baptist Congregations." *Review of Religious Research* 42:2 (2004): 119.

Eldridge, Daryl, et al. *The Teaching Ministry of the Church*. Nashville: B&H, 1995.

Fowler, James. *Stages of Faith*. San Francisco: HarperCollins, 1981.

Haywood, Janice. *Enduring Connections*. St. Louis: Chalice, 2007.

Isbell, Rebecca, and Shirley Raines. *Creativity and the Arts with Young Children*. Canada: Thomson Delmar Learning, 2007.

May, Scottie, et al. *Children Matter*. Grand Rapid: Eerdmans, 2005.

Poteet, Jerry. Live interview by Karen Kennemur, June 14, 2007, Southwestern Baptist Theological Seminary, Ft. Worth, Texas.

Rainer, Thom. *High Expectations*. Nashville: B&H, 1999.

Santrock, John. *Life-Span Development*. New York: McGraw-Hill, 2008.

Singhal, Arvind, Michael Cody, Everett Rogers, and Miguel Sabido, comps. *Entertainment-Education and Social Change*. Mahwah, NJ: Lawrence Erlbaum Associates, 2004.

Stonehouse, Catherine. *Joining Children on the Spiritual Journey*. Grand Rapids: Baker, 1998.

Stringer, Paula, and James Hargrave. *Crayons, Computers and Kids*. Nashville: Convention, 1996.

Trent, John, Rick Osborne, and Kurt Bruner. *The Spiritual Growth of Children*. Carol Stream, Ill: Tyndale House, 2000.

Ward, Chris, David Morrow, and Anne Tonks. *Teaching Children: Laying Foundations for Faith*. Nashville: LifeWay, 2004.

Westerhoff, John. *Will Our Children Have Faith?* New York: Seabury, 1976.

White, James Emery. *A Mind for God*. Downers Grove, IL: InterVarsity, 2006.

Woolley, Jacqueline, and Katrina Phelps. "The Development of Children's Beliefs about Prayer." *Journal of Cognition and Culture,* no. 12 (2001).

Zuck, Roy. *Precious in His Sight*. Grand Rapids: Baker, 1996.

Chapter 17

TEACHING YOUTH

Johnny Derouen

They are to make a sanctuary for Me so that I may
dwell among them. You must make it according to
all that I show you—the pattern of the tabernacle
as well as the pattern of all its furnishings.
(Exod 25:8–9)

O ver the years I have had many significant conversations
with teenagers and their parents. The following speaks to
the heart of their concerns:

Erika (8th grade):

> It's Erika again. I wanted to thank you for what you said in
> my last e-mail, but once again something has been bother-
> ing me. Whenever I hear a great sermon, I question what
> was said. Whenever I read the Bible, I question it; and
> whenever I have a conversation with God, I question if I
> really am. I've talked to other Christians about their faith,
> and they always tell me how God showed them something
> that changed their lives. I feel like God hasn't sent me that
> kind of message yet, and this makes me wonder: How do
> I know when God will [speak] to me? How do I know it
> won't just be me thinking it? I want to have the faith, but
> it's just so hard. . . . I just don't like this feeling I have, and
> I want to fix it. Thanks for any help you can offer.

Josh (8th grade): "Do other religions have their own apologetics? If
so, then who is right? How do I know that what I believe is the truth?"

(Johnny): "I love your children. They are such good leaders and
live genuine godly lives at church."

(Parent): "Thank you for your kind words, but you don't live with them."

How would you respond? We'll talk more about these at the end of the chapter.

Thinking through these conversations confirms for me how critical our teaching ministry with teenagers is. They question what they hear at home and at church in order to make their faith real, genuine, and personal. They are struggling with how to live out what they believe, relating biblical truths to real life. At the same time an increasingly non-Christian culture attacks what they learn in their local church youth groups and at home. These are difficult times for youth and even more difficult for adults who respond to God's call to work and teach with them.

The world of teenagers is constantly changing with stakes that are continually getting higher and higher. The 1950s to the present bear witness to this change as the list of teenage media interests shifts and changes—James Dean, Marlon Brando, Buddy Holly, *I Love Lucy*, *Leave It to Beaver*, Steve McQueen, The Beatles, Twiggy, Sean Connery, The Mamas and the Papas, *Beverly Hillbillies*, *Bonanza*, *High Chaparral*, Robert Redford, Paul Newman, *Saturday Night Live*, John Travolta, Fleetwood Mac, *Happy Days*, *Welcome Back Kotter*, Abba, Peter Frampton, Asia, Harrison Ford, Prince, Michael Jackson, Eddie Murphy, McGyver, Steve Perry and Journey, *Family Ties*, Aerosmith, Cyndi Lauper, The Bangles, Adam Sandler, *Saved by the Bell*, Will Smith, Nirvana, the boy bands, *Fresh Prince of Bel Air*, *Dawson's Creek*, Will Farrell, The Spice Girls, Maroon Five, Brittney Spears, Johnny Depp, Pink, Fergie, *Survivor*, *Lost*, *24*, *CSI*, and *American Idol*. Whew! The list goes on and on.

Within this flux today's teenagers "stand at a critical crossroads in history: floating in a sea of relativism, of nonlinear thinking, of broken homes and shattered dreams, and weary of anything phony, this generation cries out for significance."[1] How are these changes affecting our teaching ministry to students, how they learn, and what they need?

---

[1] Josh McDowell, quoted in Alvin Reid's *Raising the Bar* (Grand Rapids: Kregel, 2004), 11.

Theology of Youth Ministry

Your theology of youth ministry will affect how and what you teach teenagers. Our journey into the world of teaching teenagers begins by developing a correct theology of working with them. This will, in turn, influence how and what we teach them.

Jewish Culture

In Jewish culture adulthood begins at the end of childhood and the beginning of what we have labeled as the teenage year. Under Jewish law, children are not obligated to observe the command-ments although they are encouraged to learn obligations they will have as adults. At age 13 the Jewish male become bar mitzvah and the Jewish female at 12 become bat mitzvah. Bar/bat mitzvah is Hebrew for "one to whom the commandments apply" or "son/daughter of the law." Even though celebrations for the bar mitzvah did not become formalized until medieval times—or the bat mitzvah until 1922—the thirteenth birthday for a boy and the twelfth birth-day for a girl were established as the recognized ages for becoming a responsible adult in Jewish culture according to the Talmud in *Pirkei Avos.*

Five things occurred. They were *responsible* for their own actions. They could *read* from the *Torah* (Scriptures). They could *partici-pate in the Minyan* (minimum number of people needed to perform certain parts of temple religious services). They were old enough to *marry* but were encouraged, in the Talmud, to wait until 18. They were *required to follow the 613* laws of the Torah. In other words, they were considered adults and an active part of the temple religious services. The fact that teens were considered adults in biblical culture does not negate youth ministry today any more than the absence of baptistries, pews, church buildings, and tracts from the Bible negate them. Air-conditioning and jet planes aren't in the Bible either, but they are helpful. It does mean that the youth of our churches should be taught to be active and vital members of the church and not seg-regated outside the mainstream of church life. It tells us that we can challenge teenagers as we would young adults.

The Bible

Scripture gives us several principles that apply to teenagers as well as adults. We are to teach our youth, as well as adults and children, to construct their lives exactly as God has commanded in His Word. In Exod 25:8–9, God states to Moses that if the temple/tabernacle is built specifically as He commands, He will put His presence in that place. The actual physical temple was destroyed in 70 BC. The New Testament in 2 Cor 6:16–17 points out that we are now the temple of the living God. We all are meant to be sanctuaries of the Lord, built for His presence (Exod 25:8–9). Teenagers need to understand the beginning point of this construction is to invite the Master Builder—Jesus Christ—into their lives. Part of constructing our lives His way is to accept salvation His way—by inviting Jesus, the Messiah/Christ, into our lives. God will then put His very presence into our lives. We are to teach youth to continue the construction exactly as God commanded in His Word.

Part of treating teenagers like adults is to equip them for ministry: "for the training of the saints in the work of ministry, to build up the body of Christ" (Eph 4:12). We are to teach/equip them to be a functioning part of the church body, to have the tools to walk with God for the rest of their lives, and to accomplish His purpose for them through works of service.

For what purpose? So that they will mature in their faith ("will no longer be little children") and not be "tossed by the waves and carried about by every wind of doctrine, by the trickery of men, by craftiness in deceitful scheming" (Eph 4:14).

James 2:14–22 points out that our faith is to be practical. It is to be lived out—"faith without works is dead"—and not just words that we know and repeat. This faith is to be applied to our everyday life, or they become simply words.

Since youth over the age of 12 were considered adults, 2 Tim 2:1–2 gives us direction for teaching truths to teenagers. We should have similar teaching goals as we would with young adults. As they learn, they are to teach others what they have learned. One of the goals of teaching youth is intentionally to equip them to teach other youth. John Santrock challenges us to use skilled peers as teachers because this process benefits both youth teacher and youth learner.[2]

Youth tend to learn best when a three-step model is employed—dialogue, model, guide. First we dialogue (lecture and/or discuss) the biblical truth we are teaching, its explanation, and its practical usage. Second we supply models for how that truth looks in the lives of others. Third we guide them to act on or live out that truth in their own lives along with practical opportunities to live it in the present.

Remember, I heard/discussed and I forgot (dialogue), I saw and I remembered (model), I did and I understood (guide). This is the basis of teaching youth. Presenting a biblical truth in a lecture/discussion style only may lead to forgetfulness. Providing models establishes the truth in one's mind. Guiding one to perform an action based on that truth supports understanding of the truth.

Youth Ministry Research

Current research supports the need to be effective in our reaching/teaching/discipling of youth because nearly half of all Americans who receive Jesus Christ as Lord and Savior do so by age 13 (43 percent). Two-thirds (64 percent) will accept Jesus before their eighteenth birthday and 77 percent by their twenty-first birthday. This means that less than one out of four (23 percent) will accept Jesus Christ after age 21.[3] It is critical we make a strong effort to reach youth and teach Christian youth how to reach their peers before they reach 21 years of age, remembering that "the gate is narrow."

George Barna discovered (2006) that more than four out of five teens (81 percent), nationwide, attended a church for at least two consecutive months during their teen years. This reveals that churches have the ears of 81 percent of teenagers for a short period of time, providing a wonderful opportunity to teach/disciple them. Only 20 percent of young adults maintain the same level of spiritual activity as they had in high school. This indicates that much of our

---

[2] John Santrock, *Lifespan Development* (Boston, MA: McGraw Hill, 2008), 251–52.

[3] George Barna, "Evangelism Is Most Effective Among Kids," October 11, 2004, http://www.barna.org/flexpage.aspx?Page=Barnaupdatenarrow&barnaupdateID=216&Pa.

teaching of the life-changing message of Jesus Christ does not penetrate the hearts of teenagers in a life-changing way.[4]

A 16-year study (2006) by UCLA professor Gary Railsback revealed that 50 percent of incoming university students who claim to be born-again Christians reject their faith in Jesus by the time they graduate.[5] The data suggests that our teaching/discipling of these spiritually interested teenagers is not preparing them for the challenges to their faith that they receive in university/young adult life.

So where do we begin to make a change? How do we help teenagers move beyond church words to find Christ? How do we prepare them to defend themselves against secular arguments in the college years? The problem goes beyond the youth years. Preparing children wisely, equipping parents to be the primary spiritual influencers of their children, strengthening youth discipleship to give students the tools to walk with God for a lifetime, and developing college/young adult ministries to take youth to the next stage of growth and not just drop them to fend for themselves during the university years are helpful steps.

Factors Affecting Adolescent Learning

Tony Campolo admitted:

> There is one vocation that would frighten me if I were required to get into it. That is being a church youth worker. I shudder at the thought of having to go into a group of some 30 to 40 teenagers to try to elicit some kind of enthusiastic participation. To get them to sing a gospel chorus or get them to be genuinely involved in discussion would require a charisma and a talent that only a superior species might possess. I can just see myself standing in front of them, strumming my guitar and doing my best to generate some kind of enthusiastic response. A firing squad seems less threatening.[6]

---

[4] George Barna, "Most Twentysomethings Put Christianity on the Shelf Following Spiritually Active Teen Years." Ventura, CA: September 11, 2006. (download)

[5] Gary Railsback, quoted in David Wheaton, *University of Destruction* (Minneapolis, MN: Bethany House, 2006), 176.

[6] Tony Campolo, *Carpe Diem* (Waco: Word, 1994), 55.

Working with a group of teenagers is completely different from working with older adults. A misunderstanding of developmental factors that affect adolescent learning can frustrate adults who genuinely care about teenagers.

> I feel seriously stressed out most of the time. My guidance counselor says my tests show I'm smart, but I'm having trouble getting B's and C's, let alone A's. I went for math extra help every day last week—I even skipped lacrosse practice—and I still only got a C on the test. I'll never get into a good college at this rate. Then the lacrosse coach threatened to suspend me for cutting practice. Wonderful! Then at home I found a note from my mom saying to fix dinner because she was working late . . . again. Then my baby-sitting job canceled, and I really needed the money.
>   I was ready to scream. I'm only 16! If these are the best years of my life, would somebody please shoot me? So, yeah, I went to a party that night and got bombed.[7]

Further, the problems facing teenagers of the future continue to grow. Today's children are experiencing many firsts. They are the first day-care generation; the first truly multicultural generation; the first generation to grow up in the electronic bubble, the environment defined by computers and new forms of television; the first post-sexual-revolution generation; the first generation for which nature is more abstraction than reality; the first generation to grow up in a new form of dispersed cities that mix elements of urban, suburban, and rural cultures.

> The combined force of these changes produces a seemingly unstoppable dynamic process: childhood today is defined by the expansion of experience and the contraction of positive adult contact. . . . Because children seem to know more about the world, adults are more likely to assume, sometimes wishfully, that kids can take care of themselves. As a result, children and adults pass each other in the night at ever-accelerating speeds, and the American social environment becomes increasingly lonely for both.

---

[7] High school girl, "Quotes," cited in *Family Circle* (April 5, 1994): 3.

The way to reverse this process is to find ways to increase positive contact between adults and children.[8]

Factors That Influence Ministry to Youth

There are critical factors in youth ministry essential for anyone choosing to minister to teenagers.

Youth alternate between childishness and maturity.

Youth live on an emotional elevator caught between two floors: below them is childish dependence and above them is adult interdependence. Further, the speed at which they can switch from maturity to childishness and back again is amazing. One moment they are unselfishly leading younger students, showing responsibility, and the next moment they whine about cleaning their room. Understanding this aspect of teenage life is important to a youth worker's sanity and effectiveness.

I love a note I discovered in our youth room: "Dear God, I hate you. Love, Stephanie." What a dichotomy!

Youth need patient leaders.

Youth are realizing their dreams will not come true or may come true. Youth begin to realize that their exaggerated childhood dreams—to become a famous athlete, movie star, or princess—may not come true. Disappointment can grow into internal turmoil and insecurity. Teenagers struggling through these changes need leaders who are patient and compassionate.

A 16 year old in my youth group was obsessed with making the varsity baseball team at his school. When he didn't make the team, he was devastated. This well-built athlete asked me, through tears, "What do I do now? How will I tell my father I didn't make it?" This student was able to let go of his own dream and seek God's priorities through the encouragement and prayers of his loving dad. He became one of the core leaders in our youth group. His ministry on his high school campus resulted in many of his classmates coming to know Jesus.

---

[8] Richard Lour, *Childhood's Future* (Boston: Houghton Mifflin, 1990), 5.

Teenagers need adult leaders who can patiently lead them to see God's purposes, even when their personal dreams fail. By providing a model of dependence on God, despite success or failure, we help them "to love the Lord your God with all your heart, soul, mind, and strength" (Matt 22:37–39).

Youth want to belong.

Teenagers are struggling between the dependence of childhood and the interdependence of adulthood. In this adolescent neutral zone, youth want desperately to belong to a group—to be wanted and needed. In other words, relationships are the key to teaching teenagers.

Discipleship appears to occur best in the context of relationships. In this adolescent neutral zone, youth want desperately to belong to a group—to be wanted and needed. The quality of relationships *among* teenagers themselves, and *between* youth and workers, is key to providing this sense of belongingness. Further, relationships provide the best context for life-changing discipleship to happen. Teenagers who know their teachers and *are known by them*—teenagers who trust their teachers and *are trusted by them*—will be more honest, open, and teachable. As they grow, help them find a place of service where they can give and belong—where they are needed. By doing this, we make them a vital part of our churches.

Youth seek an identity.

Youth are seeking to establish their own identity. They are striving to learn "Who am I?" "What do I do well?" "How do I fit in?" "What is my purpose on this planet?"

Spending time with your teenagers inside and outside of the church setting aids you in knowing them and their families well enough to help them match their passions with their gifts.

Youth are growing.

Teenagers experience rapid growth physically, sexually, and cognitively. Expect changes and plenty of questions—especially Why? and Why not? One difficult problem here is that they all grow at different rates so some will mature in these areas quicker than others.

Adults who hang in there with them in helping teenagers to cope with these changes are extremely important.

Youth are developing values.

Youth are developing moral and spiritual values that relate to their world now! Making truth practical by asking teenagers, "Why is this important?" has implications for their developing values.

Guide them to realize that "the evidence shows that no society has yet been successful in teaching morality without religion."[9] Religion gives a reason for morality; right and wrong are grounded in the very nature of God.

Youth's parents are their greatest influence.

Youth leaders can mistakenly consider themselves the most important role model in the lives of their teenagers. The truth is that parents, even in this day and time, are the most important influence on youth. The one relationship they desire most is with their parents.[10] Work alongside parents/grandparents to encourage, train, and equip them to be that influencer. The time teenagers spend with their parents, observing them and learning from them, amplifies the importance of this critical relationship. Research has suggested that an investment of time in developing/keeping a strong emotional relationship and creativity in passing on biblical truths and moral values in this area will reap huge benefits. A teenager's self-concept, self-identity, and family satisfaction all increase with this investment.[11]

Youth are idealistic.

They see the world as it should be rather than as it is. It bothers them when reality does not match their ideals. They struggle with unfairness, injustice, and hypocrisy. Help them to understand these difficult issues and what their response should be. An example

---

[9] Guenter Dewy, quoted in Nancy Pearcy, *Total Truth* (Wheaton, IL: Crossway, 2004), 60.

[10] Paraphrase from Johnny Derouen, "A Study of the Difference in Faith Maturity Scale and Tennessee Self-Concept Scale Scores between Adolescents Taught a Bible Values Curriculum by a Parent and Adolescents Taught the Curriculum by a Non-Parent Adult Leader" (Fort Worth, TX: Southwestern Baptist Theological Seminary dissertation, 2005).

[11] Ibid.

would be helping them establish an understanding of God's sovereignty. This would help them realize that God does allow the good and the bad and is at work in both.

Youth are egocentric.

They will understand most biblical truths in light of how it affects their lives. The theorist Jean Piaget says teens have developed cognitively to be able to put this behind them. It is not that they *can't* decenter; it's that they won't. This appears to be due to selfishness in our self-centered society. Again, relating biblical truths to current needs is an important concept to teach teenagers. You must know them well in order to relate biblical truth to personal needs.

Youth are looking for purpose.

Teenagers are looking for a reason to live, a purpose in life; and we have the answer for them! Their purpose in life is given in Luke 10:27, Matt 22:36–38, Mark 12:28–30, and Deut 6:4–9. That purpose is to allow the Lord God to love us (Rev 3:20) and to love (honor, obey) Him, as the primary relationship of our life. Model both directions—opening up to God's love and honoring Him in how we live—before youth while teaching both directions regularly, with practical examples and illustrations. It is God who gives practical purpose to each individual. Purpose is discovered by receiving and obeying day by day.

Youth are abstract thinkers.

Teenagers move from concrete thinking (childhood) to abstract thinking (adults) in the adolescent years. This will lead them to question many things, even their salvation. This turbulent process is critical in helping them make faith in Jesus their own rather than something they were told and therefore accepted as a child. Teenagers are growing in their ability to understand the deeper, spiritual meanings of their faith. Address their questions concerning the realities of engaging Jesus as "the way" to live, engaging His truth, and engaging the life He gives. Show them how to use God's Word in confronting problems in life. Introduce them to apologetics, the defense of Scripture, and show them how to explain why the Bible is true and trustworthy. Lead them to compare critically and contrast media messages and God's Word. Teens hunger to be challenged, and we fail them when we soft-soap them or treat them like children. Challenge them to know what they believe and why they believe it.

Youth are emotional.

Teenagers tend to make decisions based on feelings more than reason. Brain research has discovered the underlying cause for the emotionalism of teenagers. During the adolescent years, the prefrontal cortex is still developing. This is the area of the brain responsible for critical thinking. The amygdala, on the other hand, is fully developed and fully functioning. The amygdala is the seat of fear and aggression.[12] The flightiness, turmoil, and overdramatic behavior of teens has a physiological basis. This predisposition of teens toward emotion makes the question, How do I *feel* about this? a major consideration when teaching. If teaching sessions do not "feel important" to teens (that is, *relevant to me*), we will have difficulty maintaining interest.

Youth are awakening spiritually.

The hyperdrive of adolescent emotion has a powerful potential. Throughout history God has often used young people to bring about a general spiritual awakening. This potential calls us to recognize how God values the openness of teens to be led by Him. It calls us to see this potential as well. Teach your students about the great spiritual awakenings of the past and the role of youth in God's movements. Jonathan Edwards wrote in 1834:

> The work has been chiefly amongst the young; and comparatively but few others have been made partakers of it. And indeed it has commonly been so, when God has begun any great work for the revival of his church; He has taken the young people, and cast off the old and stiff-necked generation.[13]

How Youth Learn

Youth learn in many ways, both formal and informal. The following are vital in order to teach teenagers effectively.

---

[12] "Amygdala," http://www.dictionary.com.

[13] Jonathan Edwards, "Distinguishing Marks," in *The Works of Jonathan Edwards*, ed. Sereno E. Dwight (1834; repr. Edinburgh: Banner of Truth Trust, 1986), 2: 266–268.

Youth learn from adult models.

Youth need competent, mature adult models in order to learn how to become an adult. Adult teachers are, in a very real sense, "the lesson"—the "living video"—that youth look to in order to see, "in living color," tangible Christian living. We see here the "model" and "guide" imperatives of the three-step process of teaching mentioned earlier. From my 34 years in youth ministry, I have noticed six qualities that youth look for in adult volunteers.

A Positive Attitude toward Youth. When interviewing adult volunteers to work with teenagers, ask questions like, "Do you like being around them? Do you genuinely care about their world?" It is easy for adults to become frustrated with teenagers; after all, "God made teenagers so parents wouldn't be so devastated when their children finally grow up and leave home."[14] Workers with youth need to like youth.

A Willingness to Develop Significant Relationships. The key word here is *willingness* because teenagers may never allow us to be close to them. However, when they sense we are genuine, we are willing to know them, and we care for them whether they come to our churches or not, they may allow us into *their* world. Times of crisis, which most youth face at one time or another, can provide powerful opportunities for relationships to develop.

Jack was a 15 year old on our church roll and involved in some pretty rough stuff on his high school campus. Even though we had called Jack repeatedly and visited him many times at home and at school, he would not attend church. When his grandfather became terminally ill, Jack called me to come and talk to his grandfather about Jesus and about death. On the way to the home, I picked up two students from our church to come with me to experience the visit (remember: "dialogue—**model**—guide").

Two days after our visit, the grandfather passed away. The two students and I attended the funeral. The Sunday following the funeral, Jack attended our church. Within five weeks, the entire family was attending. They all received Jesus as their Lord and Savior and were baptized!

---

[14] Loretta Kolb, cited in *The Joyful Newsletter* (April 1992): 2.

What made the difference was our willingness to establish a meaningful relationship with Jack, and this led Jack to turn to us for help in a time of crisis.

A Mature Christian Life. Students are looking for adults who are fulfilled in their life with the Lord. Teenagers respect adults who have learned to walk with Jesus in spite of life circumstances. *If adults are unable to demonstrate a consistent Christian lifestyle,* teens wonder, *why should I do what you tell me to do? It didn't work for you.*

Listen. Learn to listen, to let teenagers talk. It is not necessary to give an immediate answer to what they say or ask. My wife and I took Laurie home one evening after our Wednesday night youth worship service. She lived 30 minutes away from the church, and she talked about her life and problems the whole way. All I could get in were a few "uh-huhs," "yeahs," and "OKs." When we reached her home, Laurie got out of the car and said, "I love talking to you. This really helped." I responded, "But I didn't say anything." She replied, "I know, but you let me talk. Now I know what God wants me to do."

We need to remember to guide them into God's Word and His answers. It is wise to lead them to find the answer on their own rather than giving the answer to them. If you went to the famous Carlsbad Caverns in New Mexico, you wouldn't want to sit and listen to a description of the giant stalagmites and stalactites.[15] You'd want a knowledgeable guide to take you into the caverns and show you the wonders of these natural formations—so you could see for yourself. Do the same with God's precious Word!

Active Learners Themselves. Teenagers are better motivated to learn when their adult leaders show that they are still learning—that discipleship is a lifelong process. When adults display an attitude of "I've arrived: do as I do," teenagers quickly lose interest.

A Vibrant, Fresh Walk with God. Never love your ministry more than you love God. Is our lifelong process of growth a burdensome slog or a fresh walk? The difference is found in our focus. If we love

---

[15] Stalactite: "a deposit, usually of calcium carbonate, shaped like an icicle, hanging from the roof of a cave . . . and formed by the dripping of percolating calcareous water." Stalagmite: "a deposit, usually of calcium carbonate, more or less resembling an inverted stalactite, formed on the floor of a cave . . . by the dripping of percolating calcareous water." http://www.dictionary.com.

our ministry to youth more than we love God, our work can become a dead slog. Walk with the Lord, draw close to God every day, and He will bring freshness to your ministry. Teenagers can easily see the difference.

Youth learn best when truth meets their needs.

Teenagers have both general and specific needs of various kinds. Specific needs refer to personal concerns: family problems, conflicts with friends, difficulties at school, self-image frustrations, and the like. These needs are best engaged in private. General needs refer to those common to all teenagers, and are also very helpful to know. Here are a few of them:

1. To believe that life is meaningful and has a purpose.
2. To have a sense of community and deeper relationships.
3. To be appreciated and loved.
4. To be listened to—to be heard.
5. To have practical help in developing a mature faith.
6. To be challenged in what they believe and why.
7. To have spontaneity in life.
8. To experience consistency in adult-youth relationships.

When Bible teaching connects with these specific needs,[16] learner interest is secured and maintained, and learning is more effective. The immediate implication is that teachers need to know their students and their world. Teachers can build a bridge of interest at the beginning of the session by connecting with needs in the class. For this reason I agree with Ken Davis that the first 50 words in a teaching session are the most important.[17]

Youth learn best with objectives.

Youth learn best when a specific learning goal has been identified. The "so what?" of a lesson is better secured through a proper learning readiness experience. In most cases it is better NOT to tell learners the objective ahead of time; it's like giving away the end of a mystery novel. But objectives do give teens a sense of "going somewhere" because there is a target to be hit. By using objectives

---

[16] Recall the foundation stones of "Bible" and "Needs" in the *Disciplers' Model*, chap. 1.
[17] Ken Davis, *How to Speak to Youth* (Grand Rapids, MI: Zondervan, 1996), 114.

to structure lesson plans, we give teens a sense that we are "going somewhere." This sense of direction is, itself, motivating and helps overcome teenagers' short attention span. Without this sense of direction, teens wonder, "Why are we here?" See chapter 13, "Planning to Teach," for specific directions in how to write clear objectives.

Youth learn best when properly prepared.

The first part of a teaching session is called "learning readiness" and is the time when teens are engaged for the study to follow. Teenagers tend to be egocentric, which means they tend to see everything according to how it affects them personally. Learning readiness activities help answer the learners' sense of purpose: "So, what's the point?"

Learning readiness can raise questions in preparation for understanding a passage of Scripture or establish the proper atmosphere for sharing experiences. Chapter 13 also discusses how to plan for effective learning readiness.

Youth learn best in an atmosphere of love, trust, and acceptance.

The old adage, "People don't care how much you know until they know how much you care," is especially true for youth. Discipleship occurs best in the context of close relationships.[18] How well do teens know and trust the teacher? Do teachers encourage students to ask questions or express doubts and concerns they may be feeling? Are students demeaned or ignored when they ask difficult or probing questions? Teenagers will have difficulty learning anything meaningful when locked into an unloving, untrusting, unaccepting atmosphere.

Before our Wednesday night youth service, twenty 16-year-old boys pulled me into a small room to ask me a private question. I knew I was in for it when they all blurted out, "Is masturbation right or wrong?" When I asked them why they were asking me this question, the response was, "*Who else can we ask? We feel safe dis-*

---

[18] Jean Rhodes, *Stand by Me: The Risks and Rewards of Mentoring Today's Youth* (Cambridge, MA: Harvard University Press, 2002), 60; Chap Clark and Kara Powell, *Deep Ministry in a Shallow World* (Grand Rapids, MI: Zondervan, 2006), 79–80, 113–15.

cussing this issue with you because you know us and don't judge us."
I realized then how important relationships built on love, trust, and
acceptance are to the learning process.

Youth learn best when they are actively involved.

Active involvement in the learning process means teenagers make
discoveries for themselves. Teachers guide teenagers into active
learning by asking them questions and then giving them time to
search specified Scripture passages for answers. Follow the group
study with a time of discussion, sharing and evaluating the answers
they've developed. This discussion helps winnow biblical truth from
interactive chaff.

**Youth learn best when a variety of learning methods/activities are
employed.**

"Variety is the spice of life." It is also the spice of learning.
Without it repetition and ritual set in, producing boredom. Examples
of variety include engaging in large- and small-group discussion,
viewing videos and DVDs, solving problems, applying biblical concepts to real-life situations, taking quizzes, competing in contests,
and role playing.

Variety in classrooms is also important because, like all learners,
teenagers do not all learn the same way. Some are audible learners
(learn through listening); some are tactile learners (learn by handling
objects); some are visual learners (learn through pictures, diagrams,
videos); some are kinetic (learn through movement). Variety in
methods allows all learners to participate more in the process, to feel
more a part of the group (belongingness), and to make more meaningful applications of the truth.

Youth learn best when their minds are engaged.

Learning is more than experience. Teens are able to think more
hypothetically than children, and they need to be challenged men-
tally. One of the two "greatest commandments" of Jesus is to "love
the Lord your God . . . with all your mind" (Matt 22:37). Here the
word *mind* refers to deep thought or the exercise of understanding.[19]
Ask teenagers questions. Challenge them to consider their core be-

---

[19] Strong's Reference, *PC Study Bible*, Biblesoft 1995, #1271 "mind."

liefs: Are they based on Scripture? Are they "owned" personally or merely "rented" from parents? How do their beliefs contrast with other belief systems? Help teens consider evidence from archaeology, science, and history as they shape their beliefs.

Youth learn best when peak moments ignite general knowledge.

Effective life change in youth can occur when long-term learning comes alive in peak experiences such as summer camps, mission trips, Disciple Nows, retreats, and service projects. These kinds of opportunities are critical because they take learners out of the ordinary and challenge them to use their learning in new situations.

Characteristics of Youth Ministries That Produce Spiritually Mature Adults

A three-year study of youth programs, released in 2005, was conducted to ascertain critical characteristics that consistently produced youth who continued to walk with God as adults. [20] Drawing data from over 700 Southern Baptist, Assemblies of God, Methodist, Lutheran, Roman Catholic, Evangelical Covenant, and Presbyterian youth ministries, researchers made two important discoveries. First, there was no single youth ministry *model*—that is, no specific way to do youth ministry—that proved to be most successful in long-term life change. Research did find, secondly, that there were nine common characteristics in youth ministries that helped teens continue to grow into adulthood. The following characteristics were found to be present in holistic ministries to teenagers.

Sense of the Presence and Activity of a Living God

The students, parents, and adult workers felt that God was present when they met together. They spent time in prayer before the Lord, asking—and *expecting*—God to move in and through their youth ministry. They gave attention to being in the presence of God and to experiencing the repentance and humility that follows.

---

[20] Exemplary Youth Ministry Study, www.exemplaryym.com (August 4–6, 2006).

Emphasis on Spiritual Growth, Discipleship, and Vocation

Successful youth ministries made discipleship intentional in what was taught and how it was taught. Older teenagers were trained with the expectation that, as they matured, they would teach what they learned to younger youth. Students were equipped to walk with God in practical ways with an expectation of lifelong learning. Dialogue, modeling, and guiding were commonly employed for learning.

Promotion of Outreach and Mission

Students, parents, and adult workers were taught and expected by the youth ministry to "go public" with their witness, to serve the community, to invite others to church, and to live and speak their faith in authentic ways.

Congregational Priority and Support for Youth Ministry

The 700 churches wrapped their arms around their teenagers and youth ministries. Teenagers were engaged as an active and vital part of the church community rather than being compartmentalized away from the main congregation.

Fostering of Significant Relationships and a Sense of Community

Building on the desire of teenagers to "belong," these churches accepted teenagers and led them into genuine community. They did this with an intentional consciousness of youth needs. Their methods included mentoring, conflict resolution, formal teaching times, authentic adult and youth modeling, and congregational openness to teenagers.

Developing Committed Competent Leadership

Students, parents, staff, and adult volunteers were trained consistently in order to improve leadership skills. Churches then actively used these trained workers in youth leadership positions.

Focus on Households or Families

The churches invested time in equipping families, including grandparents, to be the primary spiritual influencers of their children. Where strong positive parental influence was lacking, trained adults were used to provide mentoring.

Common Effective Youth Ministry Practices

These nine characteristics were developed by means of several popular youth activities that are flexible and able to be adjusted as needs arise. These programs included: Bible study, discipleship, missions/service, leadership/ministry opportunities, church involvement, parent ministry, prayer ministry, worship opportunities, relationship building, and activities for bonding and enjoyment.

Custom-Designed, Integrated Approaches to Youth Ministry

Each of these churches custom-designed the characteristics and practices to develop a youth ministry that functioned well.

Erika and Josh Revisited

At the beginning of this chapter, Erika and Josh were looking for answers to questions pertaining to specific situations in their lives. Josh needed to know that his faith in Jesus is a faith based on real evidence. A study of apologetics (including scientific, archaeological, and historical evidences) would help to answer his question. Erica wanted God to speak to her and wanted to know how she would know it was really God speaking. Guiding Erica to Bible passages where God spoke to His people would satisfy her hunger to know what God wants of her and how He speaks.

Conclusion

For those of us called to work with teenagers, we desire that they fall passionately in love with Jesus, become equipped to walk with God to represent Him wisely in this generation, and grow into mature believers who:

- Seek spiritual growth, alone and with others.
- Possess a vital faith that is keenly aware of God's presence in their lives.
- Practice their faith publicly by regular worship attendance, ministry participation, and leadership in a local church.

- Recognize God's call to live their faith as a way of life in all their decisions and actions.
- Live a life of service in caring for others.
- Reach out to those in need physically, socially, or economically.
- Exercise moral responsibility in decisions.
- Speak publicly about their faith in Jesus.
- Possess a positive spirit of love and hope toward life and others.[17]

The time is critical. How do we respond? We give teenagers the best chance to walk with God into their adult years when we: (1) equip parents as teachers, (2) secure and train teachers, (3) use the dialogue-model-guide process, and (4) enlist youth as peer teachers and missionaries.

I stand squarely with Doug Fields, who wrote, "I've been living with the weighty responsibility of developing a youth ministry that equips students, rather than a youth ministry that coordinates events. I don't want to direct programs, I want to disciple students."[21]

May God bless you as you reach out, connect, and engage with teenagers to transform them and send them out in Jesus' name!

---

[21] List is quoted from Doug Fields, *Purpose Driven Youth Ministry* (Grand Rapids: Zondervan, 1998), 18.

Chapter 18

THE ADULT LEARNER

Margaret Lawson

Until we all reach unity in the faith and in
the knowledge of God's Son,
growing into a mature man with a stature
measured by Christ's fullness.
Then we will no longer be little children, tossed by the waves
and blown around by every wind of teaching, by human
cunning with cleverness in the techniques of deceit.
(Eph 4:13–14)

Introduction

Early in the 1970s Malcolm Knowles wrote a book titled *The Adult Learner: A Neglected Species.*[1] The preface suggests that, at the time, the concept of lifelong learning was beginning to dawn on society and affect education as a whole. Almost 40 years down the road, adult learning is in the forefront of education, especially since it has become available online. Institutions such as University of Phoenix offer many opportunities for adult learners. In our churches, however, adult learners are still largely a neglected species.

Adults are necessary to the functioning of the church, we are quick to admit. The church is staffed by adults. They serve on committees, teach Sunday school classes, attend Bible study classes and worship services, and support the church financially. Yet with all those responsibilities, do we approach them as lifelong learners? We quote the Scripture that reminds us that Jesus grew in all aspects of

---

[1] M. Knowles, *The Adult Learner: A Neglected Species* (Houston, TX: Gulf, 1973).

life, but most often it is associated with the development of children (Luke 2:52). When it comes to growing in wisdom and in favor with God and man, we find that adults are frequently neglected in our churches. Sometimes we fail to encourage them intentionally to grow in their faith, "into a mature man with a stature measured by Christ's fullness," as Paul expresses it in Eph 4:18.

Here are some questions to illustrate my point:

- Do you know any adults who have fallen prey to false doctrine?
- Have you experienced difficulties in maintaining a program of discipleship?
- Is it a problem to find workers for Sunday school or for the nursery?
- Are any of your new members simply "exchanges" from other churches?
- Would it make a difference in your church if every member served faithfully according to their spiritual giftedness?

If you answered yes to any of these questions, it is likely that some adults in your church have a ways to go in their journey toward maturity.

Lest you think I am painting an overly bleak picture of the situation in our churches, let me tell you about my friend Charlene. She and I are both volunteers in a nonprofit organization that raises funds for a hospital. One day each week about six of us work at a resale shop and sort clothes, household items, furniture, jewelry, and countless other items that are donated each week. All the volunteers have some characteristics in common. We are all Christians, though drawn from several denominations. Almost everyone is over the age of 60, and most are retired. Charlene is 74, a retired elementary school teacher, and she teaches a Sunday school class at her church.

The class began with one couple who were new to the church and wanted to know more about the teachings of the church. Each Sunday Charlene addresses one of the doctrines of the church in a class where there are now 75 on the roll, and they range in age from 30 to 80. I asked her why they come each Sunday. We all know that people don't want to study doctrine because it is "boring." Charlene's response was, "They come because I let them talk."

That may or may not be the reason they would offer, but in a few words Charlene had addressed several characteristics of adult learners. Why do they come, and what are they looking for in Bible study? In an attempt to provide some answers to this question, it is helpful to begin with another question: Who are the adult learners?

A Biblical Perspective

A great deal of the New Testament makes reference to adult education. The accounts of Jesus' teaching His disciples and others in the Gospels all deal with adults. Once in a while He used a child as a "visual aid," but He went to great lengths to make sure adults understood His teaching. His first opportunity to teach in the temple amazed His adult listeners. Each time He dealt with a faith issue, He was talking to adults.

Other New Testament writers, such as the apostle Paul, also make continual reference to teaching the adults in the churches. In letters to the believers in the churches he had visited, he frequently addressed the need for them to mature in their faith and grow up in Christ. Whether he was encouraging, exhorting, or chastising them, he directed his teaching toward the leaders and other adults in the churches. Sometimes he dealt with matters of doctrine or church organization or discipline, and he often reminded them to heed his teaching. He told them that this was the reason he sent Timothy to them: "He will remind you about my ways in Christ Jesus, just as I teach everywhere in every church" (1 Cor 4:17). He also urged Timothy to continue the teaching tradition: "And what you have heard from me in the presence of many witnesses, commit to faithful men who will be able to teach others also" (2 Tim 2:2). Adults were the target group, and adults were to continue the ministry.

The Adult Challenge for the Church

At one end of the adult population is the young adult generation, at the other is the senior adult group, and somewhere in between are the median adults. Each of these groups has their own particular set of needs, and the church is required to minister to all of them—and most likely all at the same time. Recent research focused on young adults points out that they are falling away from church in alarming numbers. For example, a recent LifeWay research study shows young adults in the age group of 18–34 are falling away from church, and many are finding church irrelevant to their lives:

> In 1980, more than 100,000 young adults were baptized in Southern Baptist churches. In 2005, slightly more than 60,000 young adults were baptized in SBC churches; a number drastically lower with the United States population climbing above 300 million.[2]

To identify the problem, an eight-month research study was conducted. Churchgoers or not, the study results indicated young adults are nonetheless longing for community and fellowship with peers, looking for ways to reach people in need, and circling the church but not always finding a home in it.[3] This discovery raises more questions. Why is it that the thing young adults are looking for is supposed to be characteristic of the church, but they are not finding it? Is this not the place where we want them to experience a sense of connectedness and belonging?

A different study by George Barna states that one-third of the adult population is yet unchurched. Although there have been many changes in American life in the last 10 to 15 years, the proportion of unchurched adults has remained the same. "During that period there have been noteworthy shifts in religious behavior, but the percentage of adults who have steered clear of churches for at least the past six months has remained stable since 1994."[4]

At the opposite end of the age range is the senior adult population. Another phenomenon confronting the church is the baby boomer generation that is just entering senior adult status. An article in *Time* magazine describes baby boomers this way:

> When they were 18 years old, their rites of passage into adulthood—civil rights protest, the war in Vietnam, the counterculture—filled the nation's front pages. When they finally married and began families—often much later than

---

[2] "LifeWay Research Uncovers Reasons 18 to 22 Year Olds Drop Out of Church," LifeWay Research online, http://www.lifeway.com/lwc/article_main_page/0%2C170 3%2CA%25253D165949%252526M%25253D200906%2C00.html.

[3] Ibid.

[4] "Unchurched Population Nears 100 Million in the U.S.," March 19, 2007 (Ventura, CA) http://www.barna.org/FlexPage.aspx?Page=BarnaUpdate&BarnaUpdateID=267.

their own parents—their family issues became the stuff of
sitcoms. Throughout their now advancing lives, the baby
boomers have always stood at the demographic center of
American life. Their concerns have been the dominant concerns, their passions the dominant passions. So it stands to
reason that as the baby-boom generation begins its massive
sweep into old age, the age-old problems of this transition
into seniority are being rediscovered and re-examined as
never before.[5]

A cursory Internet search will reveal just how many books, articles,
and products are being produced to deal with this shift in the generation. What is the church doing? What preparations have you made
for the influx of baby boomers into the realm of senior adulthood?
The mind-set they will bring will introduce a completely new focus
on the senior age group as it has been conceived until now.

The Church's View of Adult Ministry

Those who work with adults of all ages in the church have a
great deal of work to do. We focus on the other age groups in the
church and even have a children's minister or youth minister to
give special attention to the age group. We know that preschoolers
are different from children, and children are not the same as youth.
Developmentally they are different so their needs are different. As a
result, we minister to them specifically and uniquely.

As soon as learners become adults, however, we often leave them
to fend for themselves. Leaders often assume they will work and witness and fellowship and grow on their own. We train them to perform tasks but often neglect their spiritual growth. They make decisions in our churches and our businesses and our government. They
teach our children, go to camp with our youth, lead in our worship
services, serve on committees, and do ministry. How do we minister
to them?

When I make this point in my classes, I always hear some whis-
per, "I work with youth," or "I work with children," as if this lets
them off the hook. Not so fast! Before you move on to another chapter, consider that all those who work with younger age groups must

[5] Andrea Sachs, "Coming of Age," *Time*, Jan. 18, 1999, http://www.time.com/time/
magazine/article/0,9171,990009,00.html.

of necessity encounter adult teachers and workers. And adults also have responsibility for the parents of those age groups. We will all be more effective as ministers in the local church, whatever our specific age group, if we give attention to the importance of educating adults. Just as we emphasize the focus on preschoolers, children, and youth in the church, so we would do well to make a similar emphasis on teaching adult learners, giving attention to what makes them unique and how they can best be taught.

In Phil 3:12–14 Paul urges the believers at the church at Philippi to move forward.

> Not that I have already reached the goal or am already fully mature, but I make every effort to take hold of it because I have been taken hold of by Christ Jesus. . . . Brothers, I do not consider myself to have taken hold of it. But one thing I do: forgetting what is behind and reaching forward to what is ahead, I pursue as my goal the prize promised by God's heavenly call in Christ Jesus.

Paul was a lifelong learner and encouraged his readers to be the same. No excuses, no hesitation, no consideration of the cost. Consider the following questions before you read on:

- Is lifelong learning the goal of all the adults in your church today?
- Does your church focus as much attention on developing adults as it does on children and youth?
- Are you personally pressing on toward a goal? Can you look back over a year, over five years, and see progress?

Who Are the Adults We Teach?

When is an adult an adult? When I ask students this question, there is always great variety in the answers. Some would suggest that age 18 is when one achieves adulthood because in America that is when a person can vote. Others say it is when a young person leaves home. Some would consider childbearing as a symbol. Or sometimes marriage defines us as "adult." Yet another thought is that adulthood occurs when a young person can obtain a driver's license. Culturally and contextually, this definition also varies. One of my Laotian friends speaks of his "young people's class" spanning from teenage to age 35. Research in the mid-1990s on Erikson's "Identity—Role Confusion" stage (teenagers), which he identified as 12–18 in the 1950s, now spans 10–35, which is why so many 20- and 30-somethings act like teenagers.[6]

Webster's Dictionary defines *adulthood* as "fully developed and mature," but it does not tell us when this happens.[7] Coleman says:

> No matter what direction it takes, our search for a concrete definition of adulthood keeps bringing us back to the same conclusion. The definition is a moving target. There is no way to fix adulthood chronologically or define it biologically. . . . The Latin participle, *adultus*, to grow up, emphasizes the dynamic of growth, rather than some state of being already attained. An adult is a person who is *growing* up, not *grown* up.[8]

The same perspective is true in Scripture where the *process of maturing* in Christ is described as an ongoing task. And yet we do not arrive at *spiritual maturity* this side of heaven. Paul says, "I press toward the mark for the prize of the high calling of God in Christ Jesus" (Phil 3:14).

A definition I have developed combines several ideas: Adulthood is reached when individuals become personally accountable for themselves and accept adult responsibilities. Adulthood is another stage of life that, in itself, has many more stages. Shakespeare expressed it a long time ago when he said, "All the world's a stage and all the men and women merely players. They have their exits and their entrances, and one man in his time plays many parts."

Our role in ministry is to help adults continue on in their journey toward Christlikeness. In the words of the apostle Paul, "We proclaim Him, warning and teaching everyone with all wisdom, so that we may present everyone mature in Christ. I labor for this, striving with His strength that works powerfully in me" (Col 1:28–29). Paul expressed a compelling sense of urgency, whether he was with

---

[6] W. R. Yount, *Created to Learn* (Nashville: B&H, 1996). See notes on Erikson in chapter 3 for this research.

[7] M. Webster online Dictionary, http://mw1.merriam-webster.com/dictionary/adult, accessed September 13, 2007.

[8] L. Coleman, *Understanding Today's Adults* (Nashville: Convention, 1969), 49.

an individual, with a group, or with a church he had left behind, to encourage them to grow. We would see tangible results in our ministries to adults if we reflected Paul's sense of urgency.

Over the years there have been many approaches to ministry with adults in the church. Grouping, or grading, learners into Bible study classes always presents difficulties when it comes to adults. Should they be categorized according to age? Or perhaps it would be better to divide them into classes by common interests? Some adult leaders simply give up and allow them to go wherever they want to go for Bible study. The truth is that some adults will do that anyway, no matter what approach we use. And yet we have a given number of meeting spaces for however many adults so we must organize them for study in some way. What is the best approach to organize adults into groups for Bible study?

The *simplest* but often the most controversial organizational pattern is grading by age, and in a couples' class it is usually by the wife's age. Age-grading is the *best* approach for long-term stability in learning and growing because adults of similar ages tend to have similar life situations, and teachers can better address life needs in age-graded classes. If my adult members complain about the structure, I suggest we should do it by weight instead, and that seems to subdue the grumbling.

Sometimes classes are organized by ages, such as

- Married Adults, 25–35; 36–55; 55 and above
- Women, 25–35; 36–55; 55 and above
- Men, 25–35; 36–55; 55 and above
- Singles, 25–35; 35 and above

Larger churches may narrow these age brackets, producing more divisions. It has also been found to be successful to grade classes for the younger adults by interest groups:

- Single Adults
- Married Adults
- Formerly Married
- Married, No Children
- Married and Single with Preschoolers

Each church will have to determine for themselves the best plan. Some churches simply suggest that people try several classes to decide where they feel the most comfortable. The possible danger of this *self-choice* pattern of organization is the creation of personality-centered classes, which could hinder the growth of discipline, service, cooperation with leaders and other groups, and the like. Some of the research of educational psychologists will provide guidance in designing a ministry model for adults.

Insights from Developmental Theorists

Adult educators have sometimes used developmental stages provided by educational psychologists to describe adults as learners. It is usual to recognize that wholistic adult development takes place in six major domains: physical, spiritual, cognitive, affective, moral, and social. Theorists have developed each of these and give insight into the needs and characteristics of the lives of individuals at particular phases. The categories usually apply to the entire lifespan and not just adulthood, but they do offer insight into the developmental issues confronting adults.

Regarding senior adults we often hear comments like, "My arms are not long enough to hold the hymnbook where I can see it." Another common one is, "When I bend down to fasten my shoelaces I look around to see if there is anything else I can do while I am down there." If you have reached that stage, you know exactly what I mean. Impairment of hearing or sight, less stamina, and "the battle of the bulge" are frequent allusions to changes that are happening in the maturing individual's body.

Robert J. Havighurst divided adulthood into three phases and outlined a series of developmental tasks for each stage. The noted psychologist Jean Piaget, parallel with Havighurst, recognized stages of cognitive development known as mental maturation. Six stages of moral development were researched by Lawrence Kohlberg. Psychosocial development was identified in eight stages by Erik Erikson. Finally, Robert Fowler attempted to show that faith development was also incremental. Each of these theories has formed the basis of discussion and debate in relation to adult education, and from them theories of teaching and learning have been derived. There is much literature available on each of these theorists and a study of their results is certainly helpful in ministry to adults in the church.[9]

Another popular approach is to consider adulthood from a generational perspective. A generation is usually defined by the major events that occurred within its time span.

Generations

In recent years there has been an increased emphasis on the concept of generations as a basis for organizing teaching opportunities for adults in the Christian context. The word *generations* is not new. From the beginning of the Old Testament to the end of the New Testament are references to the effect of one generation on another. Currently generations are used to place adults into categories where they share similar life-defining events. In *One Church, Four Generations*, Gary McIntosh discusses all the generations in one context—the church—and shows the intergenerational challenges.[10] Others have extracted sub groups of adults such as baby boomers or gen-Xers and focused on their characteristics with implications for the church. Unfortunately, this trend toward division has seeped over into the church, and increasingly *segregation* is taking place there too. Churches are usually made up of a combination of generations, and each suggests a unique approach. Gary McIntosh states, "Not only are these generational waves causing turbulence in our society, they are also causing turbulence in our churches."[11] This is our challenge as we determine the best way to organize the adult ministry so that maximum learning will occur. Barna designates the generations in this way:

- Mosaics—those born between 1984 and 2002
- Buster—those born between 1965 and 1983
- Boomer—those born between 1946 and 1964
- Builders—those born between 1927 and 1945
- Senior—those born in 1926 and earlier[12]

[9] For more information about each of the theorists see Yount, *Created to Learn* (Nashville: B&H, 1996).

[10] G. McIntosh, *One Church, Four Generations* (Grand Rapids: Baker, 2002).

[11] Ibid.

[12] "Generational Differences," http://www.barna.org/FlexPage. aspx?Page=Topic&TopicID=22, accessed September 13, 2007.

Organization of adult learners is just one factor for consideration. It is also important to address the matter of the best way to teach adult learners. Do adults learn the same way as children and youth?

How Do Adults Learn?

Most of us are familiar with Matt 28:18–20, Jesus' Great Commission to His followers. We see its implication for evangelism, for missions, and for discipleship. Often, however, we overlook its significance for teaching. I often ask groups of adults what the thrust of this verse is, and I hear "going" or "disciple-making," and occasionally someone mentions "teaching." What did Jesus say here about teaching? The command is for us to teach those whom we reach for Christ *to obey* everything that He has commanded. Some translations use the word *observe*—to pay attention, to give careful consideration to—everything that Jesus commanded. Sometimes we miss another focus of the passage, and that is to teach them to *obey* all the things Jesus commanded them.

How do we help them practice what they hear in church every week? Perhaps something in the way we teach could be redirected towards this end. For some of us it may be the total rethinking of the way we do adult education. Consider the following as food for thought.

- How do we teach so that adults will experience a change in lifestyle?
- How do we teach so that we know adults are learning?
- How do we teach so that spiritual transformation takes place?
- How do we get our learners to move information from the head to the heart?

Before we answer these questions, think of a *learning* situation you experienced as an adult. What made you enjoy the class? What made the greatest impression on you? Was it the material? Was it the personality or the ability of the teacher? Or was it, perhaps, that you were challenged because you were able to contribute to the class as well as learn from it. Your opinion was valued and your contribution helped others. Now cast your thoughts back to a *teaching* opportunity you have experienced with adults. Maybe you taught a Sunday school class, or trained teachers, or led a discipleship group. How did you approach that lesson? Did you think of it in terms of what you needed to tell them, or what they needed to learn?

The key to learning for adults is found in shifting the focus from the teacher to the learner. Focusing attention on the adult as a learner in the context of the church, the definition Ford provides is helpful. He defined *learning* simply as "a lasting change in knowledge, understanding, skill, attitudes and values, brought about by experience."[13]

Malcolm Knowles's theory of adult learning has influenced adult educators for several decades. His theory is based on the conviction that adults and children learn differently. Therefore, just as *pedagogy*[14] refers to the art and science of teaching children, so Knowles coined the term *andragogy*[15] to refer to the art and science of leading adults to learn.[16] In John 14:25–27, Jesus says, "But the Counselor, the Holy Spirit, whom the Father will send in My name, will teach you all things and remind you of everything I have told you." If the Holy Spirit is indeed the Teacher, and He indwells each adult believer, then each has the ability to discern the truth of the Scripture as it is revealed by the Spirit. Thus, every adult believer is both teacher and learner and should be encouraged to share his or her experiences with others, and so build up the body of Christ. Involving the learner actively in the study experience usually reaps rich dividends.

Andragogy

Andragogy assumes that the point at which an individual achieves a self-concept of essential self-direction is the point at which he psychologically becomes adult. A critical thing happens when this occurs: the individual develops a deep psychological need to be perceived by others as being self-directing. Thus, when he finds himself in a situation in which he is not allowed to be self-directing, he ex-

---

[13] L. Ford, *Design for Teaching and Training: A Self-Study Guide to Lesson Planning* (Eugene, OR: Wipf and Stock, 2000).

[14] From the Greek word *paid*, meaning "child," and *agogus* meaning "guide or leader."

[15] From the Greek *aner*, meaning "adult."

[16] K. Gangel and J. Wilhoit, *Handbook on Adult Education* (Grand Rapids: Baker, 1993), 96.

periences a tension between that situation and his self-concept. His
reaction is bound to be tainted with resentment and resistance.[17]

Knowles would suggest that the following points are important for
adult learning:

- **The Need to Know.** Adult learners need to know why they
  need to learn something before undertaking to learn it.
- **Learner Self-Concept.** Adults need to be responsible for their
  own decisions and to be treated as capable of self-direction.
- **Role of Learners' Experience.** Adult learners have a variety
  of experiences of life, which represent the richest resource for
  learning.
- **Readiness to Learn.** Adults are ready to learn those things
  they need to know in order to cope effectively with life
  situations.
- **Orientation to Learning.** Adults are motivated to learn to the
  extent that they perceive that it will help them perform tasks
  they confront in their life situations.[18]

Richard Patterson suggests that andragogy was Knowles's effort
to counter a nearly total dependence on pedagogy as a teaching and
learning approach for adults. He further suggests that in a pedagogi-
cal classroom model, the teacher is the expert in the content area and
presents information to the learner who passively absorbs whatever
is required.[19] Since what many adult educators had observed about
adults and their learning preferences argued against pedagogy, andragogy became the alternative.

Adults do not learn simply because we talk. They learn the most
when they feel that their personal needs are being met. And to do
this they must feel their own experiences are recognized. Adult
learners feel their needs are being met when they are involved in
planning the learning experience and when they can contribute in a
meaningful way.

Consider some of these questions as you teach adults in the
church:

---

[17] M. Knowles, *The Modern Practice of Adult Education: From Pedogogy to Andragogy*,
rev. & updated (Chicago, IL: Follett, 1980), 56.

[18] Adapted from Knowles in *The Modern Practice of Adult Education*, 1978, 56.

[19] R. Patterson, "How Adults Learn," in *Handbook on Adult Education*, 125.

- Do you know each learner's spiritual condition?
- Do you know who is lost, growing, or struggling spiritually?
- Do you provide opportunities for learners to make commitments to Christ or other decisions during a Bible study session?
- Do you emphasize further study of the lesson?
- Do you emphasize developing a daily quiet time?
- Do you ask for reports on what God has done based on a previous Bible study lesson?
- Do you provide opportunities for learners to practice a Bible study lesson through ministry and outreach?
- Do you encourage learners to use the lesson as part of a family Bible time?
- Do you vary your teaching method? How could you move out of your comfort range and try something different? For example, teachers who are comfortable explaining a term or phrase in the Bible might share a personal experience and invite others to share theirs.
- Do you pray specifically for each learner before you teach?[20]

As a volunteer, Charlene is typical of her age group and the volunteer generation. Why did the adult learners choose her class for Bible study? One reason is that she prepares thoroughly and is ready to teach when she enters the classroom. In addition, the learners were able to attend a class of their choice, and they were able to participate in the discussion using personal experiences from the past. New members were also able to put the course material to immediate use as they joined a new congregation. Charlene gave them assignments and asked them to be responsible for portions of the lesson from time to time. Their contributions were affirmed and helpful. As a by-product, Charlene has said to me, "I have learned so much in preparing to teach this class." From the youngest to the oldest, learning presents a challenge, and the reward is satisfaction.

---

[20] Adapted from questions by John McLendon, *Beyond the Walls: Multiply Your Adult Ministry*, LifeWay Christian Resources online download: Multiply Your Adult Ministry (PDF) http://www.lifeway.com/lwc/article_main_page.html, accessed September 13, 2007.

Conclusion

Our desire in all our opportunities for teaching adults is that they would be excited about their learning and would practice their lessons in daily living. If we focus on their needs and invite them to be lifelong learners alongside the teacher, we, too, will enjoy seeing them mature in Christ. The apostle Peter explained it this way: "You yourselves, as living stones, are being built into a spiritual house for a holy priesthood to offer spiritual sacrifices acceptable to God through Jesus Christ" (1 Pet 2:5). May God bless you as you contribute to the living stones under your care, building a spiritual house in Jesus' name.

Discussion Questions

1. Evaluate your church's generational profile. What proportion of adults fits into each of Barna's generational divisions?
2. What evidences of spiritual growth do you see among the adults in your church?
3. What changes would you have to make in your teaching to implement some of the tenets of andragogy?
4. How do you organize your adults for Bible teaching? Based on the chapter, how would you recommend organizing adults for Bible study?

Additional Resources

Edwards, Rick, comp. *Teaching Adults*. Nashville: LifeWay, 2002.
Gangel, Kenneth O. *Ministering to Today's Adults*. OR: Wipf and Stock, 1999.
Gangel, Kenneth O., and James Wilhoit. *The Christian Educator's Handbook of Adult Education*. Grand Rapids: Baker, 1993.
Hanks, Louis. *Vision, Variety, Vitality*. Nashville: LifeWay, 1996.
McLendon, John. *Beyond the Walls: Multiply Your Adult Ministry*. Lifeway Christian Resources, online download. Multiply Your Adult Ministry (PDF), http://www.lifeway.com/lwc/article_main_page.html.
Raughton, Alan, and Louis B. Hanks. *Essentials for Excellence*. Nashville: LifeWay, 2003.

Stubblefield, Jerry. *A Church Ministering to Adults*. Nashville: Broadman, 1986.

Bibliography

Coleman, Lucien. *Understanding Today's Adults*. Nashville: Convention, 1969.

Ford, LeRoy. *Design for Teaching and Training: A Self-Study Guide to Lesson Planning*. Eugene, OR: Wipf and Stock, 2000.

Gangel, Ken, and James Wilhoit. *Handbook on Adult Education*. Grand Rapids: Baker, 1993.

Knowles, Malcolm. *The Adult Learner: A Neglected Species*. Houston, TX: Gulf, 1973.

_____. *The Modern Practice of Adult Education: From Pedogogy to Andragogy*. Rev. & updated. Chicago, IL: Follett, 1980.

McIntosh, Gary. *One Church, Four Generations*. Grand Rapids: Baker, 2002.

Patterson, Richard. "How Adults Learn." *Handbook on Adult Education*. Grand Rapids: Baker, 1993.

Yount, William R. *Created to Learn*. Nashville: B&H, 1996.

Part Four

STRUCTURING THE TEACHING

MINISTRY OF THE CHURCH

Chapter 19

SELECTING AND EVALUATING CURRICULUM

Margaret Lawson

I have fought the good fight, I have finished
the race, I have kept the faith.
(2 Tim 4:7)

What Is Curriculum?

C hurch leaders responsible for Bible teaching programs frequently hear questions or comments like this: "Our class does not like the curriculum we use. Can we use something else?" Perhaps it is phrased this way: "Our curriculum does not meet the needs in our class. We would like to study a book." Or more extreme than either of these: "We don't like the curriculum so we have decided to write our own!" What is the best response to these questions? How would you answer?

Ministers of education and pastors ask me more questions about curriculum than about any other issue in Christian education. It is a challenging issue. It is a relentless issue, confronting us at least every quarter. And it is even more of a challenge when it is needed for the many ethnic churches in a cultural context other than our own as the world has come to our front door. Further afield yet, missionaries face additional challenges when securing teaching resources for their work. Their limited resources and cultural and language differences mean that they often adapt existing materials for their particular situations or write their own.

The truth is that the questions and comments above have the wrong focus. It follows that if we keep asking the wrong questions we are bound to get the wrong answer. First, there is a misunderstanding of the term *curriculum*. For many, the term conjures up an image of "the quarterly," but curriculum is much more. There are essential differences among the related terms *curriculum*, *curriculum plan*, and *curriculum resources*.

Curriculum—from the Latin *currere*, to run—means "race course." It refers to a sequence of intentional experiences where learning takes place.[1] LeRoy Ford defined curriculum in terms of the apostle Paul's statement to Timothy, "I have fought the good fight, I have finished the *race*, I have kept the faith" (2 Tim 4:7). Ford points out that Paul finished the "curriculum" that was laid out for him to do, when he finished life's race. Curriculum includes all of life's events, some of which are planned and some unplanned, that contribute toward maturing the individual. He diagrams it like this:[2]

A *curriculum plan* is the organized process by which the teaching-learning process is systematically undertaken under the guidance of

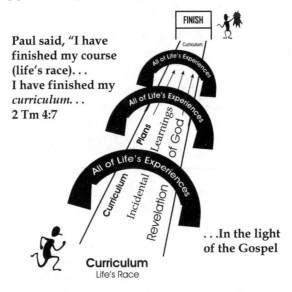

---

[1] L. Ford, *A Curriculum Design Manual for Theological Education* (Nashville: Broadman, 1991), 34.
[2] Ford, letter to writer, January 24, 2005.

the church. A curriculum plan is a detailed blueprint for learning in the church.[3] The difference between a curriculum and a curriculum plan is analogous to the difference between "a race completed" and "a race planned."[4]

Curriculum resources are the materials used to accomplish the purpose of the educational ministry of the church. These would include printed materials, such as study guides ("quarterlies") and teaching aids, as well as the necessary equipment for ongoing activities. Even hymnbooks form part of our resources, providing learners theological meanings and analogies. In churches we often refer to these resources, in general terms, as "the curriculum."

Selecting and Evaluating the Curriculum

Is a church curriculum plan necessary? Many of us grew up in churches where there was no obvious churchwide plan, and where the same programs and the same resources were used year after year. Few ever thought of questioning why. Some churches are filled with members who attend services regularly yet show little evidence of spiritual growth or life transformation. No plan or program alone will produce spiritual transformation. Only the Holy Spirit can do that. But we can provide an environment in which He is able to work. As we plan for teachers, learners, and learning experiences for all ages, we can choose to be intentional and focus the education ministry toward particular goals.

Curriculum resources are a significant component of a curriculum plan. Choosing these wisely contributes to the vital role the church plays in teaching and equipping individuals toward maturity in Christ. Resources alone will not produce mature Christians, but when chosen and used correctly, curriculum resources go a long way toward assisting teachers to make disciples.

The purpose of curriculum planning is not merely an administrative function but rather it reflects the church's view of discipleship. It answers the first question, What does a fully developed follower of Christ look like? And it gives rise to the second, How do we equip people to become increasingly mature in Christ? Perhaps Paul's

---

[3] Ford, *Curriculum Design Manual*, 34.
[4] Ibid., 43.

stated desire in Phil 3:10 would be an appropriate goal: "to know Him and the power of His resurrection and the fellowship of His sufferings, being conformed to His death" (Phil 3:10). As disciple-makers it becomes our responsibility to help others to grow in Christ, and as the apostle says, "We proclaim Him, warning and teaching everyone with all wisdom, so that we may present everyone mature in Christ" (Col 1:28–29).

How do we select curriculum resources that will help teachers encourage spiritual growth in their students? The decisions we make affect Bible study, discipleship, missions, and any other programs through which the church teaches. The Sunday school hour is when dated materials are most frequently used, although the same criteria for selection apply to all the educational programs of the church. The many available resources on the market today cause us to ask, "Which curriculum series best serves the interests of a specific local church?" Using the Sunday school as common ground, to which most of us can relate, consider the following criteria to determine the most appropriate materials for your situation. The purpose of the following statements is to assist in selecting from many good items the one curriculum series that is best for your situation.

Biblically Based

The Bible is foundational for teaching and the first factor for consideration. There are many different kinds of Bible study materials. Sometimes a Bible book is selected and studied each week so the content is the starting point, and over a period of time the entire Bible is presented. Other curriculum series identify significant life issues for learners in each age group and select Bible passages that address the topic. Some Bible study series today provide relevant subject matter but quote just one text to support the topic chosen. In the final analysis it is not how much Scripture is used, or if the curriculum is learner centered or content centered, but the way in which learners are engaged in the study. Does the material lend itself to leading the learners to study and interact with the Scripture passage?

Theologically Sound

While the matter of theological soundness is closely related to a biblical base, there is a distinction. Materials can be considered theologically sound yet not match specific doctrines of various denominations. Churches desire curriculum resources that reinforce their own theological views. Denominational distinctives—such as open or closed Communion, mode of baptism, and eternal security of the believer—emphasize this or that particular theological perspective. Most churches will consider a curriculum theologically sound only if it agrees with their doctrinal stance. This is called denominational alignment. Most publishers of curriculum materials post a doctrinal statement on their Web sites, so it is possible to examine the theological stance from which the resources are written.

Denominational Alignment

One advantage of using denominational publications is that the church's doctrine is recognized and reliable. Baptists should be able to trust Baptist resources, Methodists ought to know what to expect with materials from Methodist publishers, and so on. Southern Baptists have a unique approach to missions and mission support through the Cooperative Program. Other annual denominational emphases are recognized in churches, such as weeks of prayer for missions, special emphasis lessons on ethical issues, or stewardship; and these are built into the resources.

Is it appropriate, then, to use nondenominational materials as long as their statement of doctrine is acceptable? That is certainly a possibility as long as the leaders and teachers using the resources understand that any particular doctrinal issue may need to be interpreted. For example, the approach to topics such as baptism or the Lord's Supper may offer the alternatives of several denominations rather than advocating one specifically. Nondenominational publishers market their products to a wide variety of denominations and try to avoid taking a stance on controversial issues.

When a church makes a decision to use interdenominational resources, specific theological emphases are missed. The individual church leadership is responsible for providing supplements at the appropriate times to provide focused lessons.

Educational Objective

Curriculum resources also reflect the educational purpose of the church. Traditionally Southern Baptist materials have included in their objectives the following: leading individuals to Christ, involving them in church membership, and equipping them to live as Christians in the world. Encompassed in this is a focus on assisting people to grow toward maturity in discipleship and become involved in service in the church, the community, and the world. In selecting resources it is important to examine the educational objective of the materials to ensure their focus is in keeping with the church's purpose, mission, and annual goals.

Correlation of Curriculum

The various parts of the total curriculum should be properly correlated, and this necessitates a close relationship among all the programs of the church. These programs all lead toward the same general purpose and should support one another but not overlap. Curricula used in the Sunday school hour, discipleship groups, and men's and women's ministries, for example, should be complementary but not usually repetitive.

Sometimes a deliberate decision may be made for all classes in the Sunday school to study a particular topic in line with an emphasis in the church. A stewardship lesson, for instance, might be provided for all age groups for one Sunday.

Sequence of Study

It is common for publishers of curriculum materials to provide the "scope and sequence" of topics for an extended period of time, such as a year or even five years. Publishers' Web sites will often overview the content in each unit over a year or several years. This enables leaders to determine if the presentation of the segments is in the best order for learning in any age group. The best order for lessons to be presented is in relationship to learning readiness in each age level.

Materials ought to reflect the ability of learners at any given age to assimilate concepts. Preschoolers are imaginative and active thinkers, children are logical (concrete) thinkers, while youth can process the abstract (kingdom of heaven) and hypothetical (What if?). Adults are able to think abstractly but often choose to live in earlier stages. For example, the apostle Paul chided the Corinthian believers for still being infants. He said, "I fed you milk, not solid food, because you were not yet able to receive it. In fact, you are still not able" (1 Cor 3:2). Curriculum resources should provide both milk and solid food.

Sequence of units of study is also a consideration, especially if different age groups in the church are using different curriculum series. A fourth grader may have been involved in a cycle of topics one year, and upon promotion to fifth grade could conceivably repeat those same topics in another series. One advantage of the whole church using the same curriculum series for a Bible study program is the matter of coordinated sequence over a span of years.

Comprehensiveness of the Curriculum

The goal of Christian teaching—the development of well-rounded learners—is the guiding principle here. Is the curriculum framework of content, learning activities, and suggested experiences adequate for such development? Does it provide for a variety of learning styles and teaching methods so that the educational needs of learners are included? Does the course content assist the learner to grow in all aspects of spiritual development? This kind of evaluation requires training in both educational process and theological content.

To those who would write their own curriculum, a word of caution is in order here. Make sure the specifically designed lessons are indeed the best for the development of the learner rather than a platform for the writer's favorite topic. The following principle of balance relates to this.

The Principle of Balance

How do curriculum designers decide what to include and what to leave out of their resources in any given period? Consider a learner in a church who attends Sunday school from preschool through adulthood. How can we be assured he has learned all he needs to live the Christian life?

One sure measure is to consider the weight given to topics in the Scripture and to provide the same balance in teaching. Failing to do this—that is, emphasizing a few topics over others—leads to imbalance in teaching. A learner may have been in church all his life without having read the Bible through. If church leaders have steadily selected *life-issues* curriculum materials, the student may know a great deal about some topics but nothing about what the Bible says on other important topics. If leaders take into account the long-term overview of curriculum materials rather than a week-to-week glance, they are more likely to provide adequate balance in teaching topics.

Learner Interests

Curriculum resources should also reflect sound principles of learning. Christian learning takes place when an eternal truth of the gospel coincides or intersects with a persistent life need of the learner.[5] If the resources focus on the needs of the learner as well as ways in which students learn in each developmental stage, they will assist in bringing about change in the individual's life.[6]

The ultimate goal of all Christian teaching is spiritual transformation. The materials should be focused to lead learners to an encounter with Christ at the appropriate stages in their spiritual journey and help them grow toward being like Him.

Carefully designed resources help make the truth of Scripture come alive. The aim or goal of the lesson[7] should be clearly stated so that teachers can focus learning toward a particular response and not merely "finish the lesson."

Supporting materials such as artwork and illustrations should reflect the culture of the learner. Do African-American, Asian, or Hispanic children ever see pictures of children "like them" in the materials? Do illustrations overemphasize middle-class suburbia and underemphasize urban and rural settings?

Teacher Ability

Teachers of Bible study classes come from a variety of walks of life, and so curriculum resources should be geared to accommodate them. Teachers and leaders may have little training in educational practice so the materials need to be written in such a way that volunteers can easily obtain resources and use teaching methods suggested in the materials.

---

[5] Howard P. Colson and Raymond M. Rigdon, *Understanding Your Church's Curriculum* (Nashville: Broadman, 1981), 81.

[6] The Bible (Eternal Truth) speaking to Needs of the Learners: the foundation of Disciplers' Model, chapter 1.

[7] See chapter 13, "Planning to Teach," for a discussion of goals, objectives, and "targets"

Leaders and teachers should be provided adequate training[8] in the use of the curriculum materials as helps for teaching preparation. Many undated resources provide additional help for teacher planning. Books on age-group characteristics—such as *Understanding Preschoolers*—and suggestions for teaching—*Teaching Youth*—provide a wide variety of learning activities from which to choose.

Choosing Acceptable and Effective Resources

Denominational publications are produced for many churches, all of which are different. It is a challenge to meet the requirements of every church, everywhere. Producers of curriculum materials often provide options from which churches may choose. Church leaders determine which option is most effective for their own situation.

Young adults and senior adults have significantly different expectations for resources. Color may be a factor for a young adult while economy may be the focus of the senior. Producers of resources consider the diverse population in their churches and do their best to meet their needs. Some publishers even consider senior adults who want a large-print learner's guide that is small enough to fit in their Bibles! It is a well-known fact that it is impossible to please all of the people all of the time, but if we make our selections carefully and explain those selections to users, materials can be used effectively to help learners grow.

Cost of the Curriculum Materials

The cost of the materials is certainly a consideration for many churches, though we hope, given all we said above, not the primary one. Basic curriculum pieces include the teacher's and learners' guides. Will you purchase just enough for members, or will you purchase additional copies for visitors and new members?

Publishers often provide teaching helps in the form of kits, which include posters, maps, lists, artwork, and the like. Bible commentaries are also available. Some churches provide these "free" to any teacher who asks; others order materials for purchase by teachers who want them.

---

[8] See chapter 20, "Equipping Teachers," for practical suggestions for training.

We can save money by carefully managing ordering and use patterns every quarter (or order cycle) and order only what teachers and leaders actually use. We can save money by impressing on teachers the cost of materials and helping them become good stewards of budgeted monies. We can save money by comparing various curricula, purchasing the materials that provide the best materials (content, sequence, aims) for the least money. By doing all these things, we can provide the best mix of content and cost, helping both the leaders and the church as a whole.

Contextualizing Resources

It is important to consider the context in which the materials are to be used. Language differences, methods of teaching, financial and human resources available, and appropriateness of activities and artwork are among the items to be evaluated. A student once told me about an experience she had on a mission trip. She filled small containers with rice to make different sounds, as an activity for young children. The activity was age appropriate, and the children enjoyed it immensely. After she finished, she threw the dirty rice away. The children were horrified that she had been so wasteful. They would have taken it home for a meal. The aim of the lesson was totally overlooked. She had forgotten to consider context: she was in a country where food was very scarce. Increasingly, our churches are becoming a mix of cultures and ethnicities. Choosing appropriate Bible study resources is all the more important if we are to reach out to the world and teach them what Jesus commanded.

The Curriculum Planning Team

The selection and management of curriculum resources is best handled by leaders of the organizations using the materials. For example, if a church has a preschool division director and several preschool departments (director and teachers), these leaders are the best qualified to determine which preschool curriculum resources to use. The Sunday school director provides coordination across preschool, children, youth, and adult divisions.

If a church is fortunate enough to have age-group staff ministers (children, youth, adult), they can provide excellent support for selecting the curriculum, particularly when they have been specifically trained in educational processes. A minister of education provides overall supervision to the process. Regardless of how much professional support a church provides to lay leaders, it is important that lay leaders and teachers be involved in the process of evaluating and selecting curriculum materials. When teachers and leaders assist in the selection of resources, they will use them more readily. In smaller churches, lay leaders work with the pastor in selecting a curriculum series for their various areas.

Management of resources requires an established process for ordering materials and evaluating their use. Publishers may provide an order form, which is helpful for leaders/teachers to complete each year (or quarter) to request the materials they would like to use. Analysis of ordering patterns can be done using these completed forms. Regular evaluation of resources used will enable the leaders to exercise stewardship in handling the finances of the church.

Teachers' meetings and/or individual consultations with teachers will allow leaders to determine the usefulness of resources. Adjustments are then made accordingly.

After selecting the materials, hold a training event to help teachers use the materials effectively. This is especially important for those who are using the materials for the first time. Understanding purpose and design of each curriculum series will assist in accomplishing the desired results. Printed resources, as good as they may be, are just part of the curriculum plan necessary for helping followers of Jesus Christ to grow in Him.

Using a Checklist

A checklist is an instrument devised to help teaching leaders make appropriate choices in curriculum resources. Below are two examples of curriculum checklists.[9] You would do well to use one of these examples as a model to custom design a list especially for your specific church situation. A checklist for children's materials will look different from one for adults. The checklists also help leaders emphasize important curriculum considerations beyond the pictures on the

---

[9] Norma Hedin, "How to Select and Evaluate Curriculum Materials," in D. Eldridge, *The Teaching Ministry of the Church* (Nashville: B&H, 1995), 291–93. Hedin created these two checklists for the first edition of the text.

cover. By working through the checklists, leaders provide helpful
training in what actually makes curriculum resources effective.

Sample Checklist One: General Characteristics

The first sample checklist emphasizes questions that are most important to your church. Simple yes/no responses provide a quick way
to compare two curriculum pieces.

CURRICULUM EVALUATION CHECKLIST		
Curriculum		
Age Group		
Educational Goals		
Use of Content		
Regards the Bible as the authoritative guide to faith and practice	Yes	No
Emphasizes biblical essentials: salvation, discipleship, service	Yes	No
Emphasizes the doctrinal distinctive of your particular denomination	Yes	No
Encourages commitment to Jesus Christ as personal Savior and Lord	Yes	No
Encourages independent thinking and questioning	Yes	No
Uses personal life experiences of members as occasions for spiritual insight	Yes	No
Recognizes and affirms the uniqueness of each person's spiritual journey	Yes	No
Emphasizes applying faith to moral decision-making and life issues	Yes	No
Relationship to Goals		
Focuses on outreach and ministry to others	Yes	No
Provides resources related to the needs of singles	Yes	No
Provides resources for all age groups for family Bible study	Yes	No
Focuses on spiritual disciplines with practical suggestions for family relationships and growth	Yes	No

Educational Approach and Organization		
Gives clear and understandable objectives for teaching and learning	Yes	No
Offers a balance of biblical exposition and application to life	Yes	No
Uses materials appropriate to learner's needs, abilities, and interests	Yes	No
Needs of Church and Teachers		
Allows for flexibility to meet the needs of various size churches and diversity of teachers and pupils	Yes	No
Gives teachers guidance and insight into educational theory and methods for adults	Yes	No
Provides inspiration, biblical background, and teaching principles for teachers	Yes	No
Provides at least one detailed lesson plan with additional teacher helps and resources	Yes	No
Provides illustrations and application suggestions appropriate for the age group for which it is written	Yes	No
Suggests a variety of learning activities based on sound educational principles	Yes	No
Mechanical Features		
Material is well-written and readable, using short paragraphs and sentences	Yes	No
Graphics and layout are attractive, contemporary, and interesting	Yes	No
Designed for ease of use for teacher and student	Yes	No
Comments and Overall Assessment		

Sample Checklist Two: Evaluation Worksheet

The second checklist provides a means to measure the strength of essential characteristics. By rating each item on a scale from 5 (high) to 1 (low) and adding the scores together, you can compare two different curriculum series. You may certainly add questions to reflect the curriculum preferences of your church, based on the value given to each of the criteria above.

CURRICULUM EVALUATION WORKSHEET	
As you evaluate each curriculum piece, answer the question: To what extent does this curriculum reveal this characteristic? A score of 1 = very poor; 2 = poor; 3 = average; 4 = good; 5 = excellent.	
Centered in the Word of God	1 2 3 4 5
Emphasizes salvation, discipleship, service	1 2 3 4 5
Emphasizes the doctrinal distinctives of our denomination	1 2 3 4 5
Encourages commitment to Jesus Christ as personal Savior and Lord	1 2 3 4 5
Emphasizes biblical knowledge and understanding, and application of Bible truths	1 2 3 4 5
Encourages independent thinking and questioning	1 2 3 4 5
Uses educational processes that actively involve learners	1 2 3 4 5
Gives teachers guidance and insight into educational theory and methods	1 2 3 4 5
Gives clear and understandable objectives for teaching and learning	1 2 3 4 5
Is flexible enough to meet the needs of various teachers and pupils in our church	1 2 3 4 5
Provides biblical background, illustrations, and teaching helps for teachers	1 2 3 4 5
Provides at least one detailed lesson plan with additional teacher helps and resources	1 2 3 4 5
Provides illustrations and application suggestions appropriate for the age group for which it is written	1 2 3 4 5

Is well-written and readable, using short paragraphs and sentences	1 2 3 4 5
Features attractive, contemporary, and interesting graphics and layout	1 2 3 4 5
Is easy for teachers and students to use	1 2 3 4 5

Return to the Dilemma

At the beginning of our chapter, we raised questions often heard by educational leaders: "Our class does not like the curriculum we use. Can we use something else?" Or, "Our curriculum does not meet the needs in our class. We would like to study a book." Or, "We don't like the curriculum so we have decided to write our own!" In the light of this chapter, how would you respond to these questions?

Before rushing to change curriculum lines or publishers, consider other factors that may be creating problems in classes. Consider the teacher (unprepared; always critical), the teaching approach (uses only one teaching method; wandering discussion), level of skill in the use of the current resources (lacking training), and the age group of the learners (too broad an age range; first-time teacher with the age group). Also important is the specific reason for the dissatisfaction. Can it actually be traced to the curriculum itself? In many cases one of these extraneous factors is more problematic than the printed resources themselves because, truth be told, a good teacher can convert almost any printed curriculum into an unforgettable learning experience.[10]

If indeed the resources are the problem, we solve this by finding a more appropriate curriculum. If church leaders apply the criteria in the checklists above and choose their curriculum resources with care, the church will make great strides toward providing solid support for educating individuals to grow in their faith and "run the race" set out for them.

A Personal Reflection

The principles of curriculum planning and resource selection have broad application. My personal experience has demonstrated clearly

---

[10] See chapter 14, "Creating an Unforgettable Learning Experience."

to me that it is worth the time and effort it requires. I am convinced of this because I have made all the mistakes! I lived in a country where resources were limited, and it was the desire of the people to have indigenous materials. With limited knowledge of all the principles I have offered above, we developed materials that consisted of one book of teacher's materials and a separate book of lesson activities for preschool, children, youth, and adults. We decided to begin with the book of Romans. We had a clear rationale and believed that Romans would introduce the learners to the gospel. It would also be a cost-effective approach.

What we did not consider was the educational background of the people or their *level of Bible knowledge*. The materials were targeted for the people, and we meant well, but it missed our target completely: it is difficult, if not impossible, to teach the same Scripture passage to all four age groups using the same teacher's book. This experience helped focus my interest on curriculum design when I entered seminary to study Christian education.

Conclusion

The Father has a plan for each one of our learners, and He allows us to participate in it. It is a great responsibility to choose the best resources to develop and equip believers of all ages. In the words of the apostle Paul, our goal is to "proclaim Him, warning and teaching everyone with all wisdom, so that we may present everyone mature in Christ" (Col 1:28). The right curriculum materials will assist us in accomplishing this goal.

In 1971 Howard Colson wrote an article on "adequate curriculum" that began with these words:

> One of the most encouraging aspects of Southern Baptist church life today is the increased attention being given to the curriculum of Christian education. Church leaders are focusing attention—long overdue—on curriculum matters. This new interest has the possibility of bringing about real improvement in church educational work in the years ahead.[11]

---

[11] Howard P. Colson, "Tests of an Adequate Curriculum," *Facts and Trends*, vol 15, no. 4, 1971.

Although these words were penned nearly 40 years ago, the sentiment is still applicable today. Some things may have changed, but as we call the churches back to the task of "present[ing] everyone mature in Christ" (Col 1:28), we will do well to recognize that curriculum resources can make a significant impact on educational ministry today.

Discussion Questions

1. What curriculum resources does your church use? What are the reasons for selecting these?
2. How do you deal with questions regarding substitution of curriculum resources? How would you address the issues at the beginning of this chapter?
3. Design a checklist to evaluate the curriculum resources your church uses. Choose an age group to evaluate.
4. Who makes the curriculum decisions in your church? Formulate a plan to evaluate the process you have in place.

Bibliography

Colson, Howard P. "Tests of an Adequate Curriculum."*Facts and Trends*, vol 15, no. 4, 1971.

Colson, Howard P., and Raymond M. Rigdon. *Understanding Your Church's Curriculum*. Nashville: Broadman, 1981.

Cully, Iris V. *Planning and Selecting Curriculum for Christian Education*. Valley Forge: Judson, 1983.

Ford, LeRoy. *A Curriculum Design Manual for Theological Education*. Nashville: Broadman, 1991.

Harris, Maria. *Fashion Me a People*. Louisville, KY: Westminister/ John Knox, 1989.

Mager, Robert F. *Preparing Instructional Objectives*. 3rd ed. Atlanta: The Center for Effective Performance, 1997.

Mims, Gene. *Kingdom Principles for Church Growth*. Nashville: LifeWay Church Resources, 1994.

Ornstein, Allan C., and Linda S. Behar. *Contemporary Issues in Curriculum*. Needham Heights: Allyn and Bacon, 1995.

Posner, George J. *Analyzing the Curriculum*. 3rd ed. New York: McGraw Hill, 2004.

Tyler, Ralph W. *Basic Principles of Curriculum and Design.* Chicago: University of Chicago Press, 1949.

Wyckoff, D, Campbell. *Theory and Design of Christian Education Curriculum.* Philadelphia: Westminster, 1961.

Chapter 20

EQUIPPING TEACHERS

Rick Yount

Now may the God of peace,
who brought up from the dead our Lord Jesus—
the great Shepherd of the sheep—
with the blood of the everlasting covenant,
equip you with all that is good to do His will,
working in us what is pleasing in His sight,
through Jesus Christ, to whom be glory forever and ever. Amen.
(Heb 13:20–21)

"Don't Waste My Time!"

I was so excited with my new ministry position. Five years before, my wife and I had left this wonderful church to attend seminary. A warmhearted, mission-minded, growing church. A loving pastor-teacher. Many close friends. And now, with an MRE[1] and an ABD[2] doctorate in education, we headed back "home" to assume the newly created position of minister of education. I had studied the *ideals* of education ministry for years, but now I faced the *ordeal* of education ministry in the real world.

One of my first goals was to establish a training program for the 68 teachers of adults in the Sunday school program. I already knew it wasn't going to be easy. In initial meetings I had heard from a dozen teachers that the *last* thing they wanted was for me to "waste their time with a bunch of useless meetings!" They had tried the *filet of teacher meeting* several times and found it dry and tasteless. How would I ever overcome that?

---

[1] Master of Religious Education degree
[2] "All (doctoral work completed) But Dissertation."

381

The Need for the Systematic Equipping of Teachers

Systematic teacher and leader training has fallen on hard times in many of our churches. Fifty years ago the typical Southern Baptist church provided weekly meetings of teachers and directors in which preparations were made, educationally and administratively, for up-coming Sunday school sessions. Churches elected a lay director of Sunday school, as well as lay directors of age divisions (preschool, children, youth, adults), who coordinated the work of their areas—which included training.[3]

Larger churches called vocational ministers of education, professionals trained in a variety of seminary courses, to guide these efforts. The largest churches provided a full educational staff whose primary purpose was to "equip the saints for works of service"—teaching, reaching, ministering. In the late 1940s and early 1950s, Southern Baptists could boast of a veritable army of trained workers, tens of thousands of trained teachers and leaders in thousands of churches nationwide. Two regional training centers in Glorieta, New Mexico, and Ridgecrest, North Carolina, were filled to capacity during multiple weeks of Sunday school training sessions. Convention Press produced scores of training booklets, which provided opportunities for church members to study individually, or in groups, to earn certificates. Regional associations of churches and state conventions provided regular training events. Today's efforts at helping local church teachers in "rightly dividing the word of truth" (2 Tim 2:15 KJV) are a shadow of what they once were. Even when the training events are provided, only a fraction of our teachers take advantage of them.

There are many reasons for this, I suppose, but I will mention two, both societal. First, we are far more individualistic than we used to be,[4] less given to surrendering personal time for the good of the group. When men like my father and father-in-law enlisted to

---

[3] I say "Southern Baptist" here not to exclude other evangelical groups but because I know of Southern Baptists' work in this area firsthand. Only once was my family a member of an independent Baptist church, on Long Island, New York, and they had no Bible study or discipleship training for adults at all.

[4] Existential philosophy (self, free choice, revolt from the societal norm) took hold in the 1960s. Humanistic psychology (personal values, emphasis of emotion over reason) struck in the 1970s. Both quickly rose to prominence in schools of education, training a generation of teachers, principals, and future deans. In the late 1980s and early 1990s, these two streams morphed into postmodernism.

fight in World War II, they believed they were joining something larger than their own lives, engaging a struggle larger than self. Today, it seems, there is nothing larger than self. Even the U.S. Army engages prospective recruits with the self-obsessed slogan, "Be an Army of One!" When recruits arrive at boot camp, however, they find themselves part of something larger than self after all—squad, platoon, and company! Military training has one fundamental goal: to build teams to carry out specific missions. We would do well to return to this mind-set in our churches, joining drill sergeants— and football coaches, for that matter—in transforming self-obsessed individuals into mission-directed team members. It is not an easy transformation.

A second societal change is the rise of entertainment as the highest virtue. A century ago the movie industry, and later, radio and television, provided the means to escape briefly the mundane responsibilities of life and work. As we moved into the twenty-first century, entertainment had all but replaced reality. Simply compare a 1960s talking-head news broadcast with today's video-intensive, animation-enhanced, sound-bite focused, runway-model delivered infotainment programs. Superbowl I (1967) focused on a championship football game; Superbowl XLI (2007) featured many eye-catching venues—a half-time spectacular, fireworks, and outlandish commercials—as well as the game itself. Commercials that once touted the advantages of products now use drama, humor, and sensuality to evoke excitement.

Churches have followed suit with an intentional avoidance of dead air during worship services and the use of segues to connect one

---

"A Million More in '54!" was the rally cry among Southern Baptists 50-plus years ago, drawing us together, submerging individual efforts into a nationwide communal effort of evangelism. Today individuals seek out churches that fit their own particular needs. In 1961, John F. Kennedy challenged the nation, "Ask not what your country can do for you. Ask what you can do for your country." Today the common view is that churches and government at all levels exist to serve the particular needs of individuals, whatever those needs might be.

This sea change of worldview is pervasive and undermines group efforts everywhere. It is a worldview that must be deconstructed in our churches so that we can, together, "grow in every way into Him who is the head—Christ. From Him the whole body, fitted and knit together by every supporting ligament, promotes the growth of the body for building up itself in love by the proper working of each individual part" (Eph 4:15–16). Believers find greater meaning as part of the larger community.

element to another. Worship has become for some little more than religious entertainment: heart-touching (emotionally laden) music, special lighting and video presentations, highly talented praise teams, and practical, self-help messages delivered with heart-warming stories. While no one suggests that worship should be boring, worship ought not be judged primarily by its entertainment value. And yet, increasingly, it is.

Teaching ministry, however, is hardly entertaining. It is hard work, serious work. Rocking crying babies while singing "Jesus Loves Me." Organizing activities and providing object lessons to keep curious preschoolers engaged. Explaining basic Bible truths that actually interest sixth-grade boys. Helping teenage girls connect God's Word with life choices. Who wouldn't prefer to sit in an adult class and soak up God's Word? Who wouldn't rather sing praise songs? Teaching exacts a cost from teachers in time, energy, and strength. But the payoff of responding to God's call to give up personal convenience, to submit to training, and to engage the task of loving and teaching people is far greater than any payoff from sitting and soaking.

Al and his wife left the comfort of their adult department to become directors of a fifth-grade department in their church. Six months after they began, while cutting firewood, I asked him how he was enjoying his ministry. "I cannot tell you what a blessing it is. I've attended adult Sunday school classes for 40 years, but I've learned more about God's Word, His ways, and the meaning of life in the last six months than I did in all those years." He was learning more because he was teaching others. He was growing more because he was sharing what he knew.

Teaching costs. But when carried out in the strength of the Lord, the payoffs are immense for both teacher and learners. The key to moving church members from *sit and soak* to *stand and deliver*, once energized to work at all,[5] is training.

Training by Meeting

By far the most common means of teacher and leader training is by calling workers together in meetings of various kinds. There is no better way to share perspective (head), passion (heart), and skill

---

[5] See chapter 22, "Ministering alongside Volunteers," for ideas on enlistment.

(hand) than in regular meetings. Authentic community in the cadre is strengthened as leaders and teachers share needs, blessings, and successes during regular times set aside to meet together.

Two essential principles guide workers' meetings of all types. The first speaks primarily to ministers moving into a new church position. Take whatever level of training meetings you find in place, and improve the focus. Then gradually expand the training focus in the direction of greatest need in the various organizations. There is no way to predict what training traditions we will find in a given church. Some churches may have a weekly workers' meeting. How is it used? Who attends? Is it effective in helping leaders and teachers? What needs to be changed? Other churches may have no workers' meetings at all. Pray for workers' attitudes toward training, and begin to plan ways to support their ministries. We'll discuss specifics in a moment.

The second principle directs the conduct of meetings themselves: "Spend your nickels wisely." I was just 28 years old when I accepted the call to become minister of education at the church mentioned above. In the first few weeks my wife and I were invited to the home of an older couple we had befriended while working at the church before leaving for seminary. After a pleasant meal and conversation, Ray, a retired Army officer of 60,[6] turned to me and said, "The people of our church are happy you are here. We have prayed for you and your ministry among us. Each of us has given you a nickel to spend any way you choose. If you spend them wisely, we will give you another. If you do not, you will quickly run out of nickels, and your ministry will be over. Spend your nickels wisely." His words guided my planning. His advice did more to help me succeed over the next five years than any other human factor. It also allowed me to begin, expand, and direct multiple levels of leader training.

Use what you have, and build on it. Use what you have well, spending nickels wisely, and you will be able to expand training opportunities.

Annual Training

Most churches use the beginning of the public school year in August or September as a time to "kick off" a new emphasis in

---

[6] Lt. Col R. Sturges (retired) commanded a thousand soldiers in the Pentagon before retiring.

educational programs—Bible study, discipleship training, missions education. This annual kickoff season usually targets a single "Promotion Sunday" when members move to new classes, younger groups by grade and adults by age or interest group. Promotion Sunday is the day new workers—enlisted by the church's nominating committee to fill places vacated by workers "going back to class" or new places created by adding new classes—begin their work. This time provides a golden opportunity for training.

Southern Baptist churches that are too small to provide training on their own are fortunate to have support from local associations and state conventions. Contact your local associational or state convention office for information on upcoming training events. These training opportunities are provided free of charge.

Another option for training rests with local Christian college professors or seminary professors—especially specialists in Christian education, teaching/learning, educational administration, age-group ministry, and family ministry. These specialists can be invited for pulpit supply, inspirational messages at appreciation banquets, or a variety of targeted workshops.[7]

Annual appreciation banquets provide a wonderful way to energize the beginning of a new year and to express gratitude to members who give themselves to others on a consistent basis year-round. Such events provide opportunity to do a minimal level of training, but more is needed to nourish workers through the year.

"A Quarter's Worth"

In the face of "don't waste our time," my first step beyond an annual training event was a quarterly meeting. The curricula we used followed a quarterly organization. Every three months new materials were purchased. New themes addressed age-specific needs across the entire Sunday school organization. Providing useful training for teachers, in all four age divisions, to overview an entire quarter of studies in a single three-hour session seemed a good place to begin.

---

[7] Any of the authors of this text would be happy to conduct training for your workers or speak at banquets or provide pulpit supply. If your church's need matches the theme of a chapter, consider contacting the author as a guest speaker.

We had a full-time children's minister on our staff who enlisted key lay leaders—department directors and teachers—in her pre-school and children's divisions to lead training sessions. We had no youth minister at the time, so I enlisted the (lay) youth division director to lead a training session for youth leaders.[8] I led the adult workers. The meetings included a focused time for sharing personal and organizational needs, and prayer; an overview of Scripture passages to be taught; suggestions for teaching[9]; and finally, a preview of the church calendar. I included this last element so that teachers would be aware of major upcoming events. We served refreshments. We held the first few Quarter's Worth meetings on Saturday mornings but later moved the meetings to Sunday evenings so that more teachers could attend.

These meetings proved helpful for teachers, and word-of-mouth publicity drew more teachers over time. The children's minister gave half her meeting time—90 minutes—for department staffs to plan on their own. Department directors and their teachers met together to sketch out the next three months: they determined which learning centers to use, who would supervise each, and which activities would be included, session by session. This 90 minutes of planning set the direction for the quarter. Monthly meetings built on this foundation. These Quarter's Worth sessions, coordinated by staff ministers and lay leaders, provided a singular focus to "equipping the saints" across the entire Sunday school organization, making tangible differences among the 1,000 people who gathered for Bible study every Sunday.

Monthly Training for Teachers

The next logical step beyond quarterly meetings was a monthly meeting. We found at this particular church that Wednesday evenings were the best time for these meetings.[10] In other churches I found Sunday evenings the best time to meet.

---

[8] Two years later the church called a full-time youth minister who took over these meetings completely. I coordinated the educational staff members, but they were tasked with enlisting, training, and leading the workers in their divisions.

[9] See chapter 13, "Planning to Teach," for specific suggestions

[10] The pastor encouraged me to hold the meetings simultaneously with prayer meeting, a gracious invitation indeed since it took nearly a third of his own Bible study/

The content of monthly meetings was similar to Quarter's Worth meetings but allowed time for providing more detailed content (passages for the month) and more examples of specific teaching methods[11] tied to those passages. We had more time to explain what to do but also, better still, time to demonstrate how to do it in specific scriptural contexts.

Monthly meetings were far more convenient for busy volunteers than weekly meetings and yet provided more focused help than the quarterly overviews. In one church we created a separate meeting time for adult division organizational leaders, allowing teachers' meetings to focus only on teachers' needs. I found that most teachers chafed when their time was "wasted" by administrative issues—attendance, space, literature orders, visitation, care groups, outreach—in more general workers' meetings.

Monthly Meetings for Directors

We handled administrative concerns in the adult division of our Sunday school in a monthly Sunday morning meeting. I met with the Sunday school director, the adult division director, and the department directors of all adult departments during the Sunday school hour.[12] Since most of these leaders finished their responsibilities at the beginning of the Sunday school hour (and since few attended class), it was easy to gather them for a 30–40 minute planning meeting once a month. During this time we discussed problems in the organization, worker needs, budget needs, and directions for the future. I found no other time where I could gather more adult division leaders than the Sunday school hour itself.

When I first proposed the leader meeting with our director, he balked. He was a truck driver and had no experience leading others in planning meetings. He was a godly man and loved Sunday school

prayer group. He did this to help families with children attend the various activities for all age groups and still arrive home early enough for the children's bedtime.

[11] *The Disciplers' Handbook*, a free download from http://www.napce.org, *Created to Learn*, and *Called to Teach* provide material for hours of teacher training sessions. For training mission teams going into different cultures, see *Called to Reach*. These last three are B&H publications.

[12] This approach to organizational meetings does not apply to preschool and children's leaders because department directors in these divisions, unlike adult leaders, are an integral part of the teaching throughout the hour.

work. But he would not agree to the meetings unless I agreed to lead them. "I'll lead the meetings for a few months if you'll work toward taking them over when you feel ready." He agreed. For six months he was an item on my agenda. Finally he agreed to begin leading the meeting if I would continue to attend. He did a great job, continuing to grow as he led us in prayer, a devotion, and discussion of our Bible study ministry. I became an item on his agenda. He continued to hold these leadership meetings for several years after my interim position came to an end—until he and his wife left the church to begin a satellite mission church across town.

In another church I conducted monthly meetings on Sunday mornings for administration of the organization and monthly meetings for teacher-training and content overview on Wednesday evenings—for a year. With the beginning of a new Sunday school year, I initiated weekly teacher meetings on Sunday evenings.

Weekly Training

Weekly training meetings provide the most consistent, most focused venue for specific training. The focus of each meeting is a single Bible study session. The narrower focus allows deeper study of passages and deeper explanation and better demonstration of teaching manners and methods. I routinely used the hour to teach a portion of the assigned passage, using specific approaches to teaching. By experiencing firsthand such approaches, teachers were better able to use the approaches themselves. By broadening the variety of methods used in teachers' meetings—rather than spending the time telling teachers how to teach—we naturally broadened the variety of methods used in adult classes themselves.

One Sunday I was standing in the sanctuary just before the worship service began when I saw one of our senior adult couples' teachers coming toward me. He was looking right at me and smiling from ear to ear. Despite his 80 years of age, there was a spring in his step. I asked him why he was so happy.

"I just had the best Sunday school class in my life!"

"Well, tell me all about it. I want to know what you did."

"I took those questions you handed out in teachers' meeting and handed them out to my class. I did just what you did with us last week in teachers' meeting. We had the best discussion I've ever had!" And off he walked, nearly floating over the carpet, to take his place for worship.

To tell the truth, I did not think my teachers' meeting had been all that dramatic. I grouped the teachers in quads, handed each group a list of questions, and let them study the text, answering the questions. Then I debriefed the groups on what they discovered. This weekly meeting was the favorite part of my ministry: these adult teachers were *my* class, and I ministered to them just as we encouraged them to minister to their own members.

Using the Disciplers' Model (see chap. 1), I focused on a different element each week, providing both variety of focus and harmony of purpose. Under "Bible" we focused on the text and the use of research aids (commentaries, Bible dictionaries, and the like). Under "Needs" we focused on the needs of members of classes and how the passage under consideration could be connected to known needs. Under "Thinking" we focused on key concepts in the text as well as ways to explain, illustrate, and paraphrase passages. Under "Feeling/ Valuing" we focused on attitudes and priorities addressed in the passages. Under "Relating" we focused on ways to use small groups— pairs, triads, quads, men/women, and random gatherings—to build relationships within the class. Under "Growth in Christ" we focused on ways to help learners grow spiritually, to help members be spiritually sensitive, and to "deny self and follow Christ." Under "Holy Spirit" we focused on prayerful preparation, including prayer for learners, for preparation, and for the session itself as well as evaluation of what happened. These seven elements provided seven different perspectives, in rotation, for the meetings—*variety with harmony.*

I used this weekly approach in five different churches. These churches ranged in Sunday school attendance from 350 to 1,100; were located in city, suburban, and small-town areas; and served a range of socioeconomic levels from blue-collar workers to white-collar professionals. I found similar results in all five.

Of all the responsibilities I had over the 20 years I served on church staff, leading the weekly teachers' meeting was my favorite ministry. I knew that as I helped teachers improve skills, ministered to them personally, and shared my life with them, I was making a tangible difference in the classes they served on Sunday morning and through the week.

When the Lord led me away from each situation into a new ministry, no other activity garnered more positive response from members than these weekly meetings with teachers. The senior adult teacher mentioned above came to teachers' meeting nearly every Sunday for the eight years of my "interim" ministry. Since I was never able to achieve 100-percent attendance of teachers in any meeting in any church in 20 years, I once asked him why he came every Sunday. He did not hesitate. "I taught for 30 years without any help from anyone. Every week these meetings help me to prepare, help to teach. I learn something new every week. I missed this for 30 years. I don't plan ever to miss it again." His words have blessed me, humbled me, and sustained me in teaching over the last 14 years. Praise the Lord for His grace.

Individual Training

Each teacher has his own set of needs and skills. Questions arise and problems surface. With openness and trust between minister and volunteer, these problems become unparalleled opportunities for listening, sharing, and equipping. Often the best ministry happens over cups of coffee or chance meetings in the hallways, hospital rooms, or funeral parlors.

Early in my ministry, I found myself struggling with the aggravation of spontaneous teacher problems. I was frustrated by having my daily schedule repeatedly interrupted by one thing or another. The Lord taught me a valuable lesson one Wednesday afternoon. I returned from lunch, needing to prepare for our teachers' meeting that evening. Not wanting to be disturbed, I asked my secretary to hold all my calls. *No interruptions, please.*

I began to read the assigned passage in Matthew 9. Jesus had been teaching about fasting (v. 14) when Jairus (Luke 8:41), the ruler of the local synagogue, came with the news that his daughter lay dying (v. 18).[13] Immediately Jesus broke off His teaching and went with Jairus. On the way a woman, suffering from a flow of blood for 12 years that left her ceremonially unclean and outcast, interrupted

---

[13] "My daughter is near death" [lit., daughter has now come to an end] in HCSB.

Him. He stopped His "Jairus mission" and turned to carry out the "suffering woman mission." After He declared the woman healed by her faith (Matt 9:22), word came that Jairus's daughter had died (Luke 8:49). Was He wrong for stopping? Should He have avoided the interruption? Jesus told them to believe, for the girl would be made well, and then proceeded on to Jairus's house. He told the mourners the girl was merely sleeping (Matt 9:24; Luke 8:52) and then entered the house and raised her back to life (Matt 9:25; Luke 8:55).

I was worried about interruptions myself. Why did Jesus handle His interruption this way? I pursued my questions into the commentaries. One scholar's statement jumped off the page at me:

> No outcome of God's Providence is of chance, but each is designed. The circumstances which in their occurrence make up an event, may all be of natural occurrence, but their conjunction is of Divine ordering and to a higher purpose, and this constitutes Divine Providence.[14]

Jesus knew no interruptions since the Father was in control. He did not hurry. He did not avoid spontaneous events because Jesus knew that everything came from the Father's hand. There is no such thing as an interruption to ministry. Indeed, "interruptions" are, in themselves, God-ordained opportunities for *His* ministry through us to others.

I buzzed my secretary: Let the calls come through. Ten minutes later my phone rang. One of the teachers in a median adult department had a problem with several talkative members in her class. She was distraught and wept as she told of the tension in the class. I listened for a while; I don't remember how long. We talked a while longer. And then we prayed about the situation. Part of me said I had "wasted" a good part of my afternoon. Another part said my conversation with this teacher was the best part of the afternoon. This teacher and I taught each other. She was able to handle the tension more effectively and eventually worked through the problem. I completed my preparation in plenty of time and learned a powerful lesson about my priorities.

---

[14] A. Edersheim, *The Life and Times of Jesus the Messiah,* vol. 1 (Grand Rapids: Wm. B. Eerdmans, 1969), 629

The most satisfying moments of ministry across the years have been these "interruptions" to my religious routine. I plan ahead more so that I can be "interrupted" more easily. I look forward to it and am always blessed by God's spontaneous plans. These times of "individual training" are the most important of all because they underscore Jesus' declaration of whose agendas take precedence:

> You know that the rulers of the Gentiles dominate them, and the men of high position exercise power over them. It must not be like that among you. On the contrary, whoever wants to become great among you must be your servant, and whoever wants to be first among you must be your slave; just as the Son of Man did not come to be served, but to serve, and to give His life—a ransom for many. (Matt 20:25–28)

Training by (E-)Mail

What do we do when teachers cannot attend meetings? I held a Quarter's Worth meeting one Sunday afternoon. Three of the oldest adult teachers in our church—all ladies—came to this training event for the first time. During the session I asked the subjective question mentioned earlier: If you had been Nicodemus, what would you have asked Jesus? One of the ladies—a retired pastor's secretary now in her late 80s—said, "Well, I wouldn't have been there because I don't go out at night."

She told me something profound in that answer. She was afraid to get out of her house at night. Our regular teachers' meetings were night meetings. For the next three years I sent her the notes from teachers' meetings by mail—week by week. The last Sunday night of July 1981 was my last Sunday at the church. I was leaving to teach at Southwestern. The pastor asked me to preach that evening, and the congregation had an after-church fellowship to send us off to Texas. A long line of members passed by to say their good-byes. Hearty handshakes from the men, hugs from the women, it was a bittersweet time of good-byes. Then out of the corner of my eye, I saw her—for the first time in three years. She had "come out at night." She had stood for a long time. When the line moved her in front of me, she took my hands in hers and said, "I just wanted to come and say thank you for sending me the teachers' notes. I've used them every week." I'd sent the notes for three years without knowing whether she used them or not.

Today the Internet and e-mail programs allow us to send Power-Points, documents, and all manner of visual aids to teachers. Teachers and leaders can write us questions 24-7. Many churches are now developing their own Web sites, which allow teachers and leaders to conduct asynchronous communication. It is hard to predict how technology will help us in the future. But there is a caution. Electronic interaction makes communication more convenient, but it does not provide for heart-to-heart relationship building like regular interactive meetings can. Pioneers in computerized education predicted that computers and sophisticated educational software would render (human) teachers obsolete. It has not happened. Neither will Internet communication in our churches replace "people with people with Jesus in the middle."

Required Participation

Should we require volunteer teachers to attend the training sessions we provide? I have seen some success in doing this, especially among youth ministers: "If a youth teacher cannot commit to attending the training we provide, we'll find someone else." I have had much less success in making this requirement for teachers of adults. I spent my nickels as wisely as I could. I was able to secure regular participation from 50 to 75 percent of adult teachers, depending on what Bible book we were studying at the time. I once achieved an average attendance of 85 percent of all adult teachers over the 13-week period we studied Revelation.

The adult division director had tried for several years to get one of our adult teachers to attend a monthly overview meeting (we did not have weekly meetings at this particular church). The teacher taught his class week after week without any help from fellow teachers or from me. As we approached my last monthly teachers' meeting at the church, the adult division director told me he had made it his goal to get this teacher to the meeting. And he came! I could only wonder what he was thinking as we made our way through the session.

At the end of the meeting, the teacher came up to talk. "How long have you been doing these meetings?" he asked. I told him we'd been providing the monthly training for more than four years. "And you've been doing things like you did tonight for four years?" Yes. He shook his head. "I've really missed something here for a long time." Oh, how I wanted to agree with him. Instead, I told him the church would be calling someone to fill my place. I encouraged him to attend a meeting or two when my replacement arrived. "Give him a chance to help you and to learn from you." He promised me he would.

I now serve our church as a volunteer teacher. I do not often attend teachers' meetings. I am so thankful for a minister of education who does not require my presence in order to teach. He provides materials through the church Web site, and I always have more than enough material for the 30 to 40 minutes teaching time afforded me on Sundays. He encourages me in my teaching ministry, even as he meets every Wednesday night with 10–15 teachers. I understand much better now why, due to life issues, some of my teachers did not attend my meetings. And the joy I feel as a volunteer, working with such a minister of education, confirms my decision in times past to draw teachers into training by spending nickels wisely. Sugar, not vinegar. Carrots, not sticks.

I encourage you to use the many approaches discussed in this chapter to make contact with every teacher you can. Your encouragement and support, training and materials, time and concern will bless them, one at a time.

"Don't Waste My Time!" Revisited

Many of the teachers who have tasted *filet of teacher training*, finding it dry and tasteless, gradually change their attitudes as we work with them through annual, quarterly, monthly, and (in some churches) weekly training meetings. But not all.

Churches differ, but all need to teach. Cadres of teachers have different sets of problems and issues, and yet there are common principles that will help any teacher become more effective. Pastors are wise to secure a staff member who can give large amounts of time to enlisting, training, organizing, and leading members of the church. Such specialists in teaching and administration have been called "ministers of education" or "directors of education" in the past. Many churches are calling "family ministers" who carry out the functions of the minister of education. But whatever name the position carries, the called ones will never waste the time of church members in meetings if they "equip the saints for works of service" in a timely fashion, spending their nickels wisely.

Conclusion

As you have noticed, this chapter has been more personal testimony than academic treatise. The creative approaches to training shared here grew out of administration courses I took at Southwestern. The ability to teach, and train others to teach, grew out of foundations of education courses. After seminary I continued to learn from staff colleagues and from minister of education conferences offered by the Baptist Sunday School Board, now LifeWay. Always, we can learn best from the One who saved us, and taught us, and called us into His ministry:

> All of you, take up **My yoke** and **learn from Me**,
> because I am gentle and humble in heart,
> and you will find rest for yourselves.
> For My yoke is easy and My burden is light. (Matt 11:29–30)

Pray to the Lord and ask Him for wisdom in creating effective ways to equip the people in your church. He will bring people and experiences into your ministry much like these I shared here. He gets the glory and we get the joy.

Discussion Questions

1. Describe training sessions you have attended. Were they helpful or not? Explain why.
2. Choose one of the training stories in the chapter. Evaluate the problem involved, the principle used, and the outcome.
3. How would you expand the ideas concerning use of the Internet and e-mail? What new technologies could be employed to improve support to workers?
4. What was your greatest discovery while reading the chapter? Why was this discovery so meaningful for you?

Chapter 21

ADMINISTERING EDUCATIONAL PROGRAMS

Bob Mathis

The Scriptural Mandate for Education in the Church:
Then Jesus came near and said to them,
"All authority has been given to Me in heaven and on earth.
Go, therefore, and make disciples of all nations,
baptizing them in the name of the Father and
of the Son and of the Holy Spirit,
teaching them to observe everything I have commanded you.
And remember, I am with you always, to the end of the age."
(Matt 28:18–20)

An obviously troubled young man came into the den and sat down in his favorite chair. He looked over at the elderly gentleman on the other side of the room and said, "Dad, I am about ready to give up."

" Oh really? What's going on?"

"Well some people in my church want me to focus on preaching and worship; some want small groups to be the emphasis on what we are doing; and some just want us to leave them alone so they can do whatever they want to do."

"What do you want to do?"

"That's just it; I don't know. It must have been a lot easier back in the old days when everyone did Sunday school and church pretty much the same way. Now everybody wants to do something different. I know what I should be doing in worship, but this education stuff is making me nuts. How did you handle it back in the old days?"

"Well I was taught to start with the Bible to see what it said to do about things like this, and I have always looked at the Great Commission as the mandate for education in the church."

The older gentleman continued, "Everything about these verses should lead the church to conclude that Jesus gave an explicit mandate to the church to be in the business of education and to be in it with a sure sense of purpose."

The Authority. The Lord has the right to define the work of the church.

The Principle Task. Make disciples. To disciple is, among other things, an educational term. A disciple is a learner but not simply a student. A disciple is one who studies, learns, commits, and puts into practice—a follower, believer, supporter, and adherent.

The Initiation into the Body of Christ. Baptize them. Some will have a negative reaction to the idea of baptism as an initiation ceremony, but it marks a significant kind of declaration about a person. At baptism the believer is saying, "I have examined the claims of the life and work of Jesus Christ and have found them to be true and effective for salvation. I desire to demonstrate my commitment to Jesus by renouncing my former existence and symbolically following Him into burial and resurrection." Gangel and Benson assert that the early church employed a multistage regimen whereby a person would move through the categories of "hearer" to "kneeler" to "chosen" before baptism would take place.[1]

The Curriculum. Teach them to obey Me. Christ did not abolish the Law; He fulfilled it. He lived it. Through Christ alone can anyone take up the command, "Be holy, because I am holy" given by Moses (Lev 11:45) and later Peter (1 Pet 1:15–16).

The Scope of the Work. Go to all nations, people, ethnic groups. (and a hint at a methodology).

The Impetus for Action and the Basis of the Testimony. Empowered by the Holy Spirit, be witnesses.

The older gentleman continued:

"The way I see it, here is everything in a nutshell needed to support an educational system—a mandate, a clientele, a curriculum, a set of

---

[1] Kenneth O. Gangel and Warren S. Benson, *Christian Education: Its History and Philosophy* (Chicago: Moody, 1983), 878–89.

student outcomes, a picture of the scope of the process, and the resources
needed to accomplish the work. These statements are also useful guide-
lines for administration: (1) This work is intentional: we are to be delib-
erate in our going; (2) it is purposeful: we are to make disciples; and (3)
it is effective: we are to be obedient to the teachings of the Lord.

"There appears to be an implicit division of the work of educational
ministries in the church: (1) providing basic Christian education for the
church combined with reaching out to those who have not heard the mes-
sage of Christ; (2) training for teachers, support staff and other volun-
teer church workers; and (3) in-depth education in personal discipleship
and corporate discipleship for church members."

"OK Dad, I'm convinced we need to be about the business of winning
people to Jesus and teaching the Bible, but how do you make that a prior-
ity? How did Baptists have such success in the old days? How did that
happen?"

"Funny you should ask about that; I was cleaning out my library the
other day, and I came across a copy of a journal I didn't remember I had
telling the story of how Sunday school developed in Southern Baptist
life."

"What did it say?"

"Well it seems . . ."

A Historical Journey

T he process that we call Christian education got off to a rocky
start in Baptist life. Early Sunday schools were not sponsored by churches; instead they were the work of dedicated
individuals. Since they were not sponsored and controlled by the
churches, ministers and laymen alike were hesitant to support them.
May states that "only when Baptist churches approved the Sunday
School as a teaching agency in the church and recognized the need
for their own schools did the denomination make significant advance
in Sunday School work." [2]

What happened to make Sunday school so attractive to Southern
Baptists? Fitch says that Southern Baptists took a different approach to Sunday school that had profound effects in gaining the

---

[2] L. E. May Jr., "The Emerging Role of Sunday Schools in Southern Baptist Life to
1900," in *Baptist History and Heritage*, vol. XVIII (January 1983): 6.

commitment of the denomination. While other denominations viewed Sunday school as merely an educational methodology, Southern Baptists were working to create an organization that would both reach and teach for the church.

A leader in this transformation was L. R. Scarborough, president and professor of evangelism at Southwestern Baptist Theological Seminary, who in 1918 introduced a resolution to the Southern Baptist Convention declaring "the primary purpose of a Southern Baptist church is evangelism." Furthermore, evangelism was affirmed by the convention to be the principal objective of all SBC organizations and churches, including the Sunday school. "These doctrinal convictions led Southern Baptist Sunday schools to be established on a foundation of biblical authority and evangelistic zeal."[3] The result of this resolution

> found immediate expression in the approaches to be used in the Sunday School . . . [which] from the beginning was the church should feel responsible for the lost and unchurched persons within the community of the church. . . . The conviction existed that in the teaching and preaching of the Word of God lay tremendous power. When a person participated in the preaching of the Word or the teaching of the Word, the Holy Spirit was expected to move and changes were expected to be wrought in the hearts and lives of the participants. Therefore, Sunday School work from its inception in the churches was considered to be a powerful spiritual force, which involved as many persons as possible in the study of the Word of God. And involvement in that study was expected to produce believers whose lives were transformed and motivated.[4]

Designated by the convention as an outreach program, men like Van Ness, Barnette, and Flake set about planning and implementing the Sunday school. Early on, procedures based on best practices in Sunday school work were developed and

> found expression finally in the writings of Arthur Flake and becoming known as the Flake formula. The formula had

---

[3] J. E. Fitch, "Major Thrusts in Sunday School Development Since 1900," in *Baptist History and Heritage*, vol. XVIII (January 1983): 20.
[4] Ibid.

> five points: (1) Know your possibilities, (2) Organize to
> reach and teach persons, (3) Enlist and train workers, (4)
> Provide space, and (5) Go after prospects.

Flake also advocated the use of a community-wide religious census to discover prospects that would then be assigned to classes. Often classes would be made up completely of prospects, and teachers were encouraged to "go get them."[5]

Another innovation of the Sunday school patriarchs was to view age grading in the youth and adult ages as the most productive for reaching people. A quality Sunday school was organized into small classes and departments based on age and gender. These classes were considered to be responsible for the people in the age group of that class.

> A class for 20–25-year-old men was given the responsibil-
> ity for reaching and teaching all the 20–25-year-old men
> in the community. The class was not just responsible for
> those who were already members, it was responsible for
> reaching all the nonmembers as well. This meant that
> every class in the Sunday School had a part of the popula-
> tion as its responsibility. Each class had a part of the Great
> Commission, and the part was determined by the age range
> of the class. This age graded approach to youth and adult
> Sunday School work became highly efficient and effective
> outreach approach for each church that used it. . . .This
> philosophical approach to Sunday School organization
> was uniquely Southern Baptist. It made the Sunday School
> an effective evangelistic and church growth organization.
> While other major denominations were using the Sunday
> School as a Christian education organization exclusively,
> Southern Baptists were using the Sunday School as a
> Christian education organization and a church growth
> organization.[6]

This balanced approach was supported by L. R. Scarborough who said, "It is not wise to say that soul winning is the main thing or that soul building is the main thing. . . . The entire work of the kingdom of God can be organized along two lines: soul winning and soul

---

[5] Ibid., 21–22.
[6] Ibid., 27.

building." Roy Fish noted that Scarborough called these "the Siamese twins of God's gospel."[7]

This was the job of Sunday school, and in the midpart of the twentieth century, Southern Baptists excelled at it, becoming the largest Protestant denomination in the United States. Clemmons reports that Sunday school as done by Southern Baptists made many contributions, including mobilization of the laity in the church; creating a unique way of doing church; assisting Southern Baptists in the transition from poor, rural beginnings to "urban, affluent, educated, and sophisticated"; tremendous increases in membership and financial resources; and a redefinition of the professional clergy in Baptist life.[8]

"Wow! That sounds great!"

"You are right. Southern Baptists were achieving great results in reaching people, teaching the Bible, winning people to Christ, and developing them into maturity. However, by the end of the twentieth century, growth in Southern Baptist churches was flat, and the luster had worn off Sunday school as a methodology."

"What happened?"

"Well there are lots of opinions about what caused this, but one of the best says . . ."

So What Happened to Sunday School?

In commenting on the general decline of the Sunday school in all kinds of churches across the United States at the end of the twentieth century, Arn, McGavran, and Arn made the following observations:

1. The focus of the Sunday School changed from those "outside" to those "inside." . . . The Sunday School fell prey to the tendency of many institutions to change from the founding goals to goals of organizational survival. Internal concerns became a preoccupation, capsizing the delicate balance of ministry to the body and ministry through the body.

2. Leadership of the Sunday School shifted from the laity to professionals. Age grading encouraged specialization. There

---

[7] Roy E. Fish, "Lee Rutland Scarborough," in James Leo Garrett Jr., *The Legacy of Southwestern* (North Richland Hills, TX: Smithfield, 2002), 26–27.

[8] W. P. Clemmons, "The Contributions of the Sunday School to Southern Baptist Churches," *Baptist History and Heritage*, vol. XVIII, no. 1 (January 1983): 31.

was less involvement by the many, and more involvement by the few. . . . Laypeople were no longer the generals in the Sunday School, but became the foot soldiers.

3. A separation of roles evolved in the Sunday School and church. The evangelist became the . . . charismatic leader, whose message was "repent and be saved" . . . during a special crusade in a church. . . . When the crusade was finished, so was evangelism. . . . The religious educator became the thoughtful, quiet planner, whose message was "let us grow spiritually" . . . [with] little time or concern for evangelism.

4. There developed a loss of community and sense of belonging. The neighborhood church changed to a drive-in church. . . . Relationships became less meaningful, resulting in the decline of a caring fellowship.

5. The Sunday School became less and less of a priority for the church. . . . As other tasks became important, the Sunday School was no longer perceived as a top priority for the church.[9]

While these comments were not specifically directed at Southern Baptists, they are appropriate in describing the decline of Sunday school in Southern Baptist life also.

"That is so sad. Do you think Sunday school (or something like it) can ever be recovered as the reaching/teaching agency of the church?"

"Well, church leaders often speak about the 'good old days' and bemoan the fact that Sunday school does not serve a useful purpose in the church anymore. But before a church can try to recover the vitality of the Sunday school of old, some 'gut check' questions about the work of the church in small-group Bible study have to be answered."

"What are they?"

1. **Evangelistic Responsibility.** Does the church really see the need to reach a lost and dying world?
2. **Priority for the Church.** Is there any desire for a strategy for a churchwide ministry mobilizing the greatest number of people to be involved in ongoing evangelism?

---

[9] C. Arn, D. McGavran, and W. Arn, *Growth: A New Vision for the Sunday School* (Pasadena: Church Growth, 1980), 25–27.

3. **Methods:**
    a. What is the best way both to teach and reach new people?
    b. What is the best way to stay in touch with and provide ministry to your people?
    c. Can a large-group master-teacher approach maintain a ministry/outreach priority?
    d. Can a church find enough good teachers to staff a small group approach?
4. **The Name, Sunday School.** What should we call a comprehensive approach to reaching for Christ and teaching people the Bible? This is not a new issue. Over 50 years ago this was already an issue. Gaines Dobbins said, "The name has become something of an anomaly. . . . Sometimes it is referred to as "Bible school" . . . [or] "Church school."[10] Today we see different words emphasized: *fellowship groups, Bible study groups, community groups, home groups, care groups.* Is there a best name?
5. **Schedule the Day and Time.** When are the best day and the best time to do the Bible study experience?
6. **Location.** Should Bible study be done at the church campus or anywhere?
7. **Curriculum.** Many issues:
    a. Do we study the Bible, or anything that is spiritual?
    b. Do we use denomination curriculum or anything we want?
    c. Who controls the curriculum choices we have?

"These really are gut-issue questions. Do you think there is any way to answer them?"

"I think so. For some time I have been working on a way to develop a simple, streamlined, strategic approach to Christian education that supports the primary role of a Bible teaching/outreach organization in the church. This effort would then be sustained by programs of personal discipleship development and church member training. I call the central feature of this approach Foundational Bible Study (FBS), which has many commonalities; to Sunday school as advocated by Flake, Barnette, Anderson, and Piland; but you could call it anything you want. I chose foundational because it lays the foundation for the church to mobilize

---

[10] G. Dobbins, *The Church Book* (Nashville: Broadman, 1951), 96.

the membership to reach people, teach them, and care for them. It is foundational for the lost person because it is the beginning place for him/her to consider the Holy Scriptures. It is foundational for the saved person because it underscores the need for consistency in the Christian life."

"I like the sound of that, but how would you describe it in terms of what it would do?"

"Well I view the purpose of F BS to be . . ."

Reaching. Intentionally to create a systematic process of enlisting people to be involved in small-group Bible study with the goal of bringing them to faith in Jesus Christ and into the faith community of the local church where they will grow to spiritual maturity.

Inviting. To provide an open, inviting, safe opportunity for all people to consider to claims of the Bible in a small-group, informal teaching setting.

Teaching. To teach the Scriptures from the perspective that the Bible is the unique, true Word of God that is powerful to bring people to salvation and purposeful life.

Church Supporting. To promote and support the programs and ministries of the local church such as worship attendance, the leadership of the pastor and ministerial staff, and the work of church committees or ministry teams.

Developing the Church as an Organization. To provide meaningful opportunities for places of service for church members.

Leading in Personal Spiritual Development. Support and instruct the spiritual disciplines of biblical stewardship, personal Bible study, and prayer.

Supporting the Denomination. Instruct and encourage participation in mission endeavors and other work of the denomination.

"Any church would want to see these things being done, but how would you actually do it?"

"I have thought about that a lot and have put together an administration plan where one thing grows out of another. You would start off . . ."

The Administration of Foundational Bible Study

Implement a leadership council or team consisting of the pastor or designated staff member, age-group coordinators, a training coordinator (probably the minister of education or discipleship), and lay members of the church in sufficient numbers to ensure church-wide support. The leadership council is essential because its job is to keep FBS on track on its teaching/reaching purpose by setting enroll-ment goals, planning prospecting events, identifying areas where new units are needed, overseeing the selection of workers, coordinating and planning training events, and evaluating the effectiveness of the overall program. The council would meet as needed but at least quar-terly to evaluate processes, plan special events, and set goals.

"This leadership council has to be completely sold on the idea of open, small-group Bible study as the strategy of the church to reach, win, as-similate, and engage people in the work of the gospel."

"I hear you. What do you do next?"

"You begin by enrolling people."

Enrollment

Enrollment maintenance/enlargement is a never-ending job. Setting enrollment growth goals is only part of the problem, and it is hard enough. As a department or class gets to a large, comfort-able size, the pressure to enroll diminishes. The leaders of FBS must constantly keep in mind that the priority is to keep enrolling people. New enrollment must take place to replace persons who move away and to maintain the enrollment of people who are less dedicated or have stopped coming altogether. FBS leaders must be continually mindful to take care of the ones who are on the roll but are chroni-cally absent. Has anyone actually talked to these folks? It is rare that someone will call the church to say, "I don't want you people to pray for or be concerned about me."

"You know, son, enrolling and keeping up with people seems like an easy thing to do, but you will be surprised at how difficult it is. To make it work, everyone in the church has to be continually looking for new folks."

Prospecting

Attention needs to be continually given to the effort of finding new people and enrolling them into the FBS program. Identify a sys-tematic process for prospecting.

Use prospecting methods like People Search, neighborhood canvassing, FRAN (Friends, Relatives, Associates, Neighbors) lists, phone surveys, or e-mail/Web surveys to secure the names of people who are not in any Bible study program.

Anytime the church is planning an event of any kind, someone in leadership has to ask, "How are we going to get the names of the people coming to this event as prospects for FBS?" Be intentional about age-group crossover. A teenager starts coming to a Wednesday night event; get the names of the parents and give them to an appropriate department as prospects. A preschooler comes to your day-care program; turn over the names of the parents to the appropriate class.

"Prospecting gets old until you realize that it is the main way you keep the momentum going. Also, I have seen that if you are continually seeking people, the Lord blesses your activities by sending people your way."

"How do you take care of all those new people?"

"The key administrative action here is to begin new classes to take care of them."

Starting New Classes

New classes mean you are trying to reach a new group that is not being reached, putting to work people who need to be serving the Lord in a meaningful way, and keeping the organization focused on reaching. People will argue that classes are small and need to be filled to capacity first. They may suggest that an old class is shrinking, so why start new ones? However, new classes grow faster, reach more people, and provide more eager workers than old ones. Whenever the total enrollment is higher than 20:1 of the number of units, it is time to begin some new classes. This 20:1 ratio allows you to have some larger classes but still ensures that units are small enough for new members to get to know people.

"So where do we start?"

1. **Age and Gender Specific Groups**. Whether we like it or not, age and gender are the simplest ways to group people. You will have people who prefer same-gender classes to coed classes and vice versa. Offer them as an option.

2. **Affinity or Life-Stage Groups**. Adults often find themselves relating to other adults based on the age of their children. Perhaps the retirement ages create an opportunity for a new class either for those who are not retired or for those who are.

3. **Cover the Special Needs**. Don't just think about adult classes. Make sure you have the preschool, children, and youth units to balance what you are doing with adults. One of the persistent problems with off-campus small groups is taking care of small children.

4. **Interest Groups**. Different learning styles and curriculum interests might offer a way to identify an opportunity for a new group. However, remember that FBS is an open-group approach, so be careful not to make the content so deep that a non-Christian or baby Christian would feel out of place. Provide short-term, in-depth classes at other times to provide for this need.

5. **Location Groups**. Out of space at the church? Could a home FBS group or a lunchtime class work?

6. **Work Schedule Groups**. For those who work on Sundays or can't come to FBS on Sunday morning for any reason, why not begin a Sunday night or Wednesday night class (or any other night)?

"This sounds like you can start classes just about anywhere or anytime."

"That's true, you can, as long as you have the teachers and workers to support a class."

Recruiting and Training Workers

At least 10 percent of the number of the enrollment of your church should be working in some capacity in FBS. Sometimes ministers say that their church can't grow because they just don't have any people who could be teachers or workers. This is both a damning admission of irresponsibility, and blasphemy. God has sent people to the church who could (if asked and trained) be wonderful Bible teachers. To deny this is to call God impotent. Remember, God even used a jackass to teach Balaam, so who is to say you don't have those who are qualified to serve?

"Why are workers so important?"

"The pastor should take the lead here because this is his greatest opportunity for long-term impact. Ephesians 4:12 states that equipping

people for service is part of the work we ministers are called to do. Recruiting and training people to serve shows that you value what God is doing in those persons' lives. Equipping will bring a harvest of loyal followers because it says you trust them to share in your work of the gospel."

Putting people in places of service is the church's greatest opportunity to mobilize an army for the Lord. Why would we shrink from giving someone the opportunity to share regularly what God has said in His Word and what God is doing in that teacher's life? This is meaningful and fulfilling work.

Recruiting, however, needs to be done properly. Recruiting workers, especially teachers, should not be a hallway ambush on Sunday morning but a deliberate, prayerful process whereby a person is informed of the responsibilities of the task as well as the awesome opportunity to be in on God's working in the lives of people.[11]

"This is beginning to sound like work. What happens after you start classes?"

"Well before you start these new classes you have to figure out where they will meet."

Securing Adequate Space

Every class or teaching unit needs a place to meet. Lack of space is frequently the reason a church stops growing. There are many ways to get additional space.

1. **Multiple Use.** Churches are notorious for wasting resources. Why build a building, equip it, heat/cool it, only to use it for one hour on Sunday mornings? Granted, multiple usage will require people to cooperate with others and practice courtesy for the goal of reaching more people for Christ. Multiple use of buildings requires planning for additional parking on site as well as additional preschool units.

2. **Temporary Space.** Modular classrooms may be available for rent. Pay attention to zoning restrictions and the fact that such buildings may take up parking spaces.

---

[11] Refer to chapter 22, "Ministering alongside Volunteers," for detailed suggestions for doing this.

3. **Off-campus Space.** Sometimes space can be obtained in nearby schools, hotel meeting rooms, or business conference rooms for Bible study groups, especially at lunchtime. One advantage with these kinds of spaces is that parking comes with it. Among the disadvantages is that this space usually can only accommodate adult classes. This is also the case with home study groups.

"So now I have all these people, workers, and classes. What happens next?"

"You have to keep up with them, and you do that by getting out of the church building."

Conducting Outreach

One often hears that church visitation is dead. Perhaps this is the excuse of lazy ministers, but it is hardly the truth. Outreach is a daily activity in all kinds of businesses. Why would it not be an essential activity of the greatest enterprise in the world?

Make a first impression that says, "We care about you and your family." After someone visits your church, a contact needs to be made in person. This does not need to be a long visit; just a stop at the door with a gift, or a reminder and an invitation to join an FBS class, is usually sufficient. Set a consistent day and time for outreach. Visitation programs that are planned with a regular procedure for making assignments and receiving reports are more likely to occur than spontaneous ones.

Remember, earlier is better. The quicker a church prospect can put a human face with the church, the more likely a good impression can be made. Also, make good use of e-mail and the telephone to contact busy people.

"If you do FBS right, you will notice when people are absent. If you check on them, you will often find out that there is some kind of a need. Then you can see how God puts us together in the church so we can help carry one anothers' burdens."

Ministry

FBS classes provide ministry in times of crisis as well as promoting the socialization component.

Care Groups. In times of personal crisis, the FBS class should be considered a first line of support for the church. This is one of the reasons classes need to be small enough so that members know and care about the family that is hurting.

Fellowship Groups. The nonchurched world has the view that people in church sit around complaining that someone somewhere might be having fun. We need to involve people in fun times as well as serious Bible study times. FBS classes should have some kind of social event to which prospects are encouraged to attend at least once per month.

Attendance Support

High attendance days and other churchwide special emphases are sometimes needed. This will allow class members to see how the organization fits in with the whole of the church.

Evangelistic Harvest

As teachers observe the interaction and questions of members of the class who have not made a personal commitment to Christ, they should arrange for some personal one-on-one time with those class members.

"I am beginning to see what the scope of the job is, but how does a church keep everything on track?"

"Well son, that is the real leadership question, isn't it?"

Evaluation and Planning

At least quarterly the leadership council should receive reports from all age groups and evaluate the FBS as a whole, focusing on questions like the following:

1. Are you hitting your enrollment goals?
2. Do you have an adequate number of prospects to conduct outreach and start new classes?
3. Have you added enough new units to take care of the enrollment?
4. Do you have trained workers in sufficient numbers to adequately staff your classes?
5. Are you offering training opportunities on a regular schedule?

6. Are your workers taking advantage of regular training?
7. Do you have sufficient space for each unit?
8. Are you making enough contacts to maintain attendance?
9. Do you have enough people involved in outreach to be effective?
10. Does you attendance reflect a healthy FBS program (40–60 percent)?
11. Are FBS members participating in worship?

Once evaluation is made, the council can take appropriate corrective actions to improve ministry operations. See chapter 23, "Evaluating the Teaching Ministry," for more information about evaluation of educational programs.

"I am puzzled by one thing—where do you get all those qualified workers?"

"Remember one member of the leadership council was a training coordinator. This person would have the job seeing that workers are properly recruited and trained. This could be done in a small church by one person, but in a larger church it would probably require a team representing all the age groups."

Training for Teachers, Support Staff, and Other Volunteer Church Workers

The Task of Church Training

Support FBS by providing a well-trained staff of workers to teach, conduct outreach, evangelize, and minister to members and nonmembers and support the overall work of the church by training people to serve in a variety of roles as identified and needed by the church.

Goals of Training

1. **Quality FBS Faculty**. Conduct training in teaching methods, age-group needs, learning styles, and educational technology.
2. **Quality FBS Staff**. Provide instruction in effective outreach activities and ministry performance.

3. **Church Support**. Train church members to serve on church committees, on ministry teams, in deacon ministry, and in special church projects.

Administration

The training coordinator of the leadership council plans training events and enlists personnel to conduct training. These would include such things as:

1. **FBS Worker Training/Planning**. Annual training events should be planned for FBS teachers and staff.
2. **Ongoing Training**. Such as weekly teacher training and outreach ministry planning.
3. **Church Training**. Annual training for church ministry teams/ committees, and deacons.

"Well that takes care of the church workers, but what about those people who want more?"

"The training coordinator takes care of those needs too."

Comprehensive Programs for In-Depth Education in Personal and Corporate Discipleship for Church Members

Purpose of Discipleship Training

Develop an ongoing curriculum of classes, private study, and mentoring experiences to lead the individual believer to be able to survive in today's culture and contribute to the work of the church. New Testament discipleship is a corporate matter. "Disciple" (*mathetes*) is used, with a few exceptions, in the plural. In the language of the epistles, it is replaced with corporate images and metaphors— brothers, sisters, body, building, family of God, nation. Training members how to live as the body of Christ is essential.

Goals of Discipleship Training

1. Assist new believers to grow in their spiritual life through instruction in the spiritual disciplines, Christian doctrine, and application of Christian principles for everyday living.

2. Develop personal habits of Bible study, stewardship, prayer, and devotional reading through classes, personal study, accountability groups, and mentoring.

Administration of Discipleship Training

The training coordinator of the leadership council identifies congregational needs and interests and plans discipleship classes and studies to meet these needs. This can be done through use of congregational surveys, discussion groups, and suggestion boxes. In medium to large churches, there may be a need to create a discipleship council to coordinate offerings specifically designed for women, men, parents, and families.

The training coordinator, working with other interested church members, develops an ongoing curriculum of classes, private study, and mentoring experiences. The training coordinator enlists personnel to conduct classes, seminars, and retreats to facilitate personal and corporate discipleship.

Evaluation and Planning of Discipleship Training

As the leadership council prepares to have its quarterly meeting, the training coordinator will evaluate the classes conducted to measure their effectiveness and ensure adequate coverage of courses in the curriculum. As requests for new classes or repeated classes are received, options for new courses are developed.

"Well Dad, it sounds like you have given this a lot of thought. Would you like to start off by helping me get ready to talk to my church leaders about moving to Foundational Bible Study in my church?"

Discussion Questions

1. How would you view the "gut issue" questions? Are they really that important?
2. This approach views evangelism and assimilation as responsibilities of the whole church rather than a separate program. Do you agree? Explain your answer.
3. What are the pros and cons of open, small-group Bible study?
4. What should we call our main, churchwide Bible study program?

5.   How important is scheduling in making Bible study effective?
6.   List advantages of on-campus and off-campus Bible study classes.
7.   Concerning curriculum, what should we study—the Bible or anything that is spiritual?
8.   Should we use Southern Baptist curriculum or anything we want? List pros and cons.
9.   Who should control the curriculum choices we have—the church or the class? Why?
10. What problems do you envision with the leadership council?
11. How much priority does your church give to enrolling new people?
12. How important are recruitment and training new workers?
13. What does your church do to create new, usable space?
14. What kind of outreach program does your church use? Is it effective? Whom does it reach, non-Christians or transfer Christians?
15. How do you use evaluation in your church?

Bibliography

Anderson, Andy, and Linda Lawson. *Effective Methods of Church Growth.* Nashville: Broadman, 1985.

Arn, Charles, Donald McGavran, and Win Arn. *Growth: A New Vision for the Sunday School.* Pasadena: Church Growth, 1980.

Barnett, J. N. *A Church Using Its Sunday School.* Nashville: Convention, 1937, revised 1955.

Clemmons, William P. "The Contributions of the Sunday School to Southern Baptist Churches." *Baptist History and Heritage*, volume XVIII, number 1, January 1983.

Dobbins, Gaines S. *The Church Book.* Nashville: Broadman, 1951.

Flake, Arthur. *Building a Better Sunday School.* Nashville: The Sunday School Board, 1934.

_____. *Sunday School Officers and Their Work. Revised.* Nashville: The Sunday School Board, 1952.

_____. *The True Functions of the Sunday School.* 3rd ed. Nashville: Convention, 1930.

Fish, Roy E. "Lee Rutland Scarborough." In *The Legacy of Southwestern,* ed. James Leo Garrett Jr. North Richland Hills, TX: Smithfield, 2002.

Fitch, James E. "Major Thrusts in Sunday School Development since 1900." *Baptist History and Heritage,* volume XVIII, number 1. January 1983.

Gangel, Kenneth O., and Warren S. Benson. *Christian Education: Its History and Philosophy.* Chicago: Moody, 1983.

May, Lynn E. "The Emerging Role of Sunday Schools and Southern Baptist Life to 1900." *Baptist History and Heritage,* volume XVIII, number 1. January 1983.

Piland, Harry M., and Arthur D. Burcham. *Evangelism through the Sunday School.* Nashville: Convention, 1989.

Sizemore, John T. *Church Growth through the Sunday School.* Nashville: Broadman, 1983.

Chapter 22

MINISTERING ALONGSIDE VOLUNTEERS

Esther Díaz-Bolet

Based on the gift they have received, everyone
should use it to serve others,
as good managers of the varied grace of God.
(1 Pet 4:10)

If the church would see the life and work of
each member as part of the mission of the church,
then every member would be active.[1]

The Green Meadow Blues

Bro. Luis Sánchez, pastor of Green Meadow Baptist Church, sensed his apprehension mounting. Time was nearing for him to meet with Olga and Brian, the co-chairs of the committee that recruits and nominates volunteers to serve in various church ministries. He prayed for an optimistic report. Surely things would be different this year, considering they had added two staff positions and the membership had increased significantly. A knock at the door interrupted his thoughts. It was Olga and Brian, looking exhausted and frustrated. Olga explained that once again they had a shortage of volunteers to fill the vacant slots for the upcoming church year. Brian added that most of the volunteers that had been serving for the last few years were either burned out or unreliable. They

---

[1] G. Nelson, *Service Is the Point: Members as Ministers to the World* (Nashville: Abingdon, 2000), 7.

417

knew that it was time for an extreme makeover of the volunteer ministry, but where would they begin?

Sound familiar? Perhaps you, too, have encountered a similar situation and have wondered what to do. Regrettably, this is a recurring dilemma that has many churches singing the blues. But what is the source of the problem? Is it spiritual? Is it administrative? Is it a leadership issue? Is it a lack of commitment? Or is it all of the above? There is no one simple answer to this complex issue, but there are viable solutions.

In this chapter we will examine the terms *volunteer* and *laity* and the perceptions associated with these. Then we will establish a biblical and theological rationale for volunteer service in the church. Finally, we will focus on the practical aspects of recruiting, placing, training, monitoring, motivating, and retaining lay leaders.

What Is in a Name?

The purpose of this section is to dispel negative implications that may be associated with the words *volunteer* and *laity* in reference to the unpaid servants of the church. *Webster's New Collegiate Dictionary* defines the two words in this manner. *Volunteer* is one who enters into or offers himself for a service of his own free will. *Laity* refers to the people of a religious faith as distinguished from its clergy.

Although the definition of *volunteer* itself is impartial, numerous negative perceptions are associated with the word. In the minds of some, *volunteer* may create erroneous images, resulting in faulty concepts: "Volunteering in the church is optional." "No expectations can be placed on volunteers; they are not paid employees." "No commitment is required of volunteers." "If the work is done poorly, well, they are only volunteers."

The definition for *laity*, however, helps to perpetuate some of the negative connotations associated with the term, such as "second class," "lower standard," "not as capable," "perform only menial jobs." As the definition indicates, *laity* is distinguished from *clergy*, which is defined by *Webster's New Collegiate* as "a group ordained for religious service." In other words, it is unpaid versus paid, common versus elite, mediocre versus excellent. This distinction lends itself to an unwholesome and unproductive attitude resulting in a "we" and "they" mentality. Such distinction, not present in the early church culture,[2] produces a ministry that is mainly clergy centered, that determines the validity of a ministry according to remuneration, and that hinders the work of the church by minimizing the involvement of all believers in service.

Throughout this chapter, the terms *congregational minister*, *servant*, and *leader* will be used interchangeably with *volunteer* and *laity*. These terms are regarded as titles of honor because volunteers have been called into the body of Christ, sharing the same privileges and responsibilities as other believers. Thus, any negative meaning associated with the words *volunteer* and *laity* is discouraged. Lay leaders are equal partners in ministry with paid staff.

What is your opinion? What are your beliefs or perceptions concerning church volunteers? Since our beliefs drive our perceptions and behavior, let us review the basis of our beliefs. We will examine the Scriptures to establish a foundation for Christians serving in the church.

Serving God Is Not Optional: A Biblical and Theological Rationale

Bestowing the privilege and responsibility of service on all believers had its inception in the mind of God. "For we are His creation, created in Christ Jesus for good works, which God prepared ahead of time so that we should walk in them" (Eph 2:10). God designed a strategy of service for His chosen people. "But you are a chosen race, a royal priesthood, a holy nation, a people for His possession, so that you may proclaim the praises of the One who called you out of darkness into His marvelous light" (1 Pet 2:9). Jesus modeled it. "For even the Son of Man did not come to be served, but to serve, and to give His life—a ransom for many" (Mark 10:45).

God, our Creator, Sustainer, and Redeemer, *called*, *gifted*, and *empowered* each of us for service. Let us look at each of these verbs more closely.

---

[2] See Ephesians 4.

Called

The term *church* in the New Testament is *ekklesia*, a compound Greek term of *ek* and *klesis*, literally meaning "the called-out ones." This Greek term was used in the Septuagint to translate the Hebrew word used in the Old Testament that referred to the nation of Israel convened before God, submitted to His divine authority, and called out for His purpose.[3]

The New Testament church succeeded the Old Testament Jewish community. The early church was a close knit body of believers, Jews and Gentiles, who lived in a new relationship to God. The term *church* in the New Testament has a twofold meaning. First, the term most often refers to a local group of born-again, baptized believers of Christ, who are called out to accomplish God's purposes. Second, the church is regarded as the body of Christ, which includes the redeemed of all the ages.[4]

Paul states in 2 Tim 1:9 that God "has saved us and called us with a holy calling, not according to our works, but according to His own purpose and grace, which was given to us in Christ Jesus before time began." Christians have been set apart to carry out God's mission. We are God's servants called by God Himself.

Gifted

Through the Holy Spirit, God has gifted each believer with one or more spiritual gifts to fulfill the call. "A spiritual gift is an expression of the Holy Spirit in the life of believers which impacts them to serve the body of Christ, the church."[5] The gifts are exercised by the believers under the direction of the Holy Spirit, enabling us to respond to the call of God. Diverse yet working in harmonious unity, spiritual gifts are the spiritual tools for service with the purpose of building up the body of Christ. The spiritual gifts are discussed in Romans 12; 1 Corinthians 12; Ephesians 4; and 1 Peter 4.

Just as each part of the human body has a particular and necessary function, each gift is essential and equally needed in the proper functioning of the body of Christ. Paul expressed it this way: "From Him

---

[3] Morlee H. Maynard, comp., *We're Here for the Churches* (Nashville: LifeWay, 2001), 7.
[4] Ibid.
[5] C. G. Wilkes, *Jesus on Leadership: Becoming a Servant Leader* (Nashville: LifeWay, 1996), 38.

the whole body, fitted and knit together by every supporting ligament, promotes the growth of the body for building up itself in love
by the proper working of each individual part" (Eph 4:16). Each of
us has a contribution that is ours alone to make. There are no worth-
less parts in the body of Christ. Therefore, "based on the gift they
have received, everyone should use it to serve others, as good managers of the varied grace of God" (1 Pet 4:10).

Called and gifted by God, each Christian has a significant contribution to make to maintain the church in proper working order
as intended by God. Romans 11:29 reminds us that "God's gracious
gifts and calling are irrevocable." Each one of us has a sacred call, a
solemn responsibility to identify our gifts, and a blessed privilege to
exercise them for the glory of God.

Empowered

At the moment of salvation, we are sealed by the Holy Spirit:
"when you believed in Him, you were also sealed with the promised
Holy Spirit. He is the down payment of our inheritance, for the redemption of the possession, to the praise of His glory" (Eph 1:13b,
14).

Once saved, we remain in God. "This is how we know that we
remain in Him and He in us: He has given to us from His Spirit"
(1 John 4:13). We know that God has given us diverse gifts to accomplish His work. "Now there are different gifts, but the same
Spirit. There are different ministries, but the same Lord. And there
are different activities, but the same God is active in everyone and
everything. A manifestation of the Spirit is given to each person to
produce what is beneficial" (1 Cor 12:4–7).

Serving our Lord is a high privilege and a weighty responsibility.
We may feel overwhelmed by the realization that we are inadequate
of ourselves to accomplish anything for God. This is a human reaction, indeed, but rather than responding from a place of scarcity, let
us be encouraged in knowing that God has empowered us by His
Spirit.

> We have this kind of confidence toward God through
> Christ: not that we are competent of ourselves to consider
> anything as coming from ourselves, but our competence is

from God. He has made us competent to be ministers of a
new covenant, not of the letter but of the Spirit: for the letter kills, but the Spirit gives life. (2 Cor 3:4–6)

We are made competent, that is, we are empowered by God to serve
Him. Thus, maintaining our focus on God's possibilities rather than
our impossibilities encourages us to persevere in His service.

We have established that each believer is called, gifted, and empowered to serve God.

Let me ask again: What are your beliefs or perceptions concerning church volunteers? Unless we understand and believe
what constitutes a biblical and theological basis for serving in the
church, our actions will be based on uninformed practices and un-
founded habits that will produce negative results. Therefore, it is
crucial that the church staff as well as the trained and experienced
congregational leaders understand their role in equipping potential
church leaders.

The Role of the Staff and Experienced Laity

At any given time in the life of the local church, God places the
number of servants needed to do the work of ministry. Thus, staff as
well as experienced laity should be intentional in instructing members in the knowledge of their role as ministers as well as in helping
them to accept that role. Randy Pope underscores the need for an
informed and committed laity when he states, "The first Reformation
gave the Word of God back to the people of God. Today we need a
second Reformation that gives the work of God back to the people
of God. That will not happen until the laity accepts their role as
ministers."[6]

This is possible when the staff and experienced leaders accept
their responsibility to identify potential leaders, encourage them,
help them to identify their giftedness, and provide them opportunities to serve according to their giftedness, abilities, and passions.
Lynn Anderson admonishes us about the importance of our role as
equippers: "If a Christian leader is not equipping someone to live

---

[6] R. Pope, *The Intentional Church* (Chicago: Moody, 2006), 131.

the Christ-life through works of service, then to that degree that Christian leader is not living up to his or her calling."[7]

In Matt 20:25–27, Jesus describes the kind of behavior that is to be exhibited by and expected of the equipping leaders:

> But Jesus called them over and said, "You know that the rulers of the Gentiles dominate them, and the men of high position exercise power over them. It must not be like that among you. On the contrary, whoever wants to be become great among you must be your servant, and whoever wants to be first among you must be your slave."

Kenneth Gangel inspires us to apply the teaching of Jesus by reminding us that "we are the servants of the servants of God."[8]

Blanchard and Miller offer an acronym for *serve* that outlines important principles to assist church leaders in responding to the noble call of equipping others.

See the future.
Engage and develop others.
Reinvent continuously.
Value results and relationships.
Embody the values.[9]

The church's ministerial staff as well as established lay leaders will find great success in equipping members for service as they apply the principles outlined by Blanchard and Miller: (1) to visualize the church mission and vision; (2) to share these with the potential leader; (3) to enlist and equip the leaders; (4) to perpetuate the need for improvement; (5) to esteem the individuals, not merely the accomplishments; and (6) to model integrity and credibility.

As we prepare others for works of service, let us express our concern by genuinely caring for them, respecting their efforts, and treating them as equal partners in ministry. Let us be faithful to our calling as Christian leaders to equip believers to serve. Let us be committed to help volunteers reach their God-given potential in pursuit of the call of God in their lives.

---

[7] L. Anderson, *They Smell like Sheep, Volume 2* (New York: Howard, 2007), 235.

[8] K. O. Gangel, *Feeding and Leading* (Wheaton: Victor, 1989), 35.

[9] K. Blanchard and M. Miller, *The Secret: What Great Leaders Know and Do* (San Francisco: Berrett-Koehler, 2007), 95.

A Strategy to Equip the Saints

The goal of equipping the laity is attainable when there is an effective strategy in place, which is undergirded by prayer and aligned with the mission and vision of the church. The strategy proposed here is made up of seven basic components: (1) establish the standards; communicate expectations; (2) commit to ongoing recruitment; (3) achieve a good fit: placement; (4) provide quality training; (5) monitor to promote spiritual growth and improve performance; (6) be mindful of retention generators; and (7) provide a nurturing environment that motivates volunteers to achieve great things for God and to stay committed to their area of service.

1. Establish the Standards; Communicate the Expectations

If we expect nothing, we will get it every time. On the other hand, when expectations are placed on the membership, they will rise to the occasion. Therefore, standards, expectations, and qualifications for service in the church should be established and communicated clearly, upfront, and in writing. This will result in a strong sense of ownership and commitment on the part of the volunteer to accomplishing the task at hand.

In his book *High Expectations*, Thom Rainer observes:
(1) "Churches that expect more from their members are more likely to retain them in active membership." (2) "The vast majority of the churches [surveyed] (95 percent) believe that a new Christian should become involved in a place of service as quickly as possible." (3) "Churches that have a system for spiritual gifts discovery and utilization had a higher assimilation rate than other churches."[10]

The unwillingness on the part of some church leaders to inform volunteers of what is expected of them will yield mediocre results. Low expectations are just as detrimental. We pay dearly in integrity and effectiveness when we water down expectations of volunteers simply because they are unpaid. We secure many benefits when we set high expectations for all leaders, whether remunerated or not. There is no place in the body of Christ for qualifications such as "a warm body," "alive," or "with a pulse," which ignore the God-given

---

[10] T. S. Rainer, *High Expectations: The Remarkable Secret for Keeping People in Your Church* (Nashville: B&H, 1999), 27, 125, 136.

talents and gifts that each believer has received to serve God and others. Such terms are counterproductive and inappropriate, but most importantly they violate the essence of God's call on His chosen people.

Generally qualifications will vary from church to church; however, some may be more universal. For example, for several decades, the acronym FAT—faithful, available, and teachable—has been quoted in reference to the qualifications of volunteers, especially as it relates to volunteers in the educational ministries of the church. An updated version is FAST—faithful, available, Spirit filled, and teachable.

Here is a third set. I call it the three Cs of service: *Calling*, *Character*, and *Competencies*. *Calling* refers to the call of God to serve and the empowering of the Holy Spirit to obey the call. It includes passion, attitude, and timing. *Character* pertains to holiness, integrity, and humility; that is, evidence of maturity toward Christlikeness. *Competencies* involve knowledge and understanding, abilities and skills, and attitudes. The three Cs of service emphasize the importance of having a sense of God's call and the Spirit's guidance, maturing spiritually toward a Christlike character, and developing the competencies needed to serve God.

Expectations are two-way propositions. Just like there is a set of expectations for the volunteers, the same should be true for the church. Congregational leaders can expect the church to support them in a number of ways: (1) commit to pray regularly for lay leader; (2) identify and record volunteer's giftedness, interests, skills, and abilities; (3) maintain open and clear lines of communication; (4) provide adequate resources, competent training, effective supervision, and hefty portions of encouragement; (5) provide documents that communicate expectations such as service (job) descriptions, church or workers' covenants, service applications, and samples of Bible study literature when applicable; and (6) conduct a responsible level of screening, including background checks that verify the existence or absence of prior criminal or other injurious behavior.

Standards are the boundaries within which one must navigate. Standards serve their purpose best when they are established, communicated, and monitored. Expectations help volunteers serve effectively within their commitments as well as guide leaders in the recruiting effort.

2. Commit to Ongoing Recruitment

Effective recruitment is ongoing and applies the rule of reproduction. A once-a-year recruitment effort does not suffice if we are to have the number of volunteers needed to minister effectively. Keeping our eyes and ears open as well as being consistently sensitive to the leading of the Holy Spirit will help us identify potential servants. As mentioned previously, the expectation is that the staff as well as the recruited volunteers will in turn recruit others who will recruit others because "if you can successfully inspire your existing volunteers to replace themselves, volunteerism has the opportunity to grow exponentially. The grassroots goal is to make sure every volunteer makes it his mission to recruit another volunteer."[11] This will result in significant growth of the church's volunteer base.

Of particular import to effective recruitment is the use of proper techniques. Gangel underscores this when he states, "Remember, people rarely perform above the level at which they were recruited."[12] In other words, if in a desperate effort to recruit, we tell members that "there is nothing to the task" or "that anybody can do it," we should not be surprised when volunteers do not prepare beforehand, do not attend worker's meetings, and sometimes do not even show up for their assignments. In such cases we are not only underestimating the God-given potential of the volunteer and being untruthful; we are also "underselling" the work of the Lord. Instead, let us respect and affirm the laity by offering them meaningful ministry opportunities with clear expectations, specific goals, built-in accountability, and training. Let us believe in the abilities of the volunteers and in the importance of the ministry.

Here are some guidelines to keep in mind:

1. Think in terms of a ministry opportunity rather than a need. There are more responses to opportunity than to need.

---

[11] A. Stanley, R. Joiner, and L. Jones, *7 Practices of Effective Ministry* (Colorado Springs: Multnomah, 2004), 163.

[12] Gangel, *Feeding and Leading,* 146.

2. Ask for a commitment to serve rather than to "help," which connotes temporary, short-term, or one-time assignments. The highest call deserves the highest level of commitment.
3. Seek for mutual understanding and commitment to the expectations by communicating them clearly, thoroughly, and in writing.
4. Ask for servants or ministers instead of "volunteers" to communicate the importance of the call and ministry opportunity.
5. Allow potential leaders adequate time to pray before giving a response.
6. Appreciate their willingness to consider the position regardless of the answer.
7. See a no response as an opportunity to minister to the member.
8. Continue to respect and love the members as well as pray for them even when the answer is no.

The effectiveness of the recruitment process depends largely on the commitment of the staff and the experienced leaders actively to enlist potential leaders, using appropriate recruiting techniques. Essential also is for leaders to believe in the importance of the church's ministries and in the potential of the volunteers as well as to accept their responsibility to equip the laity for effective service.

3. Achieve a Good Fit: Placement

Placement is matching potential leaders with ministry opportunities. Placement is more than just filling a vacant spot. The idea is to achieve a good fit, which will result in a win-win-win situation for congregational leaders, ministries, and the church at large. When lay leaders minister according to their giftedness, skills, and passions, others receive the benefits of an effectively led ministry.

Without a good fit, however, the results are burned out and frustrated volunteers who generally shy away from serving in the future if ever. Thus, insisting on forcing "a square peg in a round hole" yields adverse results for everyone involved. For example, placing a congregational leader who does not have the gift of evangelism or the passion to share Christ as the outreach leader for the church's educational ministries because "after all, there is nothing to it" is irresponsible and inconsiderate.

Achieving a good fit requires having the pertinent information about the potential leader and the service position. Information about the service position may include purpose, qualifications, requirements, specific tasks, and accountability. Information about the potential leader may comprise spiritual giftedness, talents, passion, abilities, skills, experience, and so forth.

Interviews are indispensable links in the placement process. Such interview links are easy ways to exchange information effectively and build rapport with potential volunteers. Interviewing potential leaders helps to secure a good fit between them and the positions.

So the placement process involves a number of intentional steps from identifying qualified potential leaders, to asking them to consider prayerfully a position that may be a good fit, to placing them. When we depend on God's wisdom and discernment to guide us in the process, He enables us to accomplish this momentous, ongoing task.

4. Provide Quality Orientation and Training

When cutting down a tree, a sharp ax is preferred to a dull one. Thus, God can use us more effectively when "sharpened." Training sharpens our spiritual sensitivity as well as our ministerial skills.

Imagine any company launching a new product or service without training its personnel. Absurd, right? Corporations train their personnel extensively before any product or service is available for public consumption. However, this is not the case in many churches. Sue Mallory's statement alerts us to this ludicrous reality: "The church is one of the few, if not the only, nonprofit organization that does not require training for service in leadership. Churches tend to assume that people of faith will automatically have the kind of commitment, skill, and experience to carry out whatever is asked of them."[13]

Several factors may contribute to this situation. A church may not have a philosophy of training, may have a faulty one, or may lack understanding of the one that is in place. This results in training that is haphazard, lacking intentionality and direction. I call it "popcorn" training.

---

[13] S. Mallory, *The Equipping Church: Serving Together to Transform Lives* (Grand Rapids: Zondervan, 2001), 150.

When working toward a sound philosophy of training, consider this: First, recognize that training is an integral component of discipleship. Training is for spiritual development as well as for skills development. Second, align the training needs with the mission and vision of the church. Such alignment will result in training that is purposeful and relevant to the accomplishment of the church mission. Volunteers in particular and the church as a whole will profit from training.

Marlene Wilson offers a succinct definition of orientation and training as well as some of the benefits.

> In a nutshell, an orientation program answers the question: What is it like to live or work here? A training program answers the next question that usually follows: what does it take to be successful here?
>
> When a volunteer has the answers to both those questions, you dramatically increase that volunteer's comfort . . . effectiveness . . . and likelihood of sticking in the job.[14]

An effective orientation program sets the tone for the staff and the lay leaders. It communicates the importance of preparing volunteers adequately and the commitment of the staff to support them in their various ministries. Other benefits of training include (1) preparing the lay leaders to teach the Bible properly, (2) equipping more members to assume leadership roles, (3) developing a better understanding of the job, (4) giving clear direction to the volunteers' efforts, and (5) motivating them to do their best.

There are many ways to train congregational leaders. These range from certification courses to apprenticeship opportunities, mentoring, online training, training DVDs, CDs, or audiotapes, and so forth. We improve attendance at planned training events when we (1) focus training on the needs of volunteers, (2) schedule training at times that are convenient for them, and (3) ensure that the sessions are helpful and interesting.

---

[14] M. Wilson, ed., *Volunteer Orientation and Training,* Group's Volunteer Leadership Series, Volume 5 (Loveland, CO: Group Publishing, 2004), 6. Group's Volunteer Leadership Series, comprised of six volumes, and Group's Church Volunteer Central Web site www.churchvolunteercentral.com offer practical and valuable helps for staff and lay leaders.

It is important to have a budget to support quality training. Such a budget would include funds for training materials, guest speaker fees, training retreats, and conferences. Expenses such as the cost of registration, mileage, and meals associated with attending a training conference should also be included. Providing the financial support for training is another way to show volunteers that the church is committed to equipping them to reach their God-given potential.

5. Monitor Performance Effectively

Overseeing the work of volunteers is an important administrative task for staff and other experienced leaders. Although sometimes misunderstood, ignored, or abused, monitoring is a crucial component of the overall strategy to equip congregational leaders. Monitoring performance for growth provides an avenue to keep the church mission and vision in focus while enabling lay leaders to serve to the best of their ability.

Terms associated with monitoring are *overseeing, accountability, relationship, commitment, improvement, evaluation*, and such. For Christians serving together, the terms *relationship, cooperation*, and *commitment* take on a special meaning. Since supervision exists in the context of a relationship, it is vital that the worker and the overseer maintain edifying relationships that demonstrate their spiritual maturity as well as strengthen their relationship in Christ. Mutual cooperation and commitment place the responsibility for results on both the volunteer and the supervisor.

Standards are crucial to the process of measuring, evaluating, and correcting performance. Without standards we cannot monitor progress. We cannot ask the question: How are we doing? Thus, it is vital that standards be established and communicated clearly and in writing and that there be a mutual understanding and commitment to the expectations as well as the goals and objectives. See Chapter 23, "Evaluating the Teaching Ministry," for more details.

Effective supervision is possible when there is a support system for the personal and spiritual enrichment of the volunteer as well as for the improvement of performance. Walter C. Wright Jr. offers a simple strategy, which he calls the CARE Plan for Volunteer Development:

Clarify expectations.
Agree on objectives.
Review progress.
Equip for performance and growth.[15]

When performance is inadequate, the supervisor and the volunteer should identify the cause. Subsequently, they should admit their responsibility for the failure and proceed to remedy the situation. The solution may involve reviewing or clarifying the expectations, the procedures, or the guidelines. Other situations may require retraining. And still others may involve reassigning volunteers to other ministry areas where their giftedness, abilities, and talents are better matched with the tasks and responsibilities of the ministry position.

Monitoring the level of performance of volunteers is central to the accomplishment of the church's mission. Successful monitoring is conducted through an adequate plan that enables the unpaid ministers successfully and effectively to achieve ministry goals and objectives as well as to grow in their competence and confidence.

6. Retention Generators

Most challenges related to the attrition of volunteers may be resolved at the front end by the proactive application of the principles in this chapter to each phase of the equipping process. Having the proper procedures and guidelines in place from the beginning will help to prevent or circumvent many of the recurring problems. In the same way that placing a bandage on a cut that has severed a bone is counterproductive, so is providing a simplistic solution to a problem that has compounded due to inattention. Retention, however, is generated when we: (1) offer meaningful work that has specific goals and is supported by budget and training; (2) hold workers accountable for results and offer appropriate recognition; (3) schedule orientations that promote a deeper understanding of the church's mission, establish a firm basis for effective communication, clarify expectations, and instill a sincere sense of belonging; (4) schedule training as needed; (5) respect volunteers as they are; (6) model community; and (7) show appreciation frequently, specifically, and personally.[16]

---

[15] W. C. Wright Jr., *Relational Leadership: A Biblical Model for Influence and Service* (Waynesboro, GA: Paternoster, 2002), 161–79.

[16] D. Pinsoneault, *Attracting & Managing Volunteers* (Liguori, MO: Liguori Publications, 2001), 83–88.

In most situations we can enhance retention. Modeling perseverance in our lives and ministries, letting the volunteers know that
their contributions count, remembering to minister to and with them
as well as applying the principles mentioned above will reduce the
attrition rate of volunteers. Let us make this our prayer: "May the
Lord direct your [our] hearts into the love of God and into the steadfastness [perseverance] of Christ" (2 Thess 3:5 NASB).

7. Provide a Nurturing Environment: Motivation

"Only fear the Lord and serve Him in truth with all your heart;
for consider what great things He has done for you" (1 Sam 12:24
NASB). God's love and grace toward us are powerful internal motiva-
tors. Likewise, loving our fellow servants with God's unconditional
love as well as loving them for who they are—and not just what they
can contribute—helps them experience God's love and be motivated
by it. They, in turn, share God's love with others as they serve faithfully and joyfully.

We certainly cannot motivate others. This reality is illustrated in
the old saying, "You can lead a horse to water, but you cannot make
him drink." However, we can jump-start people by encouraging or
stimulating them. Thus, providing a nurturing environment in which
volunteers flourish, grow, and serve joyfully is essential. Here is an
approach to consider. It comprises four simple but powerful words:
being, connecting, caring, and *serving*.

Being refers to being physically present to guide and help the lay
leaders as well as being spiritually fit in character and integrity in
our dealings with them. *Connecting* pertains to finding meaningful
ways to relate to volunteers. This requires that we know them and
their needs. *Caring* involves demonstrating genuine concern for the
lay leaders, their family, and their ministry. Part of caring is being
sensitive to our demands on their time. *Serving* reminds us to use the
towel and basin as our symbols of Christlike service, calling for an
attitude of humility that puts the volunteers first. Notice that the important progression from "being" to "serving" requires intentionality.
One can be present physically and spiritually without connecting, or
one may decide to connect but not to care, or one may choose to care

but not enough to serve. We are most effective when we choose to be present, to connect, to care, and to serve.

A pervasive nurturing environment and a climate of acceptance will include delegating responsible tasks with built-in accountability, valuing the volunteers' contributions, recognizing that each lay leader has differing needs, appreciating them, and celebrating with them. Such an environment is fertile ground for creativity, vitality, and efficacy.

Let us be mindful that our actions can stimulate or hinder motivation. Our attitudes and motives make a difference in whether we *motivate* or *manipulate* volunteers. Since there is a fine line between motivation and manipulation, how can one know the difference? It boils down to motive. For example, if we approach a potential church leader regarding a service opportunity with the mind-set of "task at any cost," we have crossed the line to manipulation, possibly resorting to techniques such as guilt. On the other hand, if we give the member the freedom to choose and respect the volunteer's response, then we stimulate internal motivation. Crossing the line from motivation to manipulation occurs inadvertently sometimes and intentionally at other times. Whichever the case, the line is crossed too often to everyone's detriment.

As leaders we can foster a nurturing environment where motivation will thrive by following the suggestions found in this section and by avoiding the trappings of manipulation. Most importantly, realizing that true motivation comes from within, let us rely on the Holy Spirit to motivate us all to serve God as He deserves and others as He expects.

Singing a Different Tune: The Green Meadow Blues Revisited

After much prayer the church staff and congregation of Green Meadow Baptist Church hired a church consultant to help them resolve their volunteer dilemma. The consultant worked with the congregation to clarify the essential role that the church mission and vision play in the accomplishment of God's purpose. They established a clear understanding of the biblical perspective regarding congregational ministers, identified and specified the qualifications and expectations for the servants of God, and formulated an action plan, containing the essential elements discussed in this chapter. The church experienced a transformation from the inside out as congregational leaders and staff equipped and unleashed the members to accomplish God's purpose for their lives and for the church.

If your church is afflicted with the volunteer blues, you, too, may discover a different tune when the church appropriates the practical principles found in this chapter. Although their implementation may need to be customized to your church culture and needs, the principles are universal. Let me encourage you to take these principles to heart. Begin working with the staff and experienced leaders by praying first and then identifying ways to effect the changes needed. Imagine each member ministering as God intended, growing spiritually, building up the body of Christ, and bringing glory to God.

And may we hear the Lord say, "Well done, good and faithful servant!" (Mark 23:26).

Discussion Questions

1. (a) Describe your theology of service. (b) What role does a theology of service play in the development of a church volunteer ministry?
2. Discuss the role of the staff in equipping congregational leaders to serve in the church.
3. Discuss ways we can encourage lay ministers (a) to commit to serve in the church and (b) to recruit other volunteers.
4. (a) Describe your experience as a church volunteer. (b) Were there factors that encouraged or discouraged you in your service? Explain.
5. (a) List the seven elements of a strategy to equip lay leaders and describe how well your church implements each one. (b) Compare your descriptions with the chapter content and provide recommendations for improvement where applicable.

Bibliography

Anderson, Lynn. *They Smell like Sheep, Volume 2.* New York: Howard, 2007.

Blanchard, Ken, and Mark Miller. *The Secret: What Great Leaders Know and Do*. San Francisco: Berrett-Koehler, 2007.

Gangel, Kenneth O. *Feeding and Leading*. Wheaton: Victor, 1989.

Mallory, Sue. *The Equipping Church: Serving Together to Transform Lives*. Grand Rapids: Zondervan, 2001.

Nelson, Gustav. *Service Is the Point: Members as Ministers to the World*. Nashville: Abingdon, 2000.

Pinsoneault, Donna. *Attracting and Managing Volunteers*. Liguori, MO: Liguori Publications, 2001.

Pope, Randy. *The Intentional Church*. Chicago: Moody, 2006.

Rainer, Thom S. *High Expectations: The Remarkable Secret for Keeping People in Your Church*. Nashville: B&H, 1999.

Stanley, Andy, Reggie Joiner, and Lane Jones. *7 Practices of Effective Ministry*. Colorado Springs, OR: Multnomah, 2004.

Wilkes, Gene C. *Jesus On Leadership: Becoming a Servant Leader*. Nashville: LifeWay, 1996.

Wilson, Marlene, ed. *Volunteer Orientation and Training*. Group's Volunteer Leadership Series, volume 5. Loveland, CO: Group, 2004.

Wright, Walter C., Jr. *Relational Leadership: A Biblical Model for Influence and Service* Waynesboro, GA: Paternoster, 2002.

Chapter 23

EVALUATING THE
TEACHING MINISTRY

Terri Stovall

Catch the foxes for us
—the little foxes that ruin the vineyards—
for our vineyards are in bloom.
(Song 2:15)

Lord my God, You have done many things—
Your wonderful works and Your plans for us;
none can compare with You.
If I were to report and speak of them,
they are more than can be told.
(Ps 40:5)

Are There Foxes in the Vineyard?

Lott Street Baptist Church is an established church in a metropolitan area. LSBC has seen tremendous growth over the past 10 years, but along with this growth logistical issues have surfaced over what to do about Sunday school. They were out of space. The staff and church leaders decided that it was time to get creative. So the church began moving from predominantly Sunday morning Sunday school to both on-campus Sunday school and off-campus small groups for adults. LSBC is about three years into this paradigm shift with 60 percent of adults meeting in a traditional Sunday morning Bible study setting and 40 percent meeting in off-campus community groups.

There is a growing concern among the staff as they have been receiving feedback from the various groups. Jim is the minister responsible for the small-group ministry, and he has the same concerns. While some of the groups are growing and multiplying, several are not. Jim just learned that two of the groups have not met in several weeks because their teachers were sick or out of town and they didn't know what to do. On Sunday afternoon he received a telephone call from a church member who wanted to know why his small group was doing a study written by a popular Christian author that suggested a believer could lose his salvation. Then just this morning Jim heard that several of LSBC's core members have begun visiting other churches because they just couldn't find a small group that fit.

Jim thought everything was going fine. But as he began to take a fresh and close look at the educational ministry of LSBC, he began to see the signs. There were foxes in the vineyard.

A Biblical Basis for Planning and Evaluation

This chapter emphasizes the role of evaluation in educational ministry, but it is impossible to address evaluation apart from planning. Without a plan or a target, there is nothing against which to evaluate. The plan is integral to evaluation.

I have been asked on many an occasion how much we should plan and how much we should just allow the Holy Spirit to lead us. The people asking this question seem to view planning and God as being mutually exclusive as opposed to being partners. God has given us our marching orders and our overall purpose, but God has also given each of us a brain, the ability to reason, and the ability to put feet to His plan for the church. It is clear that Scripture both illustrates and admonishes that we are to be about actively carrying out the plans of God. If we don't, we leave our vineyards open to the little foxes.

Planning with Purpose and Order

Scripture abounds with examples of God's people partnering with God to carry out His plans. Moses is a clear example of an ordinary man doing extraordinary things for God. Many will go to the story of Jethro confronting Moses on his inability to delegate. I like to look earlier in his life. Can you imagine what kind of planning it took to get all of the children of Israel moving in the same direction at the same time when they left Egypt? That is more an illustration of being an extraordinary planner than Jethro's confrontation. Moses knew the destination. He knew when it was time to move. He knew God was with him. But I am sure it took every ounce of his reason—and many meetings with Joshua, Aaron, and the tribal leaders—to put feet to God's plan. Now that's what I call a planner (Exod 12).

What about Joshua? He is a true example of one who knew God's plan and how it was to be carried out. He did not waiver even if it did seem like a crazy way to take a city. After all, who marches around a city for seven days and then takes it down with a blast of trumpets (Josh 6:1–27)?

Nehemiah is the epitome of a planner and one who could make decisions and deal with the critics, the government, and the people all at once (Neh 1:1–11; 2; 4:1–6).

David is credited with putting together one of the greatest leadership teams known to man. He continually sought the Lord's direction for each step he led the people to take (2 Sam 2:1–4; 4:9–12; 5:17–25; 7:18–29).

Paul was intentional in carrying the gospel to people who had not heard. He was not one to close his eyes and throw a dart at a map to decide which town to travel to next. Paul was specific in the route he took. With that said, he is also an example of one who was ready to make changes when God redirected his path (Acts 16:9–10).

While on earth Jesus showed Himself to be the ultimate planner. He came for a purpose and a plan and did not allow anything or anyone to steer Him from that plan. He did nothing haphazardly or without intention. Every word, every step, every act—even the ultimate act of sacrifice—was carried out to fulfill the plan of the Father (John 6:38). When the religious leaders challenged Him on the plan that He was fulfilling, He was steadfast and clear on the direction He was walking (Luke 5:30–32). He stayed in constant contact with the Father who sent Him (Matt 14:23; Luke 9:28; 11:1); and when He knew the steps ahead were going to be painful, He once again went to the One who sent Him (Matt 26:36–46). Then He finished the plan set before Him.

Admonition from the Proverbs

God not only gives us examples of people who carried out His plan with purpose and order, He also gives us admonition to be in-

tentional about planning. The book of Proverbs overflows with such
admonition.

- The inexperienced believe anything, but the sensible watch
  their steps. (14:15)
- Plans fail when there is no counsel, but with many advisors
  they succeed. (15:22)
- The lot is cast into the lap, but its every decision is from the
  LORD. (16:33)
- A man's heart plans his way, but the LORD determines his
  steps. (16:9)
- Finalize plans through counsel, and wage war with sound
  guidance. (20:18)
- Commit your activities to the LORD and your plans will be
  achieved. (16:3)
- The plans of the diligent certainly lead to profit, but anyone
  who is reckless only becomes poor. (21:5)

It is clear from this small sample that God expects us to be about
planning. God expects to be a part of that process, but He also
wants us to do our part. Scripture reminds us that we are to be sensible, seek counsel, allow God to determine the steps and always be
diligent.

Evaluation and Planning

At this point you may be thinking, *But I thought this was a chapter
on evaluating not planning.* Evaluation is the beginning, the middle,
and the end of planning. Let's look at our vineyard.

- Before we can grow a crop, we must determine what we are
  working with. Different types of crops, different soils, and
  different climates require different types of care. Evaluation is
  the beginning point of assessing and analyzing where we are
  today.
- Once a crop is planted, a gardener tends his field regularly.
  Sometimes the crop needs water, sometimes fertilizer, possibly a little cultivation, or perhaps just given time to grow.
  In Christian education regular and ongoing evaluation allows

us to make sure the conditions are the best for continued growth.

- Each season the vinedresser harvests his crop and then determines what steps to take to prepare for next season's harvest. The educational ministry of the church will never end until our Lord returns, but there are significant pause points where we will evaluate our progress thus far and determine the next steps God wants us to take.

It is impossible to address evaluation apart from planning. Without a plan or a target, there is nothing against which to evaluate. The plan is integral to evaluation.

What exactly is meant by *planning* and more specifically *strategic planning?* I say strategic planning because the goal of life transformation is so critical that it must be part of a plan that takes into account as many variables, conditions, and opportunities as possible while never wavering from the ultimate objective.

As I have tried to settle on one definition of strategic planning that can be applied to the ministry of the church, I discovered that this is not a cut-and-dried task. Many definitions have been given and restated.

- The process of thinking and acting.[1]
- A disciplined effort to produce fundamental decisions and actions that shape and guide what an organization is, what it does, and why it does it, with a focus on the future.[2]
- A multifaceted plan designed to reach an objective.[3]

Webster's dictionary does not define *strategic planning* per se, but defines *plan* as "a method for accomplishing an objective." The term *strategy* has multiple definitions. The primary definition has a definite military application: "the science and art of military command aimed at meeting the enemy under conditions advantageous to one's own forces." That was it!

---

[1] A. Malphurs, *Advanced Strategic Planning: A New Model for Church and Ministry Leaders* (Boston: Baker, 2005), 11.

[2] J. M. Bryson, *Strategic Planning for Public and Nonprofit Organizations* (San Francisco: Jossey-Bass, 1995), 4–5.

[3] K. Hemphill and B. Taylor, *Ten Best Practices to Make Your Sunday School Work* (Nashville: Lifeway Church Resources, 2001), 25.

Paul reminds us in his letter to the church at Ephesus that "our battle is not against flesh and blood, but against the rulers, against

> GOD-CENTERED strategic planning is a disciplined, intentional effort to develop and follow a method to accomplish God's objective for His church in order to meet the enemy under conditions that give us the advantage.

the authorities, against the world powers of this darkness, against the spiritual forces of evil in the heavens" (Eph 6:12). The teaching ministry of the church is not just another program. It is making disciples for the kingdom of God. It is carrying out God's plan that has eternal ramifications. We are in a spiritual battle, and the enemy will do what he can to move the church off course. Many times, I believe, one of the enemy's most effective tactics is to draw the church into a laissez-fare attitude toward the teaching ministry of the church by convincing us that everything is fine.

Solomon warned that we are continually to be on the lookout for the little foxes that enter our vineyard. If we do not stay alert, before we know it, our vineyard will be invaded, trampled down, and devoured by little foxes.

Understanding Your Part of the Vineyard

The Overall Teaching Ministry

Earlier in this text a foundation was laid that addressed the role of the church, pastor, and family in Christian education. The ultimate goal of all we do in Christian education is life transformation. The Great Commission clearly states our command to make disciples by baptizing (evangelism) and teaching (discipleship). The teaching ministry of the church is integral to accomplishing the mission of the church. But how do we make sure we truly are making disciples?

Leonard Sweet, in his book *Aqua Church*, states, "Every successful [ministry] is successful in its own way. However we may try to pass ministries off as our own intuitive insights, settling for mimicry and impersonation only offers up a recipe for extinction."[4] Too many churches today jump on the latest program or methodology band-wagon without realizing where that parade is taking them. The ultimate goal for which God wants a church to aim will dictate how the teaching ministry of the church is carried out. The church's responsibility is to execute the ministry in the best possible way to reach that goal, regardless of what everyone else may be doing.

A local church—that is, a New Testament church—has been placed by God at a particular time, in a particular place, with an ability to reach a particular people. A church in San Jose, California, is able to reach a particular people to whom a church in Tyler, Texas, may not have access. Florida works in a culture that is different from the culture of a church in Minnesota. A church in Minnesota has opportunities to reach people in 2007 that the same church did not have in 1955. Each local body of believers is unique, and God has a unique way of carrying out His ultimate plan in that context.

A series of questions will help us determine what is to be accomplished and how to get there.

- Why does this church exist?
- What are we to be as "church"? (Who and what are we?)
- What is our church profile? (age, family demographics, work patterns, and the like)
- What are the spiritual needs of the people we are reaching? (seeking, new Christians, growing believers, leaders)
- How are we doing? (attendance, baptisms, leadership, outreach)
- Where does God want us to go from here? (What does God want this local body of believers do in this community and in our world?)
- How will we get there?

Answers to these questions, while generally similar, will be different for each church. While all churches have the same universal mission—God's mission—each church plays a unique role with its own specific methods in accomplishing it.

---

[4] L. Sweet, *AquaChurch* (Loveland, CO: Group, 1999), 257.

Setting Goals within the Teaching Ministry

A popular adage says, "If you aim for nothing you are going to hit it every time." God's target is specific and intentional. Our targets, however, tend to be so broad and general that we never really know when we hit them. Once you have answered the questions listed on the previous page, you will have a clearer picture of what God may be leading you to accomplish through the teaching ministry at your church. Given this picture, you can set objectives and goals within that ministry.

Each program within the teaching ministry of the church should have goals and objectives. The previous chapter, "Administering Educational Programs," introduced you to the process of developing goals, objectives, and actions for the various programs. The questions that must be answered at this point are:

- How does each program help us accomplish the overall goal of the teaching ministry?
- Are the goals and objectives set for each program and ministry a true reflection of that program or ministry?
- How does each program or ministry fit into the context of our church?
- Is there anything that we are trying to accomplish through the teaching ministry that has nothing in place to help us get there?

When you answer these questions, you may find that some of the goals or objectives or actions will need to be changed, adjusted, or even eliminated. It is important to keep coming back to the question, What are we trying to accomplish and how are we getting there? You may also find that your goals and objectives are right on target. When that is the case, it is time to move on to the next step.

Tending the Vineyard

Having set program goals and objectives, it is then time to work the field. The wise gardener monitors his field regularly to determine what is needed to produce the greatest growth. If we are wise, we will also regularly monitor our programs to determine our progress toward what we believe God wants us to achieve. Evaluation involves gathering information and data that tell you where things stand today and measuring that information against a standard or criterion.

Evaluation is only as good as the information on which it is based. Information and data should be current, accurate, and reliable. If the information is inflated or a mere supposition, then the picture that is painted is not a true reflection of what is happening in the teaching ministry of the church.

The question often asked here is, "What kind of information do I need, and where do I get it?" Tools and resources are available that will give you the standards to set. The resource *Essentials for Excellence* provides work sheets, checklists, and tools to measure space requirements and student-teacher ratios.[5] The earlier chapter on "Evaluating Curriculum" gave you criteria on which to evaluate curriculum. The objectives and goals, too, serve as benchmarks to compare the collected information.

Evaluating the Tangibles

You will want to evaluate several areas, areas that are objective and easily measured. How often each of these elements is intentionally evaluated will depend on the situation and the setting. I have yet to meet someone who is responsible for an area of the educational ministry of a church that is not constantly evaluating whether there are enough teachers on any given Sunday. On the other hand, evaluating space may happen less frequently. Here are several suggested questions to answer that will aid you in the evaluation process. They can, of course, be adapted to your church's unique setting.

Administration

- Is our record-keeping system effective, accurate, and adequate?
- Are we capturing the information that we need?
- Where does each program fit into the overall organizational structure of the church?

---

[5] The resource *Essentials for Excellence* (see resource list) provides a CD with printable work sheets and tables. Some of the tables that are most helpful give standards for student/teacher ratios and space recommendations by ages.

Leadership

- How many teachers do we have for each unit? How does this compare with the teacher-student ratio guidelines?
- How many people do we have in leadership positions other than teachers?
- What kind of regular training do we provide for our teachers and leaders?
- How many teachers and leaders attend training opportunities?
- What is the attendance record of the teachers and leaders for program meetings?
- How many teacher or leader vacancies do I have today?

Space and Equipment

- Is the space for each unit adequate?
- Are there classes/departments/groups that have outgrown their current space or are in too large a space?
- What equipment needs to be replaced or repaired?
- Does the classroom environment promote learning?
- Is there a need for additional spaces for groups to meet?

Programming

- What programs are designed to reach people for Christ or to introduce them to the church?
- What programs are designed for discipleship?
- What programs are designed to develop leaders?
- What percentage of your church membership is actively involved in the Foundational Bible Study of your church?
- How many outreach contacts are made by your church members?
- How are members educated in doctrine, church polity, missions, or how to share their faith?

Working through these questions will help you see areas that need to be addressed. It will also reveal the strengths of the educational ministry of your church, highlighting the things that are going well. This is by no means an exhaustive list of questions, but it can be used to help the educational minister objectively evaluate the teaching ministry of the church.

Evaluating the Intangibles

The previous section addressed the tangibles; those things that can be measured in an objective way. There are also intangibles. If you were to ask a farmer how he knew when it was just the right time to harvest his crop, he would try to give you some objective answer, but it generally comes down to "when it feels, looks, and smells right." While depending too much on feelings and experience can mislead us, God has given us intuitive insight to know when something is working well.

One way of getting a feel for how things are going is to observe classes while they are in session. When I served as minister of education, I made it a point to visit each Sunday school department at least once a quarter to observe and evaluate. When you observe a small group, ask yourself questions like these:

- What is the general feel of the group?
- Does everyone seem to be engaged?
- Does the teacher appear prepared?
- Is the space conducive to learning?

As you are observing, take note of anything that you sense can be improved. These notations can direct your further investigations.

Another way to get a feel for what is happening is to solicit feedback from the participants. While a formal evaluation is helpful, I have found the best information comes from casual conversation. For example, as I am talking to Laurie about the women's Bible study, I may say, "I know this is the first time Jane is leading this group; how is it going?" In the course of a conversation, Laurie may be more open to give me honest feedback than if she were formally to evaluate Laurie's performance. You can gain feedback from participants on any aspect of the learning experience, but I have found it most helpful to hear from participants regarding schedule, curriculum, space, and leadership.

One final area to consider is teacher evaluation. A large church in Texas tells its teachers that they will be evaluated at least twice a year. The teachers are videotaped, and then the minister of education sits down with the teacher and evaluates his teaching. This intentional evaluation has resulted in teachers who are maturing, honing their skills, and more committed than ever. You may not wish to do something quite as formal, but evaluating teachers—encouraging them in their strengths and helping them with their weaknesses—can only improve the learning experience and give your teachers a boost of confidence.

Pests, Foxes, and the Unexpected

The best planned and well-tended vineyard cannot account for the unexpected events along the way. External forces that are out of our control, unforeseen events, or overlooked problems can have significant impact on the harvest that is produced.

Prioritizing and Addressing Needs

In any given church on any given week, issues may arise from lack of teachers to disgruntled members. I saw a Sunday school come to a screeching halt one week because we had run out of coffee. Now that was a significant problem!

A farmer, struggling with a withering crop due to lack of rain, will put thoughts of water aside when a swarm of locusts swoops in and begins to eat the fruit. While water is important, the immediate priority is getting rid of the locusts. When you are being pulled by several issues at once, the best thing you can do is to stop and prioritize what is most critical. As you deal with the most critical first, it is not uncommon for lesser issues to correct themselves.

After determining the most critical problem, next identify the steps or create a plan of action to address the most critical need first. When you begin to implement each step, it is important to determine the timetable, who is involved, and what is your expected result. Let's look at a couple of specific problems and how this might work.

Teachers

The need for more teachers is often a priority problem. In order to develop a strategy, leaders will first determine how many teachers they need, for what ages, and by what deadline. From here they can

begin to set a specific course of actions such as how and when to enlist, when to offer training, and when the teachers will start.

Helping ineffective teachers is another priority problem. Unlike
employees, my rule of thumb is "never fire a volunteer." Rather,
work with the volunteer to help move him to a ministry that may be
a better fit. The general steps are similar. The leader will decide by
what date he wants to have a new teacher in place. From there he
can begin to set up a specific course of action. I suggest meeting with
the teacher to determine how we might redeem him first. Work a
plan of teaching improvement. Then in time, through this process, it
is easier to determine if another place of service would fit him better.
We would then help him transition out of this leadership position
and into another, enlist a new teacher, and help the new teacher get
started.

Programming

Every now and then conditions dictate that a farmer plow his field
over and start fresh. Likewise, a time may come when a program
needs a fresh start or needs to be significantly changed. As you evaluate the teaching ministry, you may find that a program or ministry
that was once effective is now struggling. We can either work to
rejuvenate the program, or we can, in extreme cases, simply discontinue the program. God often uses these times as opportunities to
launch new programs and ministries.

This process—identify priority needs, envision a successful solution, set a course of action, and implement appropriate steps—can be
applied to any area of the educational ministry of the church, including space concerns, resources, publicity, and conflict resolution.

A Word about Sacred Cows

There are times when we have worked the process, discovered a
program that needs to be discontinued, and a plan is in place to transition the program out; but suddenly you discover that this is important to a significant group in your church. You may have stumbled
upon a sacred cow—a ministry or program that is so meaningful
to a group of people that if you were to change or discontinue this
ministry, it would have deep reaching ramifications on you and the

church. Jesus gave a warning for such times: "First sit down and cal-
culate the cost" (Luke 14:28)

The Ruth Class was mine. This group of older ladies had been together as a small group for decades. They met in a sizable room on the
bottom floor next to the preschool area. The Ruth Class had painted,
hung curtains, and furnished the room with tables, lamps, and comfy
chairs. They just loved their meeting room. As our church was growing, I had my eye on that space for a preschool room. I located a new
space for the Ruth Class that I felt would be more than adequate. But
when I approached these sweet ladies about the move, I quickly understood what this might cost me. Ruth Class members were among
my biggest supporters and prayer warriors. I knew if this was not handled correctly it could have deep-reaching ramifications. I did eventually move them, but it was on a much slower timetable. I spent almost
a full year visiting and working with the ladies (especially the matri-
arch of the group). I took them handmade Christmas cards from the
preschoolers, sharing our vision for the church and preschool ministry
and involving them in finding a space where they were comfortable. I
was even able to move all of their furniture and use the same curtains.
It took a lot of work and time, but in the end it was worth it.

It is possible to change and even discontinue groups or ministries
that need to be changed even when they have deep stakeholder roots.
When faced with this task, ask yourself, "Is the cost of leaving a sacred cow in place less than what it would cost us if we changed it?"
A cost can be felt in loss of membership, loss of trust, loss of credibility, and even loss in finances. Sometimes, the church—*and you*—are
better off letting a sacred cow continue to graze until it dies a natural
death.

The End Result

A fellow minister once said to me that all this planning and evaluating are the "not fun part of ministry. It just feels so administrative."
That may be true, but evaluation is critical to ensuring that we are
doing what we believe God wants us to do. It involves setting goals
and objectives, developing criteria against which to measure, evaluating where you are against where you want to be, and then addressing
those things that are keeping you from getting there. Then at the end

we can proclaim, "LORD, my God, You have done many things" (Ps 40:5).

Getting Rid of the Foxes: Revisited

Jim quickly realized he had some issues to deal with. He prioritized them as: (1) addressing the curriculum issue, (2) helping members connect with a small group, (3) educating small groups that the purpose of this ministry is outreach and multiplication, and (4) giving the small groups resources and support when their leaders needed to be out.

Jim knew he needed to close the curriculum hole quickly. It was important to him and the church that their teaching material be theologically sound and in line with the beliefs of the church. But he also recognized that the nature of small-group ministry required some level of choice within the groups. He evaluated a number of curriculum lines and topics and developed a list of acceptable choices, which he distributed to the groups. Now, as groups choose from this list, he is confident that the material is theologically sound. As an added benefit, the small groups were helped in finding new materials for their students. One fence hole closed; just three more to go.

The remaining holes are not as quick or easy to fix, but a process and plan are in place. He has been working with his leaders to intentionally locate those people who are having difficulty finding a small-group Bible study to attend. Slowly they are getting connected. Problems 3 and 4 have yet to be addressed, but Jim sees the long-term effects of not taking care of these "foxes." Now that he is aware of them, he is beginning to plan to keep watch over the vineyard where God has placed him.

Bibliography

Biehl, Bobb. *Masterplanning*. Nashville: B&H, 1997.

Bryson, John M. *Strategic Planning for Public and Nonprofit Organizations*. San Francisco: Jossey-Bass, 1995.

Buzzell, Sid, Kenneth Boa, and Bill Perkins, eds. *The Leadership Bible*. Grand Rapids: Zondervan, 2000.

Essentials for Excellence. Nashville: Lifeway Church Resources, 2003.

Hemphill, Ken, and Bill Taylor. *Ten Best Practices to Make Your Sunday School Work*. Nashville: Lifeway Church Resources, 2001.
Malphurs, Aubrey. *Advanced Strategic Planning: A New Model for Church and Ministry Leaders*. Boston: Baker, 2005.
Sweet, Leonard. *AquaChurch*. Loveland, CO: Group, 1999.

POSTLOGUE

Rick Yount

C. S. Lewis, premier Christian philosopher of the mid-twentieth century, was standing before his garden shed one sunny day. He opened the door, stepped inside, and found himself standing in darkness. He could just make out the garden implements, and that only by a thin beam of sunlight, piercing the darkness from upper right to lower left. Dust floated in and out of the dim, thin beam. Then he stepped over into the beam, looking up along it. In a flash the darkness was gone, the shed was gone, everything gone but the blinding beam—shining from 93 million miles away. There is a difference, said Lewis, of looking "at" and looking "along."

Our hope, as you have read these pages, is that you have seen more than a thin beam of Christian education, shining in darkness. That you've seen *people* more than programs, *life change* more than methods, a *living organism*—community—more than cold organization. That you have looked "along" Christian education into the brightness of the Son.

Christ is the great Life-changer; the church is His means of changing the world from pagan to seeker, seeker to believer, believer to disciple, disciple to teacher, teacher to missionary and leader. Such spiritual evolution is impossible outside the realm of the Spirit of God. But in Him it is a task worth every effort required of us: to awaken in learners of all ages and all nations the awareness of Christ's kingdom, *at hand*, available, and to teach them to depend on Christ as they grow in kingly citizenship and as they serve. He receives honor and glory as King; we receive joy as citizens and colaborers. Beloved, let us step into the blinding, energizing Beam and leave our darkened sheds behind. *His beam:* "for the training of the saints, to build up the body of

Christ . . . [growing] into a mature man . . . speaking the truth in love, let us grow in every way into Him who is the Head—Christ" (Eph 4:12,15). Make it so, Lord Jesus. Make it so.

NAME INDEX

455

SUBJECT INDEX

SCRIPTURE INDEX